In No Time

Windows
95

In No Time

Windows 95

Oliver Pott

Edited by
Rob Young

Prentice Hall Europe

London New York Toronto Sydney Tokyo Singapore Madrid Mexico City Munich Paris

First published in 1997 as Easy – Windows 95 by
Markt&Technik Buch- und Software Verlag GmbH
85540 Haar bei München/Germany
This edition published 1999 by
Prentice Hall Europe
Campus 400, Maylands Avenue
Hemel Hempstead
Hertfordshire, HP2 7EZ

A division of
Simon & Schuster International Group

© Prentice Hall Europe 1999

All rights reserved. No part of this publication may be reproduced, stored in a retrieval system, or transmitted, in any form, or by any means, electronic, mechanical, photocopying, recording or otherwise, without prior permission, in writing, from the publisher.

Translated by Karen Green, Elaine Richman and Martin James
in association with First Edition Translations Limited, Cambridge

Typeset in Stone Sans
by Malcolm Smythe and Michael Weintroub

Designed and Produced by Bender Richardson White

Printed and bound in Great Britain
by T J International Ltd, Padstow, Cornwall

Library of Congress Cataloging-in-Publication Data
Available from the publisher
British Library Cataloguing in Publication Data
A catalogue record for this book is available from the British Library
ISBN 0-13-977695-8
1 2 3 4 5   02 01 00 99 98

Contents

Dear readers 11

1 Basics and first steps   12

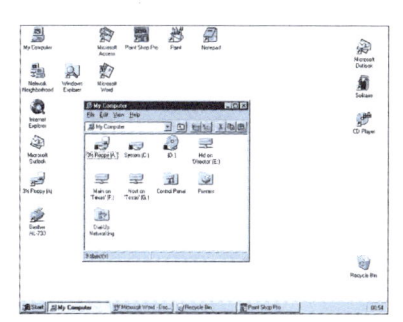

Starting Windows 14
What is the desktop? 15
Working with the mouse 17
Working with windows 23
Changing the window size 28
Moving windows 30
Scrolling through the window contents 32
Finding help 34
Exiting Windows 41

2 Working with programs   44

Using the Start menu 46
Starting a program 47
Switching between programs 51
Closing a program 53
Other ways to open programs 55

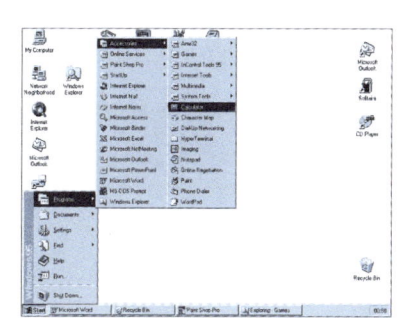

3 Using files and folders   58

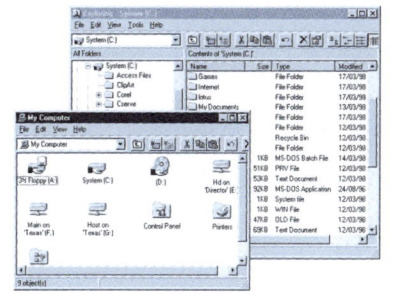

What are folders and files? 60
Using Windows drives 65
Handling floppy disks 67
Displaying drives, files and folders 68
Sorting the folder display 74
Viewing folders in Explorer 76
Moving between drives and folders 79
Creating a new folder 83

5

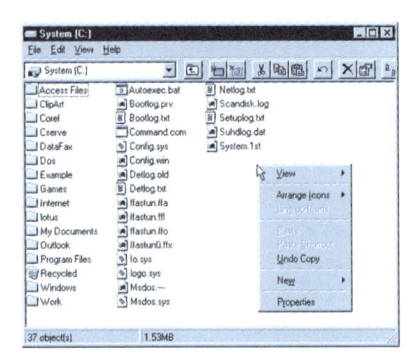

Creating a new file 86
Renaming folders and files 88
Copying folders and files 90
How to copy several files
at the same time..95
How to copy a file to the same folder 99
Moving folders and files 101
Copying a floppy disk 103
How much data is stored on a disk? 106
How much disk space does a
folder or file use? 107
Deleting files and folders 109
Retrieving deleted files from the
Recycle Bin 111
Emptying the Recycle Bin 113
Searching for files and folders 114
Formatting a floppy disk 117
A quick check on progress 121

4 Writing and drawing in Windows 124

Creating a document using Notepad 126
Editing the document in Notepad 128
Saving and opening the document..........136
Searching for text in the document 141
Printing documents with Notepad 143
Creating documents using WordPad........144
Formatting a text document....................148
Saving, opening and printing
documents in WordPad 156
Drawing pictures using Paint 159

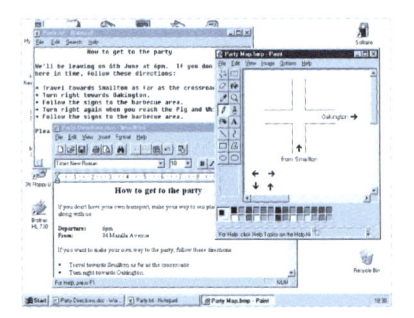

Cropping and copying graphics 170
Saving, opening and printing a
picture using Paint 173
Creating a background for the Windows
desktop....................................177
Text, pictures and other objects in
a single document 180
Progress check 184

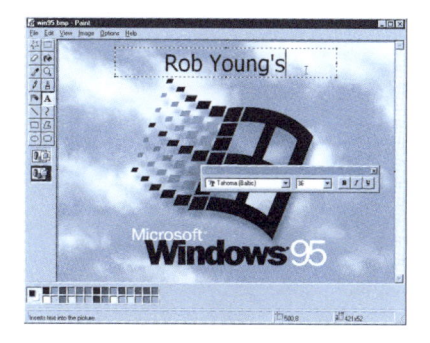

5 Handling letters, pictures and other documents   186

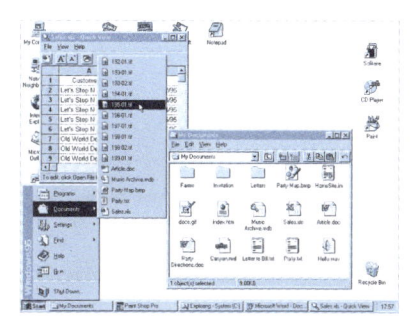

What do document files look like? 188
Opening document files 190
Keeping documents on the Desktop........192
Opening a document in different
programs 194
Displaying file contents quickly................197
Opening a list of recently used
documents 198

6 Printing in Windows   200

Setting up a new printer..........................202
Putting a printer icon on the desktop 209
How to print..212
Changing printer settings 215
Taking control of the printer 218

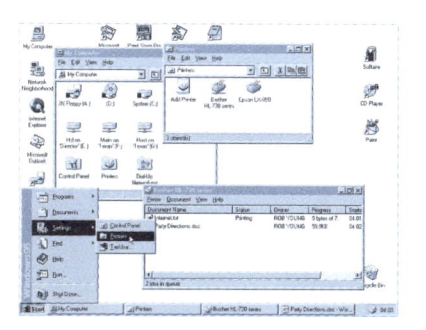

7

7 Fun with Windows 224

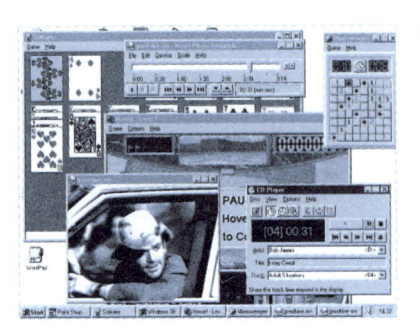

Playing music CDs on your computer 226
Working with sound files 234
Watching videos in Windows 239
Minesweeper! 245
Relax with Solitaire 248
Action with Hover! through the maze 252

8 Surfing the Web and Internet with Windows 258

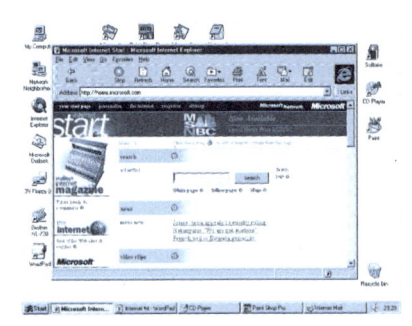

What are the Internet, Intranet,
World Wide Web and browsers? 260
First steps with Internet Explorer 264
Marking Web sites 272
Saving, loading and printing
document pages 275
Setting up your home page and
other options 280
Searching on the Internet 282
What is e-mail? 284

9 Working on a network — 288

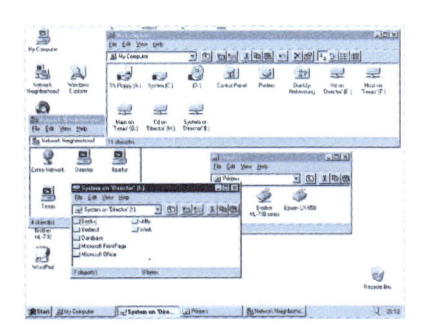

A brief survey of networks.........................290
Working on a network 292
Mapping and disconnecting
network drives 301
Printing on the network 303
How to install a network printer 305
How to share a printer 309
Sharing drives or folders
for multiple use..312

10 Care of the hard disk and defragmentation — 314

Scanning drives for errors 316
Defragmenting drives 321

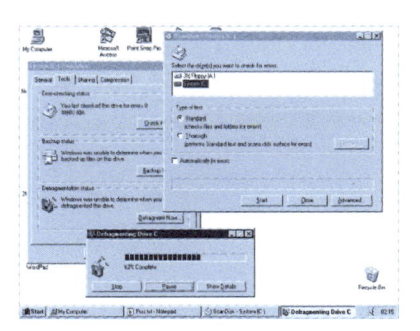

9

11 Customising Windows 324

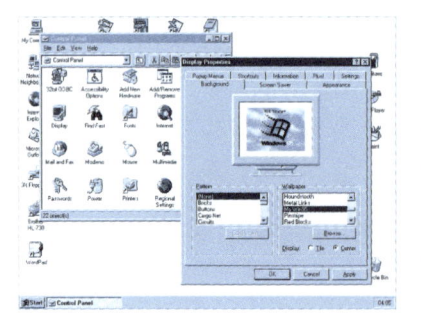

Setting the time and date 326
Changing the desktop background..........330
Installing a screen saver 336
Changing the screen resolution 338
Installing Windows components 341
Installing programs 344
Changing the Start menu 346
Installing a program icon on
the desktop..350
Installing DOS programs..........................352
Setting up the mouse 356

Help 358

Start-up problems 358
Problems with the keyboard and mouse ..359
Problems with the Windows desktop 363
Folders and files 368
Printing problems 372

The mouse 375

The keyboard 376

Glossary 380

Index 388

Dear readers,

It's so easy! That's what I was told back in 1977 when I stood in front of a computer, with a pile of punch cards, completely baffled. And little has changed! As a novice you stumble from one question to the next – how do I insert a floppy disk in the disk drive, what do I do with the mouse and which key should I press now? This was brought home to me again recently when I was writing a computer book for children.

This book is intended to help you get to grips with Windows. You will acquire the basic knowledge you need to work with the computer running Windows, step by step, from easy to quite hard. Read the first three chapters to learn how to use the mouse, windows and programs. You will also discover why files or folders are needed on the computer and how a floppy disk is inserted into the disk drive. Step-by-step instructions and illustrations show how something works.

The remaining chapters show that working with Windows can even be fun! After just a few steps you will be able to compose your first letter or design an invitation. How would you like to listen to music CDs on your computer, watch videos or relax with a game? Here's another tip for you: you'll find learning much easier if you take your time and if you're in the right mood, and you can learn a lot, coincidentally really, by repetition. With this in mind I wish you lots of fun with Windows and this book.

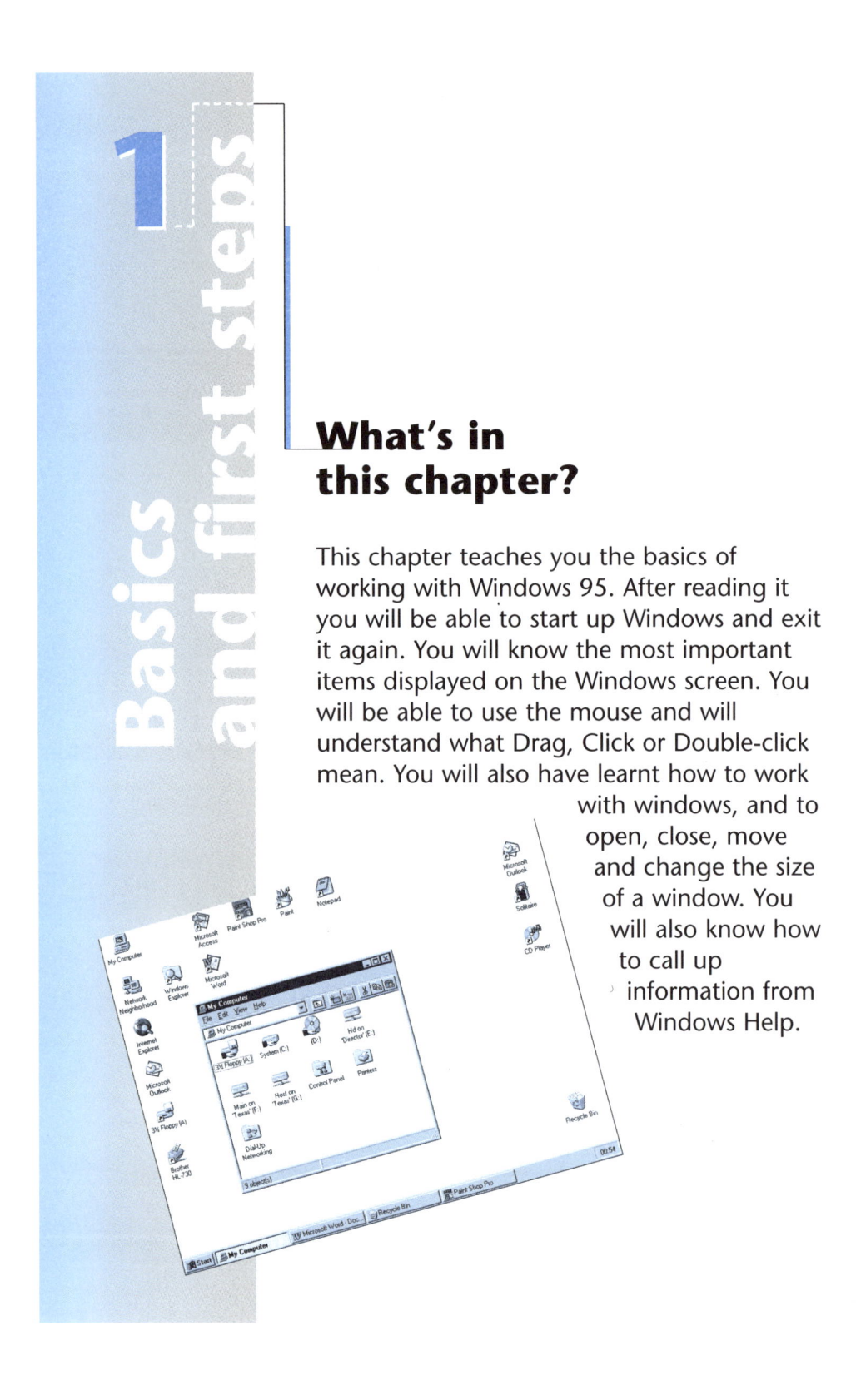

1

Basics and first steps

What's in this chapter?

This chapter teaches you the basics of working with Windows 95. After reading it you will be able to start up Windows and exit it again. You will know the most important items displayed on the Windows screen. You will be able to use the mouse and will understand what Drag, Click or Double-click mean. You will also have learnt how to work with windows, and to open, close, move and change the size of a window. You will also know how to call up information from Windows Help.

YOUR PROGRESS METER

Your are going to learn how to:

Start Windows   14
Identify items on the desktop   15
Work with the mouse   17
Work with windows   23
Change the window size   28
Move windows   30
Scroll through the window contents   32
Find help   34
Exit Windows   41

13

Starting Windows

Before you can work with Windows 95 you will have to switch on your computer and start up Windows.

1 Switch on the computer and monitor. After a few seconds Windows will be loaded.

If your computer is linked to a network, Windows will show this log-on box (more about this in Chapter 11).

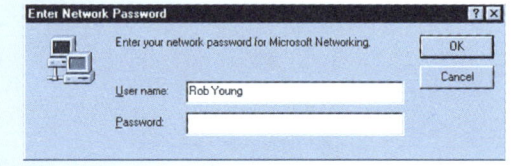

Press the Esc key to clear the log-on box.

This screen appears as soon as Windows is loaded.

2 If you can see the window *Welcome to Windows 95*, close this by pressing the Esc button. You will find further information on this window later in this chapter.

14

WHAT IS ON THE DESKTOP?

> **TIP**
> Is your screen still blank? Perhaps you forgot to switch on the monitor. Make sure all the cables are connected and the plugs plugged in. This also applies if the computer does absolutely nothing after you have switched it on.

What is the desktop?

Immediately after logging on, Windows will appear, looking like the screen below.

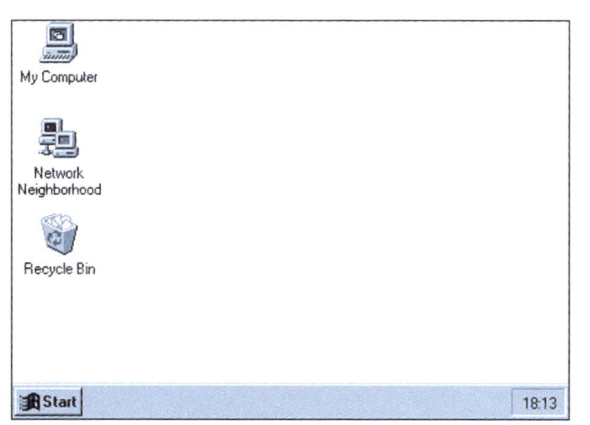

This is the Windows work area (or **User interface**) which is called the **desktop**. Here you can store the various tools (word processing programs, calculator, Recycle Bin etc.) which you often work with, in the same way as putting a pen down on a desk.

> **WHAT'S THIS?**
> User interface means the way in which the computer takes information from the user and then displays information. Windows has a graphic interface, for example, with icons and windows.

15

Does your desktop contain several icons, windows, a green background and even a picture? Don't panic. Every user can adapt Windows according to his or her requirements and the desktop is also frequently changed when installing programs. The screen above only shows a few selected items from the desktop. You will become familiar with other items and their functions in the various chapters of this book.

My Computer — The **My Computer** icon contains all the functions (also called **Resources**) for working with files such as letters, pictures etc. and programs on your computer. You will discover more in the following chapters.

Network Neighborhood — Can you see the **Network Neighborhood** icon on your desktop? Then your computer is linked to other computers in a network via a cable and by using this icon you can gain access to functions for exchanging data with the other computers in a network (see Chapter 9).

Recycle Bin — If there's something you don't need any more (a letter you wrote, for example), simply 'move' this document to the Recycle Bin. Chapter 3 will tell you exactly how this works.

The grey strip on the bottom edge of the screen is called the **taskbar**

Start   18:18

Windows displays various information for you on this bar.

18:18 — To the right of the taskbar Windows 95 shows you the **clock**.

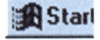

Start — The START **button** in the left-hand corner of the taskbar is used to start programs.

You will become familiar with other taskbar functions in the following pages and in Chapter 2.

16

Buttons are rectangular features which are commonly used in Windows to call up specific functions (similar to a cassette recorder, where you can press buttons to play, fast forward or rewind).

Working with the mouse

A **mouse** looks like its rodent namesake. The mouse usually has two **buttons** (sometimes three). The mouse can be moved over the surface of the desk and you can press the mouse buttons. Pressing a mouse button is generally called **clicking**. For Windows you only need the left and right mouse buttons. If there is a middle mouse button it is usually controlled by a separate program that is particular to the mouse and is usually described in the manual that comes with it. You will learn how to use the mouse in the following pages.

Put your hand over the mouse so that your index finger lies on the left button and your middle finger is on the right button. The mouse should be placed on a pad of rubber or foam (called the **mouse mat**). These mats are better suited to working with the mouse than a smooth table top.

1 Now get hold of the mouse.

2 Move the mouse on the pad. You don't need to press any mouse buttons. You can see a little pointer on the desktop.

As soon as you move the mouse, the arrow on the screen moves too. This little arrow is known as the **mouse pointer** or **mouse cursor**.

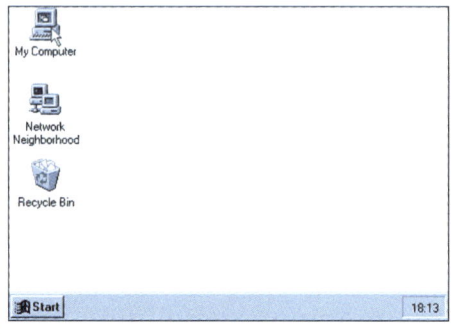

3 Move the mouse until the mouse pointer points to the *My Computer* icon. This is called **pointing** with the mouse. You can point to every item (e.g. the Recycle Bin, taskbar etc.) on the desktop with the mouse.

> **TIP**
> Really the instruction **Point to . . . with the mouse** is not quite linguistically correct. The mouse stays on the desk and you use the mouse pointer to point. This expression is in widespread use, however, and so is also used in this book.

WORKING WITH THE MOUSE

If you let the mouse pointer rest on an item, after a moment a little text window is displayed, which is known as a **ToolTip**. Windows provides you with additional information in the ToolTip window.

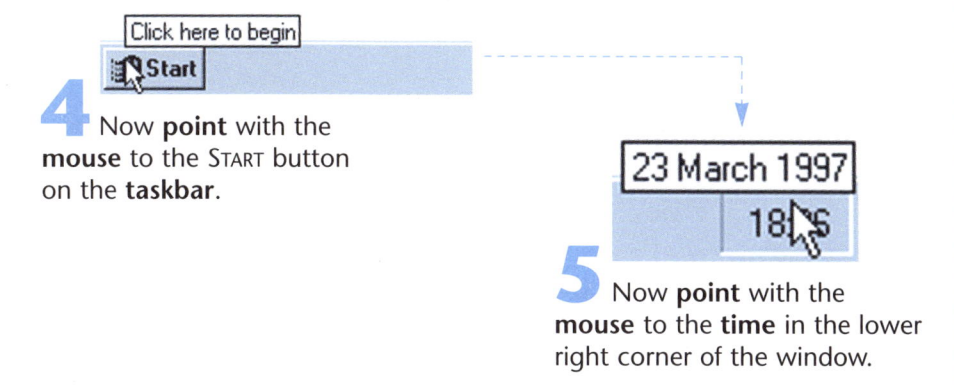

4 Now **point** with the **mouse** to the START button on the **taskbar**.

5 Now **point** with the **mouse** to the **time** in the lower right corner of the window.

Windows opens the ToolTip window and displays the **day of the week** and the **date**. When you move the mouse away again, Windows automatically closes the ToolTip window.

> In many programs you can also call up ToolTip explanations by pointing to an item such as a button.

That's all there is to pointing at items with the mouse. In addition to pointing with the mouse, there's another function, however, which is known as **Clicking**. This is also very easy.

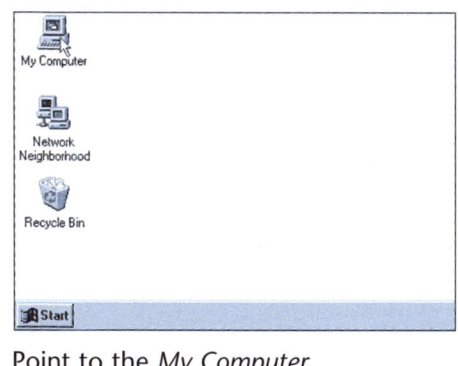

1 Point to the *My Computer* icon with the mouse.

19

2 Now press the left mouse button and then release it again. This is known as **clicking**.

The icon on which you just clicked is highlighted in colour. When you highlight an item with a mouse click, this is called **selecting**.

3 Click with the mouse on an empty space on the desktop.

Windows now removes the highlighting from the icon and only a dotted outline around the icon name remains. This outline shows which icon was last marked.

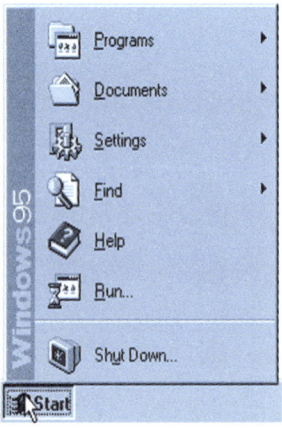

4 Now try clicking with the left mouse button on the START button. A little window will open. This window is called the **Start menu**.

WORKING WITH THE MOUSE

5 Click on an empty space on the desktop to close the Start menu again.

> You will often meet the term **Menu** in Windows. This is a small window which contains a list of items. In Windows you can select an entry in a menu by clicking it with the mouse. From the **Start menu** you can call up programs or other Windows functions (see Chapter 2).

In addition to pointing and clicking you can also **drag** something with the mouse.

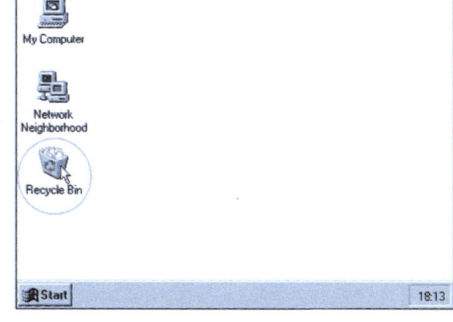

1 Point to the Recycle Bin icon with the mouse pointer.

2 Press the left mouse button again, but this time keep it pressed down and drag the Recycle Bin icon across the screen. Beneath the mouse pointer a second Recycle Bin icon is displayed, which moves with the mouse pointer.

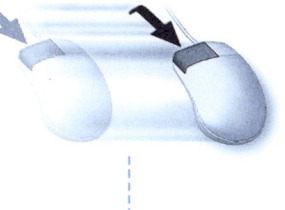

21

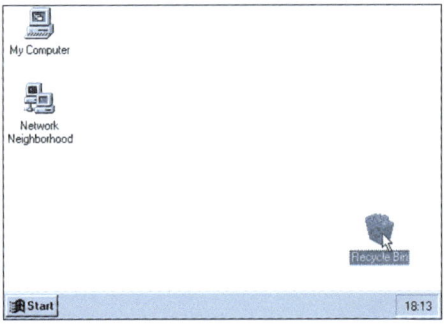

3 As soon as you have dragged the Recycle Bin icon to the bottom left corner of the desktop, release the left mouse button again. Windows now moves the Recycle Bin icon to the point where you released the left mouse button.

> **TIP**
> After dragging an icon or window it is still selected. In order to *deselect* after dragging, click with the mouse on a free space on the desktop.

The last important trick to master with the mouse is called **double-clicking**. Double-clicking is used for opening windows and starting programs.

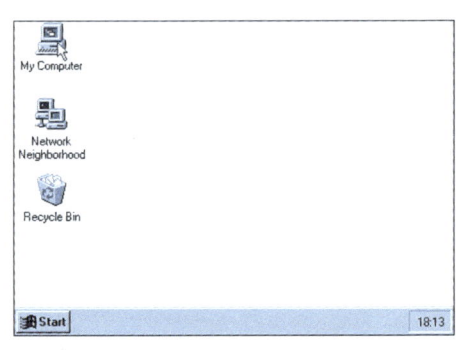

1 Point to the *My Computer* icon.

WORKING WITH WINDOWS

2 Press the left mouse button twice quickly. It is important that these clicks must be in quick succession.

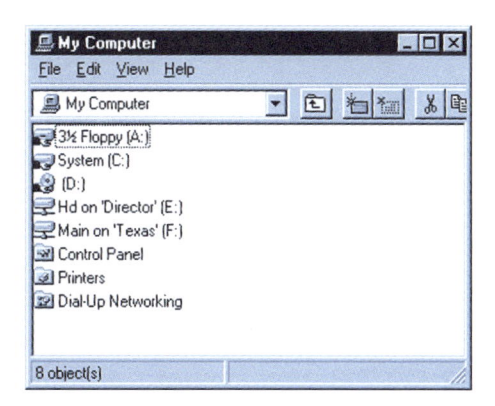

If the two mouse clicks were quick enough, Windows now opens this window, with the title *My Computer* shown at the top.

> **TIP**
> Getting the knack of double-clicking is quite difficult to begin with. Usually the gap between the first and second click is too long. Try double-clicking again, pressing the button faster. There is a summary of mouse functions at the back of this book.

Working with Windows

In Windows programs and functions are run in a window and information is displayed in them. To get to grips with Windows 95, you need to know the most important features of a window as well as how to open them, change their size and close them again.

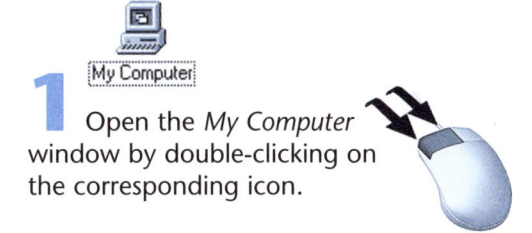

1 Open the *My Computer* window by double-clicking on the corresponding icon.

23

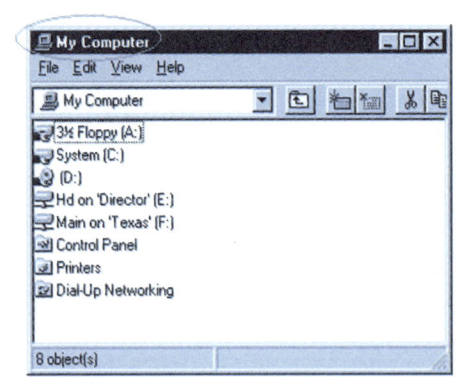

Most of the windows you'll work with will look almost identical. The *My Computer* window is typical of many Windows 95 windows.

At the upper edge of the window you will find the **title bar**, where Windows displays the name of the window.

In many windows you'll see a **menu bar** below the title bar with entries such as FILE, EDIT, VIEW, etc. The menu contains options relating to the contents of the window.

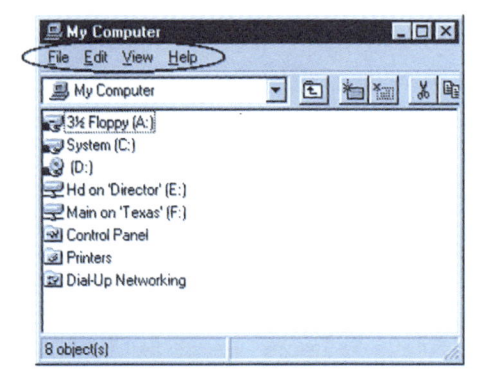

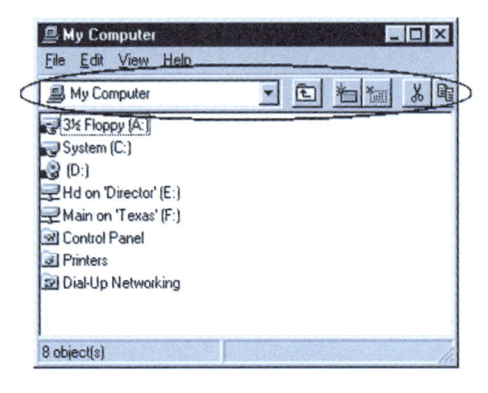

Some windows also have a **toolbar** which gives you quick access to some of the most-used options included in the menus.

24

WORKING WITH WINDOWS

Many windows also have a **status bar** along the bottom edge which displays additional information. Here the status bar tells you that the window contains 8 **objects**.

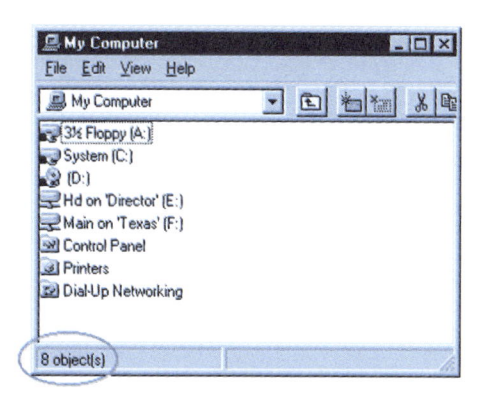

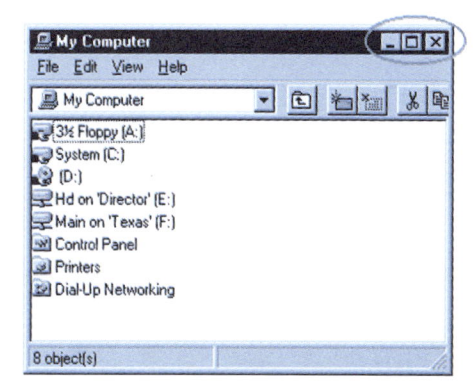

For the first stages you only need the icons on the three little buttons on the right of the title bar. These buttons close a window or change its size. Most windows have at least one or two of these buttons.

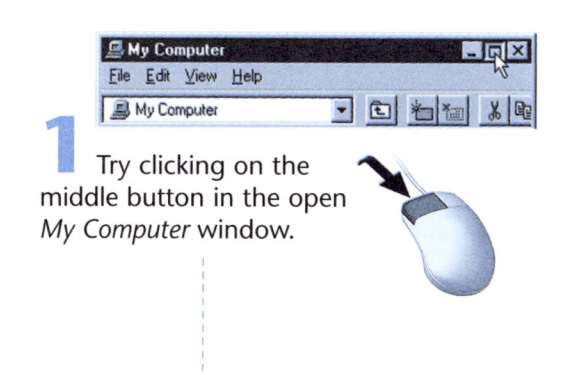

1 Try clicking on the middle button in the open *My Computer* window.

25

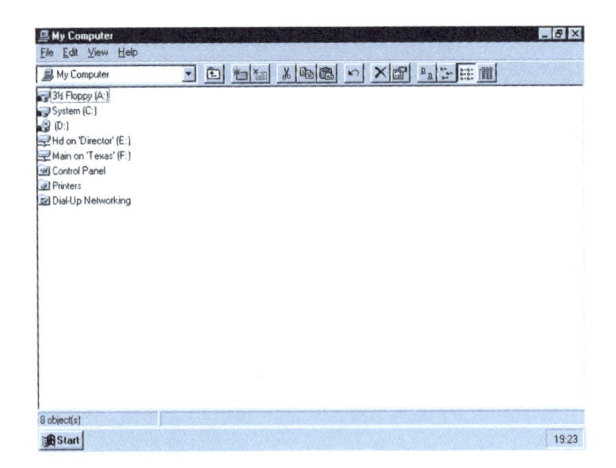

Windows now enlarges the window to make it fill the whole screen. This is known as **maximising** the window. You'll notice that the icon for the middle button has changed.

2 To return the window to its previous size, click on the middle button again.

3 Now click once on the left button of this group of three.

The window disappears from the desktop. All that's left is a button on the taskbar labelled *My Computer*. This is known as **minimising** a window.

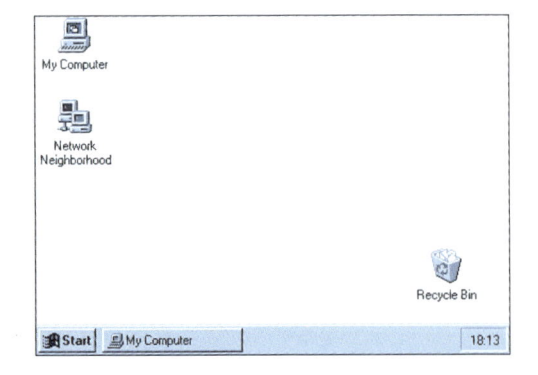

26

WORKING WITH WINDOWS

HINT

Windows displays the icons for all open windows and programs on the taskbar. If you click on one of these icons, Windows makes the related window visible on the desktop. In Chapter 2 you will find hints on how the taskbar can be used to switch between windows.

4 To make the window reappear, click the *My Computer* button on the taskbar.

The only task remaining is to close an open window.

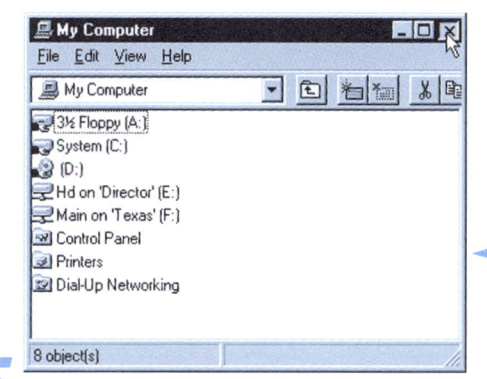

5 Click on the ⊠ button in the upper-right corner of the window. This button closes the window completely. When a window is closed, its button disappears from the taskbar.

TIP

Most windows display the ⊠ button. If you want to exit a program or close a window, all you have to do is click on this button.

27

Changing the window size

In the preceding section you have maximised a window to full screen size and minimised it to an icon using the buttons in the upper right corner. You can also choose exactly how large the window should be.

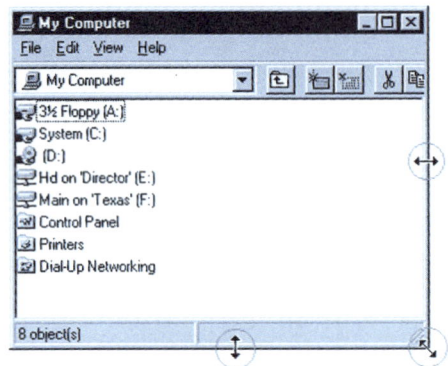

1 Point to the right edge of an open window with the mouse pointer, until the pointer changes shape.

2 Point to the lower edge and to one of the corners in the same way.

> As soon as you point to the right place on the edge of the window, the mouse pointer takes the shape of a double-headed arrow. You might have to move the mouse a bit until this double arrow appears. The double arrow displays the direction in which the size of the window can be changed. You can therefore use the left/right edge of the window to change the width of the window. The upper/lower edge of the window changes the height, and by using the corners you can stretch the window diagonally.

CHANGING THE WINDOW SIZE

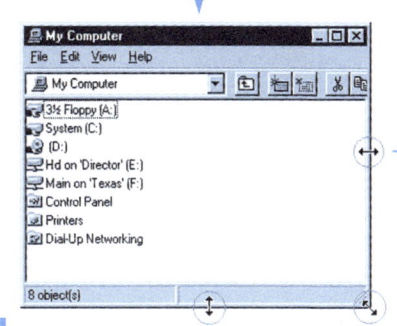

3 Point again to an edge of the window or its bottom right corner.

4 When the double arrow appears, hold down the left mouse button and drag the edge of the window in the desired direction. The new size of the window is shown by a dashed line.

5 When the window reaches the desired size, release the left mouse button. Windows now changes the size of the window accordingly.

TIP

In this way you can change the size of a window as you like. If you drag the edges outward with the mouse, the window becomes bigger. If you 'push' the edges of the window inward, the window gets smaller.

29

Moving windows

One of the strengths of Windows is that you can work with several programs or windows at the same time.

1 My Computer
Double-click on the *My Computer* symbol.

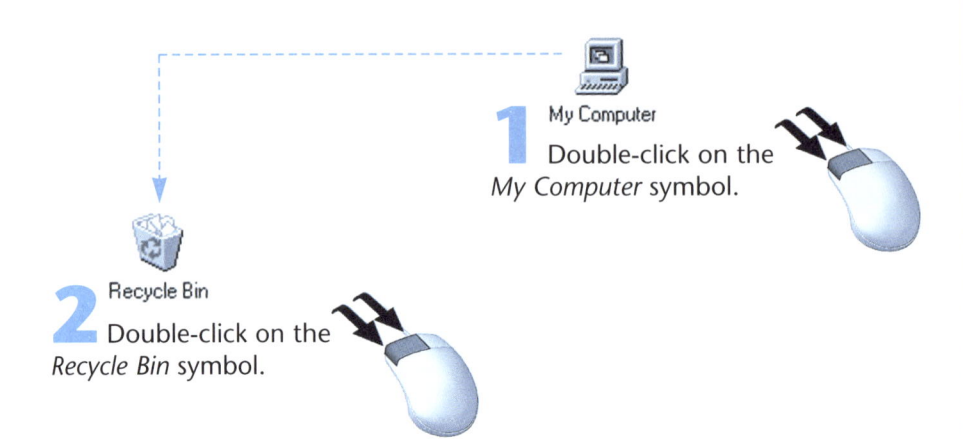

2 Recycle Bin
Double-click on the *Recycle Bin* symbol.

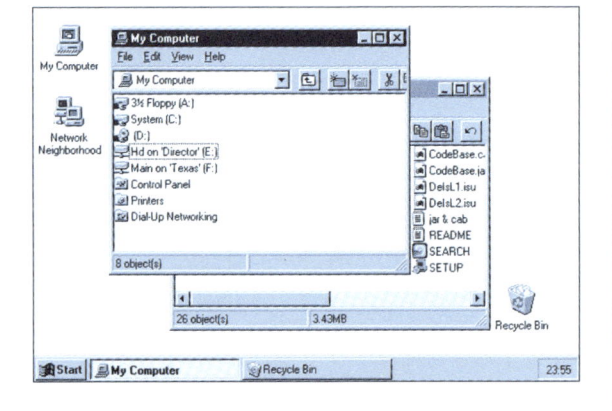

You should now see two open windows on the desktop. Unfortunately these two windows overlap, so the contents of the window in the background is partly hidden by the foreground window. You could close a window. Or you could click on the window in the background (or on its button in the taskbar) to bring it to the front. Usually, though, you will want to arrange both windows side by side so that you can see the contents of both windows at the same time. However, this is not so easy. If you drag the edge of the window, only the window size changes. You won't have much success either if you try to drag the contents of the window with the mouse. There's a certain knack to moving a window.

MOVING WINDOWS

1 Point the mouse pointer at the window's **title bar**.

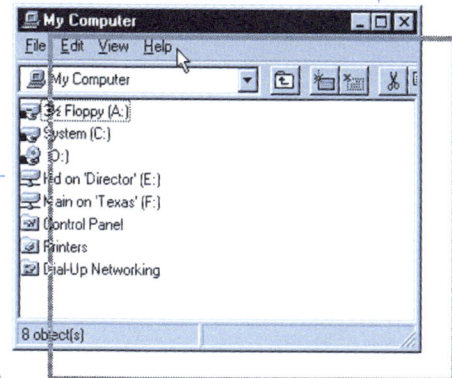

2 Then, using the mouse, **drag** the window to the desired position. As you are dragging, Windows shows the new window position with a grey outline.

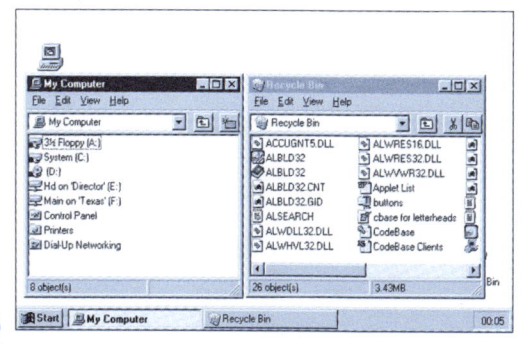

3 As soon as the window is in the desired position, release the left mouse button. Windows moves the window to the new position. By resizing the windows as well, if you need to, you can now see the whole of both windows on the desktop.

31

Scrolling through the window contents

What happens when the window contains too many items to show them all at once with the current size of window?

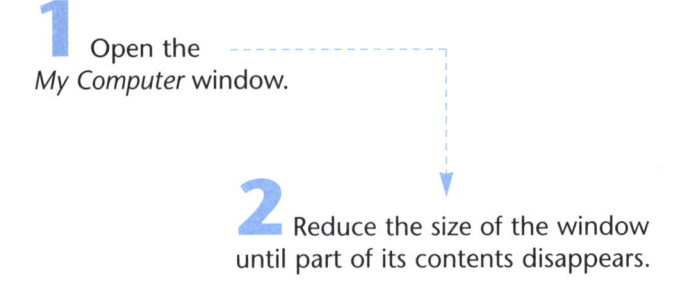

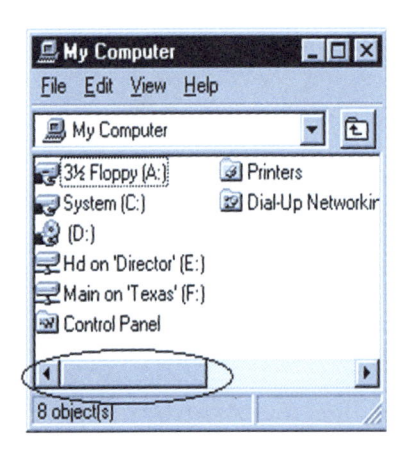

1 Open the *My Computer* window.

2 Reduce the size of the window until part of its contents disappears.

Here you can see the *My Computer* window which has been reduced like this.

As soon as the window is no longer able to display all the information, the window gains a **scroll bar** on the right or bottom edge of the window. This scroll bar makes it possible for you to choose the contents of the window which are visible.

Follow these steps to see the hidden contents of the window:

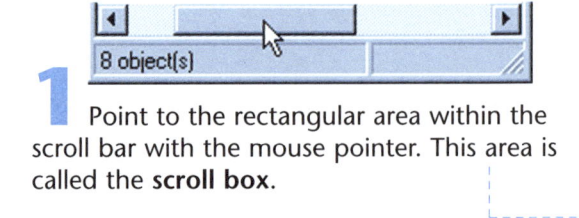

1 Point to the rectangular area within the scroll bar with the mouse pointer. This area is called the **scroll box**.

Scrolling through the window contents

2 Now, using the mouse, drag the scroll box in the desired direction. Windows then displays other parts of the window's contents that were hidden.

> **TIP** In both the preceding illustrations there is only a horizontal scroll bar. Windows can also have a vertical scroll bar. Then the contents of the window can be moved up or down. When writing a document you can browse through the text using these scroll bars.

> **TIP** At each end of the scroll bar you will see two buttons. If you find browsing with the scroll bar too swift, you can move through a document or window in small steps by clicking on the respective button.

33

Finding help

After reading this book you will probably still have questions which the Help function integrated into Windows might be able to answer for you. To display the Windows Help window, proceed as follows:

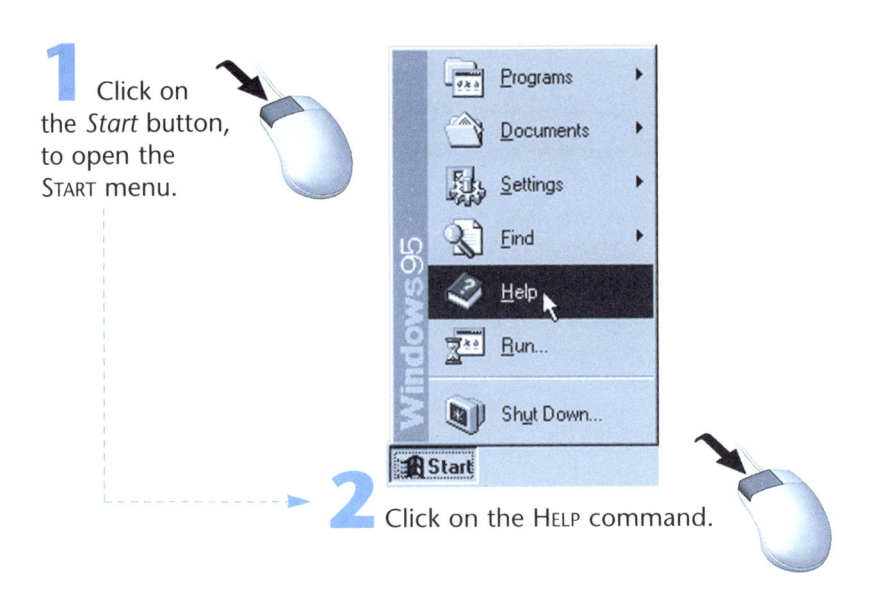

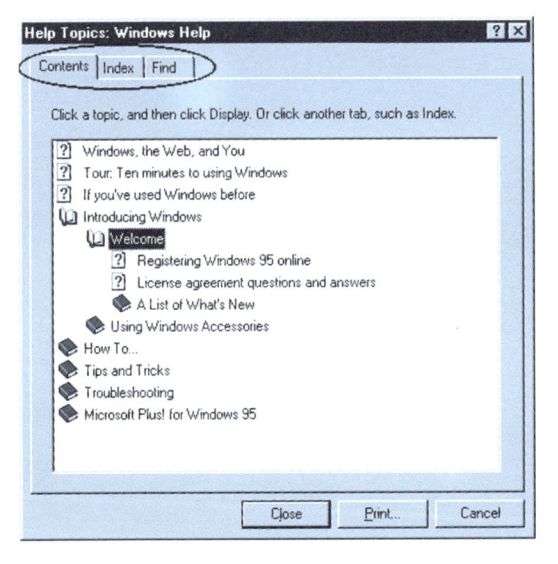

1 Click on the *Start* button, to open the START menu.

2 Click on the HELP command.

Windows now opens the Help window. This window contains three **tabs** with the words *Contents, Index* and *Find*. The *Contents* tab functions like the table of contents in a book. The individual headings are identified by icons of books or pages.

34

3 Double-click on a 'closed' book icon in order to see the headings contained in a topic.

4 A double-click on the document icon ? opens the corresponding Help page.

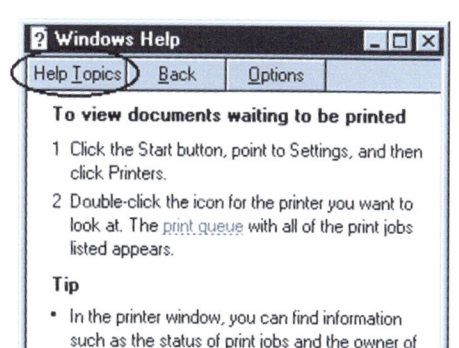

Windows then opens a window with the Help text. If the text contains buttons, you can call up other Windows functions directly using these. The *Help Topics* button takes you back to the window with the tabs.

Some areas of text in the Help window are displayed in green type and are underlined. If you click on an area of text marked in this way another window will open with additional explanations relating to the term marked in green. If you click on a further area of text in the Help window, then this additional window closes.

You can also search Help for specific terms. The *Index* tab corresponds to the index of a book.

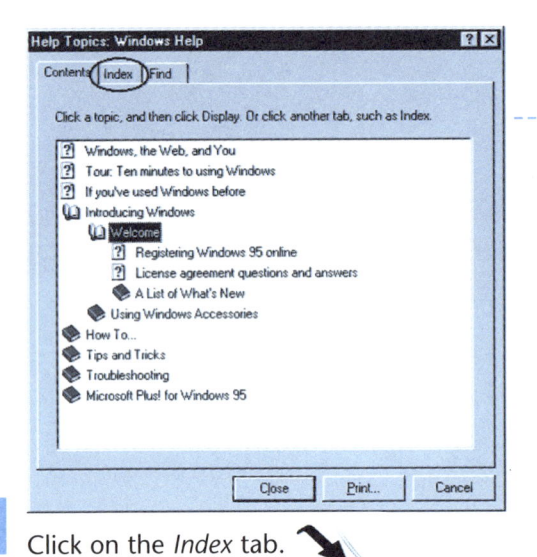

1 Click on the *Index* tab.

2 In the box marked '1. Type the first few letters of the word you're looking for' type in the **Search topic**. If a corresponding index entry exists, Windows will display it in the lower part of the window.

> You will encounter this type of 'box' for entries frequently. These boxes are called **fields** or **text fields**.

3 In box marked '2. Click the index entry you want and then click 'Display'' click on the topic you want. If necessary you can browse through the list of search topics using the scroll bar.

> If there are a lot of index entries, you can go through them using the scroll bar. Is the Help window concealing other windows? If so, minimise or close the Help window.

4 Click on the *Display* button. Windows now displays the window with the Help topic.

36

Windows Help also lets you to find help topics by searching for words or phrases.

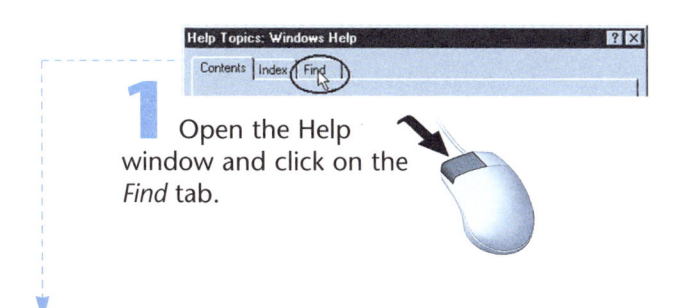

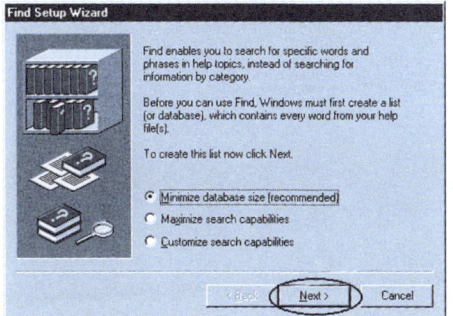

1 Open the Help window and click on the *Find* tab.

When you first call up the *Find* tab this window appears (if it doesn't, go straight to Step 4).

2 Leave all the settings as they are and click on the *Next* button.

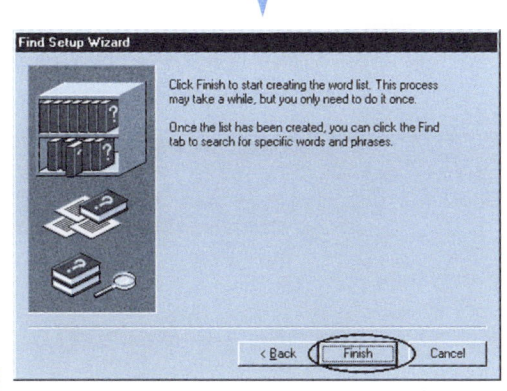

3 In this window click on the *Finish* button.

Windows uses this type of window to tell you what's going on. Therefore such windows are also called **Dialog boxes**. While Windows configures the Find function, this little window is displayed.

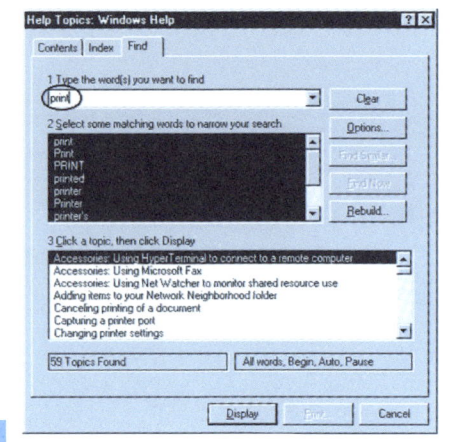

4 Now enter a word to search for in the field labelled '1. Type the word(s) you want to find'. Windows displays the terms found.

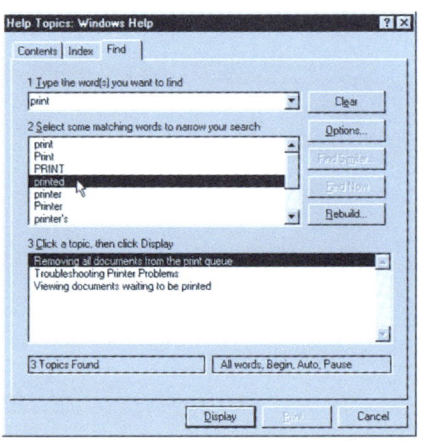

5 Click on one of the terms in the list '2. Select some matching words to narrow your search.' Windows displays the topics found relating to the selected term.

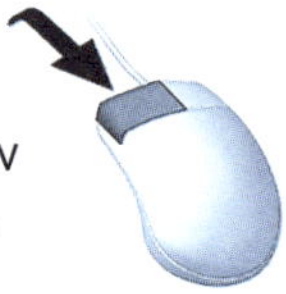

FINDING HELP

6 Click on the desired topic in the list '3. Click on a topic, then click Display', then click on the *Display* button. Windows displays the window with the Help text.

> **TIP**
> If a program window is not open then you can also call up Windows Help direct using the F1 key.

Furthermore many programs enable you to call up the Help window direct. This is shown here using the *My Computer* window as an example.

1 Open the *My Computer* window.

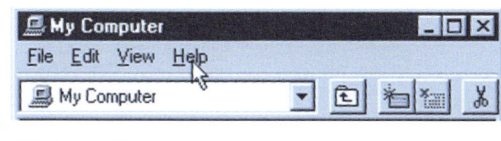

2 Click on the word HELP in the menu bar.

39

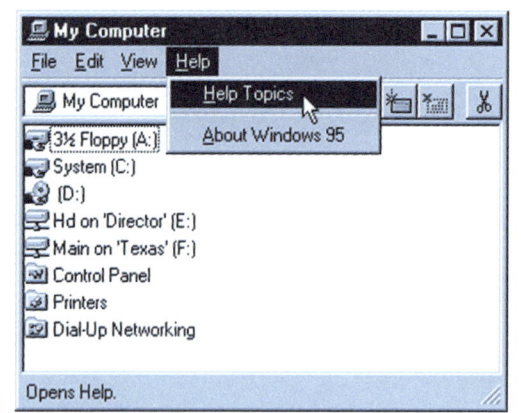

3 Click on the HELP TOPICS command. Windows displays the window with the three tabs *Topics, Index* and *Find*.

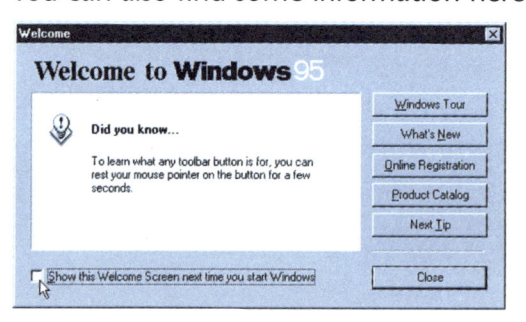

Does the *Welcome* dialog box appear when starting up Windows? You can also find some information here. By clicking the buttons you can start the Windows tour (an introduction to Windows), a Help window with new information or the next tip.

Would you prefer the Welcome dialog box not to appear the next time you start Windows?

1 Click on the **Check box** 'Show this Welcome Screen next time you start Windows'. The cross in the check box must be removed.

2 Click on the *Close* button.

> **TIP**
> **Check boxes** are small squares containing a cross if the option is activated. Depending on the current status the cross can be inserted or deleted by clicking on the box.

Exiting Windows

Before you go on to the next stages, one question remains 'How do you exit Windows?'

You might think of simply switching off the computer, but this could leave you and your computer with a lot of problems. After you have exited loaded programs and closed any open windows, you must exit Windows properly.

> **CAUTION**
> Never simply switch off the computer to exit Windows. This can cause data to be lost and Windows might possibly not start up again!

1 Click on the START button on the taskbar.

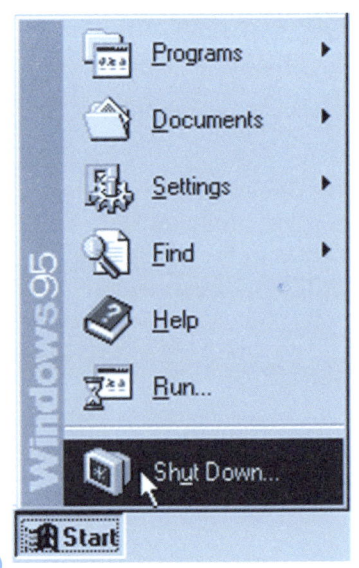

2 Click on the SHUT DOWN command in the Start menu. Windows now opens the *Shut Down Windows* dialog box.

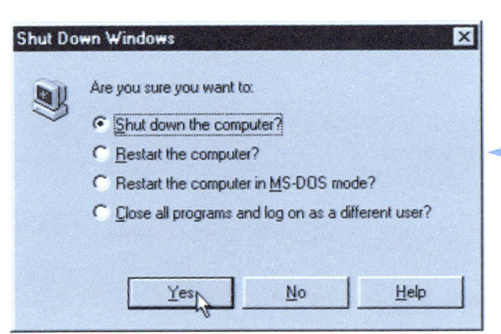

3 Click on the 'Shut down the computer' **Option box** and then on the *Yes* button.

42

EXITING WINDOWS

> **TIP**
>
> **Option boxes** are small circles within a dialog box. By clicking on them you can choose an option. If the circle has a dot in it, it shows the selected option. Unlike **Check boxes**, option boxes allow only one option to be chosen from the group.

Windows recognises the shut-down command and starts to 'tidy up'. Data is saved to the hard disk, programs which might still be running are exited and settings are saved for the next Windows start-up. As soon as this or similar wording appears on the screen, you can switch off the computer.

> It's now safe to turn off your computer.

43

2

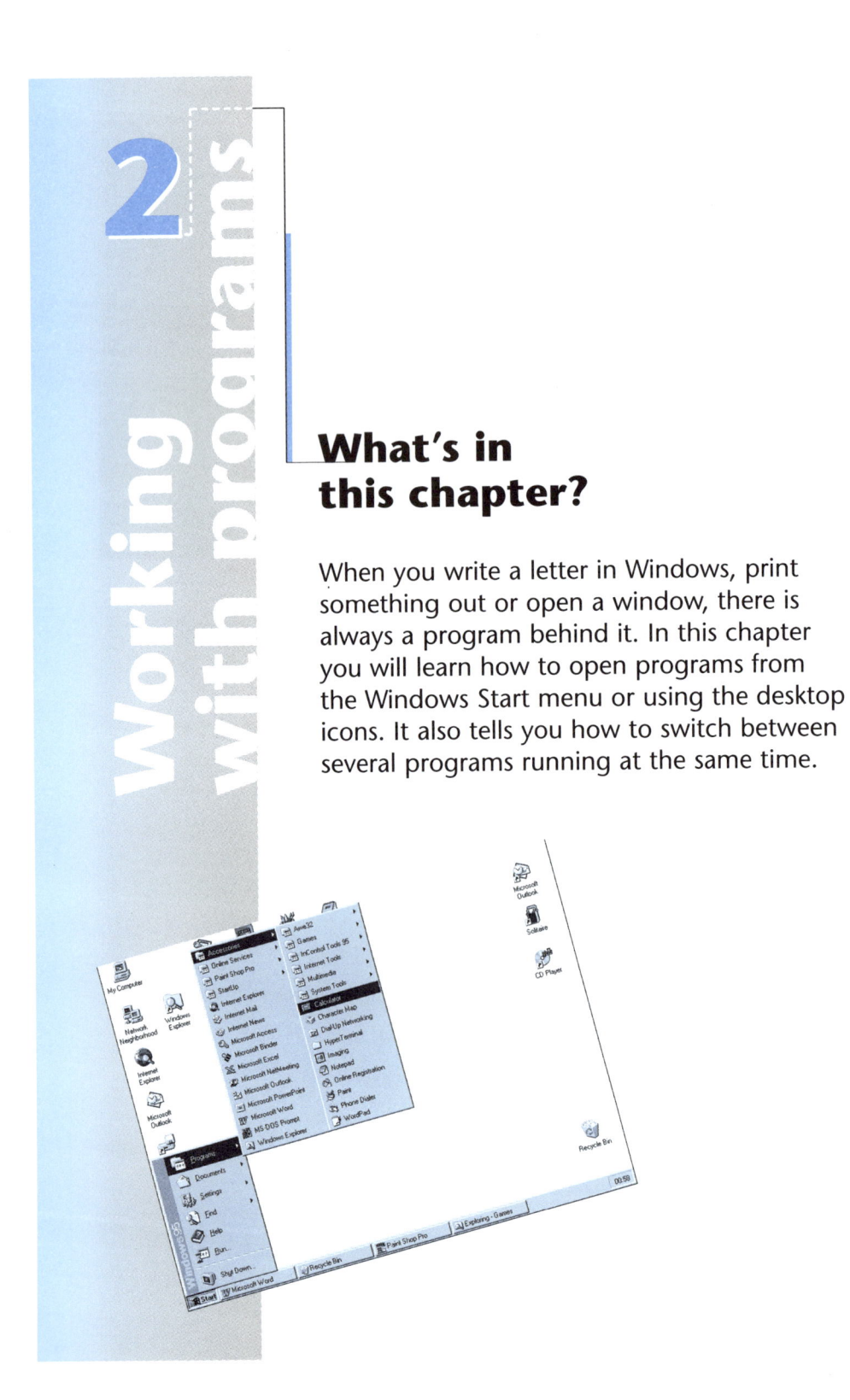

Working with programs

What's in this chapter?

When you write a letter in Windows, print something out or open a window, there is always a program behind it. In this chapter you will learn how to open programs from the Windows Start menu or using the desktop icons. It also tells you how to switch between several programs running at the same time.

You already know how to:

Work with the mouse   17
Work with windows   23
Change the window size   28

You are going to learn how to:

Use the Start menu   46
Start a program   47
Switch between programs   51
Close a program   53
Use other ways to open programs   55

Using the Start menu

You briefly got to know the **Start menu** in Chapter 1.

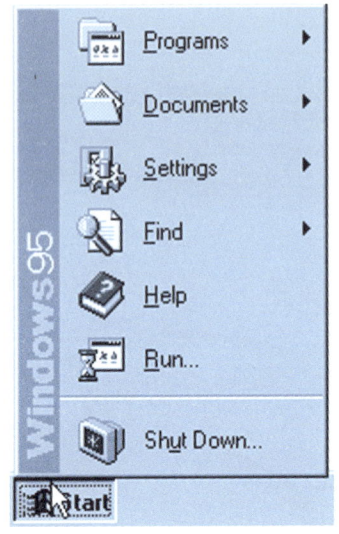

1 Click on the S*tart* button in the bottom left corner of the screen.

Windows opens a little window with various icons and names. This window is called the **Start menu**. You can choose various entries, just like a restaurant menu. These entries are Windows commands with which you can call up various functions, open drop-down lists or start programs. We already used this in Chapter 1 to call up Windows Help using the Help command.

Starting a program

You actually know how to open a program already. When working through Chapter 1, did you open the *My Computer* window with a double-click on the icon? Or did you call up Windows Help from the Start menu? When you did this you opened a program. But there are other programs in Windows and many of these programs are called up from the **Start menu**. The procedure is the same for different programs, so here is an example of how to start a program.

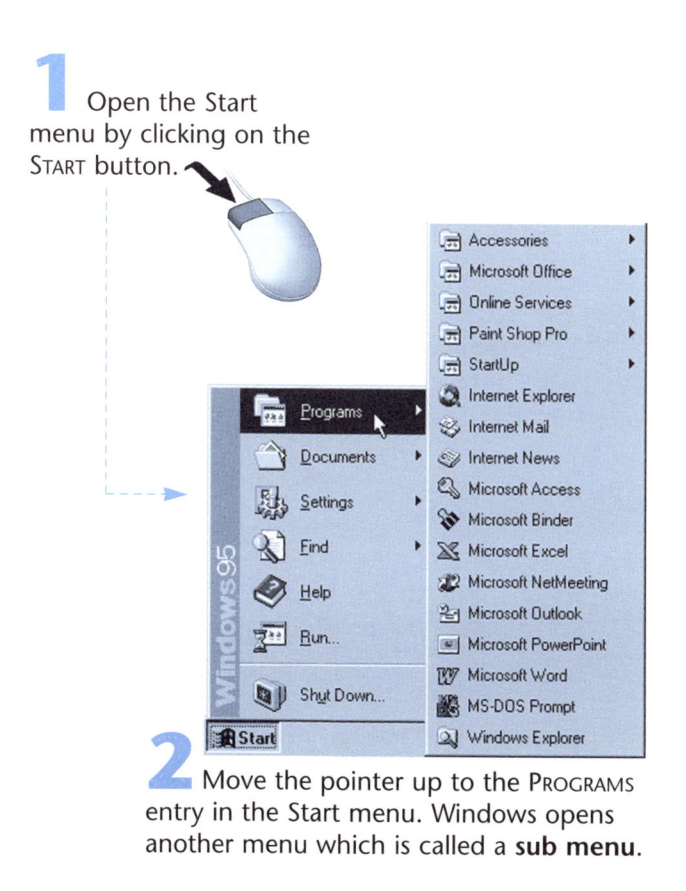

1 Open the Start menu by clicking on the START button.

- Accessories
- Microsoft Office
- Online Services
- Paint Shop Pro
- StartUp
- Internet Explorer
- Internet Mail
- Internet News
- Microsoft Access
- Microsoft Binder
- Microsoft Excel
- Microsoft NetMeeting
- Microsoft Outlook
- Microsoft PowerPoint
- Microsoft Word
- MS-DOS Prompt
- Windows Explorer

Programs
Documents
Settings
Find
Help
Run...
Shut Down...
Start

2 Move the pointer up to the PROGRAMS entry in the Start menu. Windows opens another menu which is called a **sub menu**.

There you will see the icons for programs such as INTERNET EXPLORER, MICROSOFT WORD or WINDOWS EXPLORER etc., depending on which programs are installed on your computer.

3 Click on the WINDOWS EXPLORER entry in the PROGRAMS drop-down menu.

Windows then starts the *Explorer* program. The associated window is opened on the desktop. You will learn how to use this program in Chapter 3. All the programs shown with an icon in the Start menu can be opened in this way. You will find examples of some of these on the next few pages.

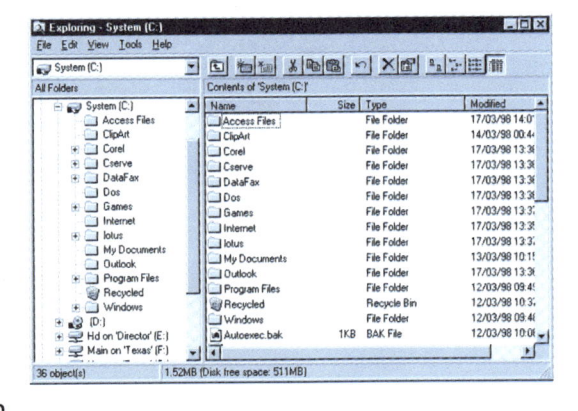

> **TIP**
> Opening a program works in just the same way as calling up Windows Help. As soon as you click on a program entry in the Start menu, Windows opens it. At the same time the window for this program is displayed on the desktop and Windows automatically closes the Start menu. Generally speaking, these icons and entries are automatically added to the Start menu when you install a new program.

48

STARTING A PROGRAM

In the previous step a program was called up directly in the PROGRAMS sub-menu. However, many programs are located in different places in the Start menu. Now call up the Calculator (a small 'pocket calculator') by following these steps:

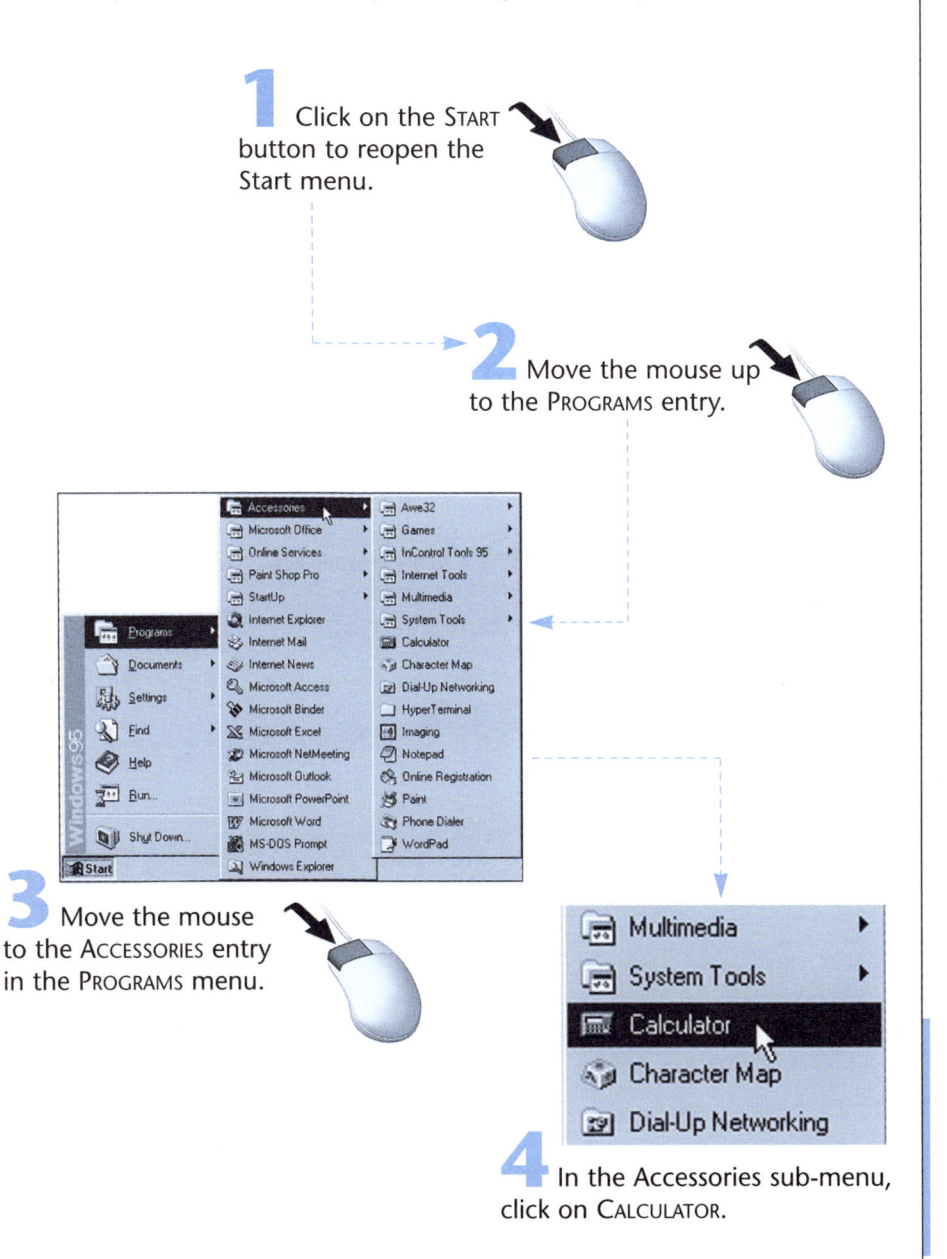

1 Click on the START button to reopen the Start menu.

2 Move the mouse up to the PROGRAMS entry.

3 Move the mouse to the ACCESSORIES entry in the PROGRAMS menu.

4 In the Accessories sub-menu, click on CALCULATOR.

49

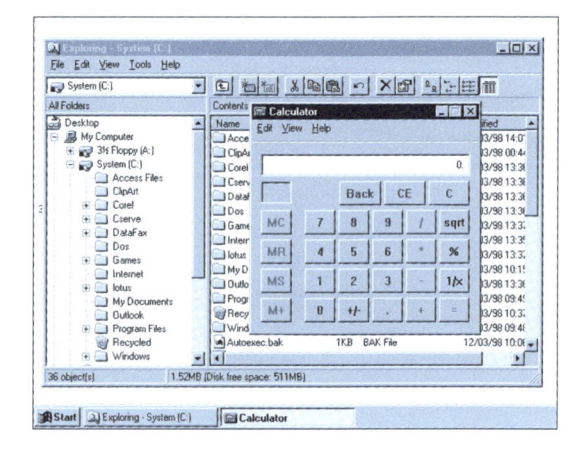

The Windows Calculator now starts up as another program. If you have not closed the Explorer window, this will probably be partly covered by the *Calculator* window.

> In addition to program entries the Start menu also contains entries with the 📁 icon. This icon (and the little triangle on the right edge of an entry) indicates a **program group** (e.g. STARTUP, ACCESSORIES etc.). Program groups gather several program icons (or other groups) into a **sub-menu**. If you move the pointer to a program group icon, a further menu opens, displaying icons for further program groups or programs. For example you may find further subgroups within the ACCESSORIES program group such as MULTIMEDIA or SYSTEM TOOLS. Which menus and sub-menus menus are displayed on your Start menu depends on the programs that have been installed on your computer.

Switching between programs

Windows makes it possible for you to have several programs open at the same time. Then you can switch between the various programs and even exchange data between them.

1 Open the Start menu and move the mouse to PROGRAMS then ACCESSORIES.

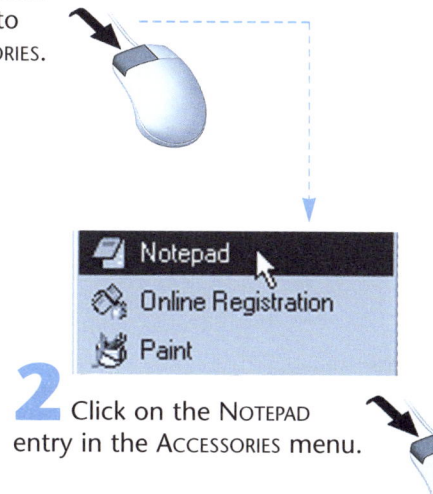

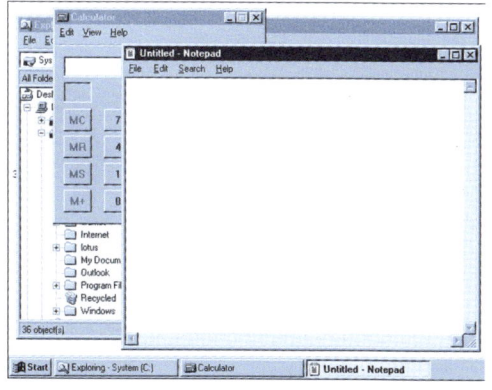

2 Click on the NOTEPAD entry in the ACCESSORIES menu.

If you've followed all the preceding steps, the desktop will now contain three overlapping windows which belong to the programs that have been opened. You can now work with the calculator, write a letter in Notepad or look at files in Explorer without having to close the program you were using previously.

51

3 To work with the calculator, for example, click on its icon in the taskbar.

The Calculator window appears in the foreground and you can then work with the program.

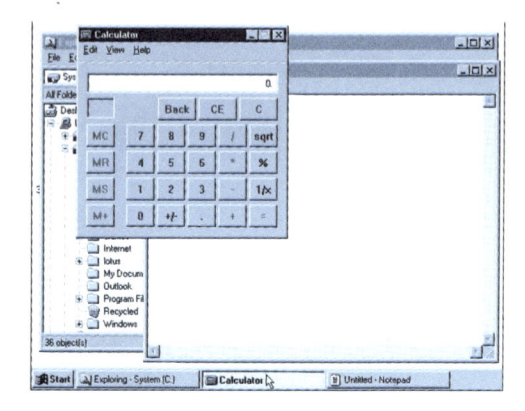

> **TIP** Windows displays the **icons** for the open **programs** in the **taskbar**. The button for the active window thus looks as though it is 'pressed in'. You can **switch** to another **program window** at any time by clicking on the corresponding **button** in the taskbar.

> **TIP** In addition to the taskbar button you can also use the `Alt` + `⇆` key combination to switch between programmes. Keep the `Alt` key pressed down and press the `⇆` key. Windows displays a window with the icons for the programs which are running. If you press on the `⇆` key it marks a different program. Release the `Alt` key and the program window you selected last is brought into the foreground.

52

Closing a program

In Chapter 1 you already learnt the techniques for closing a window. A program can be closed in a similar way.

1 Bring the Calculator window into the foreground by clicking on the corresponding button on the taskbar.

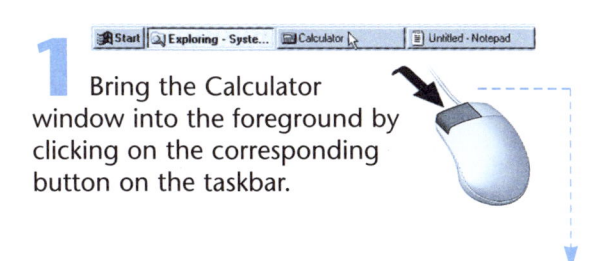

Most windows have a *Close* button.

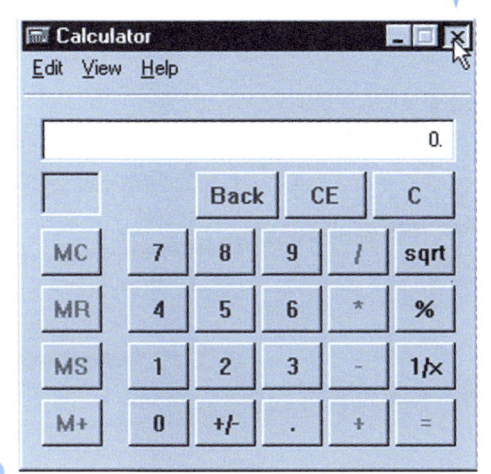

2 Click on the *Close* button in the upper right corner.

Windows closes the Calculator window and at the same time exits the related program. Closing a program's window automatically shuts down the program itself.

53

Depending on the program there are other ways to exit them.

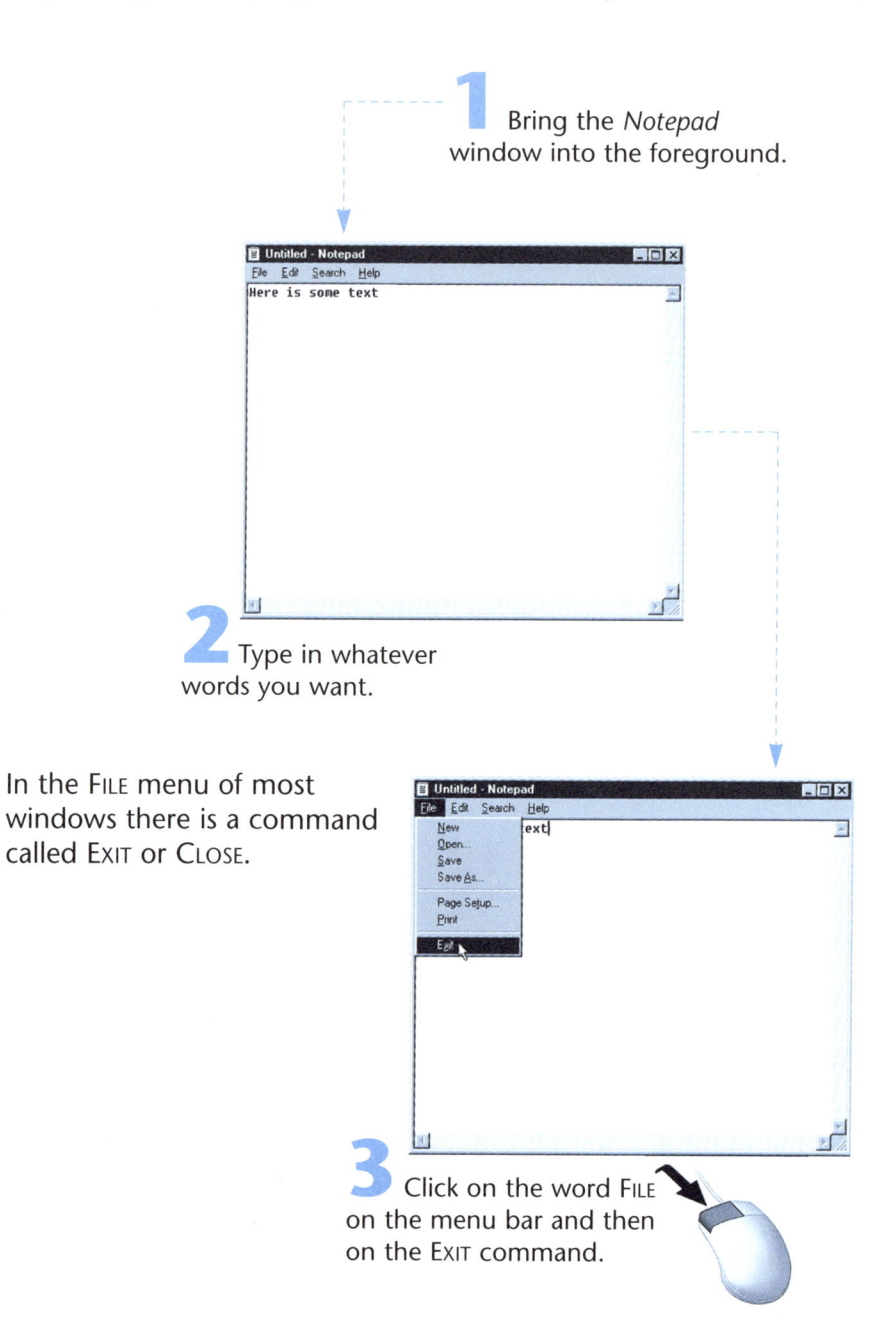

1 Bring the *Notepad* window into the foreground.

2 Type in whatever words you want.

In the FILE menu of most windows there is a command called EXIT or CLOSE.

3 Click on the word FILE on the menu bar and then on the EXIT command.

If the window contains data which has not been saved (e.g. the words you have just typed), Windows asks whether the window's contents should be saved before it is closed. You will then see the following dialog box.

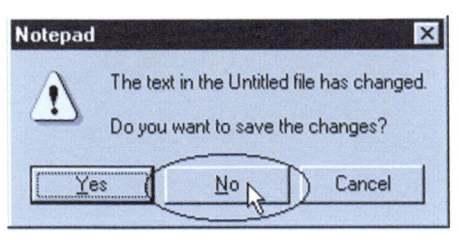

4 Click on the *No* button to exit the program without saving the words you have typed.

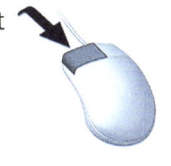

> If you have called up the Close function by mistake, choose the CANCEL button in the above dialog box. You will then return to the application window. You will learn how to save data in Notepad using the Yes button in Chapter 4.

Other ways to open programs

The Start menu provides you with a quick way to start a program, but there are disadvantages. The program must be installed in such a way that an entry is available in the Start menu (see Chapter 11). Also you might have to search though a number of sub-menus to find the entry you were looking for. Windows offers you several other ways to start programs.

55

Is the program icon visible on the desktop?

1 Double-click on the program icon.

Windows will then open the related program immediately. You already learnt this (without being aware of it) when you double-clicked on the *My Computer* icon. If the Notepad icon is visible on the desktop, for example, all you have to do is double-click on this icon. Windows opens the Notepad window right away.

> **TIP**
> You will find out how to set up a program as an icon on the desktop in Chapter 11. You'll also learn how to add more programs to the Start menu or remove them.

Finally you can also call up a program direct.

1 Open the Start menu using the START button.

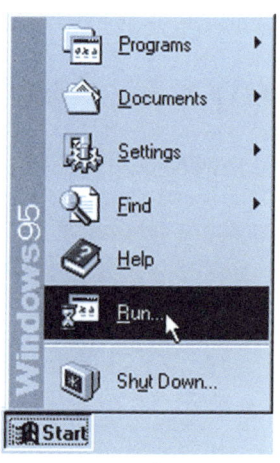

2 Click on the RUN command in the Start menu.

56

OTHER WAYS TO OPEN PROGRAMS

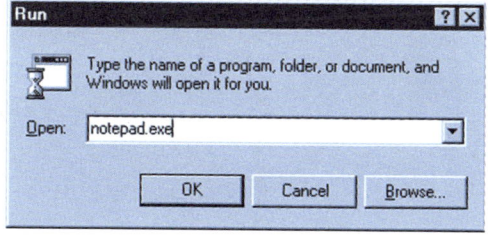

Windows immediately opens the *Run* dialog box.

> **Run**
> Type the name of a program, folder, or document, and Windows will open it for you.
> Open: notepad.exe
> OK   Cancel   Browse...

3 Type the name of the program in the *Open* entry box.

4 Click on the *OK* button.

Windows then searches for the requested program. If it finds the program, it opens it.

> **TIP**
> In Chapter 3 you will learn to use files. If a program is displayed as a file in the *My Computer* or Explorer windows, it can also be opened with a double-click on the program icon.

57

3

Using files and folders

What's in this chapter

In this chapter you will learn about drives, folders and files. You will know what type of drives there are in Windows and how disks are used to store data. You can display, copy, delete, move or rename folders and files. You will also find out how to restore files from the Recycle Bin and learn how floppy disks are formatted and copied.

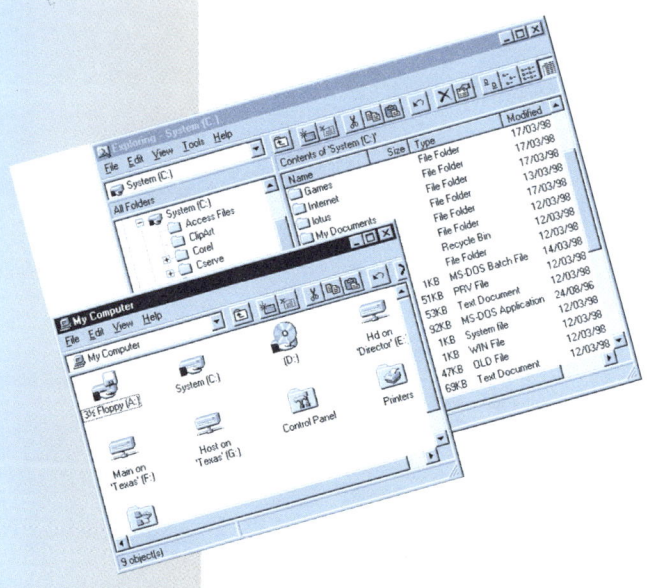

YOUR PROGRESS METER

You already know how to:

Work with Windows 23
Open a program 47

Your are going to learn how to:

Identify folders and files	60	Copy a file to the same folder	99
Use Windows drives	65	Move folders and files	101
Handle floppy disks	67	Copy a floppy disk	103
Display drives, files and folders	68	Find out how much data is stored on a disk	106
Sort folder displays	74	Find out how much disk space a folder or file uses	107
View folders in Explorer	76		
Move between drives and folders	79	Delete files and folders	109
Create a new folder	83	Retrieve deleted files from the Recycle Bin	111
Create a new file	86	Empty the Recycle Bin	113
Rename folders and files	88	Search files and folders	114
Copy folders and files	90	Format a floppy disk	117
Copy several files at the same time	95		

59

What are folders and files?

Folders and files are two terms which you will frequently encounter in Windows. If you are already familiar with these terms, you can skip this section.

Files are displayed in the windows of the *My Computer* window. For example, the window for the *Windows* folder contains the icons for various files. But what are files and what are they used for? As soon as you use a program to write a letter or to create a drawing or graphic, to draft a spreadsheet, and so on, data is generated. In many cases you will not only want to display this data on the screen or print it out, you will also want to 'store' it for later use. In computer jargon, this 'storage' is called **saving**. The computer data is (mainly) stored on the hard disk or on floppy disks. But there's more to it than the letters in a document simply being stored on a floppy disk or hard disk. How is the computer or the program supposed to find the text again if several documents are stored on the disk? A further analogy may be of help here. If you write a document by hand or with a typewriter, you fasten the pages together in an appropriate manner. You might then note the title and the contents on a cover sheet. When storing such a document in a filing cabinet, its name is probably shown on a tab. This then allows you later to go straight to the document in question. Something similar happens on a computer. This collates all the associated data (e.g. the text of a letter, a picture, a spreadsheet, a program etc.) into a **file**. You can picture a file as something like a container into which the data is packed. Each file is given a name. This name allows the computer, and ultimately you, to find the same file again later.

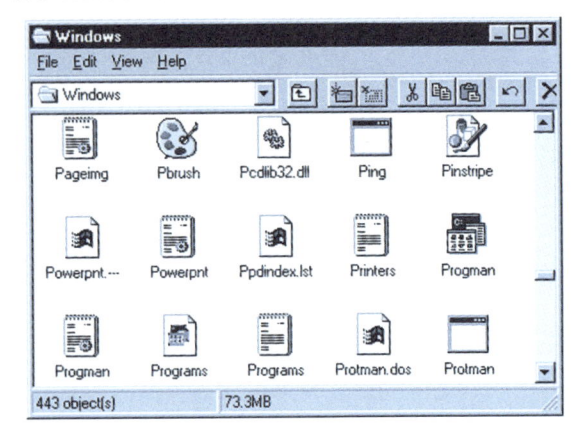

What are folders and files?

> **Rules for file names**
> File **names** must satisfy certain rules in Windows. A file name may be up to 255 characters long. The letters A to Z, a to z, the numbers 0 to 9, spaces and various other symbols can be used in the name. Letter to Bill Smith would be a valid name. The symbols " / \ | < and > are not permitted in file names.
>
> In addition to the name, files also have a **file name extension** (known as the 'extension' for short). This is a full stop, followed by three or more letters (e.g. .TXT, .BMP, .EXE, .HTML, .INI, .DOC etc.). These extensions determine the type of file, i.e. which program can be used to edit a file.
>
> You can write the file name and extension in either upper or lower case letters. Windows does not differentiate between them, i.e. the names 'Letter to Bill Smith.doc' and 'letter to bill smith.doc' are treated in the same way by Windows. The limiting of file names to eight letters for the name and three characters for the extension (often also called 8.3 file names), familiar from MS-DOS and Windows 3.1, no longer exists in Windows 95 and Windows NT. In order to save unnecessary typing, however, file names should not be longer than 20 characters.

Depending on the file name extension, files are allocated various icons under Windows. You will find a few examples of such file names below.

Icon   Description

Circles.bmp   This is a graphics file, which has the *.bmp* extension. Such files are created and edited with the Windows *Paint* program (see Chapter 4).

61

Network.txt — The writing pad icon and the *.txt* extension stand for files which contain plain text. You can create these files with the *Notepad* program, among others (see Chapter 4).

Relnotes.doc
Relnotes.doc — Files with the *.doc* extension also contain text, but may also contain graphics or specially formatted words or letters (bold, italic etc.). If a DOC file has the top icon it has been created with the Windows *WordPad* program (see Chapter 4). The bottom icon is used if the program *Microsoft Word* is available on your computer.

Accounts.xls — Files with the *.xls* extension contain spreadsheets and can be edited using a program called *Microsoft Excel*.

Notepad.hlp — Files with the *.hlp* extension contain Help documents and are displayed with a book icon. Windows uses these files if you call up a program's Help functions.

Attrib.exe — The *.exe* extension is used for program files. In the case of older MS-DOS programs the icon displayed next to the file is that of a window.

Calc.exe — Windows programs also have the *.exe* extension. Every Windows program has its own unique icon (opposite you can see the icon for the Windows Calculator).

Autoexec.bat — The *.bat* extension covers certain files which contain MS-DOS commands. These files can be executed in a similar way to programs.

WHAT ARE FOLDERS AND FILES?

> There are many more icons for files depending on the file extensions and the programs installed on your computer.

Now we come to the question **What are folders and what are they used for?** An example from everyday office practice is also helpful here. In order to work more efficiently and avoid piles of paper, letters and documents are stored in folders. A folder holds all the documents which are in some way related.

The same applies to the computer. Files are stored on the hard disk or on floppy disks. If you open the *My Computer* window and the drive window (see the following pages), then Windows displays the files stored on the drive. As with an archive, Windows reads a table of contents and displays the file names and some additional information.

The *Cap02* window opposite shows a folder with 30 files (described as objects in this window).

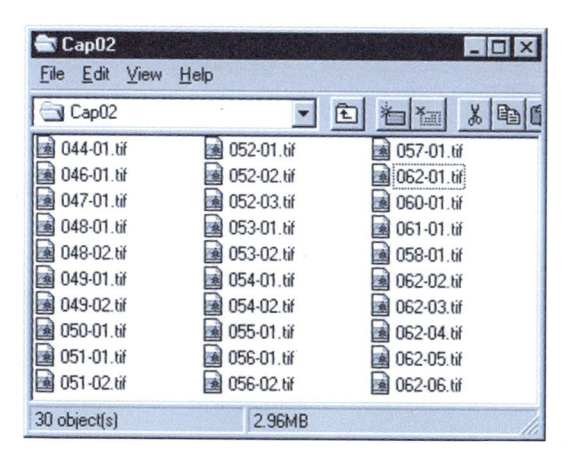

63

We soon realise that it can be difficult to find a specific file at the drop of a hat. What is it like though, when you haven't saved just 30 files, but possibly several thousand? In such a case it is very laborious to track down a specific file. Something similar happens when you have to 'fish' a certain letter out of a pile of paper. Just as in the office, Windows has a very neat solution to storing documents – files which are grouped together under a topic are stored in **folders**. Folders are stored on floppy disk or hard disk.

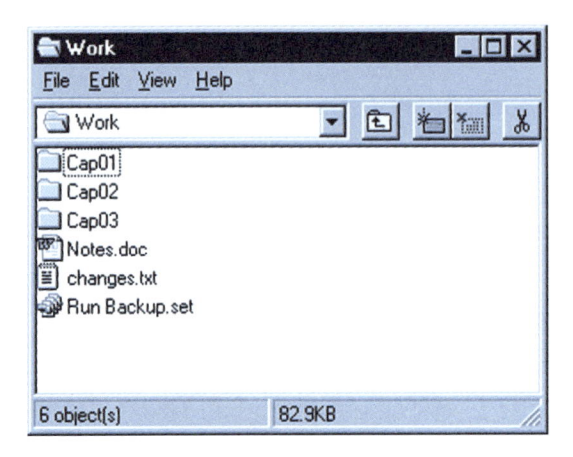

The window shows the contents of the *Work* folder. In it you can see three folder icons and three files.

> **CAUTION**
> Files and folders must be provided with a clear, unique name. You can't store two folders or files with identical names in a folder. A file may, however, be stored under the same name in different folders.

All folders are represented in windows by a yellow folder icon. This makes it possible for you to distinguish files from folders. It is left up to you which criteria you use to divide files among folders. You can store files according to certain systems (e.g. all letters are stored in a folder called *Letters*, all invoices in a second folder called *Invoices* and so on).

Folders are given a **name** in a similar way to files. The same rules apply to naming folders as to naming files. Generally however the file name extension used for files is omitted for folders. Folders are also occasionally called **Directories**. When you see this term you know that it means a folder.

Using Windows drives

Floppy disks, hard disks or CD ROMs are used to store files and folders. If you open the *My Computer* window, for example, Windows displays the drives available on your computer. The various drives are each identified by a name and an icon.

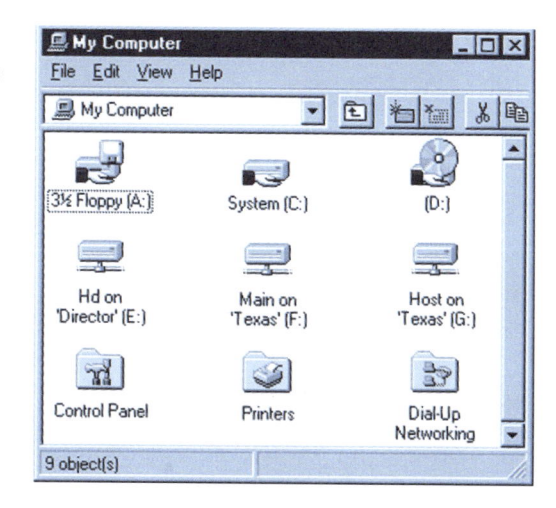

The icons provide you with a clue to the type of drive.

3½ Floppy (A:)

5¼ Floppy (A:)

Both the symbols opposite are used for floppy disk drives. The stylised floppy disk icon indicates which type of disk the drive supports. Generally speaking, new computers only use $3^1/_2$ inch floppy disks. These are disks which are approximately 9 cms square and contained in a rigid casing. Many older computers use $5^1/_2$ inch disks, which have a flexible casing.

System (C:)   Hard disk drives are allocated this icon. Such drives are built into the computer and cannot be changed like floppy disks. You can store much more data on a hard disk than on a floppy disk.

(D:)   If your computer has a CD ROM drive, this will be represented by the icon opposite.

> Sometimes drives are represented with a stylised hand in the lower left corner. This hand shows that the drive is shared on a network, i.e. other users on the network have access to this drive. This hand symbol is also used for shared printers or folders (see Chapter 9).
>
> **System (C:)**

The final question is **What are drives called?** As soon as you open the *My Computer* window you see the icons for the drives which are available on the computer including a name for the drive. The individual designations for the drives may vary according to the type of computer (e.g. Data1 (D:), System (C) etc.). But all drives are named according to a simple system which applies to all computers.

- The drives are listed alphabetically from A to Z and close with a colon. You will be able to identify these letters in the *My Computer* window.

- The floppy disk drive is generally recognised as the primary drive and is consequently named with the letter **A:**.

- If a second floppy disk drive is available, this is called by letter **B:**

- The first hard disk drive is given the letter **C:**

If **other hard disk drives** and **CD ROM drives** exist, these are given the consecutive letters **D:, E:, F:** and so on.

Handling floppy disks

If you are working with a computer you will presumably also use floppy disks. For example, you can copy files from the hard disk to floppy disks and store these floppy disks in an archive. Moreover programs are still offered for sale on floppy disks (in addition to CD ROMs). You then have to install the programs from the floppy disks to the hard disk (see Chapter 11).

> In the top right corner the floppy disk has a small rectangular opening which can be closed with a sliding plastic tab. If the opening is blocked by the tab, then files can be copied to the disk. By uncovering this opening, the disk becomes **write-protected**. An opening on the left-hand side of the disk indicates that it is a 1.44 Mb (megabyte) disk, whilst a 720 Kb (kilobyte)disk does not have this opening.

label

You should take several things into consideration when working with floppy disks. Here you can see a 3$\frac{1}{2}$ inch floppy disk which is housed in a solid plastic casing. The label is used to identify the floppy disk. You should always get hold of a floppy disk by this label. The metal slide at the bottom protects the magnetic layer on the plastic disk located in the plastic casing from dust, dirt and finger prints.

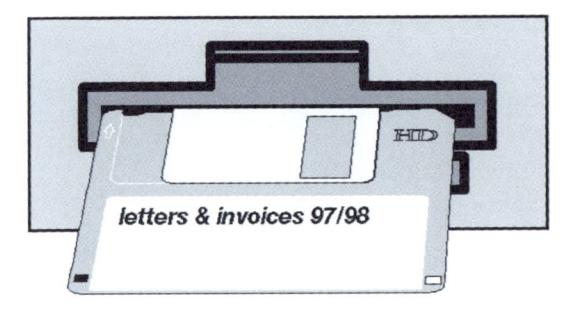

To insert the disk get hold of it by the label and push it forward as shown in the diagram opposite (metal slide to the front, paper label uppermost) until it slides into the drive. To remove the disk press the eject button located on the front of the floppy disk drive.

> **TIP**
> You should put floppy disks away in a disk box after removing them from the drive. Floppy disks should not be exposed to dust, fluids, heat or magnetic fields (from telephones, monitors or loudspeakers), because this can lead to loss of data.

Displaying drives, files and folders

Windows offers you various possibilities for displaying the contents of drives.

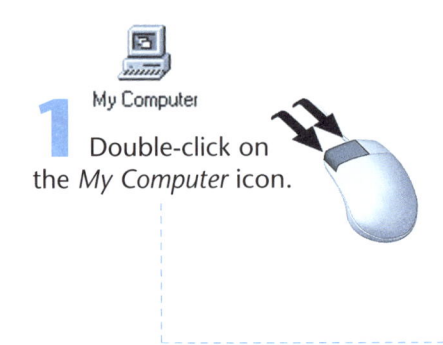

1 Double-click on the *My Computer* icon.

DISPLAYING DRIVES, FILES AND FOLDERS

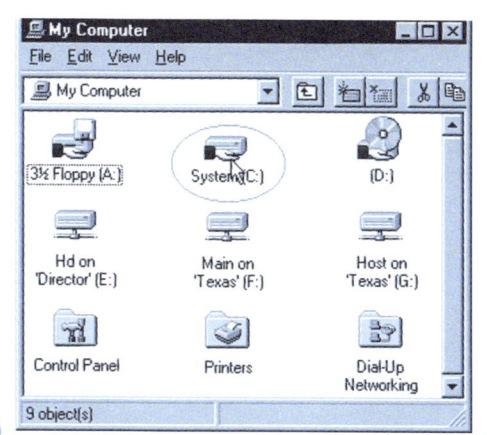

2 Double-click on the icon for the desired drive (e.g. C:) in the *My Computer* window.

Windows now opens the window which displays the drive's contents. In this window you will see the icons for the files and folders stored on this drive. You'll recognise the remaining items in the window such as scroll bars, toolbars and the buttons to close the window from Chapter 1.

You can scroll through the folder contents using the window's scroll bar. Alternatively you can change the size of the window following the steps in Chapter 1.

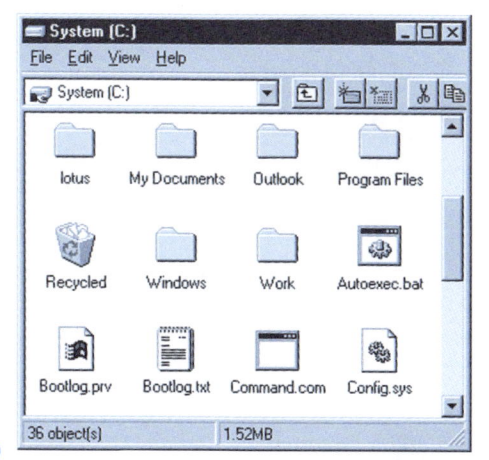

3 Double-click on a folder icon.

69

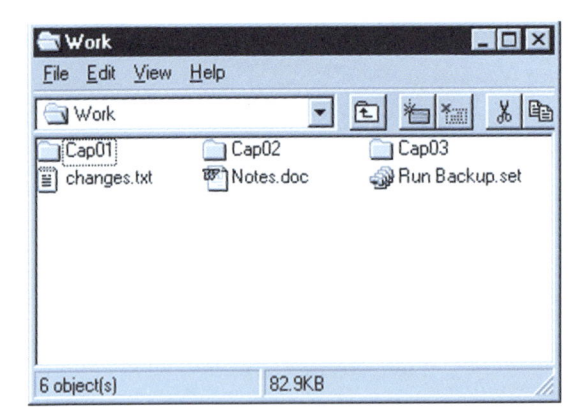

Windows opens a window for the folder you chose. In this case you can see the *Work* folder, which itself contains various folders and files. You can open the window for a folder by double-clicking its icon.

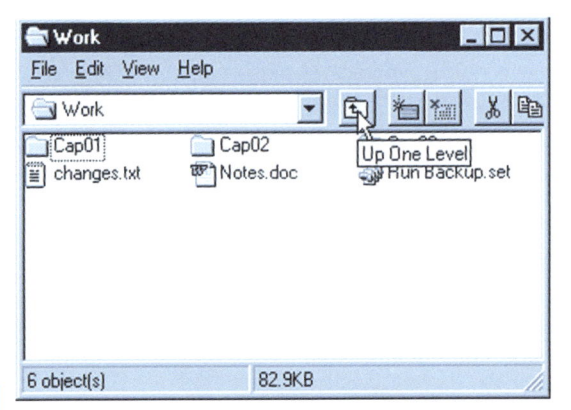

In this window you can also see the ToolTip explanation for the button.

4 In order to go back a stage from this folder to the folder above it, click on the *Up One Level* button in the toolbar.

You can also press the backspace key to return to the previous folder.

DISPLAYING DRIVES, FILES AND FOLDERS

Is the toolbar missing from your window? Would you like to insert the toolbar?

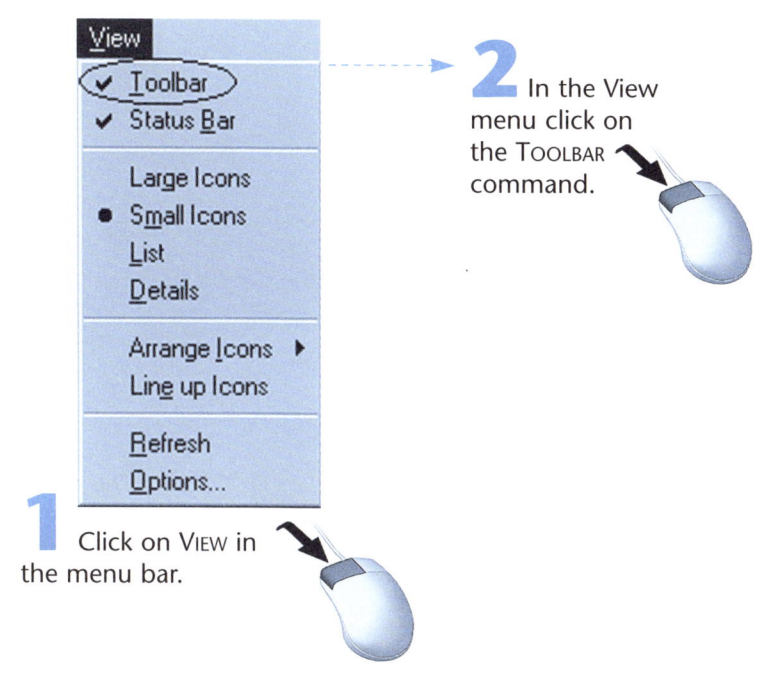

View
- ✓ Toolbar
- ✓ Status Bar
- Large Icons
- • Small Icons
- List
- Details
- Arrange Icons ▶
- Line up Icons
- Refresh
- Options...

2 In the View menu click on the TOOLBAR command.

1 Click on VIEW in the menu bar.

If the TOOLBAR command is marked with a tick, then the bar is displayed. Another click on the command switches the toolbar off again. By the way, the status bar at the bottom of the window can also be inserted in the same way. This works for many Windows application windows.

Do you find it annoying that Windows opens **a new window for each folder?**

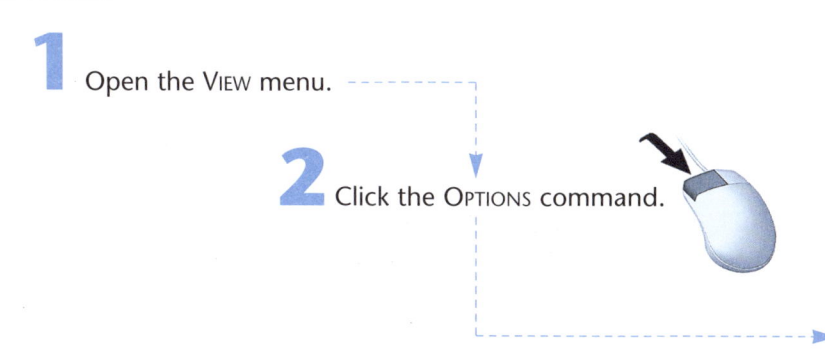

1 Open the VIEW menu.

2 Click the OPTIONS command.

71

3 Click the option box shown above.

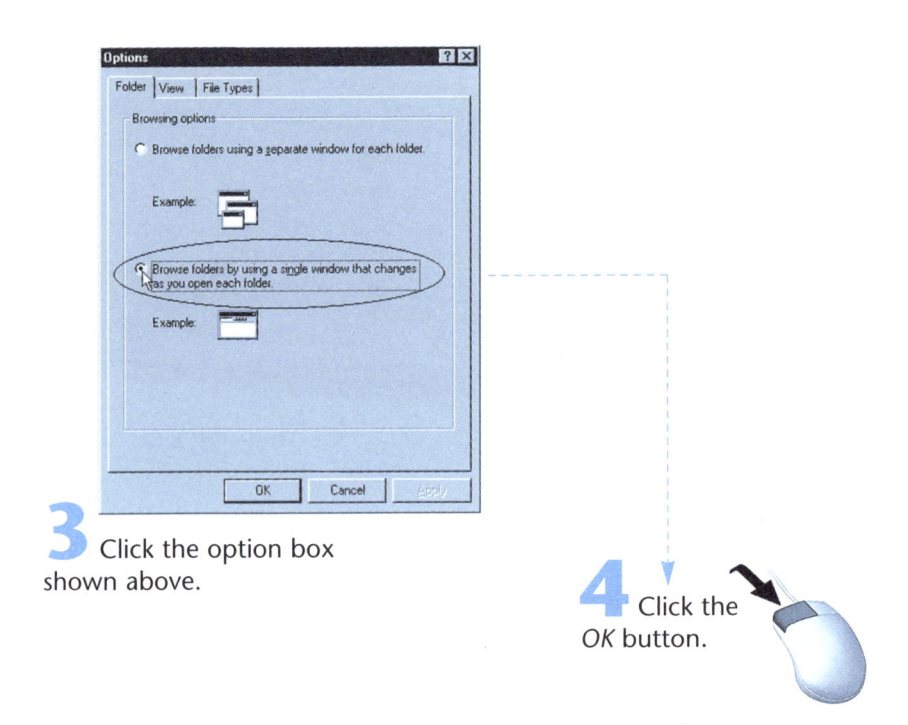

4 Click the *OK* button.

You've probably noticed that **different sizes of icon** are used in the *My Computer* window and/or the windows for other folders. Some windows use large icons for folders and files, while small icons appear in other windows. You can adjust this using the toolbar.

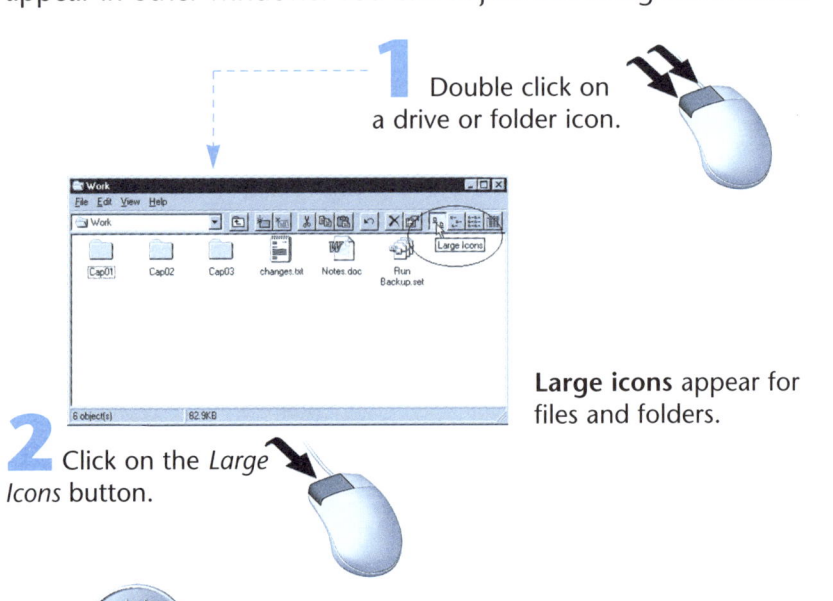

1 Double click on a drive or folder icon.

Large icons appear for files and folders.

2 Click on the *Large Icons* button.

DISPLAYING DRIVES, FILES AND FOLDERS

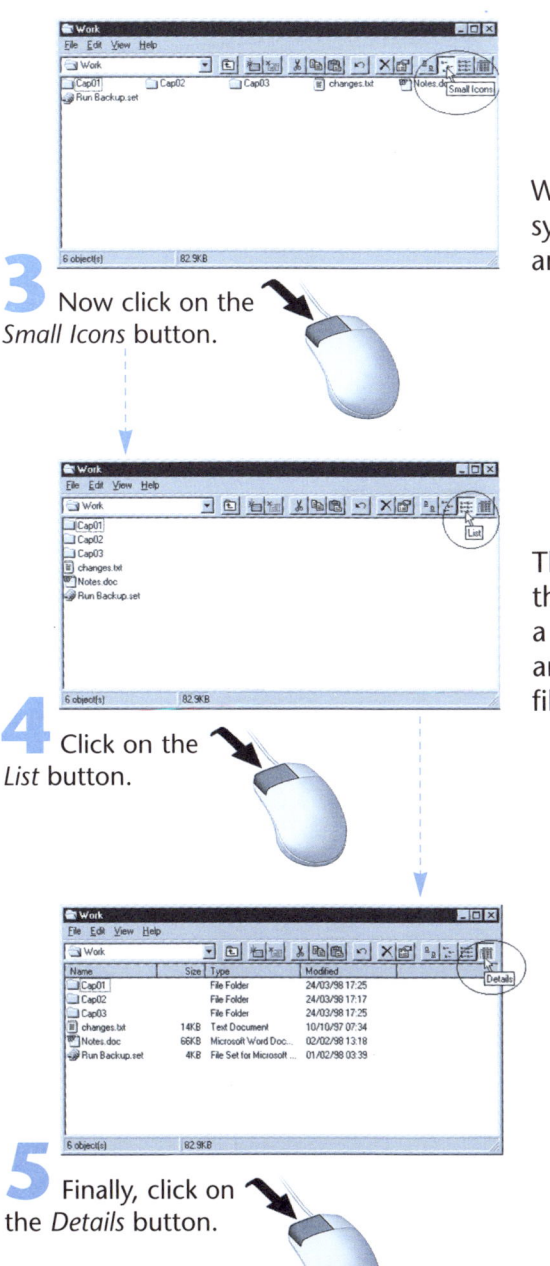

Windows now uses small symbols to display the files and folders.

3 Now click on the *Small Icons* button.

The display in the window then appears in the form of a list in which the icons and names for folders and files are shown in list form.

4 Click on the *List* button.

The display in the window is expanded with information on the file size, type of file and date last amended.

5 Finally, click on the *Details* button.

73

> You can also call up these display options using the View menu. Here you will find commands with the same names which correspond to the buttons on the toolbar shown.

Sorting the folder display

The icons for files and folders are sorted according to specific criteria in the display. You can configure these sort criteria using the ARRANGE ICONS option in the VIEW menu.

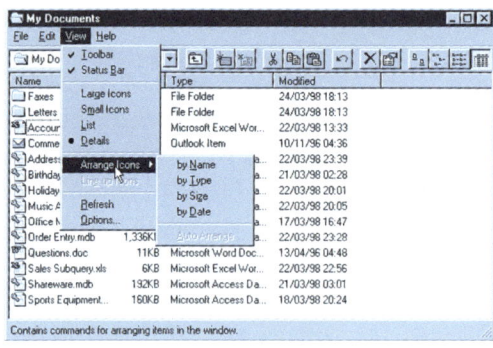

1 Click on VIEW in the menu bar and then move the pointer down to ARRANGE ICONS.

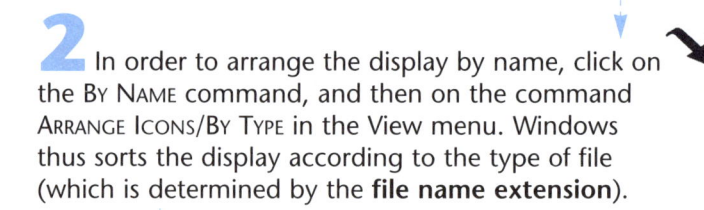

2 In order to arrange the display by name, click on the BY NAME command, and then on the command ARRANGE ICONS/BY TYPE in the View menu. Windows thus sorts the display according to the type of file (which is determined by the **file name extension**).

3 Click on the ARRANGE ICONS/BY SIZE command in the View menu. Windows sorts the display according to file size.

74

SORTING THE FOLDER DISPLAY

4 If you select the ARRANGE ICONS/BY DATE command in the VIEW menu, Windows sorts the display according to the date on which the file was last edited.

> **TIP**
> If you selected Details as the display type, the display can be sorted immediately. All you have to do is click on a column heading to sort the list by the criterion in question. In the illustration opposite the sort is alphabetical according to file name. Click on the 'Name' column heading and the sort sequence is reversed (e.g. names starting with Z are displayed first).

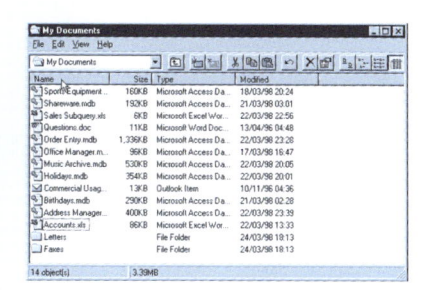

Ultimately the desktop is nothing more than a folder. You can thus arrange the icons on the desktop too.

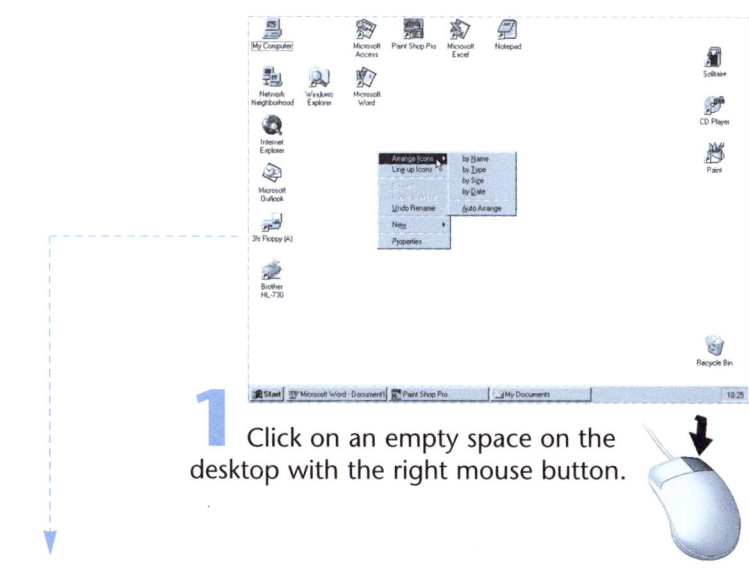

1 Click on an empty space on the desktop with the right mouse button.

2 Choose the command ARRANGE ICONS from the context-sensitive menu and select the desired sort criterion from the drop-down menu.

Windows then displays the new arrangement of icons on the desktop according to the criterion selected.

75

Viewing folders in Explorer

The *My Computer* icon provides a neat way to look at the contents of a drive or a folder. The lack of overview of folder hierarchy is a disadvantage though. Windows therefore offers Explorer as an alternative way to view the drives, folders and files on your computer.

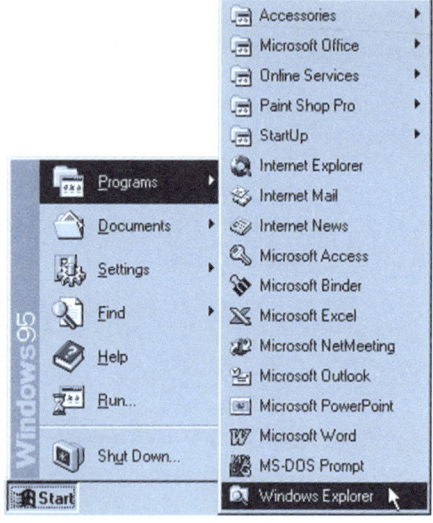

1 Go to the PROGRAMS entry in the Start menu and click on WINDOWS EXPLORER in the sub-menu.

The *Explorer* program starts and the window opposite is opened.

You already know many of this window's features from the *My Computer* window and the other folder windows.

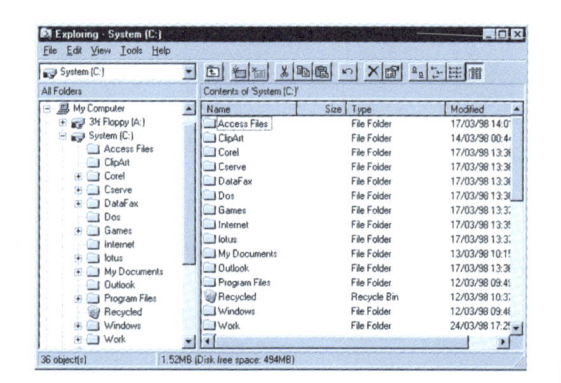

Viewing folders in Explorer

The menu bar, toolbar and status bar are the same as those in the *My Computer* window. Only the Tools entry on the menu bar is new. Unlike the folder windows, the Explorer window is also divided in two.

The **right half** of the window is similar to the display in the *My Computer* window or the contents of folder windows. You can see the icons and names of files or folders. Using the menu bar and toolbar you can change the appearance of this window (large or small icons, lists, details, display sorting). This is carried out in exactly the same way as described on the preceding pages.

The **contents of the left part** of the **Explorer** window are new. The drives and **folder hierarchy** are displayed here. For example, in the illustration opposite you can see the *My Documents* folder which in turn contains the folder *Letters*. This folder then contains further folders *(Business, Drafts* and *Personal)*.

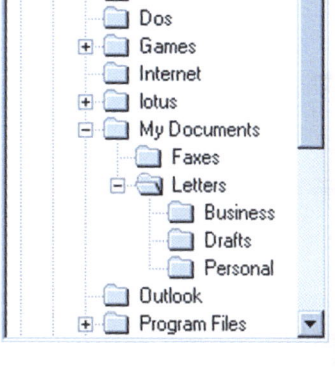

If a drive contains many folders, you can scroll through the list using the scroll bar. The drive and folder display in the left-hand window gives you a quick overview of the folder with which you are currently working.

77

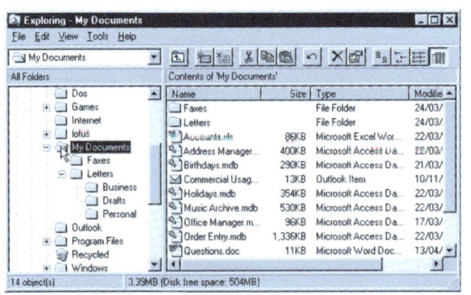

1 Click on a drive or folder icon.

In the right-hand part of the window Explorer automatically shows the associated contents.

Beside some folder icons you will see a small square with a **minus sign**.

2 If you click on this minus sign Explorer hides the related icons for the SUB-FOLDERS.

A small **plus sign** in the square preceding the folder icon shows that this folder contains sub-folders.

3 If you click on the plus sign, Explorer inserts the next level of folders into the display.

MOVING BETWEEN DRIVES AND FOLDERS

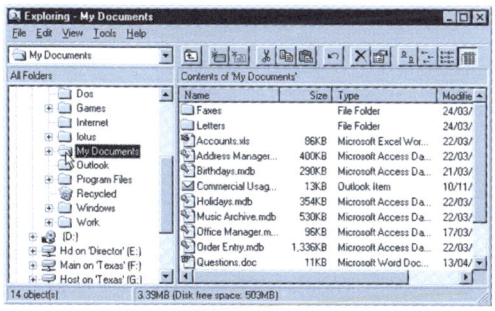

4 By clicking on a drive or folder icon in the left-hand part of the window you can quickly change to a different folder or drive. Explorer then automatically shows the contents of the folder or drive in the right-hand part of the window.

Moving between drives and folders

On the preceding pages you have learnt how to use the *My Computer* window and Explorer to display the files in folders and on drives. Now let's check that you have absorbed this information with a little test.

1 Open the *My Computer* window and double-click on drive C:.

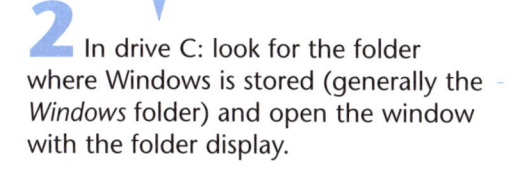

2 In drive C: look for the folder where Windows is stored (generally the *Windows* folder) and open the window with the folder display.

3 Find the *System* folder and open this folder window by double-clicking on the icon.

79

4 Now double-click on the *Cursors* folder icon. The *Cursors* folder window with the associated files is opened.

5 Insert a disk in drive A: and then switch to the window which **displays** the **contents of the disk**.

Using the *Up one level* button you have to go back to the *My Computer* window and then double-click on the floppy disk drive icon.

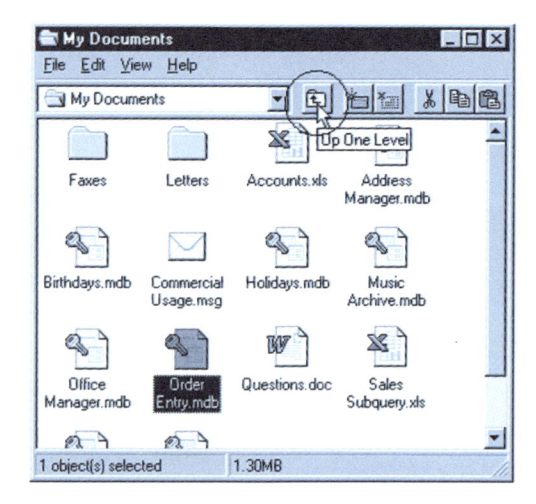

Can you follow the above steps without any problems? Then you have already mastered the most important requirements for working with files. On the following pages you will find further instructions for improving your skills in using Windows.

Practising has served another purpose though. Have you realised the laborious process that is needed to switch from the *Cursors* folder to displaying the contents of the disk? Even switching to the next folder up takes a few mouse clicks. It's a bit easier in Explorer because the left-hand part of the window displays the icons for all the individual folders and drives. Maybe you prefer working in the *My Computer* window. If so, there is a neater way for you to switch between folders and drives.

MOVING BETWEEN DRIVES AND FOLDERS

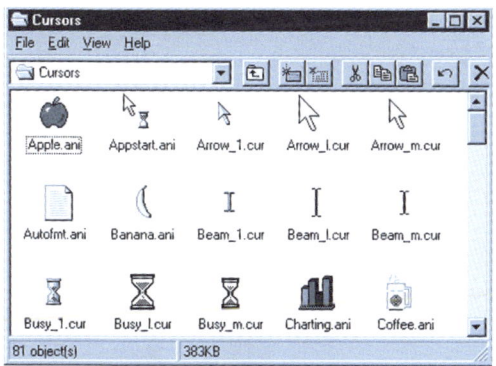

1 Using the *My Computer* icon, switch to the Windows folder *Cursors* on drive C:.

2 Now look at the toolbar.

At the far left of the toolbar you will find a **List box** with the ToolTip description *Go to a different folder*, which shows the name of the currently displayed folder.

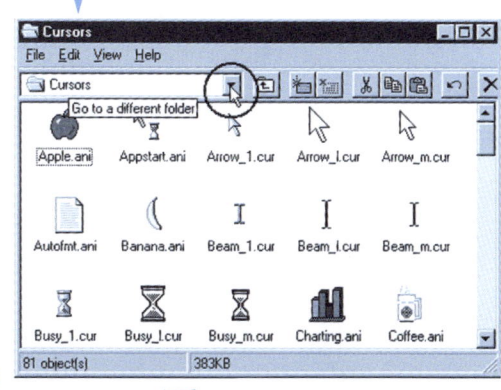

3 Click on the ▼ button for this list box.

81

Windows opens the List box which displays the hierarchy of the folder currently displayed as well as the computer drives which can be accessed from *My Computer*.

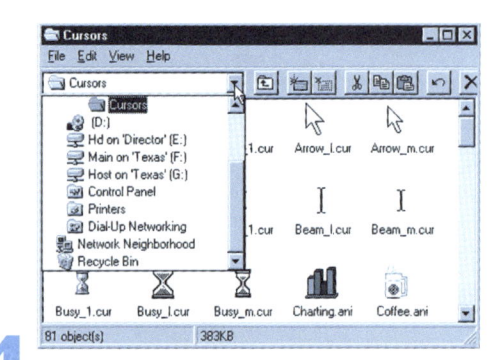

4 Use the scroll bar to scroll until the floppy disk drive is visible.

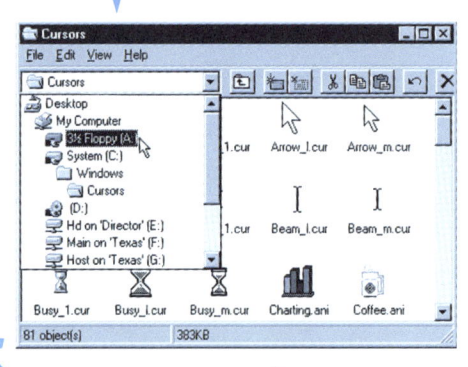

5 Click on the icon for the floppy disk drive.

Windows then immediately shows the drive contents in the window.

> The List box is a feature commonly used in Windows to select specified options. The current option (in the example above this is the open folder) is shown immediately in the list box. Usually only one line within the current selection is shown. A list can be opened to display its options using the button on the right of the List box. Then all you have to do is click on the list entry to select the item in question.

82

> You will not only find the *Go to a different folder* list box in the *My Computer* window and its windows, but also in Explorer. Many programs have dialog boxes for reading or saving data, and you'll find similar list boxes in some of these dialogs.

Creating a new folder

To create a new folder in a drive or in an existing folder, follow these steps:

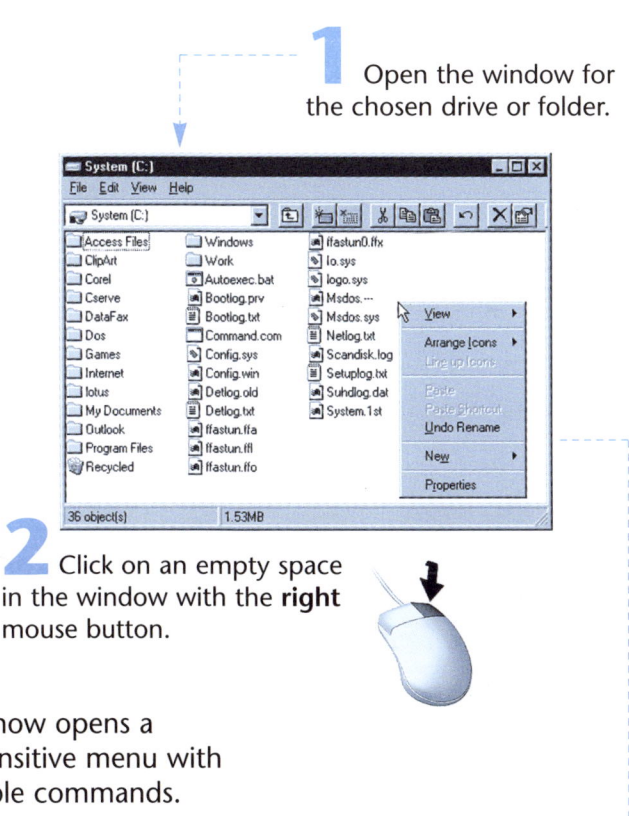

1 Open the window for the chosen drive or folder.

2 Click on an empty space in the window with the **right** mouse button.

Windows now opens a context-sensitive menu with the available commands.

3 Point to the New command.

83

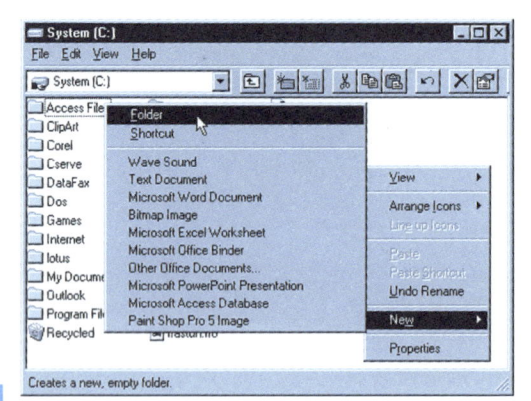

4 Click the FOLDER option on the drop-down menu.

Windows creates a new folder with the name *New Folder* in the window. The name of the new folder is highlighted, indicating that you can change this name.

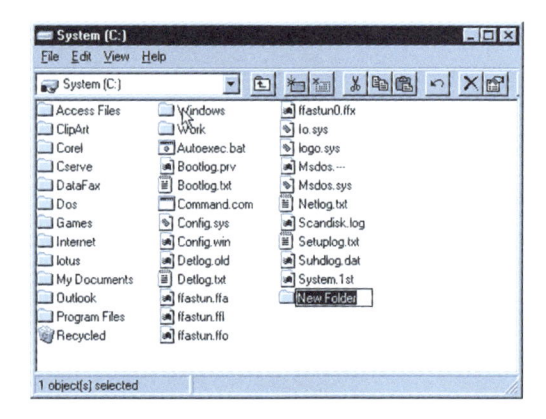

> **TIP**
>
> If you point to a command in the context-sensitive menu, a tip about what the command does usually appears in the window's status bar. In the above example, when you point to the New entry, Windows tells you that these commands let you create new **objects**. Don't be confused by the term objects. In Windows 95, drives, folders, files and icons are all referred to generally as 'objects'.

CREATING A NEW FOLDER

In the window opposite *Example* has been chosen as the name. Of course, you can use any valid folder name you like.

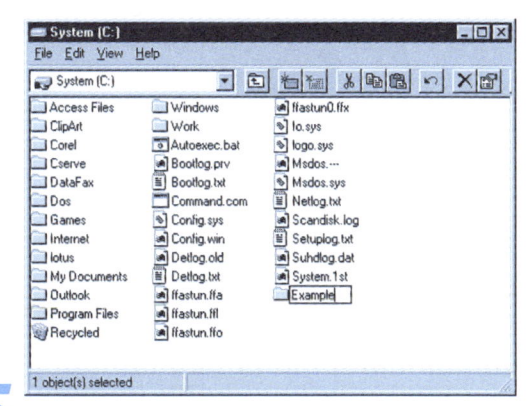

5 Type in the new name for the folder.

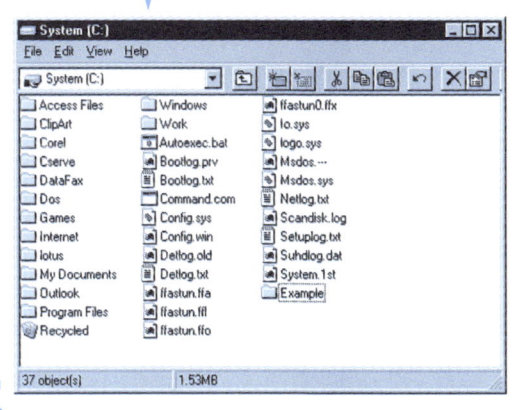

Windows removes the highlighting and allocates the name you have typed to the new folder.

6 Then click on an empty space in the window.

> You can create new folders in windows other than *My Computer* and its folder windows. You can follow the same steps in the right-hand section of the Explorer window to create a folder. The desktop is essentially a permanently-open folder, so you can use these steps to create a new folder on the desktop too. It is even possible to use the commands within some dialog boxes for creating a new folder when you save files in applications such as *WordPad* or *Paint* (see Chapter 4).

85

Creating a new file

In most cases files are created with word-processing programs, spreadsheet programs and so on (see Chapter 4). At the start of this chapter we mentioned that there are different types of files (for graphics, text, etc.). The programs automatically ensure that the appropriate type of file is used for new files. But Windows lets you create empty files of a specific file type without calling up the application program. You could create a template for a letter or a blank word processing file, for example (the advantages of doing this will become clear in Chapter 5).

1 Click on an empty space in the window with the right mouse button.

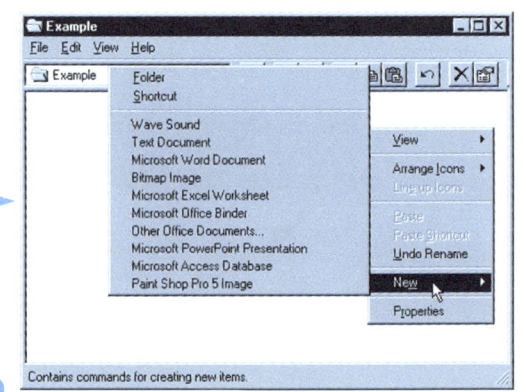

2 Point to the NEW command in the context-sensitive menu and then choose the type of file you want (e.g. word processing file).

CREATING A NEW FILE

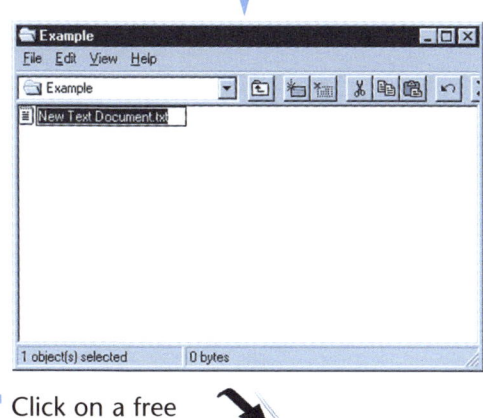

3 Type the name you want for the new file.

4 Click on a free space in the window.

Windows now creates a new file with the corresponding name.

> **TIP**
> In the early stages it often happens when creating a new file or folder that you click on another area in the window before you have typed the file name. Windows then uses the previous name for the new folder or file. In the next step you will learn how a file or folder name can easily be changed.

> **CAUTION**
> When typing the new file name the previously allocated file name extension is quickly amended. Windows uses this extension, however, to recognise the type of file. If this warning appears, close the dialog box using the *No* button and retype the name, including the file name extension.

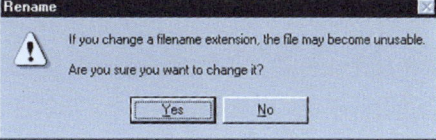

87

Renaming folders and files

File and folder names are very easy to amend later.

1 Click on the icon for the folder or file to be renamed with the **right** mouse button.

2 Choose the RENAME command in the context-sensitive menu.

Windows selects the folder or file name.

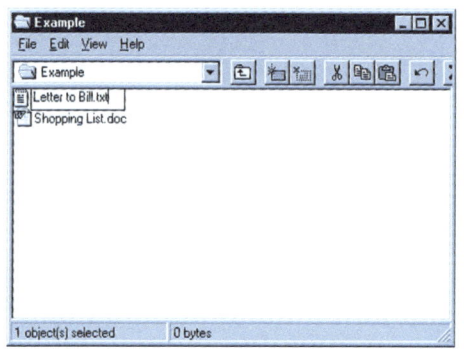

3 Type the new name.

RENAMING FOLDERS AND FILES

4 Click on an empty space on the desktop with the left mouse button.

Windows then changes the folder or file name.

5 Now click again on an empty space in the window to remove the marking.

> If you have selected a file or folder, press the F2 function key and you can also change the name this way.

The problem we encountered in the previous step occurs again when changing file names – the file name extension must stay the same. Unfortunately the Rename command selects the *whole* of the file name including the extension. When you type in the first few letters of the new name the previous name (and thus the extension too) disappears. There is a trick, though, which can help you to change just the file name, or a part of it. As soon as the pointer is located over the marked area it takes on this shape – I This symbol is called a text cursor. It shows that text can be edited.

89

1 📄 Letter.txt
Click on the first character in the name. The position is now identified by a blinking vertical line (the **insertion mark**).

2 📄 Letter to BilLetter.txt
If you now type a letter it appears where the insertion mark was. At the same time the old name is pushed to the right.

Now the only thing you have to do is remove the superfluous characters from the old name. Characters to the right of the insertion mark can be deleted using the `Delete` key. Characters to the left of the text cursor can be removed with the `○` Backspace key. If necessary, the cursor keys `←` and `→` can be used to move the insertion mark along the text.

It's worth remembering these keys; they are extremely useful when you are typing text. This will become especially clear in Chapter 4 when writing letters and other documents.

Copying folders and files

Files can be copied between folders on the hard disk or from the hard disk to a floppy disk. Take a letter for example, that you want to save for later use. You copy the file with the letter to a floppy disk and put the disk away. Would you like to use this letter as a template for a new document, without changing the existing letter? The solution is to make a copy of the original file somewhere, and make your changes to that instead.

Windows provides you with a great many possibilities for copying files or even complete folders including all the files contained in them.

COPYING FOLDERS AND FILES

The aim of the first example is to transfer a file to a floppy disk.

1 Open the *My Computer* window by double-clicking its desktop icon.

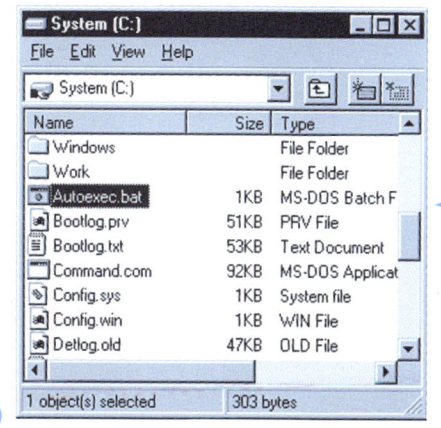

The simplest way to do this is if you select the *Details* display mode.

2 Double-click on the icon for drive C: and find the file *Autoexec.bat* in this window.

3 Insert a blank, but **formatted disk** in the floppy disk drive A: (you will find details for formatting floppy disks at the end of this chapter).

4 Double-click on the *My Computer* icon again to open a second window.

91

5 Then double-click on the icon for floppy disk drive A:.

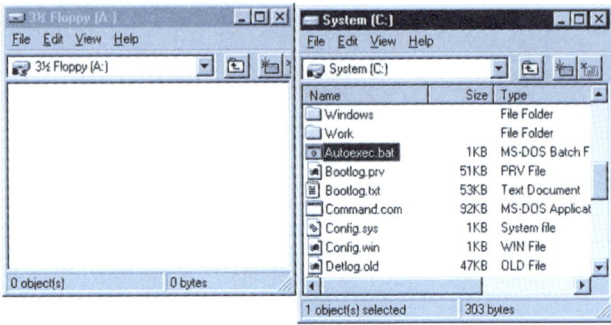

6 Position both the open windows next to each other.

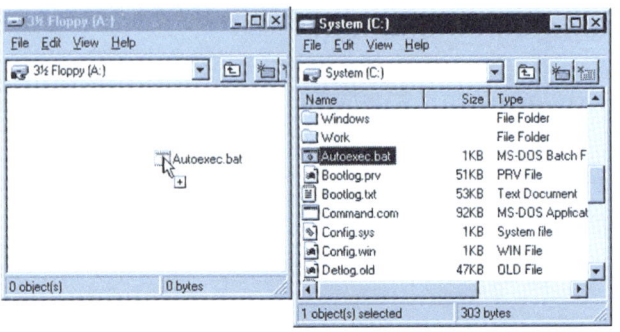

7 Drag the file *Autoexec.bat*, pressing down the right mouse button, from the original window into the second window for the floppy disk drive.

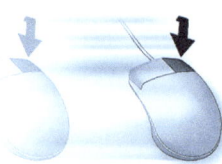

COPYING FOLDERS AND FILES

8 Release the right mouse key as soon as the file icon is located over the window.

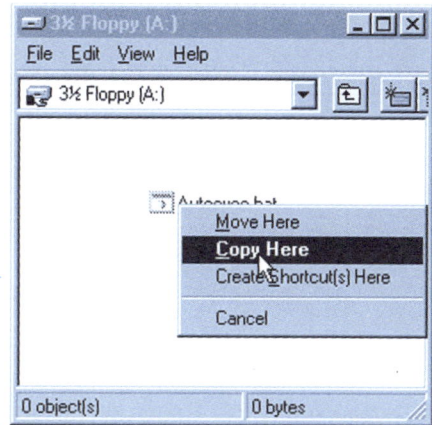

9 Select the COPY HERE command in the context-sensitive menu.

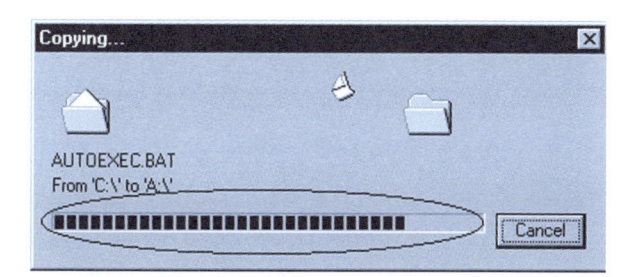

Windows then copies the file to the specified window (and thus to the floppy disk too). Progress is shown in a little window during copying.

93

WHAT'S THIS A disk must be prepared before being used for the first time. This process is known as **formatting**. Formatting creates an empty directory on the floppy disk into which Windows enters the names of folders and files as they are stored on the floppy disk. Many disks which you can buy are already formatted by the manufacturer. You can, however, format disks yourself. You will learn how to do this in the 'Formatting a floppy disk' section at the end of this chapter.

TIP Does Windows display an error message and refuse to copy to the floppy disk? Then perhaps the disk is write-protected. (You have to remove the write protection (see the 'Handling floppy disks' section in this chapter).

1 Repeat the steps above to copy the file **Autoexec.bat** to the floppy disk again.

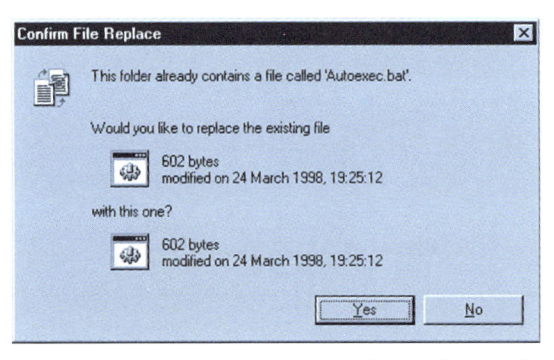

When it starts to copy, Windows realises that there is already a file with that name on the disk. The **dialog box** opposite is then displayed. You can cancel the copying process using the *No* button. If you select the *Yes* button, Windows overwrites the copy of the file on the floppy disk.

94

Whenever a file or folder already exists with the same name at the destination, Windows alerts you to this. You can then decide whether the file or folder should still be copied or not.

Windows doesn't just let you copy files and folders between the hard disk and floppy disk or other drives. It is also possible to copy files and folders between different folders in the same drive. To do this you simply open two windows to display both folders. The folder in which the file is located is known as the **source folder** and the folder to which the file is to be copied is the **destination folder**.

How to copy several files at the same time

If you would like to copy several files, then the method described in the previous paragraph is very long-winded. In this section several files are to be **copied** at the same time from the *Examples* folder to the *Letters* folder.

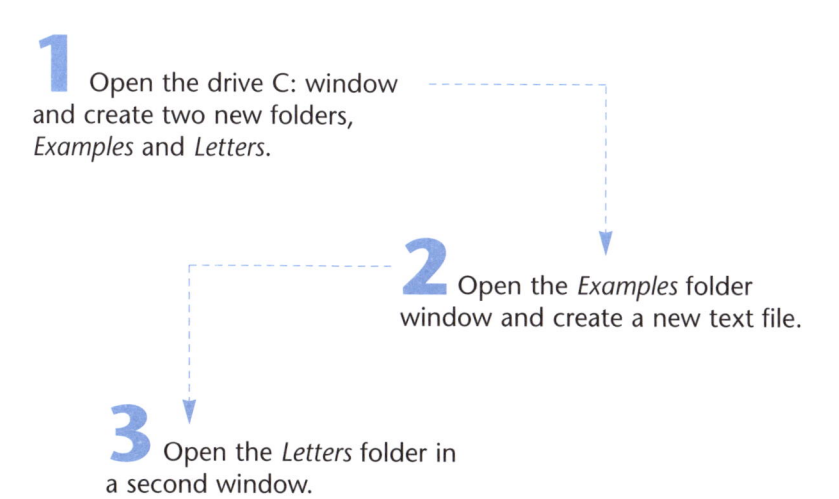

1 Open the drive C: window and create two new folders, *Examples* and *Letters*.

2 Open the *Examples* folder window and create a new text file.

3 Open the *Letters* folder in a second window.

95

The preceding pages show you how to create new folders and files and open a folder window. Now you need another method to **select** several files for copying.

1 Arrange the two windows next to each other.

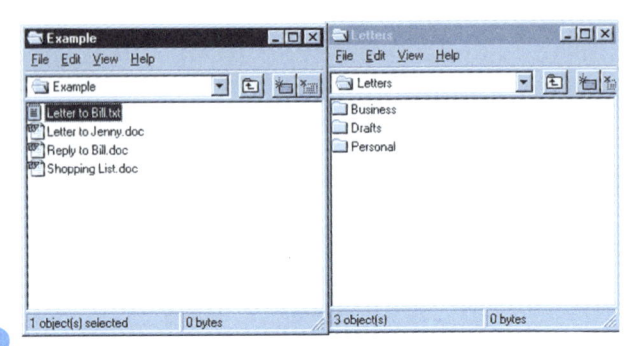

2 Click on the first file to be copied in the *Examples* folder.

Follow these steps to select several successive files:

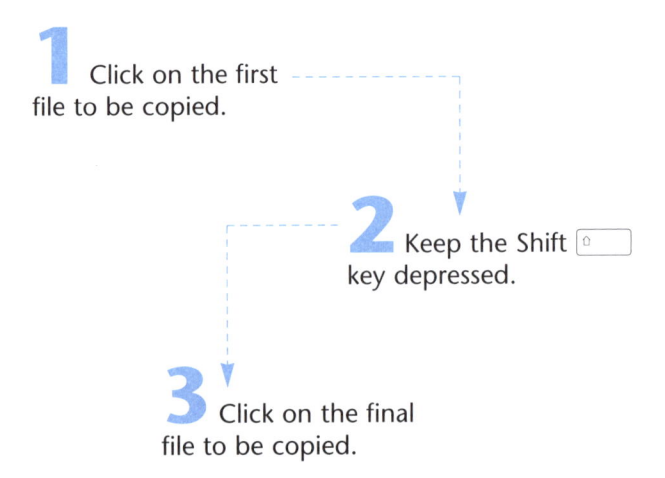

1 Click on the first file to be copied.

2 Keep the Shift key depressed.

3 Click on the final file to be copied.

HOW TO COPY SEVERAL FILES AT THE SAME TIME

Windows now selects all the files between these two. You will be able to tell this by the coloured highlighting on the file names.

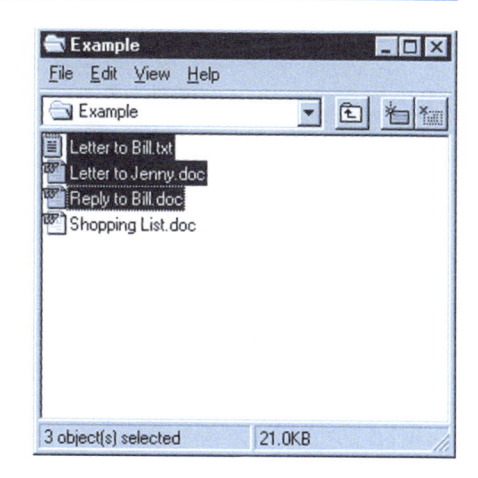

Do you want to select several files which are not successive?

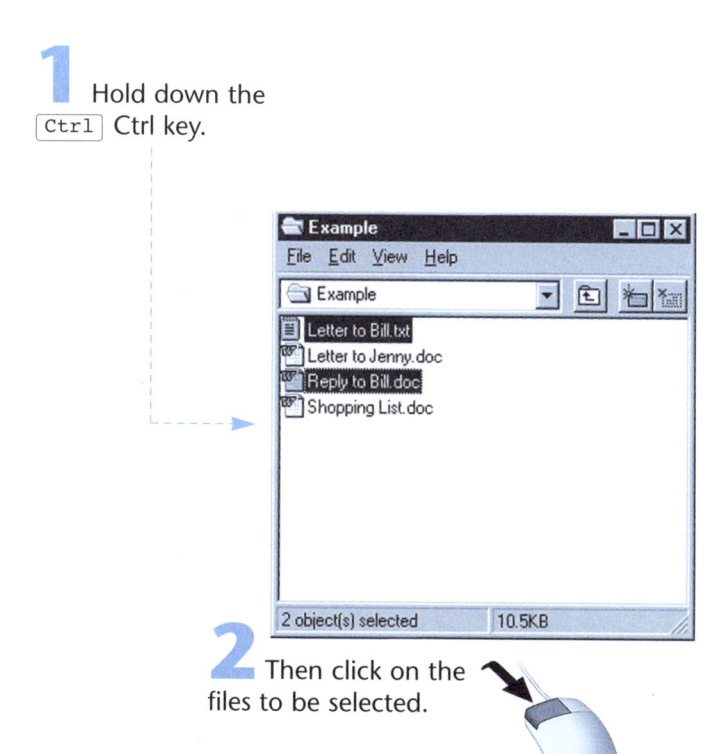

1 Hold down the `Ctrl` Ctrl key.

2 Then click on the files to be selected.

97

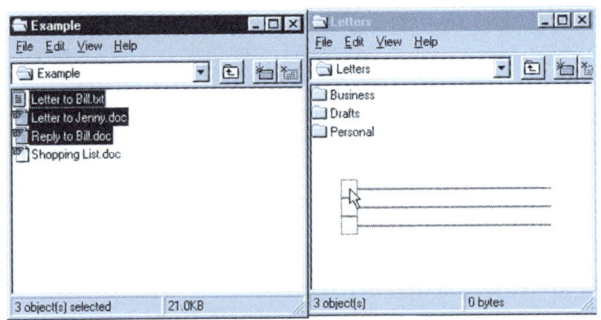

3 To copy the files, click any selected file with the right mouse button and drag the selected files to the window of the destination folder. Then release the mouse button.

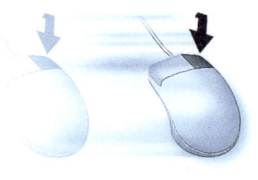

> You can of course select folders as well as files and copy them to another folder by dragging them with the mouse.

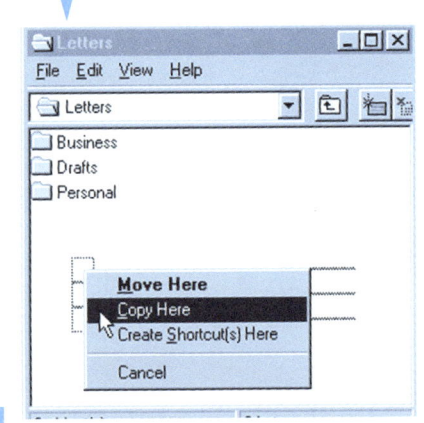

4 Select the COPY HERE command in the context-sensitive menu which has now opened.

Windows now copies the selected files from the source folder to the destination folder. Copying between folders on the hard disk usually happens so fast that the *Copying . . .* dialog box showing progress is not displayed.

How to copy a file to the same folder

Would you like to use a file, containing a letter perhaps, as the basis for a new document? Do you still wish to retain the original file? Then you need to make a copy of the file in question and work with this copy. Unfortunately there's a slight problem – you can't copy files in the same folder by dragging with the mouse. Furthermore when copying you have to ensure that the new file has a different name to the original file (a file name must be unique within the folder). There is a way of copying, however, which also works within a folder.

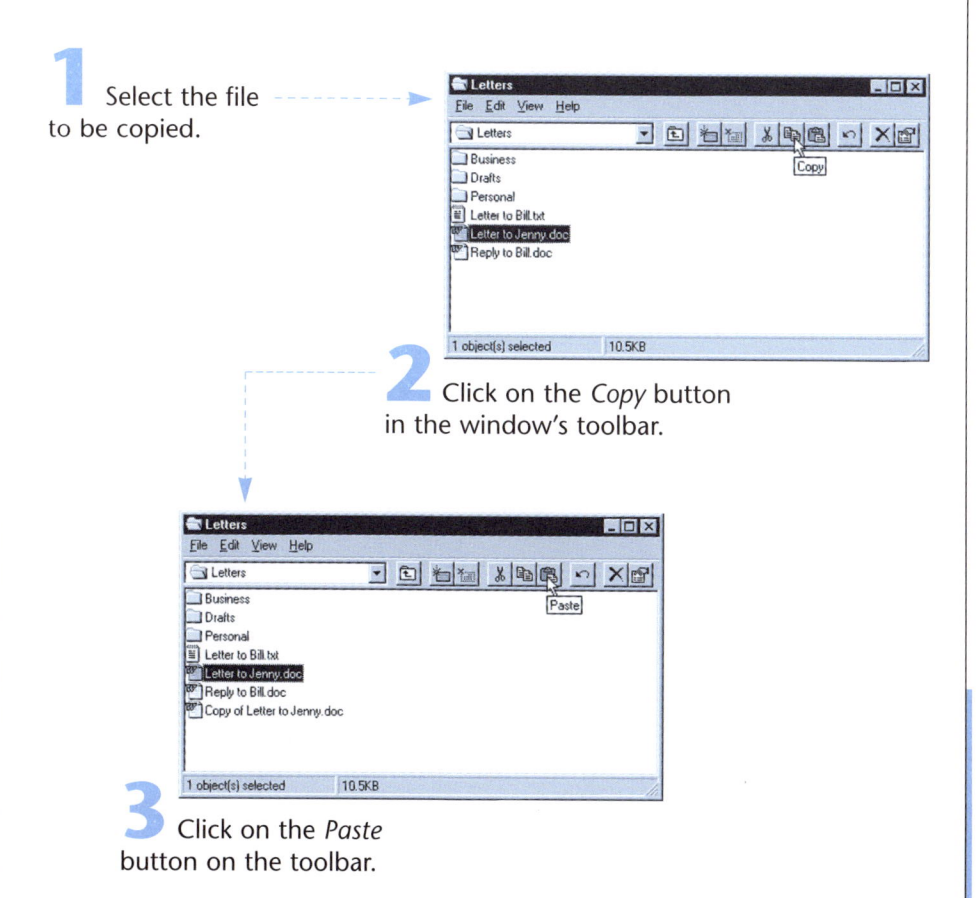

1 Select the file to be copied.

2 Click on the *Copy* button in the window's toolbar.

3 Click on the *Paste* button on the toolbar.

99

Windows pastes a copy of the selected file in the current folder. At the same time the name of the new file is amended so that it differs from that of the original file. *Copy of xxx* is used as the new name, with *xxx* standing for the old name. If you want you can also rename the copied file.

> **TIP**
> Windows has three functions for cutting selected sections (text, files, graphics etc.), copying them and pasting them again. Cut or copied sections are stored in something called the **Clipboard**. When pasting, Windows takes the contents of the Clipboard and pastes it into the current window.

With this button you can cut a selected section and transfer it to the Clipboard. The cut section disappears from the current window. Alternatively you can use the `Ctrl` + `C` key combination to cut a selected section.

This button copies the selected section to the Clipboard. The contents of the current window are not changed. Alternatively you can use the `Ctrl` + `C` key combination to copy a marked section.

This button pastes the contents of the Clipboard into the current window again. In this way you can carry over text, graphics or files. As an alternative you can use the `Ctrl` + `V` key combination to paste.

> **TIP**
> The Cut, Copy and Paste functions don't just work for files and folders, they also work for graphics, text etc. You will find further hints in Chapter 4.

Moving folders and files

When copying in the same folder or between folders or drives, you will end up with two files with the same contents. Sometimes, however, a file only needs to be *moved* from one folder into another. This means the file will be deposited in the destination folder, and, at the same time, deleted in the source folder. This is done in a similar way to copying.

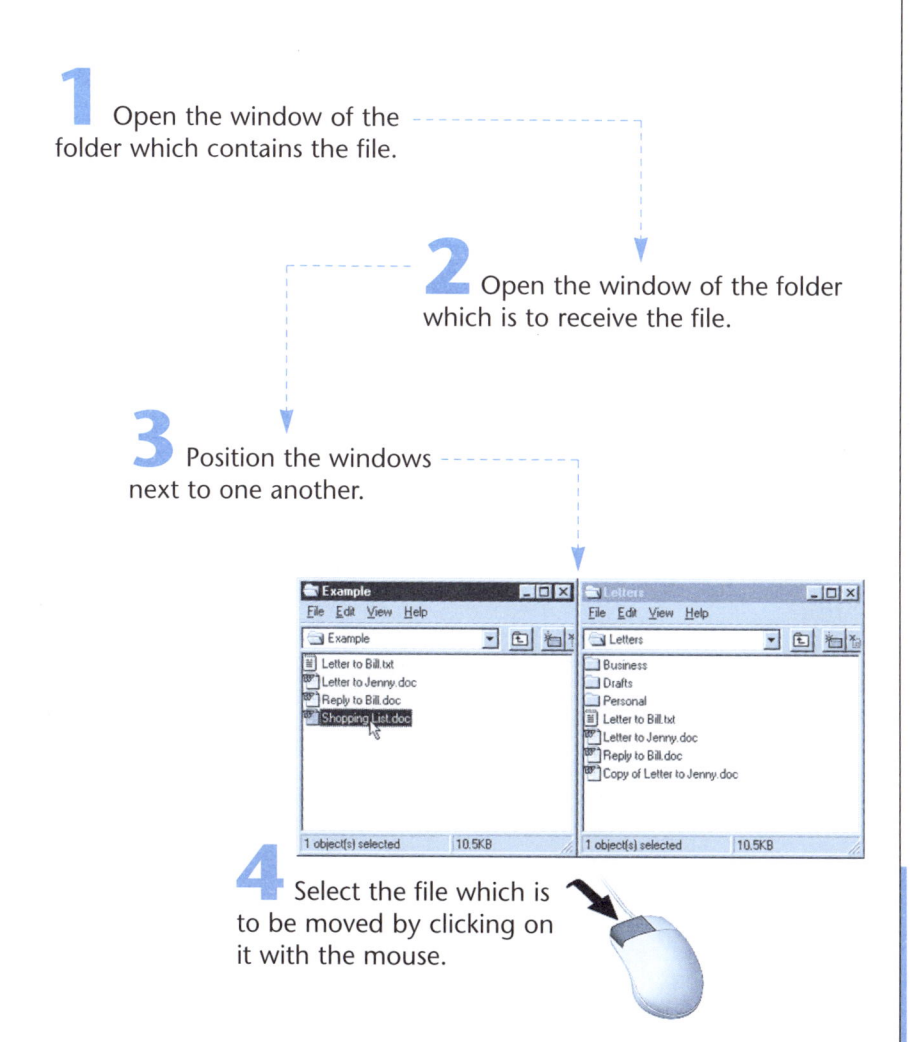

1 Open the window of the folder which contains the file.

2 Open the window of the folder which is to receive the file.

3 Position the windows next to one another.

4 Select the file which is to be moved by clicking on it with the mouse.

101

5 Drag the selected file from the source folder into the destination folder with the right mouse button clicked down.

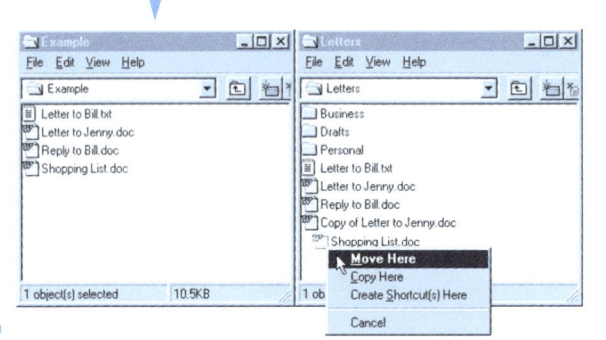

6 Release the mouse button and select the command MOVE HERE in the context menu.

Windows will now move the selected file into the destination folder, and the file will be deleted from the source folder.

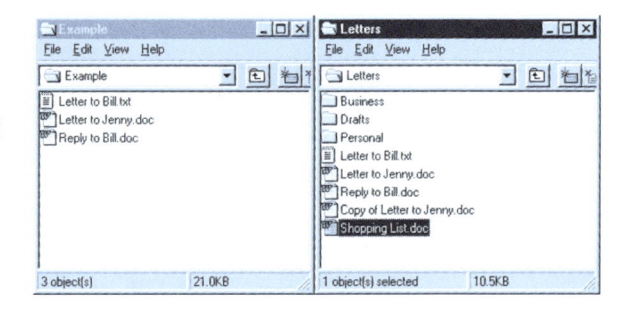

> You can drag and drop several files or folders in the same way as when copying. If there is already a file with the same name present in the destination folder, Windows will ask whether this is to be replaced by the file being dragged across.

102

Copying a floppy disk

A large number of folders and files can be stored on one floppy disk. With Windows you can copy the contents of a complete disk onto a second disk.

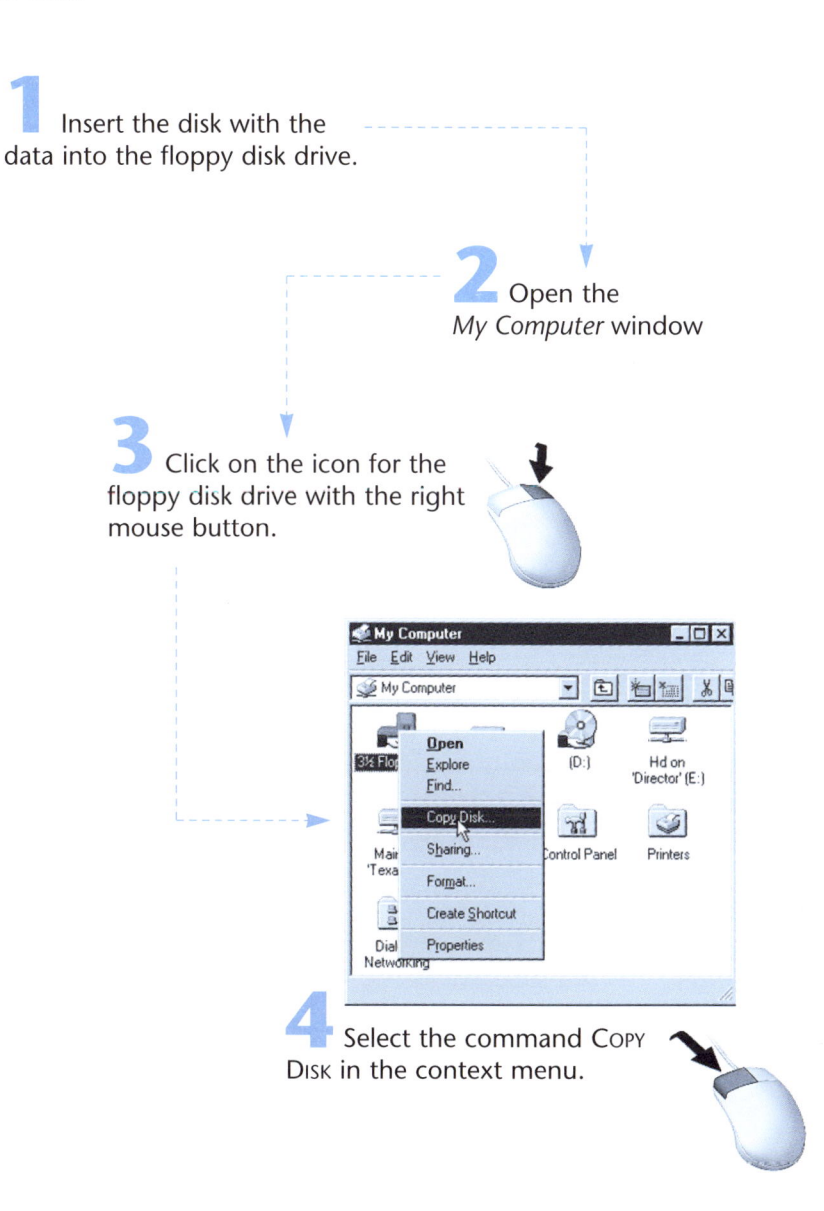

1 Insert the disk with the data into the floppy disk drive.

2 Open the *My Computer* window

3 Click on the icon for the floppy disk drive with the right mouse button.

4 Select the command COPY DISK in the context menu.

103

Windows shows the Copy Disk dialog box.

5 If you have more than one disk drive, you can select the ones you want to use for the source and destination disks simply by clicking on them.

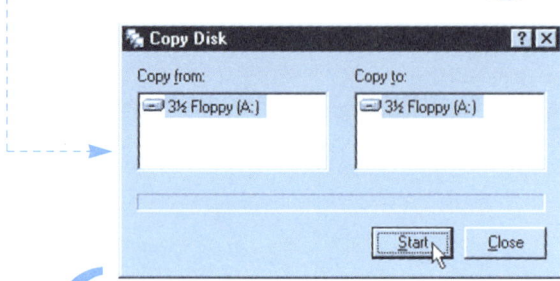

6 Click on the *Start* button to start the copying process.

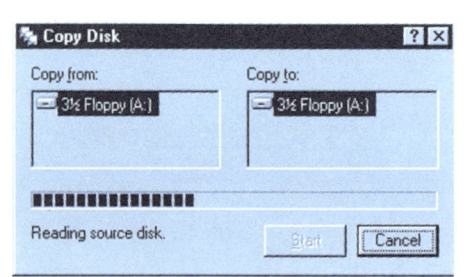

7 Take the source disk out of the disk drive, and insert the empty one.

Windows reads the data from the source disk. You will be told how things are proceeding by means of a progress display. Once the data has been read, Windows will ask you to change the disks.

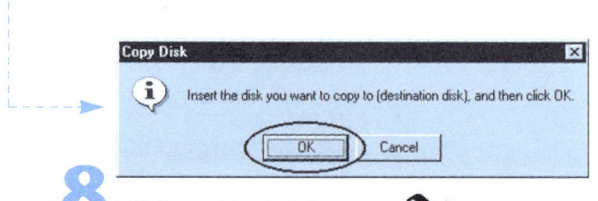

8 Click on the OK button.

COPYING A FLOPPY DISK

Windows will then write the data onto the new (destination) disk. The dialog box shown opposite will indicate how things are proceeding.

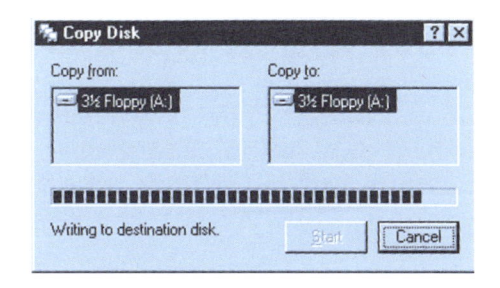

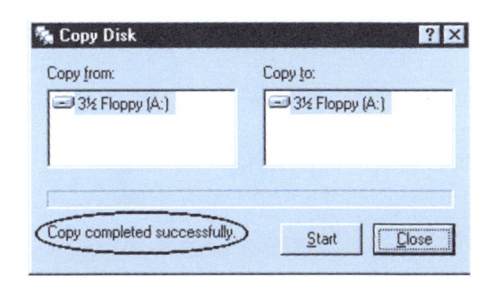

Once the copying of the disk has been completed, a confirmation message will appear.

9 Close the dialog box by clicking the *Close* button.

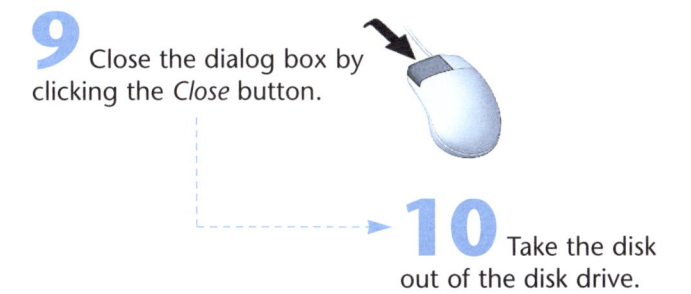

10 Take the disk out of the disk drive.

You now have an exact copy of the original disk.

> **CAUTION**
> During copying, the destination disk will be written over completely. If this disk still contains any files, they will be lost. You can only copy between two disks of the same media type, so you cannot copy a 3½ inch disk onto a 5¼ inch disk by using this method. The same applies if you want to copy a 3½ inch disk with 720 Kb storage capacity onto a 1.44 Mb disk.

How much data is stored on a disk?

Do you want to know how much data is already stored on a floppy or hard disk? Are you interested in knowing how much data the disk can store (referred to as its capacity)?

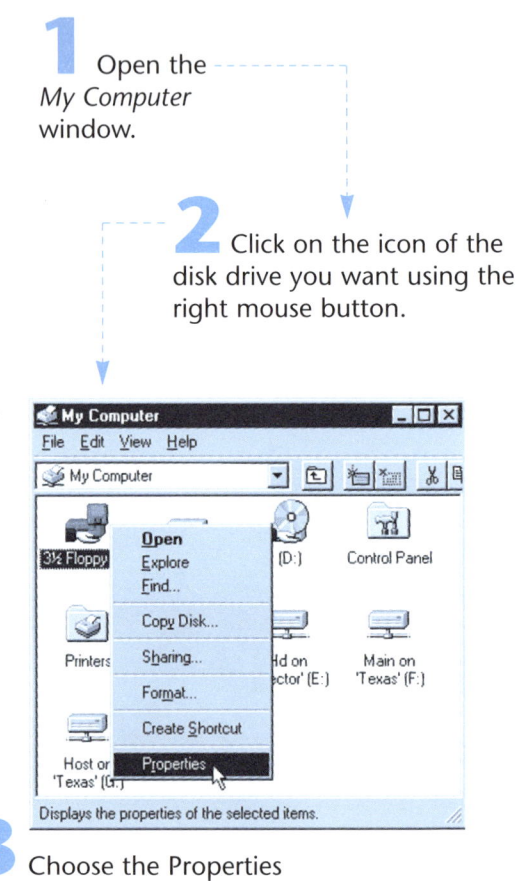

1 Open the *My Computer* window.

2 Click on the icon of the disk drive you want using the right mouse button.

3 Choose the Properties entry from the CONTEXT MENU.

HOW MUCH DISK SPACE DOES A FOLDER OR FILE USE?

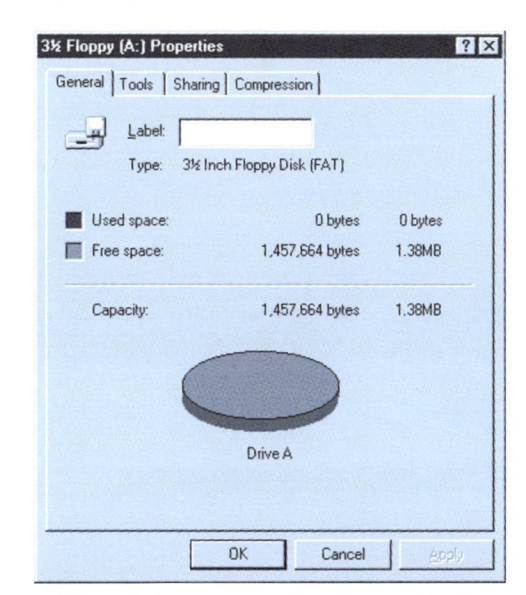

Windows opens the window shown opposite, in which the **Disk Properties** are displayed. The tabbed page called General will give you details of how much data the disk can hold, and how much disk space is already in use. The picture opposite shows that a floppy disk drive has been selected.

How much disk space does a folder or file use?

Do you want to know how many files are stored in a folder, and how much disk space this has taken up? This is important, for example, if you want to copy a folder with all its files onto a disk.

1 Open the window in which the folder is displayed.

2 Click with the right mouse button on the icon for the folder concerned.

107

3 Select the PROPERTIES entry from the context menu.

Windows opens a window in which the properties of the folder are displayed. You can also see here how many sub-folders and files the selected folder contains. At the same time you can see how much disk space these files are using.

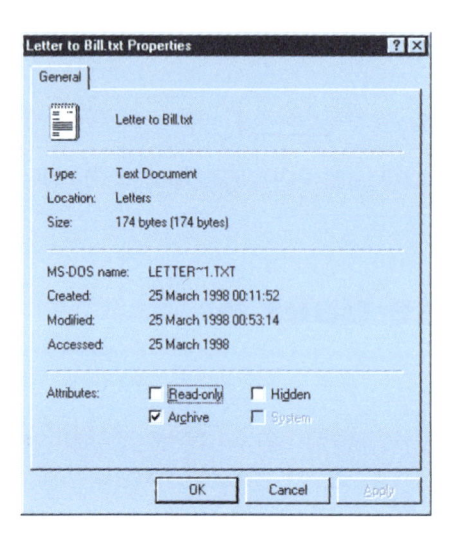

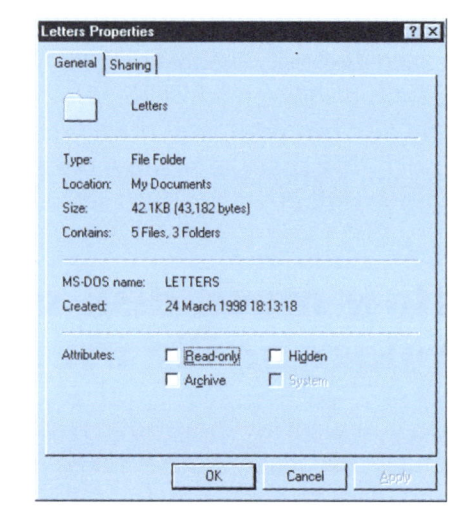

With files, the size appears directly in the display if you select Details in the Explorer window. In a similar way to a folder, however, you can select the file and choose the Properties option in the context menu. The Properties page for files look like this, and you can see not only how big the file is but also when it was last modified.

108

Deleting files and folders

Is there a file or folder you don't need any more? Here's the easy way to delete it.

1 Open the window of the folder containing the file. Click on the icon of the file that is to be deleted.

2 Drag the file or folder that is to be deleted to the Recycle Bin, with the left-hand mouse button pressed down.

3 As soon as the mouse pointer is over the Recycle Bin, release the mouse button.

Windows will now throw the selected file(s) or folder(s) into the Recycle Bin.

While this method is very convenient, it does have the disadvantage that the Recycle Bin is sometimes covered by other windows. If so, you can use another way to delete files or folders.

109

1 Open the window in which the folder or file is displayed.

2 Click on the file or folder that is to be deleted using the right-hand mouse button.

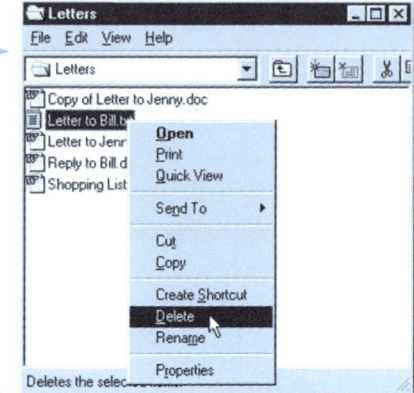

3 Select the command DELETE in the context menu.

> A selected file or folder will also be deleted if you press the Delete button.

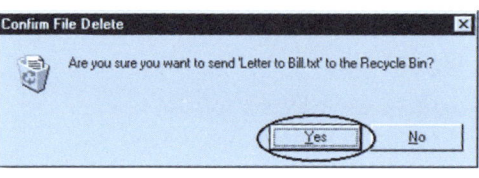

4 When the dialog box titled *Confirm File Delete* appears, click on the *Yes* button.

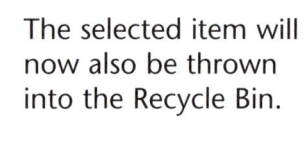

The selected item will now also be thrown into the Recycle Bin.

Retrieving deleted files from the Recycle Bin

Have you mistakenly deleted a file or folder that you may still need? As long as the file or folder is still in the Recycle Bin, you can get it out. There are two ways of recovering an item which has been deleted. If you realise what you have done immediately, recovery is simple.

1 Click with the right-hand mouse button on an empty space in the window.

2 Select the command UNDO DELETE from the context menu.

Windows will now get the deleted file out of the Recycle Bin and put it back in its original folder.

> **CAUTION**
> This method will only work if you haven't done anything else in the meantime. The UNDO option always relates to the last Windows command carried out. If you've copied or moved something since, for example, the UNDO DELETE option will have changed to UNDO COPY or UNDO MOVE.

111

TIP On the Windows toolbar you will find the button ↶ which also reverses the last command. If a file has just been deleted, this button will recover it from the Recycle Bin.

If you have carried out several actions, and only notice your mistake later, there is another way that you might still be able to rescue the deleted files.

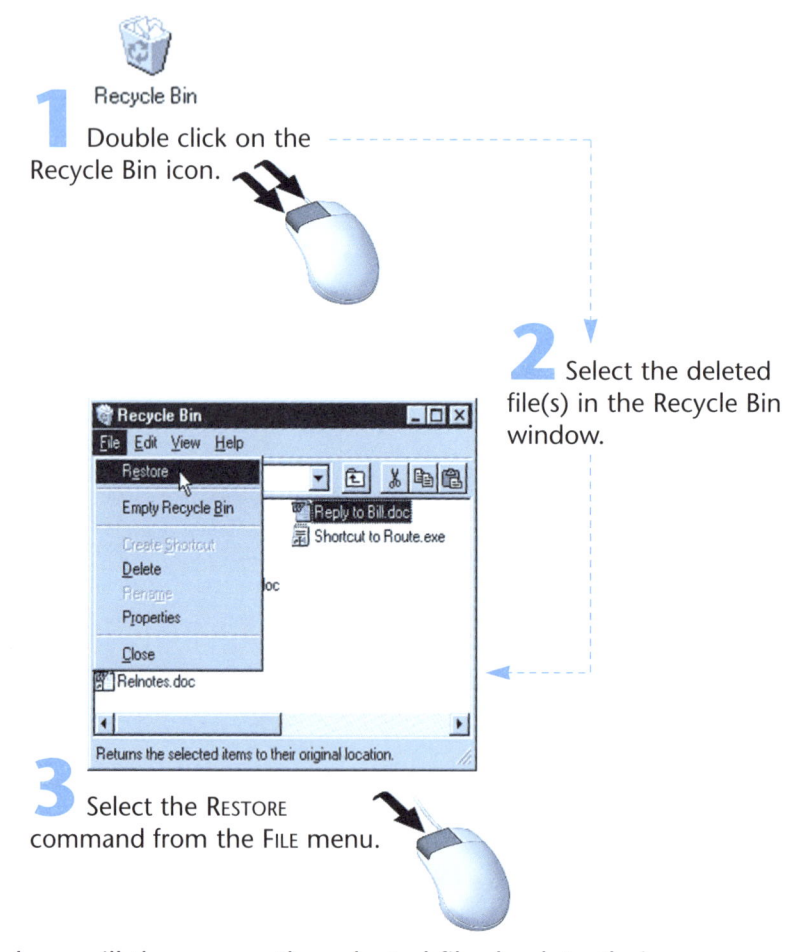

1 Double click on the Recycle Bin icon.

2 Select the deleted file(s) in the Recycle Bin window.

3 Select the RESTORE command from the FILE menu.

Windows will then move the selected files back to their original folders.

112

Emptying the Recycle Bin

When you delete a file or folder, Windows actually moves this item into the Recycle Bin. This means that the file or folder does indeed disappear from the current window, but the disk space required by the files on the disk continues to be occupied. Windows does occasionally check whether the Recycle Bin is full, and it then automatically removes the files that have been in there the longest. But it's a good idea to give it a hand and empty the Recycle Bin yourself from time to time.

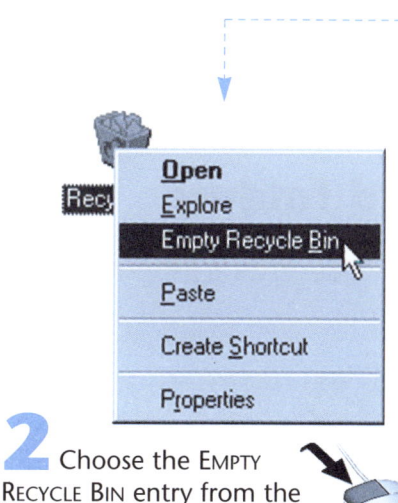

1 Click on the RECYCLE BIN icon with the right mouse button.

2 Choose the EMPTY RECYCLE BIN entry from the context menu.

Windows asks whether you really want to empty the contents of the Recycle Bin.

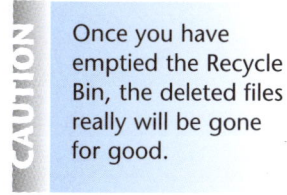

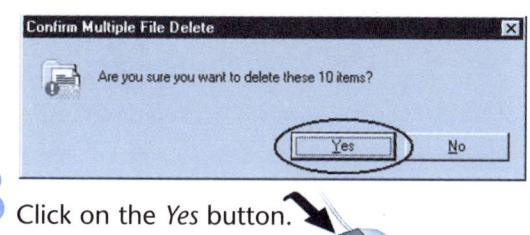

CAUTION
Once you have emptied the Recycle Bin, the deleted files really will be gone for good.

3 Click on the *Yes* button.

113

The files are removed from the Recycle Bin. At the same time, the disk space occupied by the files in the Bin is recovered, and the icon showing the empty Recycle Bin appears.

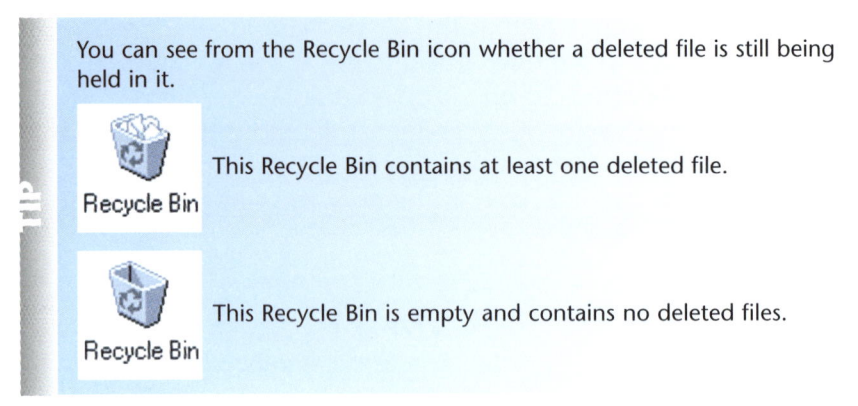

> You can see from the Recycle Bin icon whether a deleted file is still being held in it.
>
> Recycle Bin — This Recycle Bin contains at least one deleted file.
>
> Recycle Bin — This Recycle Bin is empty and contains no deleted files.

Searching for files and folders

Forgotten in which folder a file or a sub-folder is located? Windows can help you find a file or a folder.

1 Click on the START button

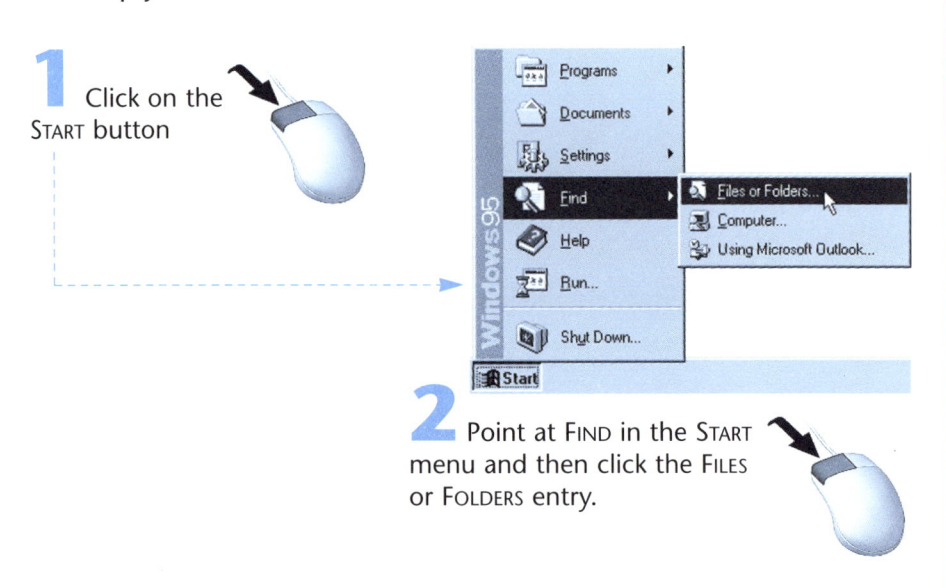

2 Point at FIND in the START menu and then click the FILES or FOLDERS entry.

114

Searching for files and folders

Windows opens the dialog box for setting the search conditions.

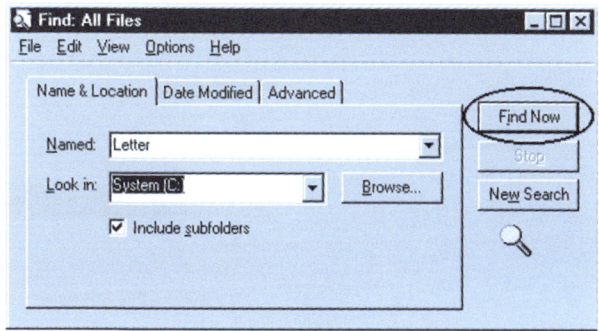

3 Type the name of the missing file or folder and click on the *Find Now* button.

The name of the file or the folder to search for is entered in the *Named* field.

- If you know the exact name, you can enter it in full.

- Of course, you may not be able to remember the exact name of the file you want. You might only know that the name begins with the letters *Letter*. In this case, enter only the start of the name in the *Named* field. The results area of the *Find* dialog will list all the files and folders that start with these characters.

- If you want to limit the search to a particular kind of file, you can use a search term in the form *Letter*.txt*. The asterisk is what is known as a wildcard character; in other words, the character * represents any letters in the name. It may, in this situation, replace one or more letters. The results area will then display any files it finds with names such as *Letter.txt, Letter3.txt, Letter to Bill Smith.txt, Letters.txt* etc. The *Letters* folder will not be displayed, because it does not have the extension *txt*. *My letters.txt* will not be found either, because the search pattern does not match.

115

In the *Look In* field, choose the drive and/or folder in which you want to search. This is what is known as a combination field. The drive station letter and the folder name can be typed directly in the field.

By using the ▼ button, a list field is opened in which you can select drives or folders.

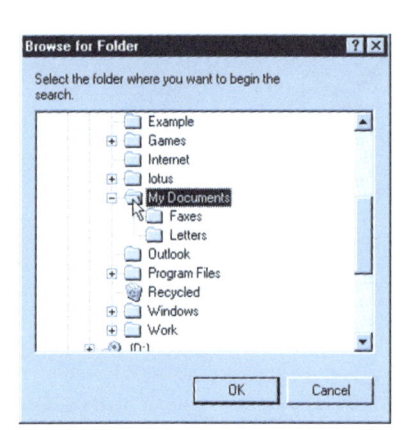

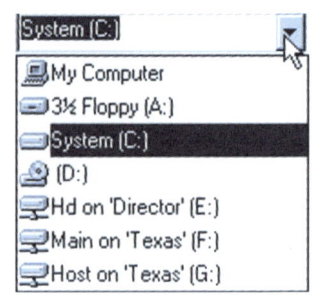

Instead of typing the name, you can use the *Browse* button beside the *Look In* field and click on the name of the drive or folder to search. This works in a similar way to selecting a folder in the Explorer window. As soon as you close the dialog field with the *OK* button, the folder selected will be entered in the *Look In* field.

> **TIP**
> Do you want Windows to search through the sub-folders of a drive or folder as well? If so, make sure the checkbox beside *Include subfolders* is ticked.

Once you click the *Find Now* button, Windows will search through the drive and/or folder, and lists the files/folders found in the results area of the *Find* dialog.

TIP The Find dialog can also be called up using the function key F3 when you're working on the desktop or in a folder or Explorer window.

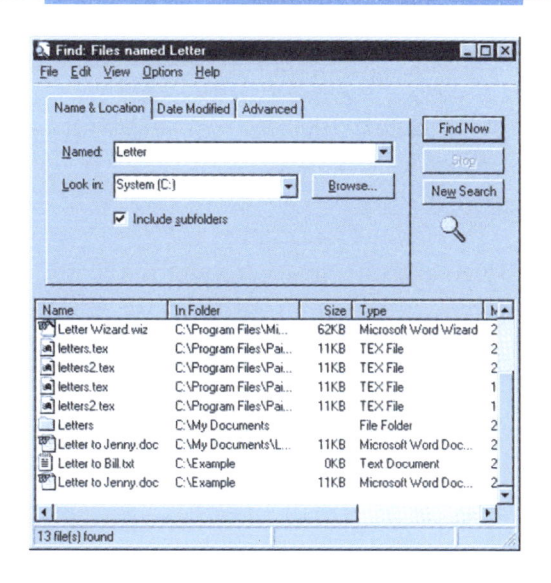

TIP Folder names are preceded by the character \ so the *Letters* folder on drive station C: will be shown as C:\Letters. If you use the *Browse* button, you don't need to bother about this, because Windows takes and enters the name itself. Something such as *C:\Letters* is referred to as a path or path name, because it indicates the direction (or the path) to a folder. Path names come up in Windows every time files are accessed.

Formatting a floppy disk

Before you can use a new floppy disk, you will need to format it. When you do this, Windows builds an empty contents list on the disk, ready for the files you'll store on it. It also checks the disk for faults.

117

TIP New disks are often pre-formatted by the manufacturer for working with Windows and MS-DOS. This is usually indicated on the disk packaging as Formatted, DOS-formatted, Preformatted, etc. This means you need not bother about formatting the disk before you use it.

To format a new disk, carry out the following procedures:

1 Insert the new disk in the disk drive. When doing this, make sure that the write-protection is not set.

2 Open the *My Computer* window and click on the icon for the floppy disk drive with the right mouse button.

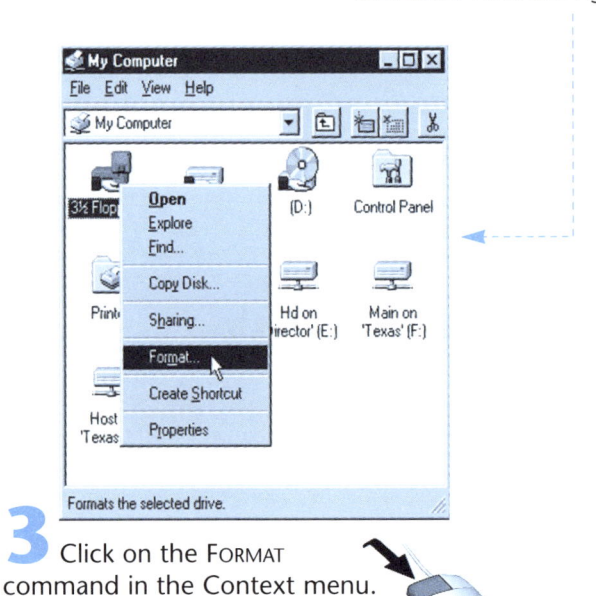

3 Click on the FORMAT command in the Context menu.

Windows opens the dialog box for formatting the disk. You can set a number of options in this dialog.

118

FORMATTING A FLOPPY DISK

CAUTION: You can of course reformat a disk which has already been used, but when you do this all the files stored on the disk will be lost.

4 Click on the *Start* button.

In the *Capacity* field, select the type of disk you are using. Two different types of 3$^1/_2$ inch disk can store either 720 Kb or 1.44 Mb of data. Make sure you choose the correct capacity for your disk. You can choose how the disk is to be formatted in the *Format type* group.

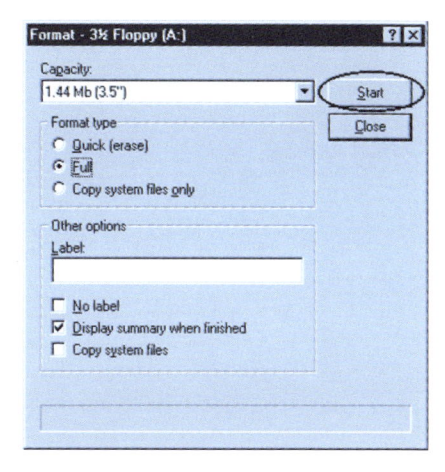

TIP: New (not yet formatted) disks are always formatted with the *Full* setting. A disk which has already been used can be reformatted with the *Quick* option, in which only the table of contents will be deleted, and the lengthy disk-checking is skipped. This makes formatting considerably quicker.

If you want, you can provide a name for the disk in the *Label* field (to a maximum of eleven characters).

Full formatting of a disk does take some time. Windows will let you know, in the lower part of the dialog box, how far formatting has progressed.

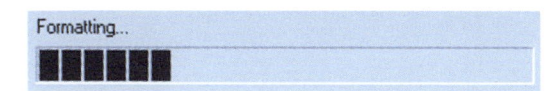

119

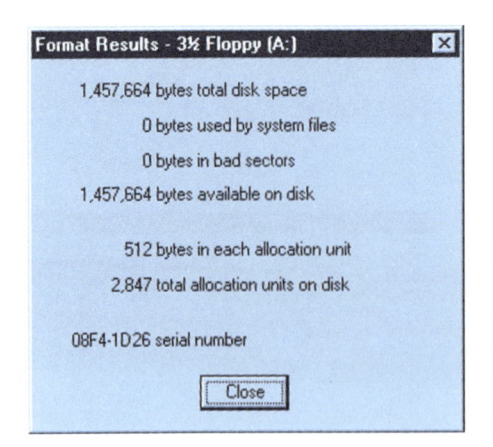

If the checkbox 'Display summary when finished' was selected, Windows will display this dialog when formatting has been completed, with detailed information about the disk.

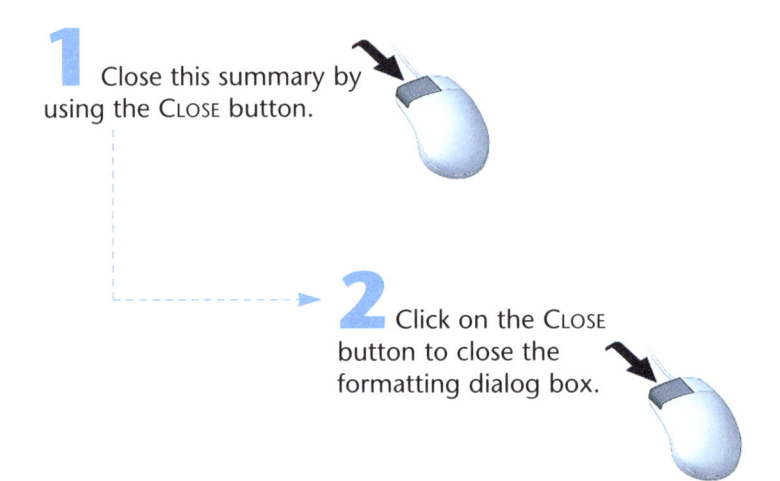

1 Close this summary by using the CLOSE button.

2 Click on the CLOSE button to close the formatting dialog box.

The disk can then be used for storing files and folders.

A quick check on progress

Have you worked through the first three chapters? If so, that means you've already mastered the basics of working with Windows. In the chapters that follow, you'll learn about individual programs and options provided by Windows. To check what you have learned so far, work through the following questions. The section which has the answers is indicated in brackets after each question.

> How do you resize a window so that it fills the entire screen?

(Answer in Chapter 1, in the section 'Working with windows')

> How is a program closed?

(Answer in Chapter 1, in the section 'Working with windows', or in Chapter 2 in the section 'Closing a program')

> Name the different ways of starting a program.

(Answers in Chapter 2, i the section 'Starting a program', or the section 'Other ways to open programs')

> How can a program (EXE file) be started from the My Computer window or Explorer?

(Answer in Chapter 2, in the tip at the end of the section 'Other ways to start programs')

121

◘ **How are file names given?**

(Answer in Chapter 3, in the section 'What are folders and files?')

◘ **How can you tell which files are stored on a disk?**

(Answer in Chapter 3, in the section 'Displaying drives, files and folders')

◘ **How can you delete a file?**

(Answer in Chapter 3, in the section 'Deleting files and folders')

◘ **How can you arrange for large symbols to be displayed in the My Computer window?**

(Answer in Chapter 3, in the section 'Copying folders and files')

Were you able to answer these questions without cheating?

Great, that means you've already mastered the basic principles of Windows. But it's not a disaster if you're still a bit shaky on a few points. Just read through the relevant sections if you need to make sure how something works. There are a lot of options and actions in Windows that are similar so, as you progress through the next chapters, some of what you'll learn, may seem familiar.

4

Writing and drawing in Windows

What's in this chapter?

With Windows, you can create plain text files, print them, save them and even merge them with files created using other programs. But you can also lay out the text in a more attractive way, or add your personal touch to letters, invitations, invoices and so on. Windows also allows you to create sketches, drawings or pictures, edit them and use them in documents or as a desktop background. In this chapter, you'll be getting to know the Windows programs that let you do all this.

You already know how to:

Work with Windows	23
Start a program	37
Use files and folders	58

Your are going to learn how to:

Create a document using Notepad	126	Save, open and print documents in WordPad	156
Edit the document in Notepad	128	Draw pictures using Paint	159
Save and open the document	136	Crop and copy graphics	170
Search for text in the document	141	Save, open, and print a picture using Paint	173
Print documents with Notepad	143	Create a background for the Windows desktop	177
Create documents with WordPad	144	Merge text with pictures and other objects	180
Format a text document	148		

125

Creating a document using Notepad

Do you want to create plain text files such as lists, notes, descriptions, etc.? Instead of writing them by hand or with a typewriter, you can write them on your computer. Documents like these can be easily stored for later use and edited later if you need to. Printouts look very clean, and you can print multiple copies of a document with no problem at all. To create a simple document, you use **Notepad**.

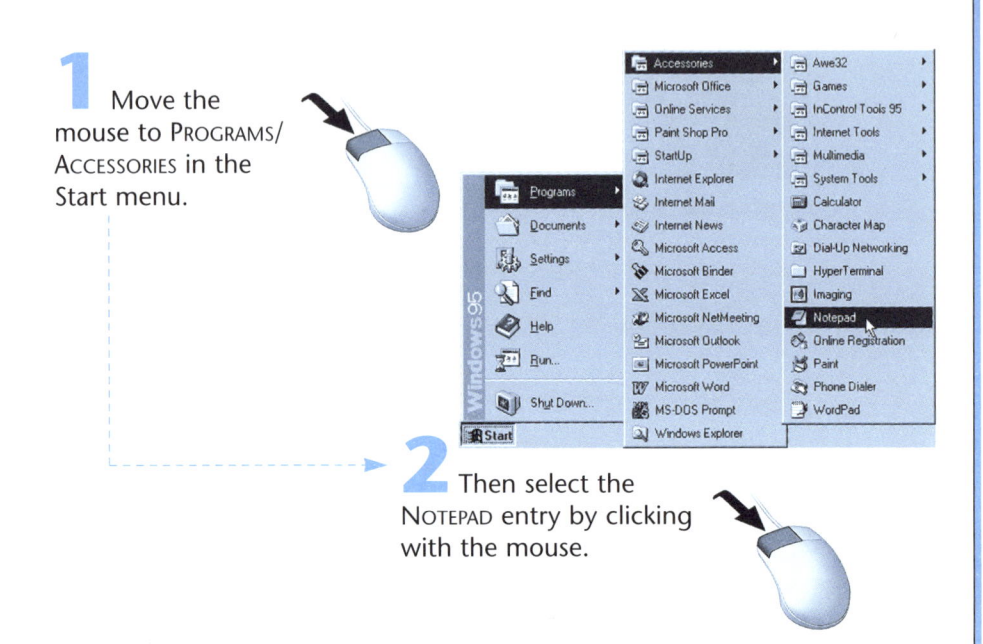

1 Move the mouse to PROGRAMS/ ACCESSORIES in the Start menu.

2 Then select the NOTEPAD entry by clicking with the mouse.

A program with which plain text documents can be produced is referred to in the computer world as a text editor. Windows provides a program called *NotePad.exe* for this, which is located in the Windows folder.

Windows now starts Notepad.

Notepad opens a window, just like other Windows programs. This window contains elements such as the title bar, the menu bar, and the scroll bars, which you learned about in the earlier chapters relating to other windows.

CREATING A DOCUMENT USING NOTEPAD

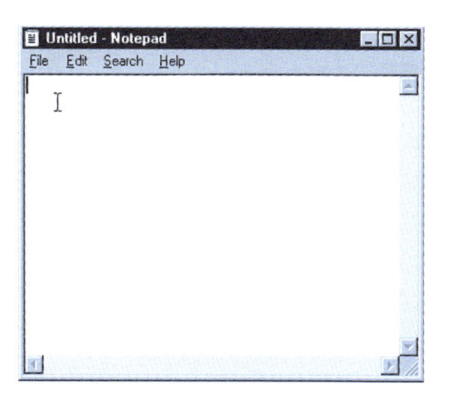

Something that's new is the white interior of the window, which is where the text is typed. When it starts, Notepad displays a blank 'white page', which does not yet contain any text. You can see the **insertion mark** in the top left-hand corner of the window.

> **TIP**
>
> The insertion mark is represented as a vertical flashing black line. This mark indicates whereabouts on the screen the next character you type will be placed. As soon as the character which has been typed is displayed, the insertion mark will move one position to the right. In Windows, insertion marks are used anywhere that text can be typed. You have already learned about this, for example, in Chapter 3 when we were renaming files. If you move the mouse cursor into the text area, the **text cursor**, which has already been mentioned, will appear instead of the mouse cursor. This can be handled in exactly the same way as the mouse pointer. You can point to a word with the text cursor, select something by clicking or double-clicking.

Here you can see some example text that has been typed into Notepad.

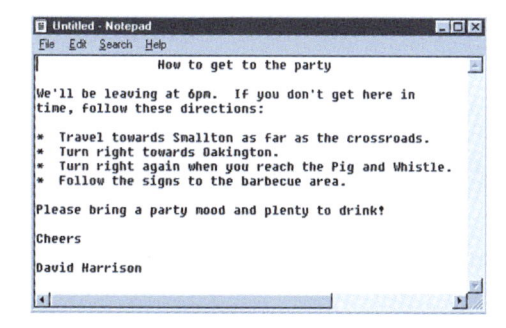

If you're not yet entirely familiar with using the keyboard, here are a few tips for typing text.

127

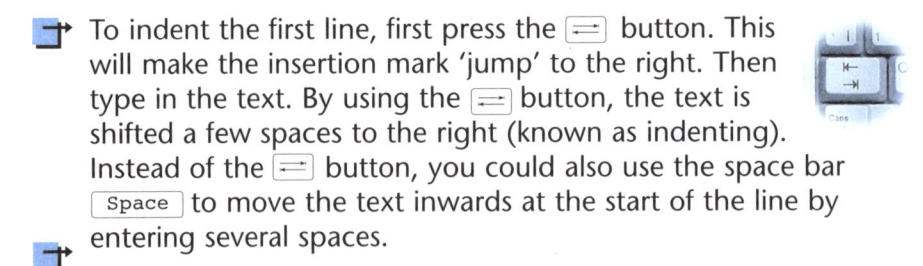

➡ To indent the first line, first press the ⇥ button. This will make the insertion mark 'jump' to the right. Then type in the text. By using the ⇥ button, the text is shifted a few spaces to the right (known as indenting). Instead of the ⇥ button, you could also use the space bar ⎵Space⎵ to move the text inwards at the start of the line by entering several spaces.

➡ Normally, when the letter keys are pressed, lower-case letters appear. In order to type upper-case letters (capitals), hold the ⇧ button down, and then press the key with the desired character.

➡ If you reach the right-hand edge of the window while typing, the text you see in Notepad will be shifted slightly to the left. To end a line at a specific point, and move on to the next line, press the ↵ key.

If you need more space between two lines, press the ↵ button twice. This procedure is used in the example above between the heading and the text section which follows.

> **TIP**
> There is an overview of the keyboard at the end of this book.

Try typing the text on this page into Notepad to get a feel for using the computer keyboard.

Editing the document in Notepad

You are bound to make a few mistakes when you type. Likewise, if you want to change a saved document, there's no alternative to *editing* the text.

Because of the rush, a number of mistakes have been incorporated in the invitation to a summer party shown here, and a few things forgotten. The aim now is to correct them. This will give you the opportunity to learn the techniques for editing text documents.

EDITING THE DOCUMENT IN NOTEPAD

The first thing is to insert the date on which the party is to be held.

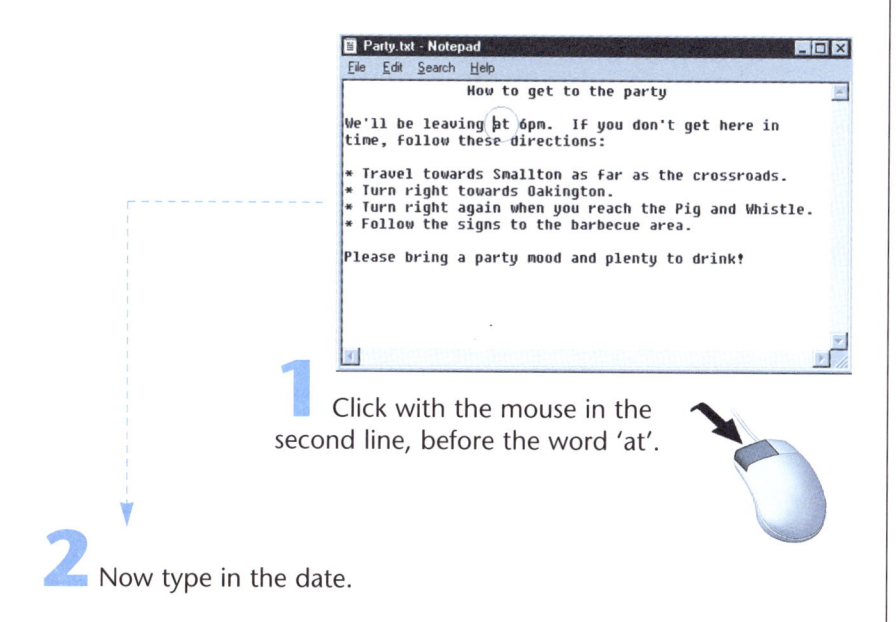

```
Party.txt - Notepad
File  Edit  Search  Help
              How to get to the party
We'll be leaving at 6pm.  If you don't get here in
time, follow these directions:

* Travel towards Smallton as far as the crossroads.
* Turn right towards Oakington.
* Turn right again when you reach the Pig and Whistle.
* Follow the signs to the barbecue area.

Please bring a party mood and plenty to drink!
```

1 Click with the mouse in the second line, before the word 'at'.

2 Now type in the date.

As you type, Notepad moves the following text further to the right.

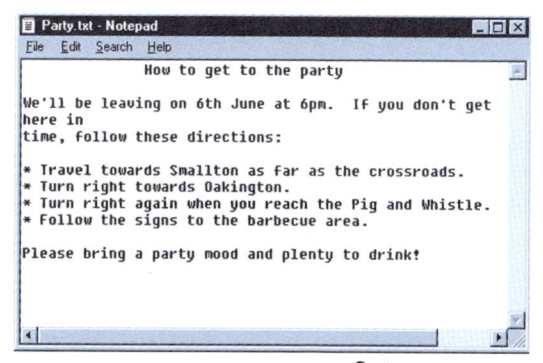

```
Party.txt - Notepad
File  Edit  Search  Help
              How to get to the party
We'll be leaving on 6th June at 6pm.  If you don't get
here in
time, follow these directions:

* Travel towards Smallton as far as the crossroads.
* Turn right towards Oakington.
* Turn right again when you reach the Pig and Whistle.
* Follow the signs to the barbecue area.

Please bring a party mood and plenty to drink!
```

This is the window with the result.

3 To make the line shorter, click before the word 'here', and press the ⬅ button.

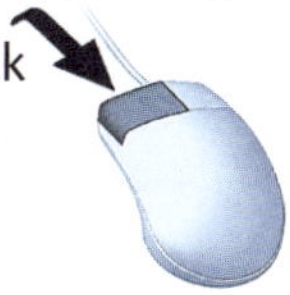

129

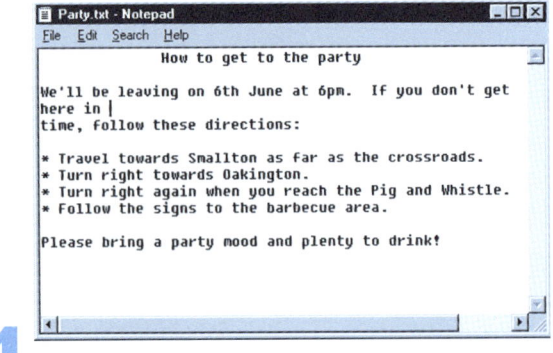

4 Now click with the text cursor after the word 'here in'.

5 Move the lower line up to meet this one by pressing the Delete `Delete` button.

> Using the Delete key, `Delete` delete the marker for the end of the line.
>
> The Delete key always removes the character to the right of the insertion mark. In order to delete a character to the left of the insertion mark, press the `⌫` button.

The insertion mark can be positioned anywhere in the text by clicking with the mouse in front of the appropriate letters. You can, however, also make use of what are referred to as the cursor keys and other keys in order to move the insertion mark around inside the text. The following key guide provides a list of the most important keys and key combinations fopr moving the insertion mark around in the text.

Moves the insertion mark one line upwards in the text.

EDITING THE DOCUMENT IN NOTEPAD

Moves the insertion mark in the text one line downwards.

Moves the insertion mark in the text one character to the left, in the direction of the start of the text.

Moves the insertion mark in the text one character to the right, in the direction of the end of the text.

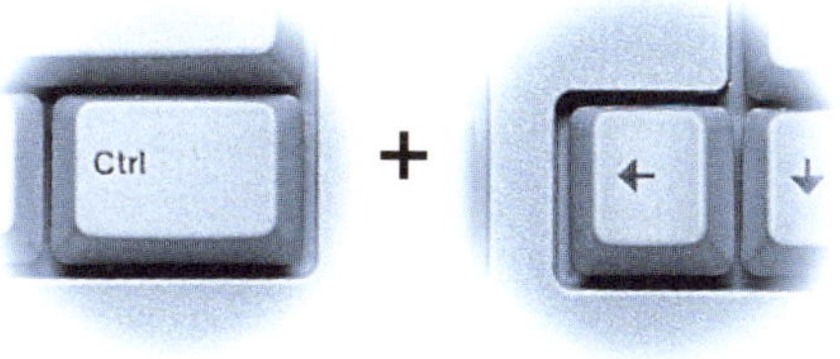

Moves the insertion mark in the text one word to the left.

Moves the insertion mark in the text one word to the right.

If you press this button, the insertion mark jumps to the start of the line.

This button moves the insertion mark to the end of the line

131

With existing text, it often happens that whole sentences or blocks of the text need to be deleted. To do this, you can place the insertion mark at the start of the text section and then press the Delete key until all the characters have been deleted. A quicker and neater solution is to **select** the text to be deleted and do the job in one go.

WHAT'S THIS? The term 'selecting' often comes up in Windows. You can select files, folders, icons, text sections, or picture sections by using the mouse. Depending on the program, Windows shows the section that has been selected by the use of a coloured background or a dotted line.

Selecting can be compared with highlighting text in colour on a sheet of paper. On paper, you draw a coloured marker across the parts of the text concerned; in Notepad, by contrast, you use the mouse pointer, which you drag across the text that is to be selected.

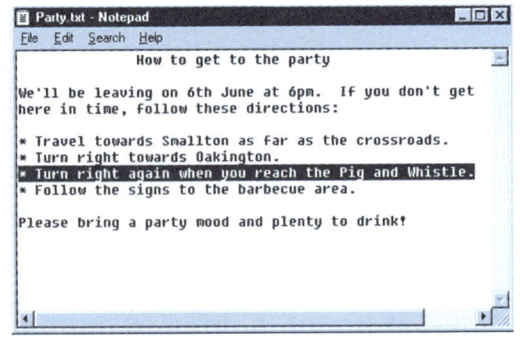

1 Click with the mouse at the start of the text that is to be selected.

2 Keep the left mouse button pressed, and drag the mouse through to the end of the section to be selected.

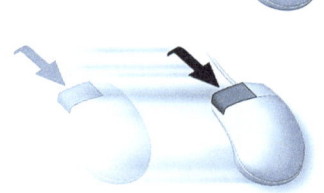

The text section that has been selected will be highlighted in colour. If you now press the Delete button `Delete`, Notepad will delete the entire selected text section.

To cancel selecting, click on a point outside the selected section.

> You can also select text using the keyboard. Move the insertion mark to the beginning of the section that is to be selected, then hold down the `⇧` key and move the insertion marker in the text by using the cursor keys. Notepad selects the characters concerned.
>
> Have you deleted something by mistake? If you press the key combination `Ctrl` + `Z`, the last change will be reversed.

The last question is how larger sections of text can be 'moved' or copied within a document. This is particularly helpful when editing old documents to create new ones.

In this window, a complete line has been selected. The intention is to move this one section upwards.

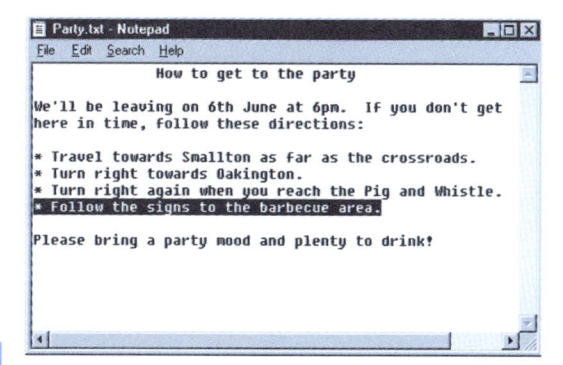

1 Select the CUT command in the EDIT menu, or press the key combination `Ctrl` + `X`.

The text will now be deleted from the Notepad window. Windows has put the selected text in the **Clipboard**.

133

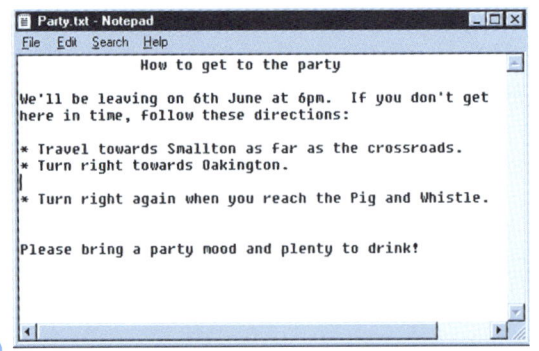

2 Click after the words '. . . towards Oakington' and then insert a new line by pressing the ⏎ key.

3 Make sure that the insertion mark is at the beginning of the new line.

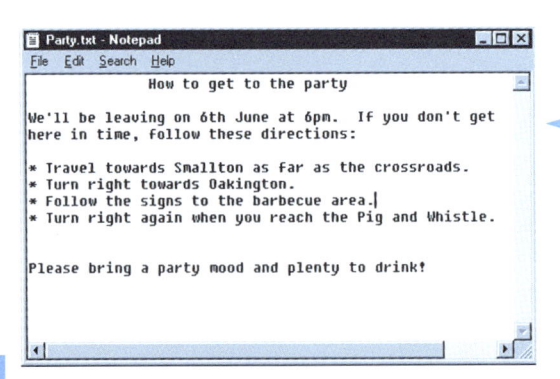

4 Select the PASTE command in the EDIT menu, or press the key combination `Ctrl` + `V`.

Notepad will now insert the text from the **Clipboard** at the insertion mark in the document. By following this step, you have effectively moved the text which you selected earlier into the new position.

EDITING THE DOCUMENT IN NOTEPAD

WHAT'S THIS? Windows has a specific memory area which is referred to as the Clipboard. If you select the functions *Cut* or *Copy* (in the Edit menu, for example), Windows will take the selected section (text, picture areas, file names, etc.) into the Clipboard. By using the command Paste in the Edit menu, the contents of the Clipboard are inserted into the current window once again.

If all you want to do is copy a piece of text (that is to say, the selected section should remain in place), the procedure is quite similar.

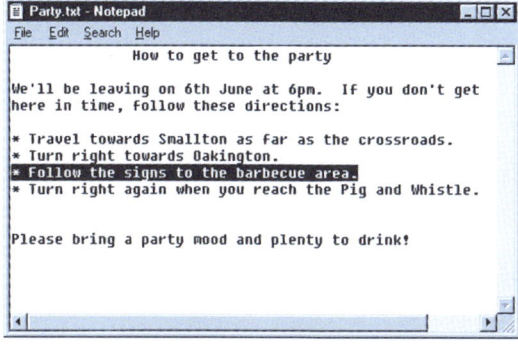

1 Select the section you want to copy.

2 Put the selected section into the CLIPBOARD by using the command COPY in the EDIT menu (or by using the keys Ctrl + C).

3 Click on the place in the text at which you want to insert the copied text.

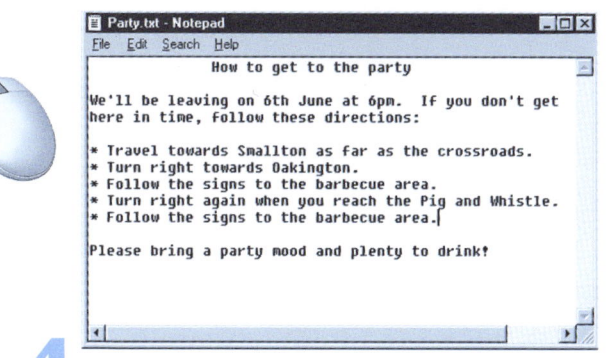

4 Choose the PASTE command from the EDIT menu, or press the key combination Ctrl + V.

135

Notepad takes the text from the Clipboard and inserts it at the position of the insertion marker. The section of the text which was selected beforehand remains unchanged when the *Copy* function is used.

> Not only can you select individual sentences to copy to the Clipboard, but also whole paragraphs. After that, the contents of the Clipboard can be inserted in the document as often as you wish.
>
> Data exchange via the Clipboard also works between different windows. You can, for example, start Notepad twice. Select the text in one window, and put this into the Clipboard, then change to the second Notepad window and paste the text from the Clipboard.

Saving and opening the document

One great advantage of a computer over a typewriter is the option to store the written text in a file. This then gives you the opportunity of reloading this text later, looking at it again, printing it and changing it if you wish to.

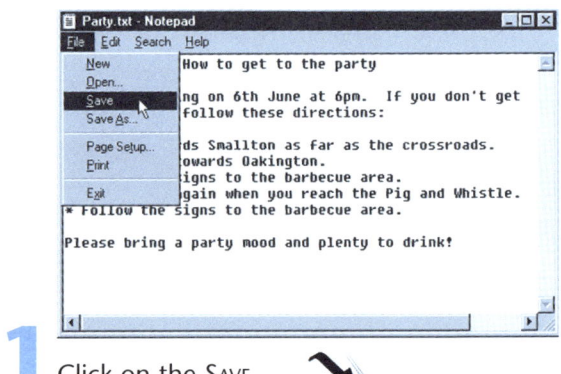

1 Click on the SAVE command in the FILE menu.

If this is a new piece of text, Notepad opens the *Save As* dialog box. In this dialog box's small window you can see the text files which are already stored in the folder which has been selected. The name of the folder is displayed in the list field *Save in*.

136

SAVING AND OPENING THE DOCUMENT

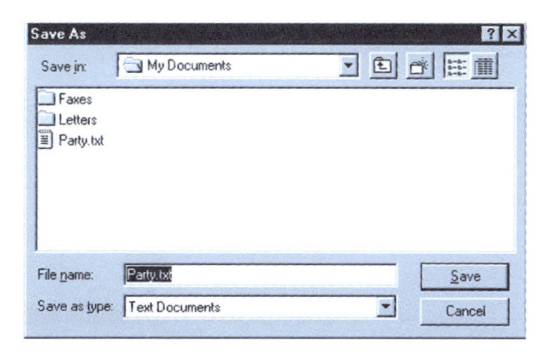

Want to save this document in a different folder?

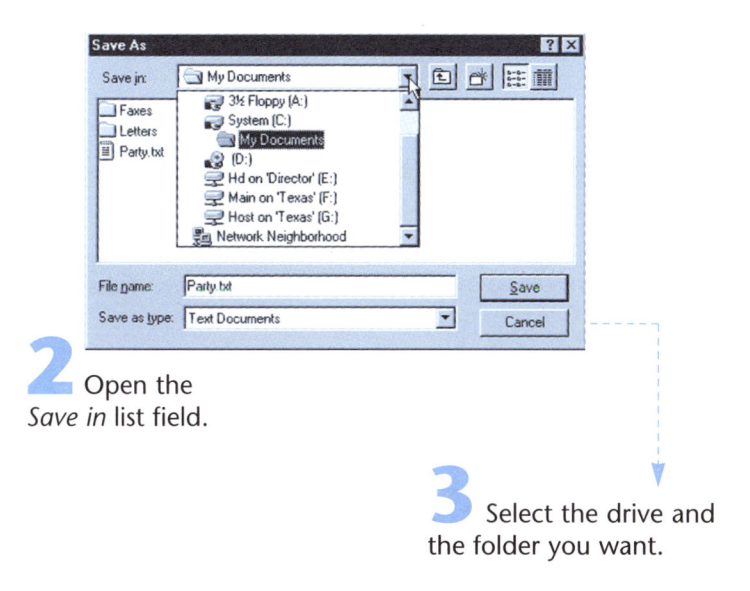

2 Open the *Save in* list field.

3 Select the drive and the folder you want.

If you get stuck, take another look at Chapter 3 for details of switching between folders.

137

Want to create a new folder before storing the file?

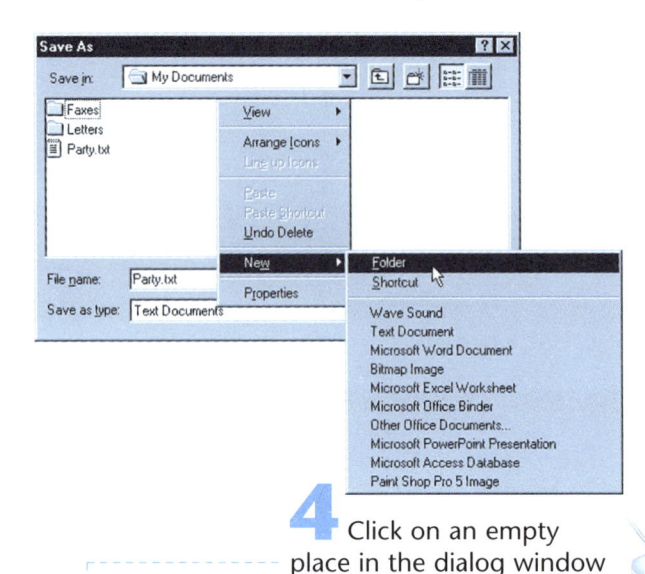

4 Click on an empty place in the dialog window with the right mouse key.

5 Select the commands NEW and FOLDER in the context menu, and type a name for the folder.

Here a new folder has been created in the dialog window.

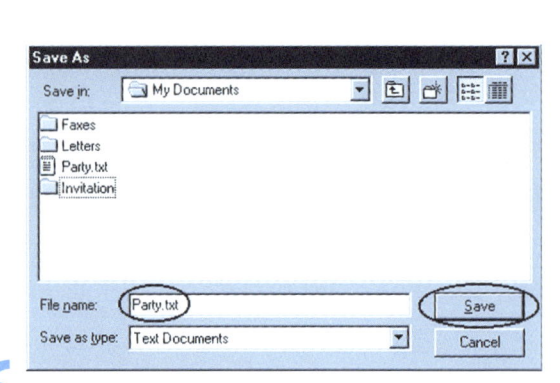

6 Now enter the name of the new file in the *File name* field.

SAVING AND OPENING THE DOCUMENT

7 Click on the *Save* button.

Notepad now creates a file with the name given and the file name extension *.txt* in the folder you chose and saves your text into it. You can now close Notepad and load this file again anytime you like.

> **TIP**
>
> In the *File name* field, you only need to enter the name. Notepad will then automatically add the extension *.txt* to it while saving. If you see a file with this extension, you know that this file can be edited with Notepad.
>
> If you have already saved the text in a file, you can update the file with any changes you have made simply by selecting the command *Save* in the File menu. The dialog field *Save as* will now no longer appear. If you want to save text under a new file name, select the command *Save as* in the File menu.

You will often come across text files in Windows. These may be files which you created yourself using Notepad. Text files are also supplied with Windows and other programs. In most cases such files have the extension *.txt*. You can load these files in Notepad, display them and, if you need to, also print them out.

1 Start Notepad with the command PROGRAMS/ ACCESSORIES/NOTEPAD in the Start menu.

2 Select the OPEN entry from Notepad's FILE menu.

139

The *Open* dialog box will appear.

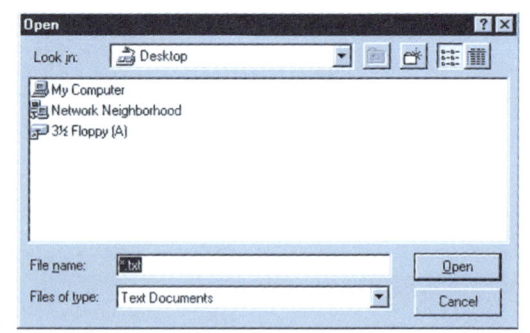

3 Now look for a folder containing a text file by double-clicking on the icons displayed for *My Computer*, the drives and the folders.

The window opposite shows a folder containing several text files.

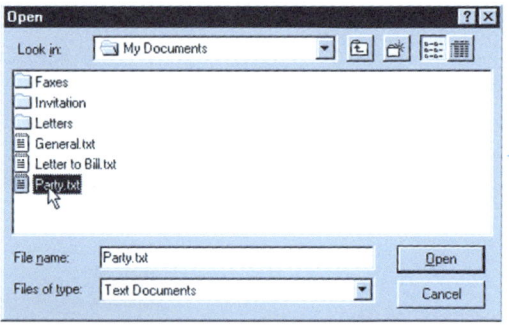

4 Click on the name of the text file you want to open.

5 Click on the *Open* button.

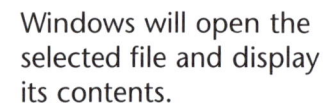

Windows will open the selected file and display its contents.

140

SEARCHING FOR TEXT IN THE DOCUMENT

Notepad is only able to read small text files (up to 64 Kb), however. If the file is too large, a dialog will appear to ask whether the file should be opened with the program *WordPad* (which is discussed later).

Unfortunately, there are text files which do not have the extension *.txt*, but instead, for example, *.ini*, *.bat* or *log*. In order for these files to appear in the *Open* dialog field, you need to select the entry *All files (*.*)* in the *Files of type* list field. You can then open these files like a text file.

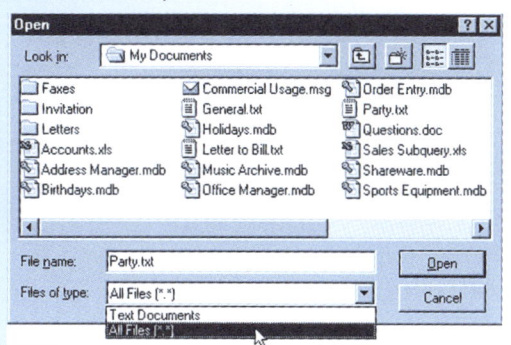

Searching for text in the document

Want to change something in a long document spanning a number of pages? It might be conceivable, for example, that a particular word needs to be replaced by another word; or perhaps you're looking for a specific part of the text. You could, of course, read the text sentence by sentence to find the term you're looking for, but that could be time-consuming and not entirely foolproof. It's a better idea to leave jobs like that to Windows.

1 Open the text file in NOTEPAD.

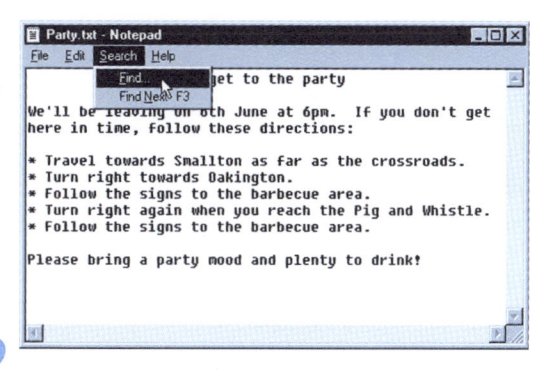

2 Select the command *Find . . .* in the SEARCH menu.

141

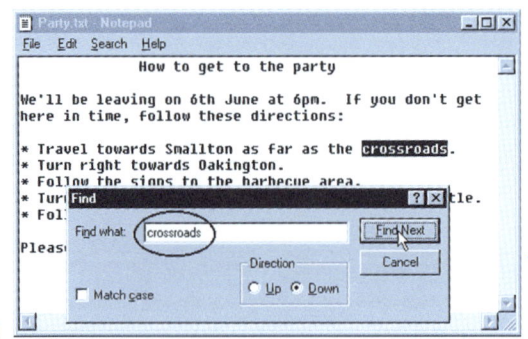

3 Enter the term you want to find in the *Find what* field of the *Find* dialog.

4 Choose options for the direction of the search (*Up* or *Down*), and whether the search should observe capital and small letters (*Match case*).

5 Click on the *Find Next* button.

If the matching text is found in the document, it is highlighted in colour. You can then close the *Find* dialog and edit the text.

6 If you want to look for more occurrences of the search term, select the command FIND NEXT in the SEARCH menu, or just press the function key F3.

If the term is not found, Notepad will display this message.

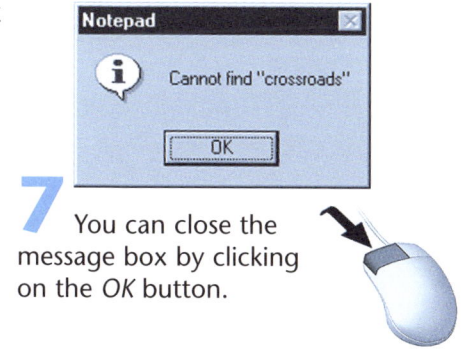

7 You can close the message box by clicking on the *OK* button.

Printing documents with Notepad

Apart from opening and saving files, one thing you're likely to want to do is to print them on paper.

1 Make sure that the printer is switched on and set to be online. Check that there is enough paper available.

2 Click on the PRINT command in Notepad's FILE menu.

During the printout, Notepad will display a small dialog box to keep you posted on the printing progress. With short documents, this dialog will disappear very quickly.

> If you have called up the print function by mistake and the progress dialog is still visible, you can click on the *Cancel* button. The printout will then be stopped and you'll be back in the Notepad window.

Creating documents using WordPad

You can use Notepad to enter simple text, print it and store it in files. Nowadays, however, many written items are laid out in a much more elaborate way. Titles and captions are emphasised in bold, or the text contains letters of different sizes and colours. Windows provides you with the *WordPad* program, which enables you to create these more stylish documents as well.

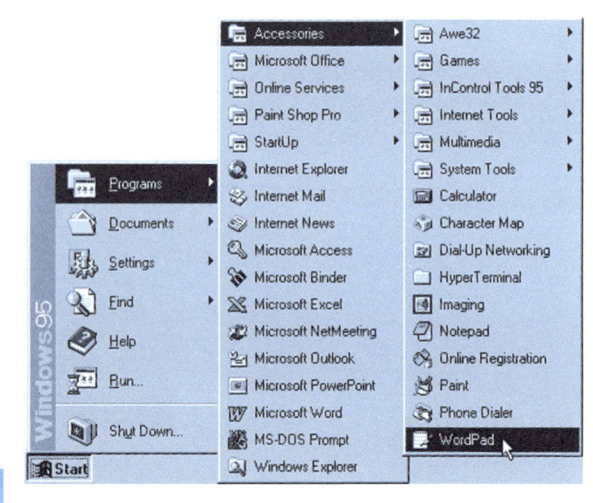

1 Click in the Start menu on PROGRAMS/ACCESSORIES/WORDPAD.

Windows will then start running the program, which has the name *Wordpad.exe*.

When the window of the *WordPad* program opens it is empty, and contains all the items you know well from other windows, such as the title bar, menu bar and toolbar.

CREATING DOCUMENTS USING WORDPAD

In a similar way to Notepad, there is also the text area with the insertion marker. Within the body of the text, the mouse pointer takes on the form of a text cursor.

This shows the empty WordPad window. By contrast with Notepad, this window has two toolbars as well as a status bar and a ruler.

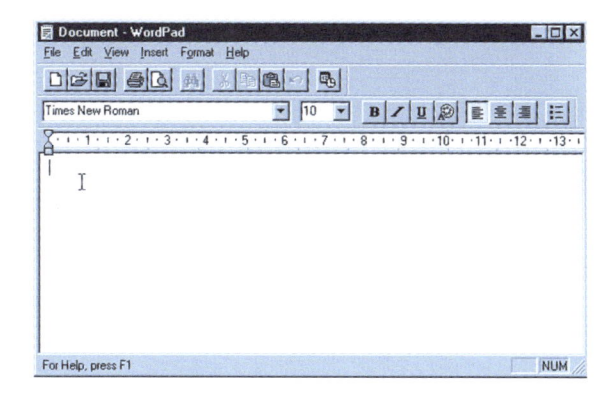

> Is the toolbar missing from your WordPad window, or is the ruler not there? You can find the commands for switching on these elements in the View menu (you have already come across these options in Chapter 3 with the folder window. You can see that there are a lot of things in Windows which are similar).

To create a new document, there are only two steps needed:

1 Click on the button (or select the NEW command in the FILE menu).

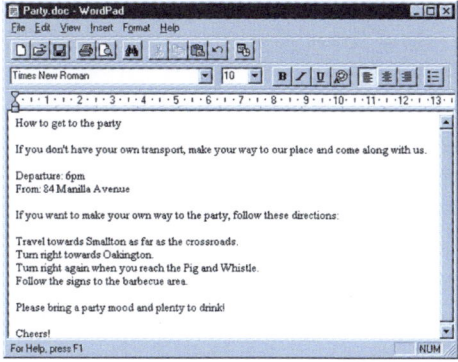

The window opposite contains the invitation to the party.

2 Enter the text.

145

When you type the text, proceed in the same way as you did previously with Notepad (the exceptions will be dealt with later).

You can use the same keys and functions to move the insertion marker, to enter the text, to select text and for other editing.

The functions for cutting, copying or pasting selected text can also be used in the same way as with Notepad. Things are actually even easier with *WordPad*, since you can use the buttons from the toolbar for these functions:

This button lets you cut out a selected text section from the WordPad window and place it in the Clipboard.

Use this button if you want to keep the selected text where it is but you also need a copy in the Clipboard.

If you click on this button, the contents of the Clipboard will be inserted in the text at the position of the insertion marker. This can be the text which was cut out or copied earlier, but you can also select pictures or other items in different programs and transfer them into the Clipboard.

> **TIP:** You should be familiar with these buttons already from Chapter 3, where we used them for copying files.

Here are the different features of WordPad we promised to talk about, which you need to take into account when you enter the text. First of all, forget about indenting individual lines with the Tab key; you will learn how to do this in a neater way later.

There is another feature which ought to be mentioned here. The Enter key ⏎ is often pressed at the end of a line, so as to start a new one. This is called the **line break** (or carriage return on a typewriter). Even if you are used to doing this from using a typewriter, don't press the ⏎ key when you reach the right edge of the window in WordPad; just keep on typing the text. WordPad has a function which spots the end of the line and automatically places the next word at the beginning of the next line. This function is called the automatic line break. This allows for texts to be set out in **paragraphs**. So what does that mean?

146

CREATING DOCUMENTS USING WORDPAD

In the text below, the ⏎ key was pressed at the end of the first line. The lines are typed continuously, and the line break occurs only at the end of the paragraph. Can you see a difference? Maybe not. So why all this fuss?

The advantages become clear as soon as the line length needs to be changed in the document. In the version below you can see the results of doing this.

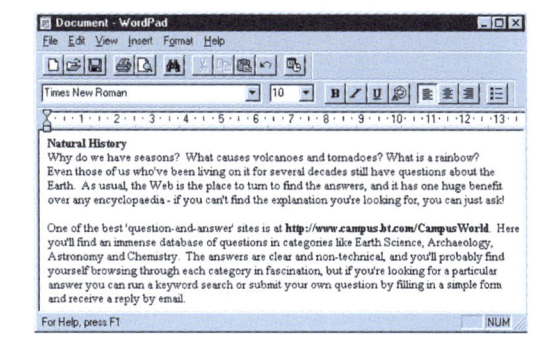

If the line length is reduced, the first lines of the document appear rather garbled. This is due to the **line break** which has been inserted with the ⏎ key.

147

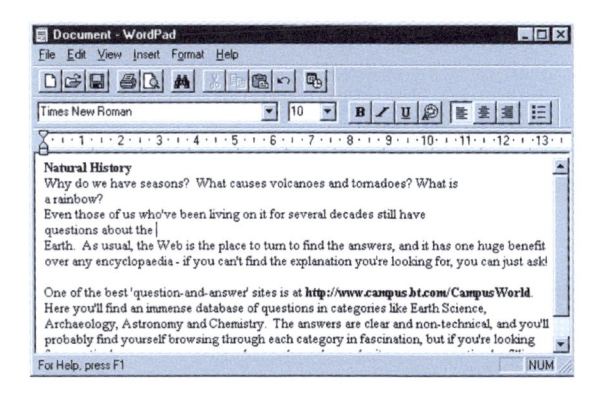

WordPad is forced to introduce a new line at the points concerned. For the text to look halfway reasonable when the line length is altered, you would have to rework all the line breaks afterwards.

The lower part of the text, on the other hand, consists of a **paragraph**, and WordPad can adjust the lines automatically to the different line lengths. There is no need for you to worry about making the adjustments yourself.

Formatting a text document

At one time or another you've undoubtedly received an invitation or a letter which has been nicely laid out. Some parts of the text may have been printed in bold, or the headings centred on the line. With WordPad you can **format** your own documents just as neatly.

WHAT'S THIS? Laying out a text document with different style effects such as bold, italics, underlining, larger letters, and so on, is referred to as formatting.

1 Click on the first line of the text.

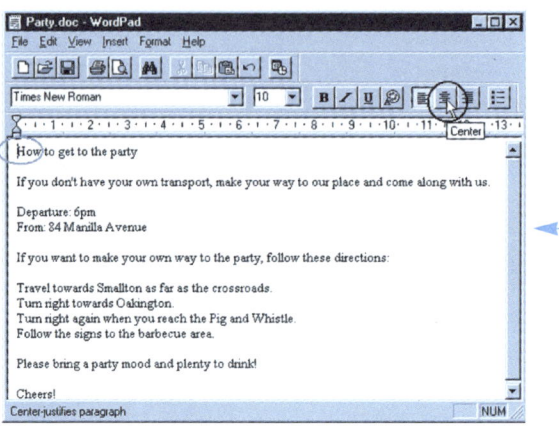

2 Click on the *Center* button on the toolbar.

WordPad will centre the first line.

148

By using the three buttons *Align Left, Center*, and *Align Right*, you can align the text at the left margin, in the middle of the line, or at the right margin.

The *Left Align* button ensures that the lines will be aligned at the left edge of the window. When the text reaches the right edge, the next word will be moved automatically onto the following line (line break). Because the lines are of differing lengths, they are described as 'ragged right'. A left-aligned style is the usual way of presenting text.

Use the *Center* button to centre text between the left and right edges. This arrangement is well-suited for formatting headings, for example.

The *Right Align* button causes the lines of the text to end at the right edge, while the 'ragged' edge occurs on the left. Unless you are working with Hebrew or Arabic texts you will rarely use this button, other than perhaps to format addresses.

> **Alignment** relates to the **selected text** or the current **paragraph**. If you pressed the ⏎ button at the end of the line when you were inputting the text, WordPad will treat every line as a paragraph, and that will make alignment a considerable effort. You can see that it is worthwhile writing the text as a paragraph right from the start.

The aim now is to emphasise the heading even further, by using bold text and slightly larger letters.

1 Select the text of the first line.

149

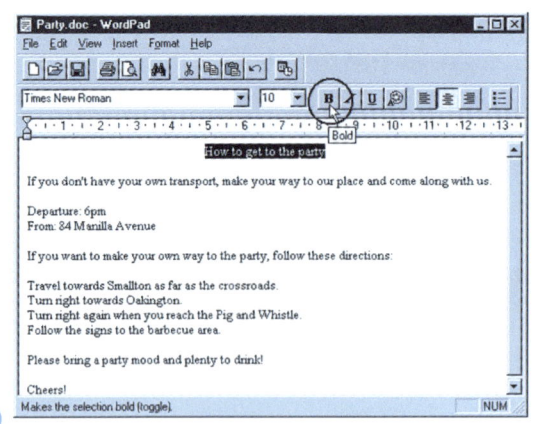

2 Click on the *Bold* button.

The text will now be displayed in bold.

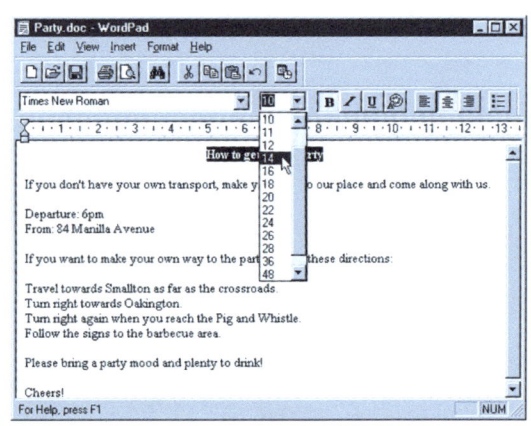

3 Click on the *Font size* list field.

4 Set a value of 14 points for the letter size.

FORMATTING A TEXT DOCUMENT

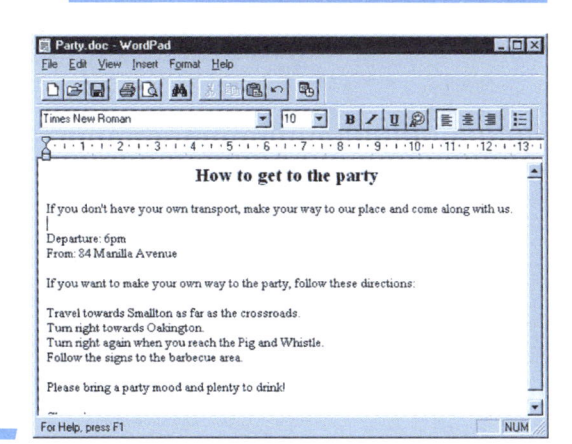

5 Click somewhere outside the selected text to remove the highlighting.

The document already looks rather better

> There are a number of technical terms used when formatting text. The size of the characters is not referred to as the character size or character height; the proper technical term is the **font size**. The numbers indicate the font size in **points**, which corresponds to a particular unit of measurement, such as millimetres, for example. For text, the term used for the different styles of lettering is **fonts**. There are many different fonts (Times Roman, Courier, Helvetica, etc.), which can be used for different styles. You are certainly aware that the letters in a newspaper differ in appearance from the advertising poster in your local supermarket. And you might remember the blocky letters in the *Wanted* posters from the Westerns, which used to be printed in a particular style (for youngsters, take a look at the leather label on your jeans. The logo of a well-known Cola manufacturer also uses a particular font).

As well as the font size and font type, you can also emphasise parts of the text by using bold, italics or underlining. WordPad offers you three buttons for this:

B This button formats the selected text in bold letters.

151

If you click on this button, the selected text will appear in tilted letters, which are referred to as *italics*.

Click on this button in order to underline a selected section of text.

In the invitation that was created with Notepad at the start of this chapter, a number of lines were 'emphasised' by an asterisk * at the start of the line. Such emphasised paragraphs are referred to as **bullets**. In WordPad, bullets can be added in a much better way.

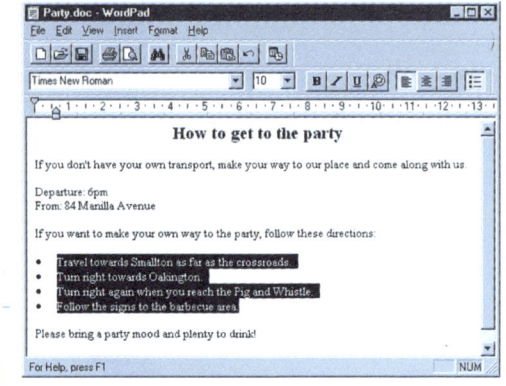

1 Select the lines or paragraphs which you intend to format with bullets.

2 Click on the BULLETS button on the toolbar.

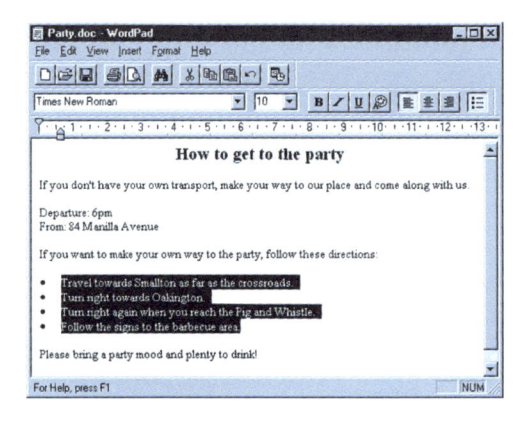

WordPad will now insert a small dot, the **bullet**, in front of the first lines of the paragraphs concerned.

152

FORMATTING A TEXT DOCUMENT

If a paragraph consists of several lines, the alignment of lines which follow will be adjusted to match the beginning of the first line. Put another way, the following lines are **indented** to the same **column** as the first line.

As the next step, we want to emphasise the time of departure and the place of departure in bold, and indented. You were told how to put the text into bold on the previous pages.

This might perhaps look like this: **Departure:** 6pm
From: 84 Manilla Avenue

Things get a little more difficult when we come to indent the two lines which were written in the normal manner. Did you use the ⇥ key as an experiment?

Departure: 6pm   Here you can see the result – not entirely
From: 84 Manilla Avenue   convincing.

Depending on the length of a word, the tabulator positions of the individual lines will not always match. In some lines, you will need to tab twice in order to get the indented words positioned precisely below one another in the same column.

WordPad sets the tabulator positions automatically (as do many other word processing programs). You do have the option, though, of setting the tabulator positions manually to suit your requirements.

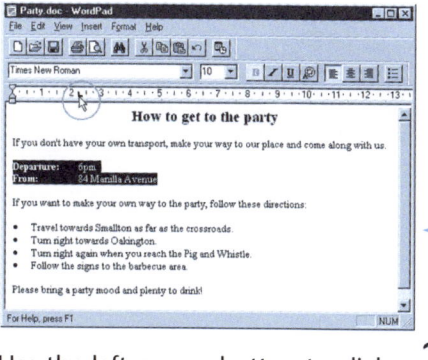

1 Select the lines or paragraphs for which the tabs are to be set.

2 Use the left mouse button to click on the point on the ruler at which you intend a tabulator position to appear.

153

WordPad marks the tabulator position by a small angular mark. At the same time, the tabulator positions in the selected text section will be indented as far as this position.

In the picture opposite, three tabulator positions have been set at 2 cm, 4 cm, and 6 cm.

These tab positions can be moved or deleted as required.

1 Set the arrow at the tabulator mark with the mouse.

2 Move the mark by dragging the mouse to the left or right (press down the left mouse button and hold it down).

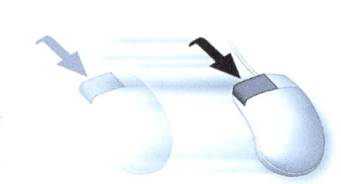

A small dotted line indicates the tabulator position in the text.

3 To delete a tabulator mark, drag it down into the text area and then release the mouse button.

> **TIP**
> Tabulators are very suitable for setting up tables (in invoices for example). The individual columns can be neatly aligned by using the key. In tables, incidentally, at the end of the line the return key is used to change the line. Once the table contents has been entered, you can select the entire table and adjust the tabulator positions if required.

A further option for formatting a written item conerns the line length for the text. WordPad starts with the line at the left edge, and makes sure that the text continues from the end of one line onto the beginning of the next. But how does WordPad know where the left and right edges are for any particular line?

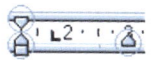

On the ruler you can see small triangles at the left and right ends.

These triangles are also known as **margin stops**. By using the lower left stop and the lower right stop you can set the start and end of the line. The margin stop at the top left sets the start of the first line in paragraphs with several lines.

It can also be said that this margin stop sets the **first line indentation** (i.e. the indentation of the first line of a paragraph). We can now use this to emphasise a paragraph in the text.

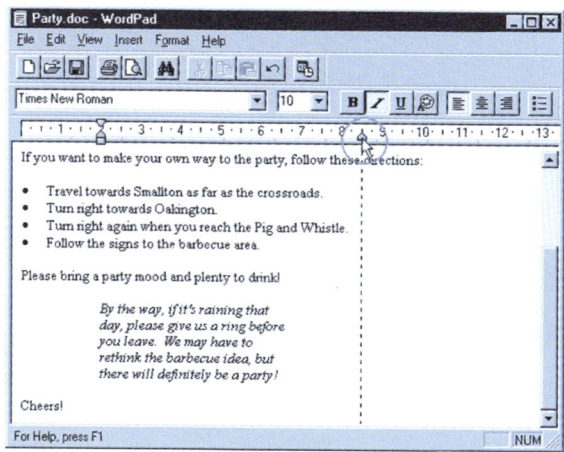

1 Move the pointer to the right margin stop and drag it to the left.

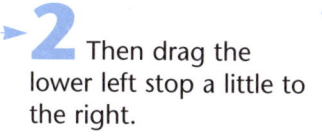

2 Then drag the lower left stop a little to the right.

This will cause the line length to be slightly reduced. WordPad will indent the text accordingly, and also provides the line breaks. The result is that you obtain a narrower paragraph text. By using this technique you can, for example, set the left or right margins.

155

> The margin stops take effect only on the paragraph being worked on (or on a selected section). If you want to adjust the margins of the entire document, you will have to select the entire document first. This can be done by just pressing the key combination `Ctrl` + `A`.

Saving, opening and printing documents in WordPad

With WordPad, like other programs, you can store the text in the form of files.

These files are given names which you choose, and the file name extension *.doc*. Saving is done in the same way as in Notepad; in other words, you can use the command Save in the File menu. But because WordPad has a toolbar, saving a file is even easier.

1 Click on the *Save* button in the toolbar.

With a new (as yet unnamed) document, the dialog box *Save As* will now appear.

2 Select the folder in which the file is to be stored.

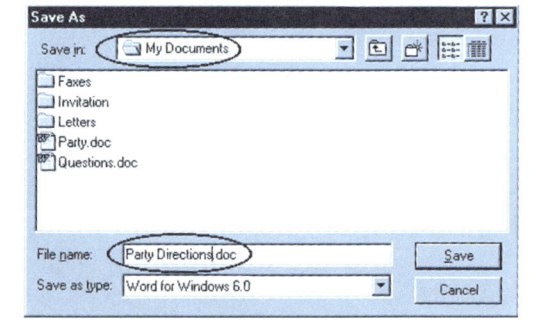

3 Type a name in the field of the *File name* field.

4 Click on the *Save* button.

WordPad will now create the file and store the text in it.

SAVING, OPENING AND PRINTING DOCUMENTS IN WORDPAD

> **TIP**
>
> You do not need to add the extension *.doc* to the filename you type. Provided the entry *Word for Windows 6.0* is selected in the field *Files of type*, WordPad will add this extension automatically. These text files can also be read and processed with the program *Microsoft Word*. This is a word-processing program which is considerably more powerful than WordPad, and is often used in the business world.
>
> There are other file formats in the *Files of type* field which can be used for saving the text. If you select the type *.txt* for example, WordPad will store the file as a plain text file, the same type of file that Notepad works with. Bear in mind that if you choose this file type, though, all your formatting will be discarded and only the plain text itself will be saved.
>
> If you want to save an edited document, which already exists as a file, all you need to do is click the *Save* button. WordPad will then save the changes without needing to ask for any more information. To save a document under a different name, select the command *Save As* in the File menu. The *Save As* dialog box, shown above, will then appear and you can enter a new file name.

Text documents can be **opened** in WordPad to be read, edited or printed.

1 Click on the toolbar button shown opposite in the WordPad window.

WordPad opens the dialog window shown opposite.

2 Choose the folder containing the file which is to be loaded.

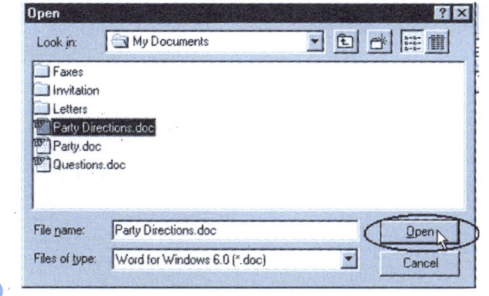

3 Click on the file which you want to open.

4 Click on the *Open* button.

157

WordPad then loads the file and displays it in the document window. If the document was formatted, this formatting will be shown on the screen.

> **TIP** WordPad is capable not only of loading files with the extension *.doc*, but also, by using the list field *Files of type*, it can load files with extensions such as *.txt* (text files) or *.rtf* (special formatted text files).

Printing a document in WordPad is even easier than it is in Notepad.

1 Click on the *Print* button, shown opposite, in the toolbar.

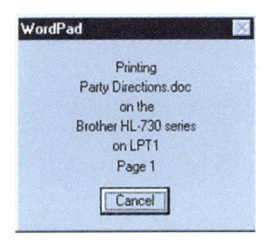

During printing, WordPad shows this dialog box to tell you how many pages have already been printed.

To stop the printing process before it has finished, click on the *Cancel* button.

What happens if you have a document with a large number of pages, but you only want to print a few of them?

1 Select the command *Print* in the File menu, or press the key combination `Ctrl` + `P`.

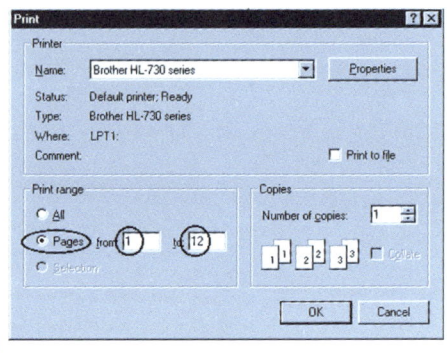

2 Click on the option field *Pages*.

158

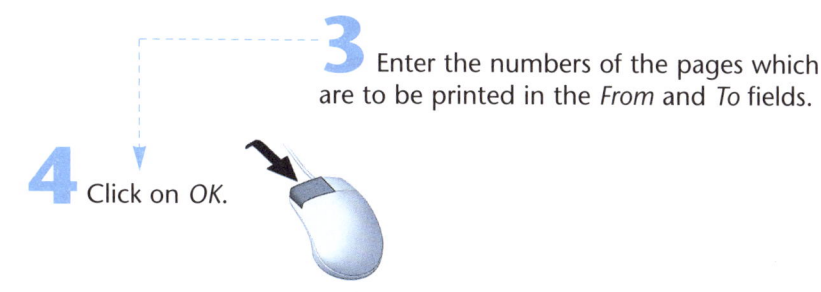

3 Enter the numbers of the pages which are to be printed in the *From* and *To* fields.

4 Click on *OK*.

> Do you just want to see what the document will look like when it is printed out later? All you need do is click on the *Print Preview* button. WordPad will then show you an overview of the document at a reduced size. WordPad can provide other functions which are not mentioned here; more information about these is provided by WordPad Help.

Drawing pictures using Paint

Along with Notepad and WordPad for working with text, Windows provides Paint, a program for creating and editing graphics, pictures and drawings.

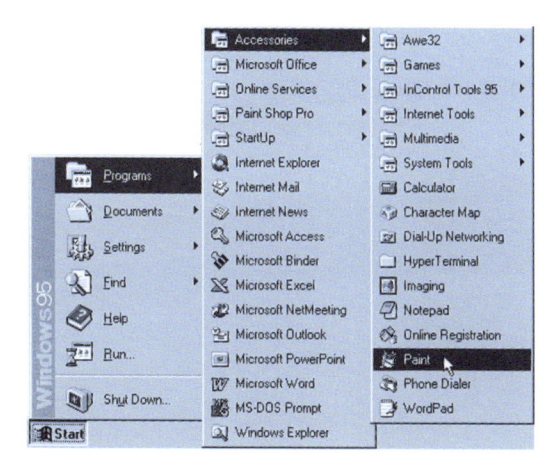

1 Click on PROGRAMS/ACCESSORIES/PAINT in the Start menu.

Windows will start the *Paint* program. Paint opens a window which contains a title bar and a menu bar. You'll recognise these from other windows you've been working with.

159

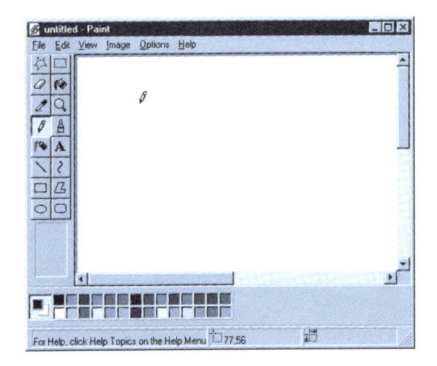

Something new here is the **drawing area**. When the mouse pointer is in this area, it takes on the form of a pencil or paintbrush.

At the left edge of the window is a toolbar with the buttons for the drawing functions. At the bottom edge of the window is a **paint palette** for choosing the colours for drawing.

Using the pencil and the brush, and keeping the mouse button pressed down (also known as freehand drawing), start drawing in the colour you have selected. With the brush, you can also select the thickness of the strokes.

To draw something, follow these steps:

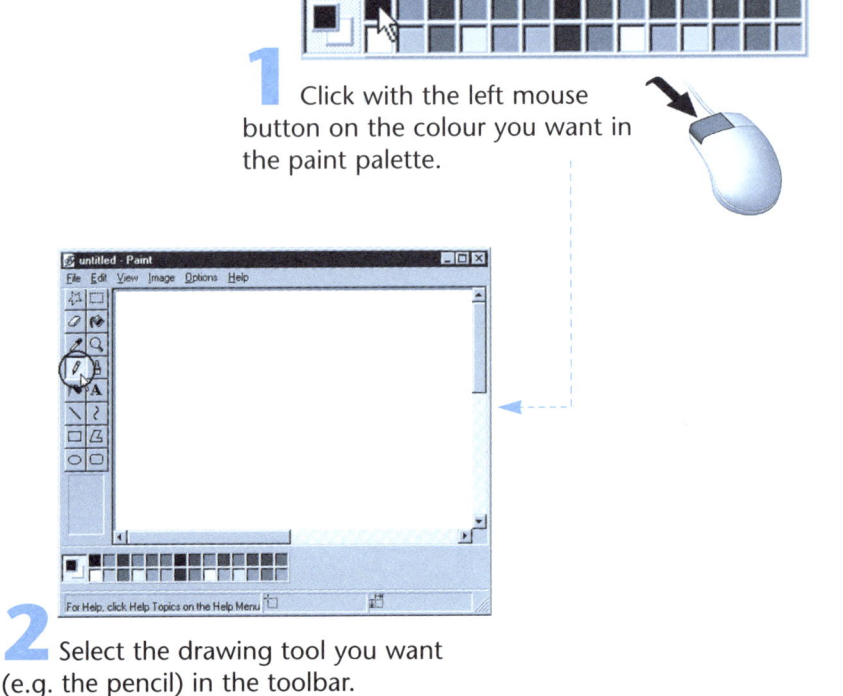

1 Click with the left mouse button on the colour you want in the paint palette.

2 Select the drawing tool you want (e.g. the pencil) in the toolbar.

DRAWING PICTURES USING PAINT

3 Put the pointer at the position in the drawing area at which you want to start drawing.

4 Drag the drawing tool over the drawing area, with the left mouse button pressed down.

5 Release the mouse button.

6 Now click on the brush as the tool

7 Decide on the thickness of the brush strokes in the field below the tool bar.

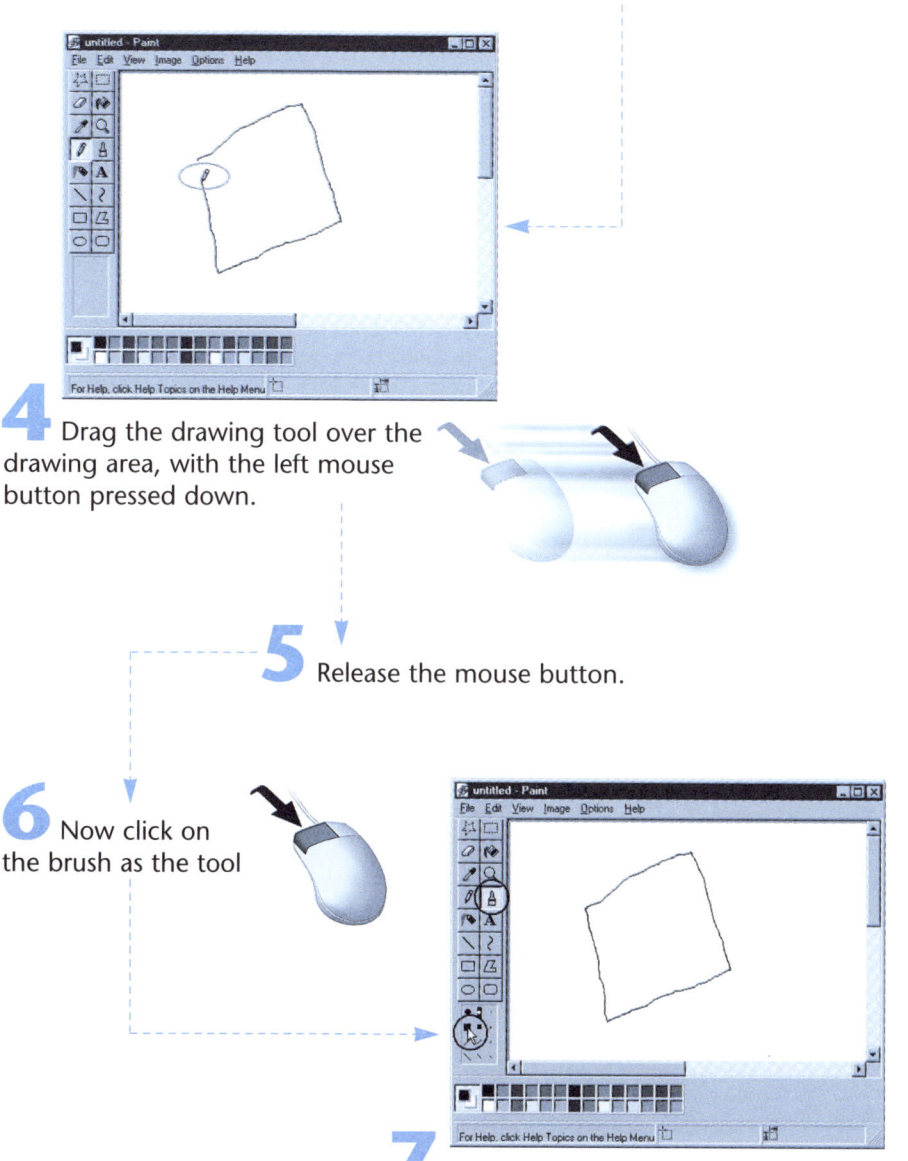

161

8 Drag the brush across the drawing area with the left mouse button pressed down.

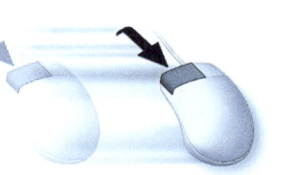

Depending on the tool which has been selected, a freehand line will now be reproduced on the drawing area in the selected colour and stroke thickness.

> The field for selecting the stroke thickness will also be displayed with other tools (eraser, spray can, etc.). By clicking on an option, the 'thickness' of the tool can be changed.
> Have you made a mistake in the drawing? Just press the key combination Ctrl + Z. The last command for drawing will then be reversed. You can use this key combination, for example, for removing the last line to be drawn.

Paint does not, unfortunately, have a function for clicking on part of a picture and then deleting it. However, it is possible to 'delete' parts of the drawing with the eraser.

1 Click on the eraser in the tool bar.

2 As required, select another thickness for the eraser (the effect of this is the same as when changing the brush thickness).

3 Move the mouse to a place on the drawing.

162

DRAWING PICTURES USING PAINT

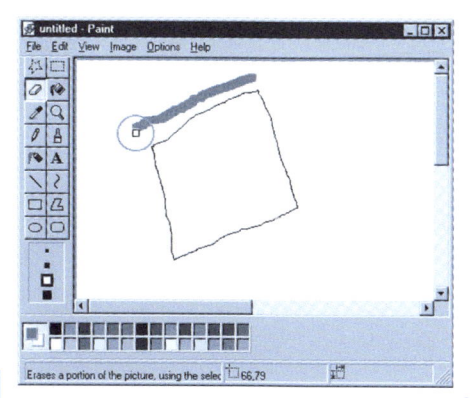

4 Keep the left mouse button pushed down, and drag the eraser over the drawing.

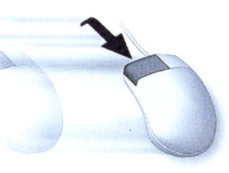

Paint will delete any area of the drawing you touch with the eraser tool.

> As a rule, you will be working against a white background. You can, however, click on a colour in the palette using the right mouse button. If you then select the command New in the File menu, Paint will delete the current drawing, and insert a new 'sheet' in the background colour you chose. During 'erasure', the tool will also use the chosen background colour. If this happens to you by mistake, simply select another background colour.

The *Paint* program provides you with other drawing tools as well. You can draw different objects with these tools, or create special effects.

The *spray can* can be used like a paintbrush, but supplies a spray effect.

1 Click on the *spray can* tool.

163

2 Drag the tool across the drawing area with the left mouse button pressed down.

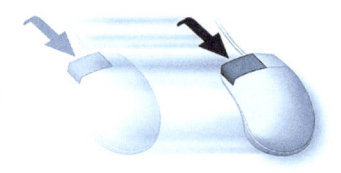

A typical spray can effect will be produced. If you drag slower, the paint will be applied more thickly. For the 'spraying', the tool uses the last paint colour that was set.

The width of the drawing tool can be adjusted in a similar manner to the paint brush, using the field shown opposite (located beneath the tool bar).

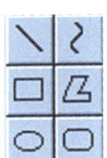

These buttons are used to select the tools for drawing straight lines, curves, polygons and other shapes.

Lines and shapes are drawn in a similar way with most of the tools.

1 Click on the tool required (in this case, the rectangle).

2 Move the pointer to where you want the rectangle to be drawn.

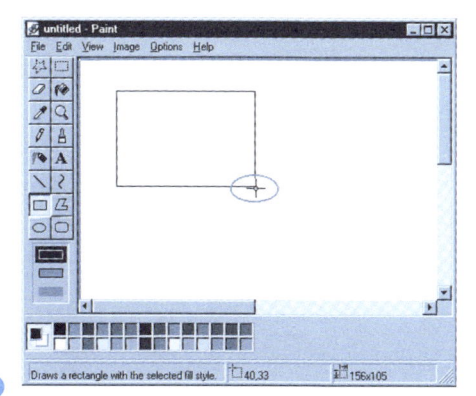

Drawing pictures using Paint

3 Keep the left mouse button pressed down, and drag the mouse to the end point of the shape.

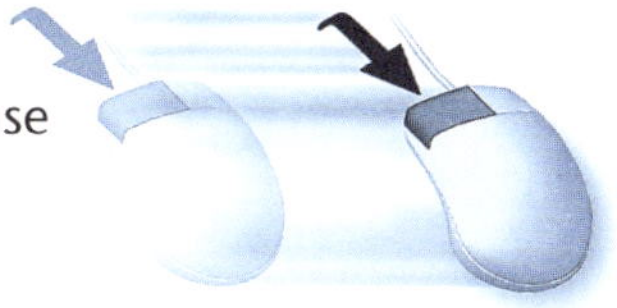

During the dragging movement, Paint will show the outlines of the line or the shape in the drawing area. As soon as you release the mouse button, Paint will draw the shape or the line at the size selected.

With surfaces (rectangle, circle) you can use the icons shown opposite to choose whether the shape should be outlined, filled in with the background colour, or a solid foreground-colour shape.

With the *Polygon* tool, more complicated shapes can be drawn by merging a number of lines onto one another. You must 'draw' the lines for this with the mouse, beginning at the starting point.

1 Click on the *Polygon* tool.

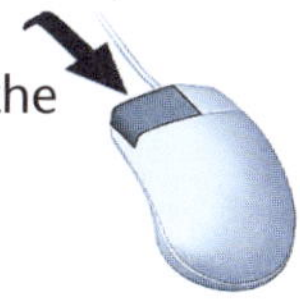

2 Move the pointer to wherever the shape should be drawn.

165

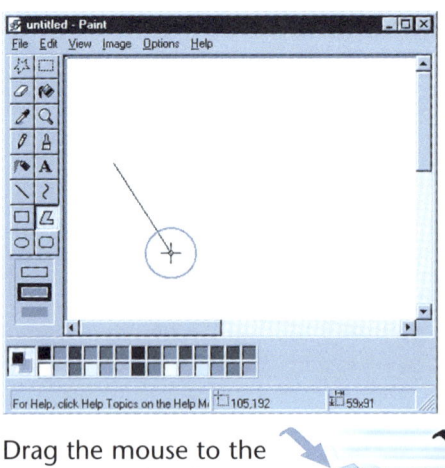

3 Drag the mouse to the end point of the first line.

4 Click on the end point to fix the line.

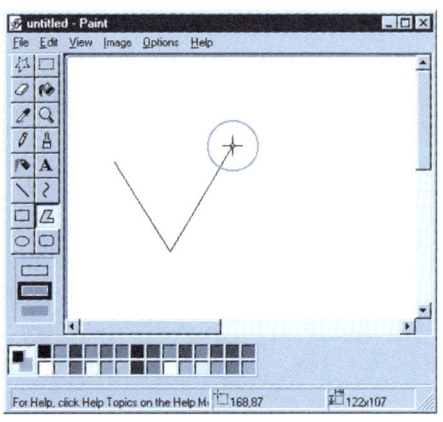

5 Repeat steps 3 and 4 to draw the next lines of the polygon.

Paint automatically joins the lines together when you double-click.

DRAWING PICTURES USING PAINT

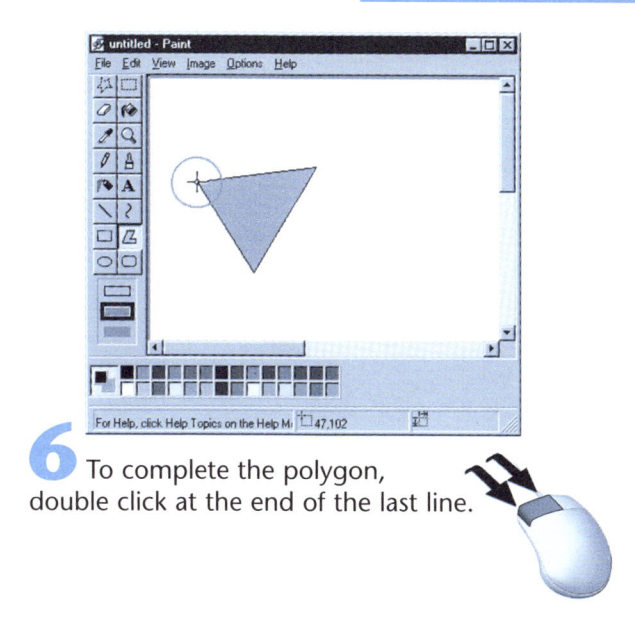

6 To complete the polygon, double click at the end of the last line.

The tool automatically merges the end points of the line sections together. When you double click on the last point, the drawing function will automatically close off the polygon with a line.

Closed shapes can be filled with the *Paint filler*.

1 Choose a filler colour from the paint palette.

2 Select the *Paint filler* tool.

Paint will display a paint bucket as the mouse cursor when the tool is selected. As soon as you click on a shape, its contents will be filled with colour.

167

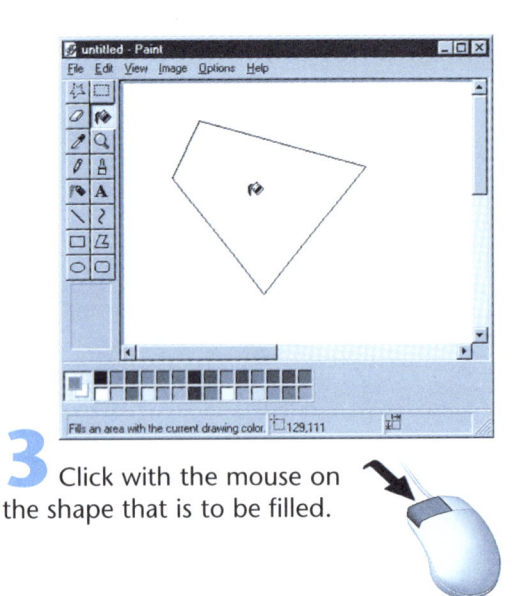

3 Click with the mouse on the shape that is to be filled.

With the artistic side sorted out, you probably want to add a label to your masterpiece.

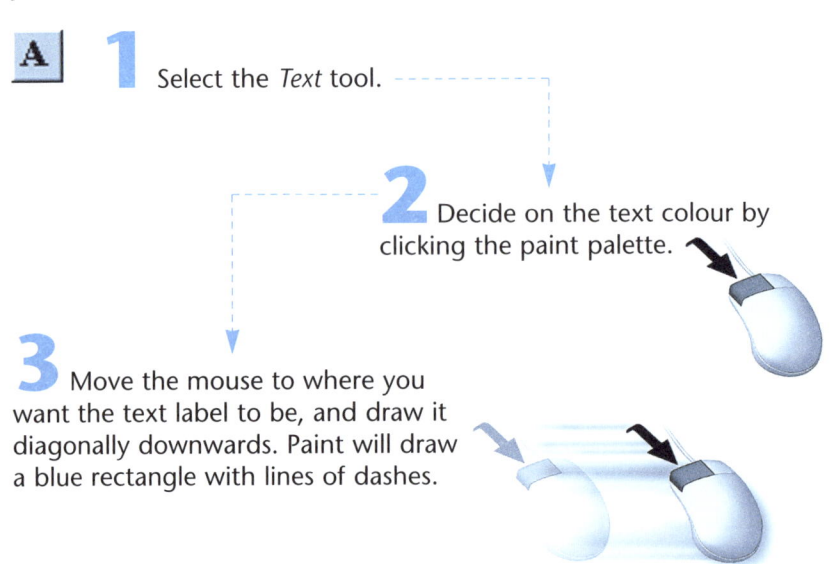

1 Select the *Text* tool.

2 Decide on the text colour by clicking the paint palette.

3 Move the mouse to where you want the text label to be, and draw it diagonally downwards. Paint will draw a blue rectangle with lines of dashes.

DRAWING PICTURES USING PAINT

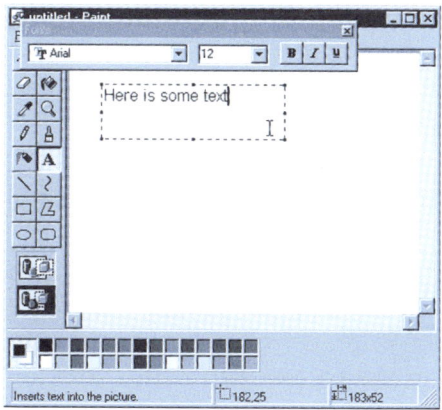

4 Release the mouse button, and type your text label.

5 Click on a place outside to the text box.

With step 5, you are fixing the text at the current position in the drawing. You will not then be able to edit the text any more, because it is now contained in the drawing as a 'picture'. You do still have the option, however, of removing the text with the *Eraser* tool.

> During text input, the *Fonts* toolbar shown opposite will appear.
>
> While you are entering the text, it can be formatted using the toolbar. You can use the toolbar to decide on the *font*, the *font size* and the formatting for *bold, italics* and *underlining*. One difference from WordPad, however, is that the formatting always relates to the whole of the text.

By using the *colour picker* tool, you can select the foreground and background colour directly in the drawing (rather than from the paint palette). Just click on the desired colour where it occurs in your picture using the left (foreground colour) or right (background colour) mouse button.

169

If the *Magnifying glass* tool is selected, you can enlarge a section of the picture by clicking on the left mouse button, while a click on the right mouse button will reverse the enlargement.

Cropping and copying graphics

You have learned the functions in Notepad and WordPad for selecting, cutting, copying, and inserting. The same capabilities are available to you under Paint as well. By using these functions you can cut out sections in the picture and copy them into the Clipboard. The contents of the Clipboard can then be reinserted into the same drawing as well as into other Windows programs (such as WordPad, for example). Here you can see a simple drawing which follows this technique, and was produced with WordPad. In the bottom left corner the drawing has a number of locations for direction arrows. The intention now is to insert the arrow pointing downwards as a copy into a part of the drawing. The first thing you must do is to select the section of the drawing in which you will be working.

1 First select the *Selection* tool.

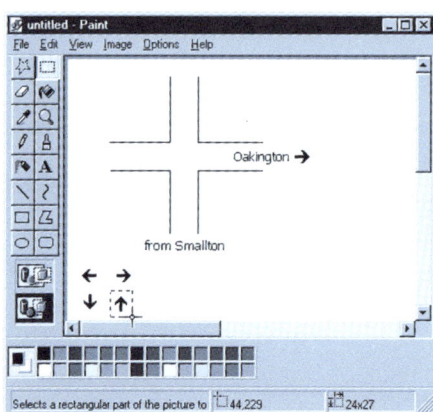

2 Move the pointer to the top left corner of the section that is to be cut.

3 Keep the left mouse button pressed down and drag the mouse into the diagonally opposite corner of the section.

CROPPING AND COPYING GRAPHICS

Paint selects the section using a dotted line rectangle. As soon as you release the mouse button, this rectangle will be secured as a selection. You can now cut out the section or copy it, and then paste it from the Clipboard.

The three functions can be called up via the Edit menu or by using the following key combinations:

`Ctrl` + `X`   This cuts out the selected section and moves it to the Clipboard. The selected section will disappear, and will be replaced by the background colour.

`Ctrl` + `C`   This copies the selected section into the Clipboard. The drawing will not be changed in the process.

`Ctrl` + `V`   The contents of the Clipboard will be inserted in the top left corner of the drawing area, as a selection. You can drag this selected area to any point in the drawing you want by using the mouse.

You are already familiar with these key combinations. Windows uses them in all programs to cut out selected sections (whether in text or in graphics), copy them and reinsert them.

1 Now press the combination `Ctrl` + `C` in order to copy the selected picture section into the Clipboard.

2 Then use the key combination `Ctrl` + `V` to reinsert the contents of the Clipboard into the window.

3 Move the pointer onto the selected section that has just been pasted into the corner.

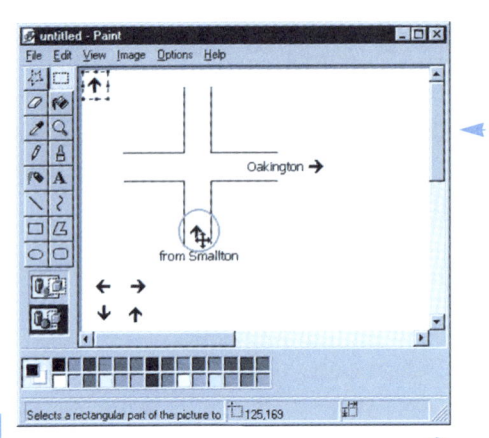

4 Drag the selected section to the desired point in the drawing using the left mouse button.

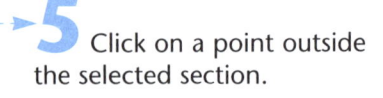

5 Click on a point outside the selected section.

This last step will remove the selection box, and the section of the picture will be fixed into position.

> **TIP**
> You may have noticed something in those last steps: to move a part of the drawing, all you need to do is to select it. The selected section can then be dragged about in the drawing by using the mouse.

Saving, opening and printing a picture using Paint

By using the options we've covered on the previous pages, you can use Paint to work with drawings, invitations or pictures.

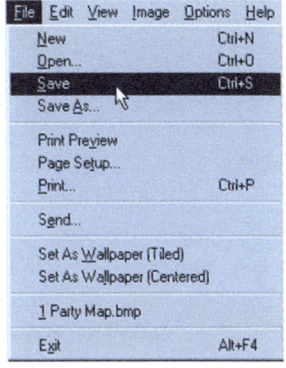

As soon as you have completed the picture you can store it in a file. This works with in just the same way with Paint as it does with other programs.

1 Select the SAVE command in the FILE menu, or press the key combination `Ctrl` + `S`.

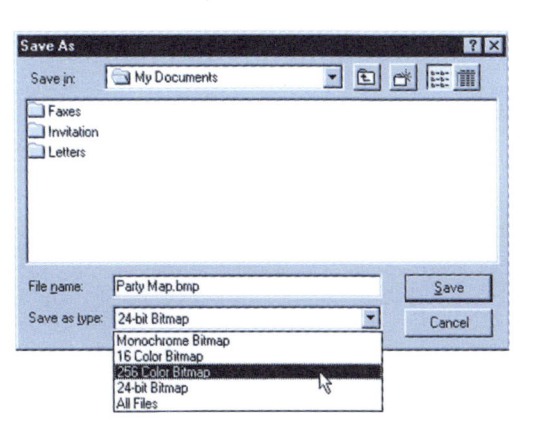

2 Select the drive staion and folder in which the file is to be saved, using the *Save in* field.

3 Type in the file name you want in the *File name* field.

173

4 If necessary, you can choose how many colours the picture is to be stored with by using the *Save as type* list field.

5 To save the picture in the file, press the *Save* button.

Paint creates a new file and stores the picture in it. The *Save As* dialog field will only appear, however, when a new picture is stored for the first time. If the file already exists, Paint's *Save* command updates the file with your changes without any further enquiry. If you want to save the file with a different name or location, you must select the *Save As* command in the File menu.

> **TIP**
> Paint stores the pictures in files with the extension *.bmp*. These files can be read by a large number of Windows programs. In this context, you can store the pictures as black and white (monochrome), with 16,256 colours, or with 16.8 million colours. The 16.8 million colours are stored by the file type *24-Bit Bitmap*. The more colours you choose when storing, the bigger the file will be (although it won't necessarily look any different).

Pictures that are stored in the file type *.bmp* can be **opened** in Paint. These may be pictures or drawings you have produced yourself. You can also load *.bmp* pictures from other sources into Paint, and work with them. For example, Windows 95 comes with a number of BMP files, and many CD-ROMs also contain BMP pictures.

1 Start the *Paint* program.

174

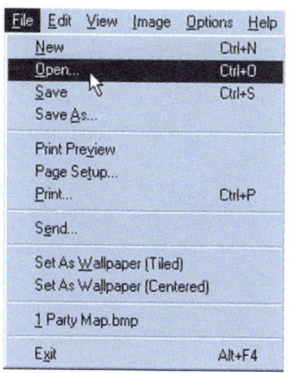

SAVING, OPENING AND PRINTING A PICTURE USING PAINT

You can also use the key combination `Ctrl` + `O` to call up the command *Open*.

2 Click on the OPEN command in the FILE menu.

3 Choose a folder containing your picture files.

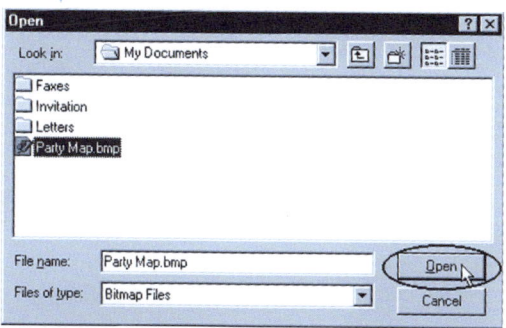

4 Click on the desired *.bmp* file.

5 Click the *Open* button.

175

Paint opens the *.bmp* file you selected, and displays the picture. You can then edit the file, save it again, and/or print it onto paper.

> **TIP**
>
> Pictures can be stored with a variety of different file types. Many windows programs use the *.bmp* file format. In the older Windows 3.1 version, pictures were created with the *Paintbrush* program, and stored in the *.pcx* file format. Pictures in *.pcx* format do not need as much disk space as *.bmp* files. In the *Open* dialog field, the option *Bitmap files* is the default in the *Files of type* field. Open this list field, and then select *PC Paintbrush (PCX)* as the file type. Picture files can then also be opened in this format.
>
> Paint (like many other Windows programs) notes the names of the last four files to be processed. You can reopen one of these quickly by clicking its entry on the File menu.

You can open pictures in Paint, and then output them on a printer. Depending on the printer you are using, Windows will, if necessary, convert colour pictures into a black and white or shades of grey representation.

1 Start the *Paint* program.

2 Load the file containing the picture you want to print.

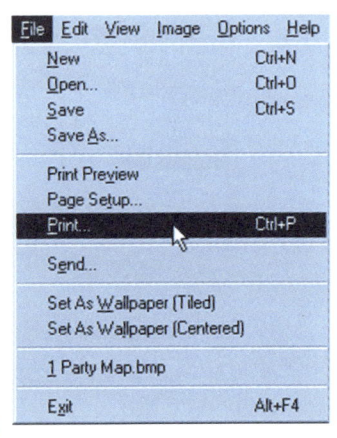

3 Select the PRINT command in the FILE menu. (or press the key combination Ctrl + P).

176

Paint opens the *Print* dialog box to let you choose the print options.

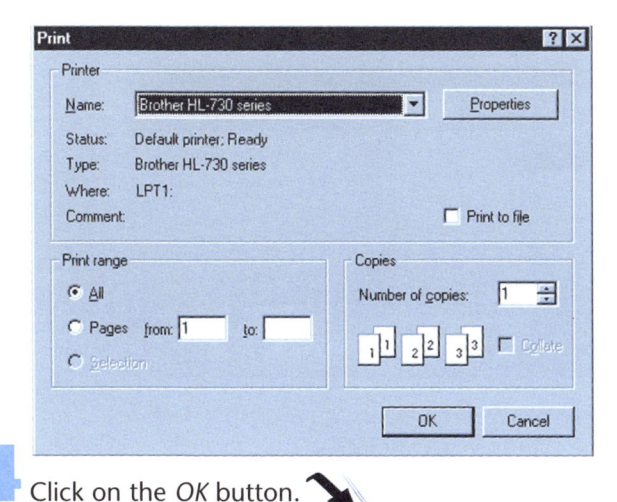

4 Click on the *OK* button.

Paint will now start printing out the picture. The complete picture will be printed, even it cannot all be seen in the window.

Creating a background for the Windows desktop

Windows can display background pictures on the desktop (see Chapter 11). These background pictures must be stored as *.bmp* files. This means that you can edit these background pictures in *Paint* or create brand new ones. The Windows 95 CD-ROM contains two *.bmp* pictures in the *\Funstuff\Pictures* folder. Using one of these pictures, we'll put our own background image on the desktop.

1 Start the *Paint* program.

177

2 Select the OPEN command in the FILE menu.

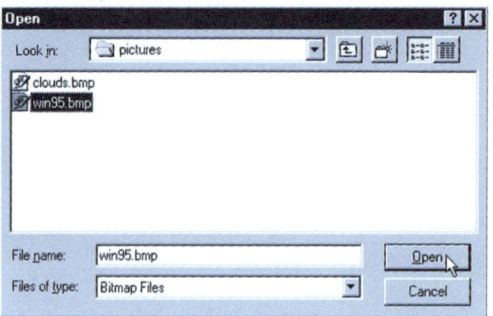

3 Load the *Win95.bmp* file in the *\Funstuff\Pictures* folder on the Windows CD-ROM.

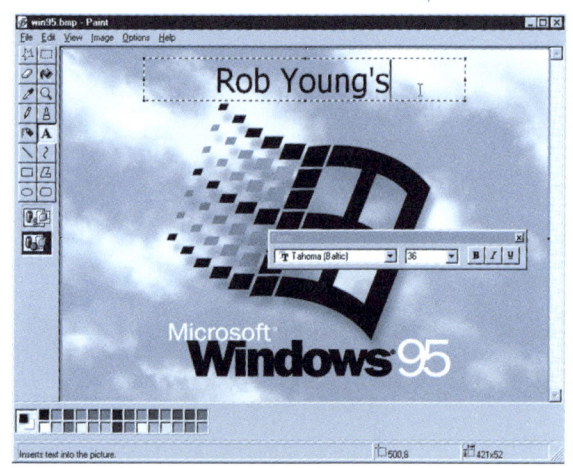

4 Edit the picture to look the way you want it. Here, for example, some text has been added to the picture.

5 Save the picture into the *Windows* folder on the hard disk using any filename you like.

You can load the picture and work with it again later. Now we need to tell Windows to use this picture as the desktop background. Windows can either display the picture in the centre of the desktop, or use it to fill the entire area.

CREATING A BACKGROUNS FOR THE WINDOWS DESKTOP

1 Choose the *Set As Wallpaper (Tiled)* option from the FILE menu if the complete background is to be filled in.

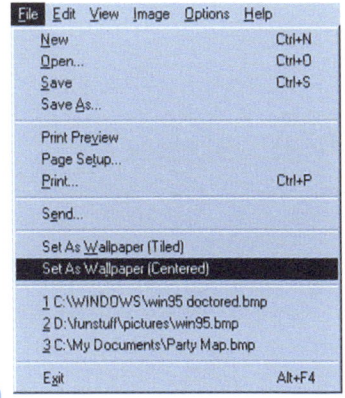

2 If you want the picture to be displayed in its present size, select *Set As Background (Middle)*.

The command *Set As Background (Middle)* is the better one for this picture. With the option *Tiled*, the picture fills the entire desktop background, but if the picture is smaller than the desktop area, the same picture will be repeated as often as necessary to fill the space.

3 Close the *Paint* program.

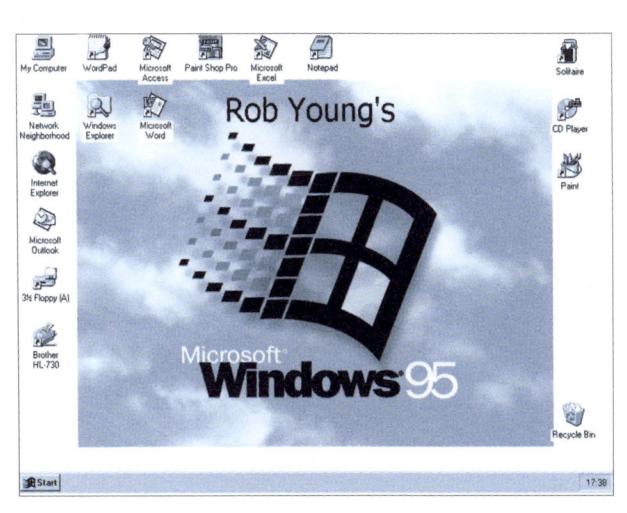

Here you can see the new-look desktop, with the picture inserted in the middle. Chapter 11 will also show you how you can get rid of this background picture again.

179

> **TIP** *Paint* has a series of further functions, which are not described in this book. If you need to, you can call up the *Paint* help section to find out more about these functions.

Text, pictures and other objects in a single document

So far in this chapter you have learned how to create text in *WordPad* and a picture in *Paint* . Now it's time to make use of the particular strengths of Windows. What about incorporating a sketch to show the way to the party in our invitation document? That way, only the text document would need to be printed out, and the sketch will automatically come with it. Does your computer have a sound card and a microphone? If so, you can even add sound recordings to the files which can be played with a single mouse click (Chapter 7 tells you how to deal with sound).

Inserting a picture into text is easy; in fact, you already know how to do it. You can select parts of documents in *WordPad* and in *Paint*, copy them to the Clipboard and paste them into a document. With most programs, Windows also allows you to take data from one program to another via the Clipboard.

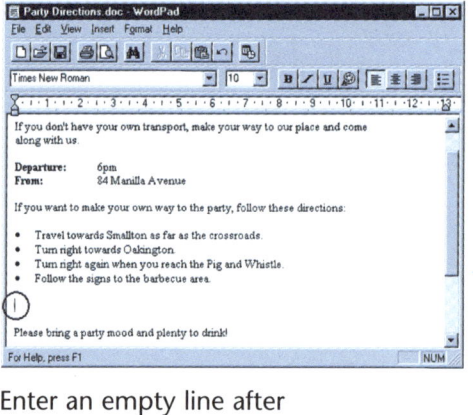

1 Start *WordPad* and load the file with the invitation text.

2 Enter an empty line after the description of the route.

This is where the sketch is to be added to the text.

TEXT, PICTURES AND OTHER OBJECTS IN A SINGLE DOCUMENT

3 Start *Paint* and load the picture with the sketch of the route.

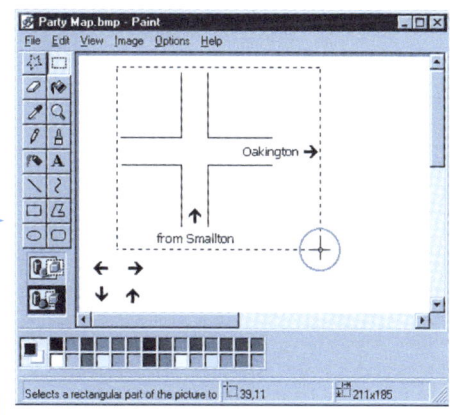

4 Select the part of the sketch which is to be included.

5 Copy the selected section to the Clipboard using the key combination [Ctrl] + [C].

6 Now switch to the WordPad window and click on the place where the picture is to be inserted.

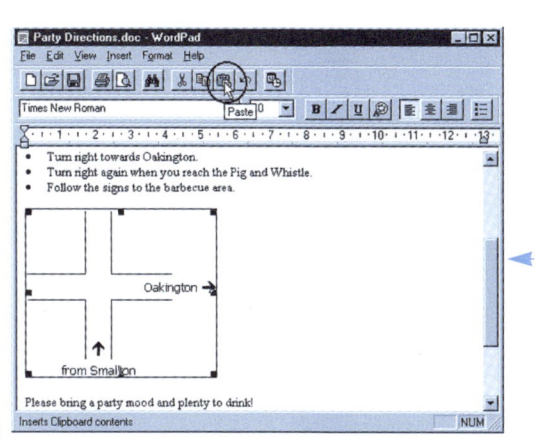

7 Insert the picture from the Clipboard into the text. To do this, you can use the *Paste* button or the key combination [Ctrl] + [V].

181

The picture will be slotted into the text. You can save the text document in the usual way, print it or continue working with it. If you want to remove the picture again, just click it to select it and press `Delete`.

When you save the picture with the text the *.doc* file becomes very large because the picture is saved with it.

WordPad also allows you to paste whole files from other programs into a text document. These files can contain texts, pictures, sound or other data. Items that are to be inserted in this way are generally referred to as **objects**. To insert an object file into a text document, follow these steps:

1 Start *WordPad* and open the document that will eventually contain the object.

2 Position the insertion mark at the point in the text at which the object is to be inserted.

3 Open the Insert menu and click on OBJECT.

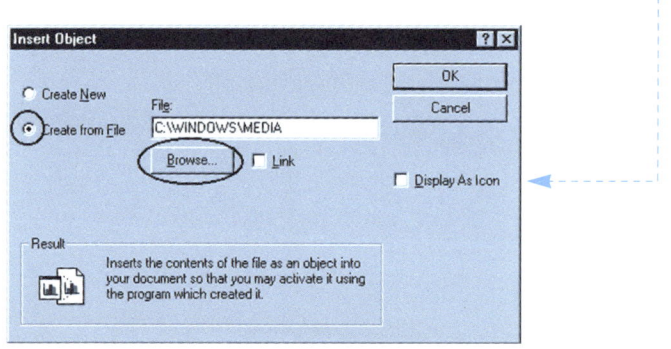

4 In the *Insert Object* dialog field, select the option 'Create from File'.

182

TEXT, PICTURES AND OTHER OBJECTS IN A SINGLE DOCUMENT

5 Click on the *Browse* button.

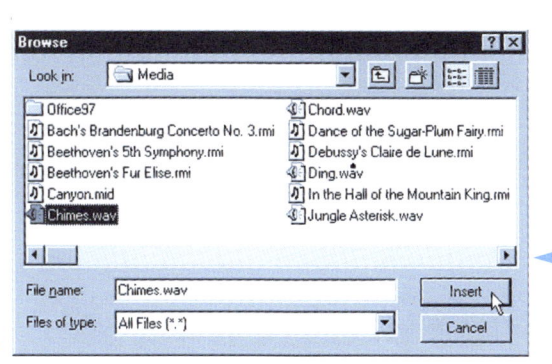

6 Select the folder and then the file you want to insert. In this case, a sound file has been chosen.

7 Close the two dialog boxes by clicking *Insert* and then *OK*.

The inserted object is then displayed in the WordPad document. Here you can see the icon for a sound file. When the icon is double-clicked, the object will be opened. In this example you will hear the sound file, if your computer has a sound card.

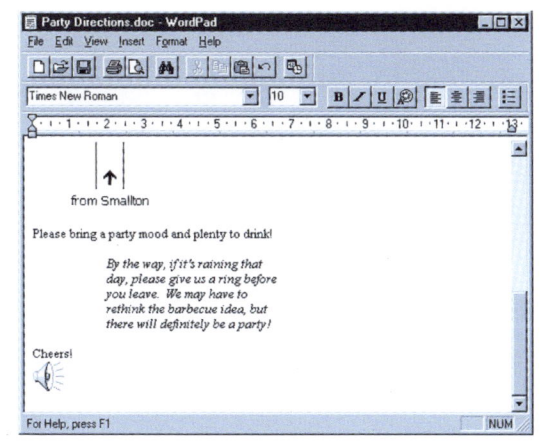

183

> The object is packed in a kind of container, and stored with the text document. This means that in some cases the WordPad *.doc* file will become considerably larger.
>
> WordPad can offer other functions which are not dealt with in this book. See the WordPad help section for more details.
>
> In addition to the programs for writing and drawing that are supplied with Windows, there are a large number of commercial accessory programs, which are considerably more powerful. If you work with Microsoft Office, for example, you can use *Word* to create and format text. This is similar to *WordPad*, but has many more features.

A quick check on progress

Now that you have reached this point, you know almost everything there is to know about getting things done in Windows. Perhaps it might be a good idea to refresh your memory and try some exercises to test out your new skills. After each exercise there are details in brackets of the section where you can find the answer.

- Create a text file with Notepad, and store it in a .txt file on a floppy disk.

    (The answer is in Chapter 4 in the sections 'Creating a document using Notepad' and 'Saving and opening the document').

- See which text files are supplied with Windows, and load them.

    (The files can be found in the Windows folder. You can find out how a .txt file is displayed in Chapter 4, in the section 'Saving and opening the document').

A QUICK CHECK ON PROGRESS

Create an invitation using the WordPad program.

(Answers are in Chapter 4, in the section 'Creating documents using WordPad').

Create your own picture for the desktop background.

(The answer is in Chapter 4, in the section 'Creating a background for the Windows desktop').

Create text document in which you can insert various objects.

(The answer is in Chapter 4, in the section 'Text, pictures and other objects in a single document').

In the next chapter, we'll look at more ways you can work with documents in Windows.

185

5

Handling letters, pictures and other documents

What's in this chapter?

You already know how to start a program and then load a document. There are, however, more elegant ways to work in Windows with documents. You will be learning how to call up the last fifteen documents which have been processed, and you will also learn how a document can be opened directly in the Explorer or in the Workplace window. You will also be shown how you can display the contents of a file without having to call up a program.

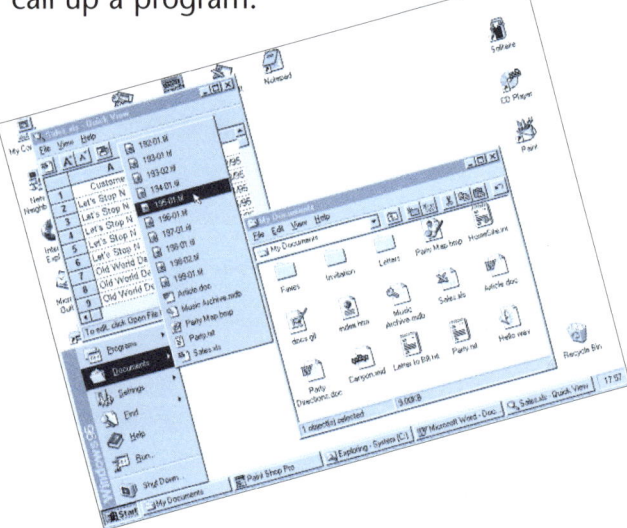

Your already know how to:

Use the Start menu	46
Start a program	47
Use files and folders	58

Your are going to learn how to:

Recognise document files	188
Open document files	190
Keep documents on the Desktop	192
Open a document in different programs	194
Display file contents quickly	197
Open a list of recently used documents	198

What do document files look like?

In Chapter 3 you learned how files are presented in the *My Computer* window (or in its sub-windows), and in the Explorer window. Now that you have some experience in handling files, we ought to go rather more deeply into the matter of handling documents. In Chapter 3 it has already been explained that files have a name and a file name extension, and are given an icon. The window opposite contains a number of files with their names and icons. Windows will recognise from the file name extension what file type is involved.

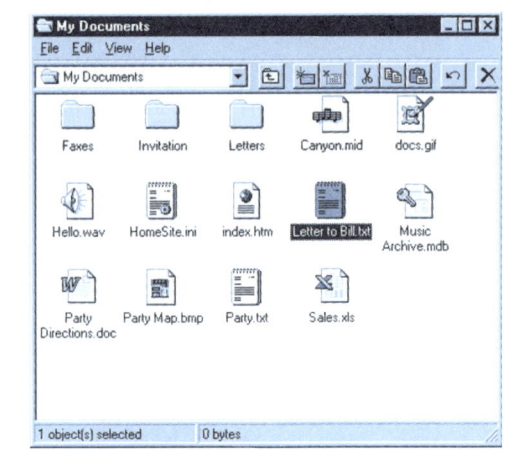

> Each program is only capable of reading files of specific file types. With *WordPad* for example, you can read and edit files of the file types *.txt, .doc, .rtf*. However, *WordPad* cannot edit graphics files (even though you can insert a picture or a *.bmp* file into a text). *Notepad*, on the other hand, only handles simple text files with the extension *.txt*. The situation with *Paint* is similar, since this can only read graphics files with the extensions *.bmp* or *.pcx*. To edit a document file, then, you need the program with which this file was saved, or one which can read that file type.

If you look at the document files in the picture above, and compare it with the display on your computer, you may notice something:

WHAT DO DOCUMENT FILES LOOK LIKE?

- One thing is that Windows always uses a specific icon for a file name extension. All *.txt* files are displayed with the icon of a little writing pad. Files with the *.doc* extension have another icon, and the same applies to picture files with the extension *.bmp*.

- In Chapter 3, in the section 'What are folders and files?' there is a table which lists the icons for a number of file types. In the picture above, however, different icons are used for files with the extensions *.bmp* and *.doc*.

Why is this, and what does it mean? The answers are fairly easy:

- If Windows is newly installed on a computer, the file name extensions and the file icons for a number of document files are already specified. Windows, for example, uses the *Paint* program for *.bmp* files, and *.doc* files are edited with *WordPad*. As a result, Windows uses these programs to open the corresponding document files. At the same time, icons for these programs are used to display the document files in Explorer or the folder windows.

- Most users install additional programs on their computers. These may be programs for word processing, graphics, multimedia, etc. If one of these programs supports a specific file type, it changes the Windows settings accordingly, which also changes the icon used for these files.

This means that you will always see the file icons that have been specified for the file types concerned by the programs installed on the particular computer.

- For example, if you have Microsoft Word installed on your computer, this icon will appear for *.doc* files.

189

If only the *Paint* program is installed for editing *.bmp* pictures, Windows uses the icon shown opposite for the files.

In the screenshot of the folder we just looked at, the icon opposite is used for *.bmp* files. The computer concerned has a program installed with the name *Paint Shop Pro*, for editing graphics. All the file types supported by this program will have this icon allocated to them.

So, if your computer displays different icons for a particular type of file, there's no need to worry. All it means is that there are a variety of programs installed on the computer with which the documents concerned can be opened. In the next section you will see what effect this has on the opening of the documents.

There are some file types, however, which are unknown to Windows. Shown opposite is a file with the extension *.asc*. Windows does not know where to begin with a file like this. These files are allocated the icon shown here. If you see such an icon, you will know that Windows does not know this type of file; we also say that the file type is not registered.

Opening document files

You already know in principle how a document file is opened.

1 You start the program with which the file was created.

2 Open the FILE menu, and select the OPEN command.

3 In the *Open* dialog box, select the folder and then the document file desired.

4 Click on the *Open* button.

The document file is now loaded into the program window.

> The technique described here will work with almost any Windows program. In Chapter 4 you used this procedure with several different Windows programs. If a program has a toolbar, you can use the *Open* button to open the document instead.

But to be perfectly honest, isn't this rather a tiresome way of doing things? In the previous chapters you have learned that programs can be started with a double click on the file belonging to them. In the window of a folder, however, the document files stored there will also be displayed. Do we always have to know whether a file is a program or a document? Why shouldn't a document simply be opened by a double click on the file symbol?

In fact, this approach can work very well:

1 Open the folder in which the document file was saved.

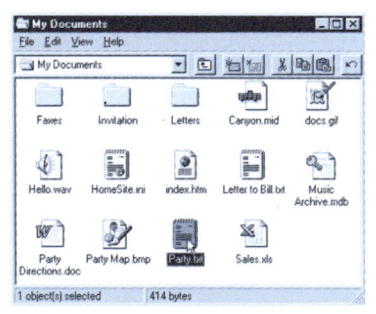

2 Double click on the icon of the document file.

191

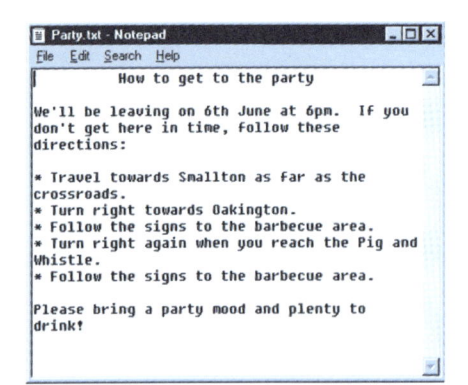

Windows starts the program responsible for this type of file, and then automatically loads the document file selected. You will immediately see the document in the program window. Here, for example, a file with the extension *.txt* has been selected by a double click.

> You can try this out with different types of files. Whenever Windows knows the file type, the appropriate program will be started, and the corresponding document file loaded. It could hardly be easier.

Keeping documents on the Desktop

Have you saved a document which you have to open frequently? This might be a template for a letter, for example. It would be nice if that document were to appear on the Desktop as an icon. A simple double click would be enough to open the program together with the document. Let's take the example of a *.doc* file to show how to set this up.

1 Start *WordPad*, or a program which can create *.doc* files.

2 Create the document which you want to use as the template.

OPENING DOCUMENT FILES

3 Save the document as a file in a folder.

4 Open the window of the folder in which the document was saved.

5 Select the document file with a click of the mouse.

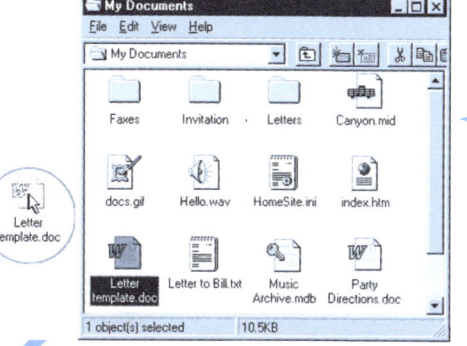

6 Hold the right mouse button down and drag the document icon to an empty space on the Desktop.

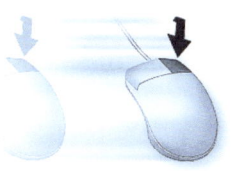

7 Release the mouse button.

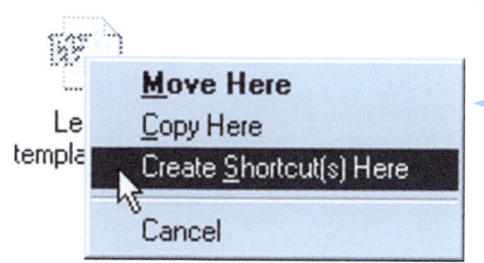

8 Select the command CREATE SHORTCUT(S) HERE in the Context menu.

193

9 If necessary, you can then rename the link.

Once the link has been created, a double click on the link icon on the desktop will be enough to open the document. You can then work in the document and, if necessary, store it under a new name.

Opening a document in different programs

Have you installed several programs in Windows which support the same file type? This is the case, for example, if you install Microsoft Word on your PC. You can then open the files with the extension *.doc* both with *Word* and with *WordPad*. The same applies to graphics programs which create *.bmp* files.

You might now have a problem: If you double click on such a file, in most cases it will be precisely the 'wrong' program which is loaded. Would you like to work in a *.doc* file with *WordPad* (because you know your way around the program better, for example), but find that Microsoft Word is started when you double click the file? One option is to start WordPad and then open the file, but there's another way:

1 Open the window of the folder in which the document file is stored.

2 Select the document file with one mouse click.

OPENING DOCUMENTS IN DIFFERENT PROGRAMS

3 Hold the ⇧ key down, and click the selected file with the right mouse button.

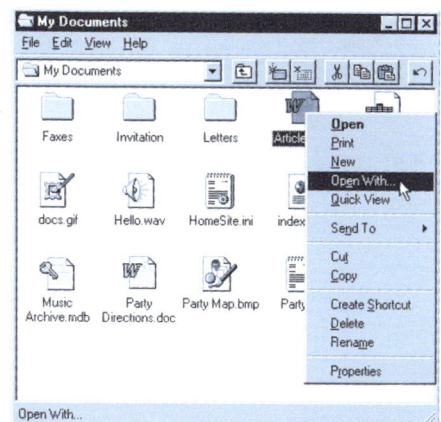

4 Click on the *Open With* command.

5 Look down the list for the program you want to use to open this file.

> **TIP**
> The trick with the whole business is that you keep the ⇧ key pressed down when you open the context menu. Windows then shows two commands for opening. The command Open in the context menu starts the standard program (in a similar way to a double click on the document file). By using the command Open With, on the other hand, you can select a suitable program from the *Open Width* dialog to edit the document files.

195

6 Click on the program name and then on the *OK* button.

Windows starts the program you have selected, and then loads the document file.

CAUTION

If you select a file by a double click with a file type which Windows does not know, the *Open With* dialog field will automatically be opened along with it. If you know what type of data is involved, you can select a suitable program from the list. If you're not sure whether the program you choose really can handle the file properly, click on the check box labelled 'Always use this program to open this type of file' to remove the check mark.

TIP

Would you like Windows always to use this program when you double click on this type of document file? If so, click the check box 'Always open file with this program' in the *Open With* dialog field, after selecting the program. As soon as you close the dialog box, Windows will change the settings for this document type. From now on, whenevr you double-click a file of this type, Windows will open it using the program you chose. This tip is also worth remembering if you want to change which program a particular type of document opens with.

196

Displaying file contents quickly

Are you familiar with this situation? You receive a disk with different document files on it. You now open the window with the file display, and try to find out the quick way to the contents of a particular file. In this case, a double click on the particular document file isn't ideal, for these reasons:

- You don't want to edit the file, and opening the document in the application might take too long. And if you want to look at three or four files by means of a double click, this becomes fairly tedious.

- The program needed to load the document is not installed on your computer.

In the second case, especially, you have a real problem. But Windows has a solution to this.

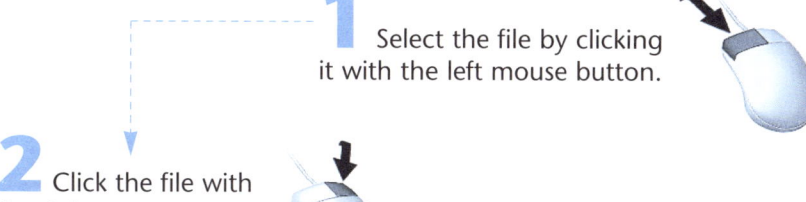

1 Select the file by clicking it with the left mouse button.

2 Click the file with the right mouse button to open its context menu.

If Windows knows the file type, the command QUICK VIEW will be included on the context menu.

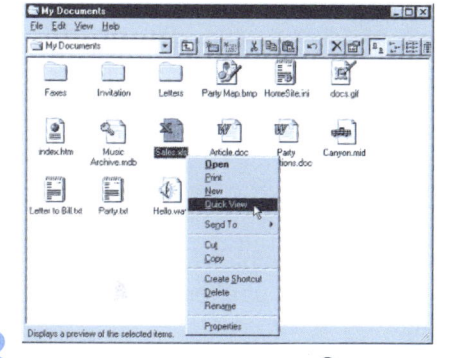

3 Click on the command QUICK VIEW in the context menu.

197

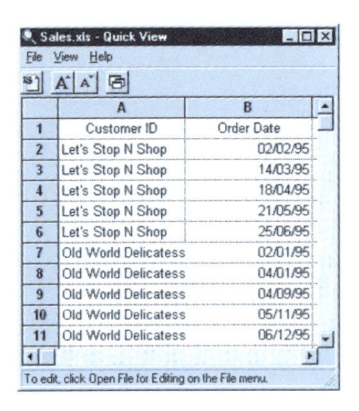

Windows opens the *Quick View* window, and shows the contents of the document file concerned. The window opposite shows an example of an Excel table.

The Windows Quick View function can show you the contents of many document files, without having to start the application concerned. This will allow you to view the contents of different files very quickly.

> In the case of document files which have been generated with Microsoft Office 97, the Windows Quick View unfortunately shows an empty window. The reason for this is that Windows does indeed know the file type, but it can't read the new Office format.

Opening a list of recently used documents

Every time you open a document file, Windows takes note of the name of the file concerned. The last fifteen documents you opened are automatically compiled into a list, which you can view on the Start menu.

1 Open the Start menu and move the pointer to the DOCUMENTS entry.

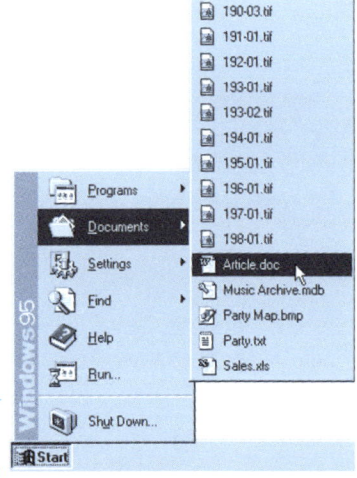

2 Click on one of the document names listed in the sub-menu.

198

OPENING A LIST OF RECENTLY USED DOCUMENTS

Windows will automatically load the program associated with the document, and the document itself.

If you want to delete the list of recent documents, carry out the following steps:

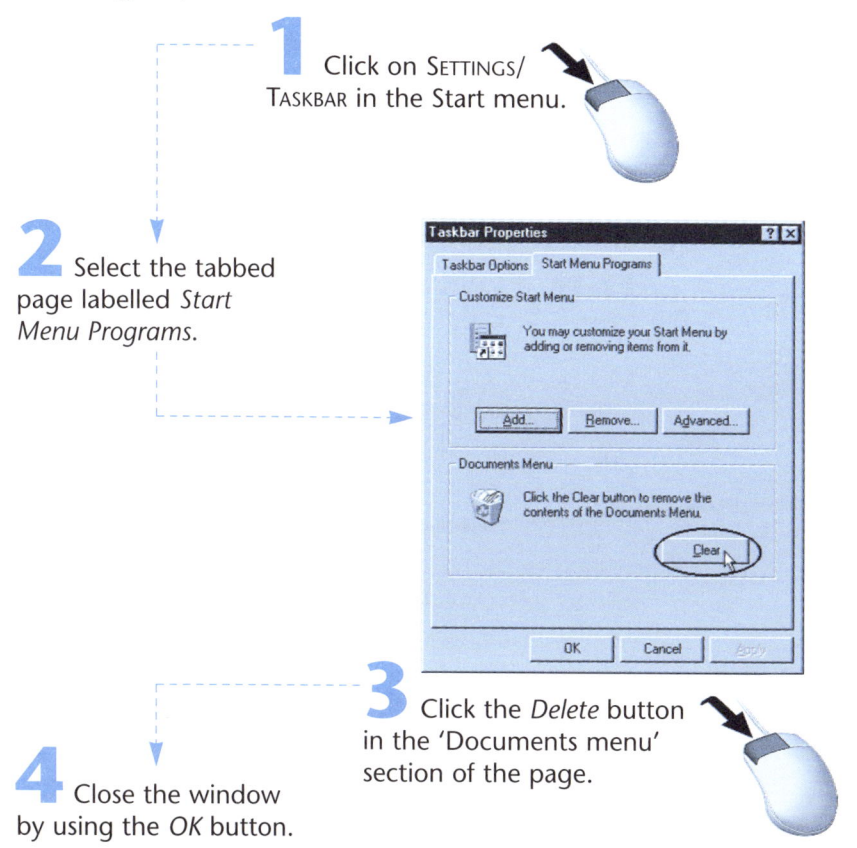

1 Click on SETTINGS/TASKBAR in the Start menu.

2 Select the tabbed page labelled *Start Menu Programs*.

3 Click the *Delete* button in the 'Documents menu' section of the page.

4 Close the window by using the *OK* button.

If you have worked through the books this far, you now know the most important features of Windows. You can start programs, and work with folders and files. You even know how documents are printed. If there is anything that you're not so confident about, it's not a disaster. If you need to, read the corresponding passages again in the relevant chapters. The chapters which follow will increase your knowledge (for example, Chapter 6), and show you other interesting things about Windows (such as Chapter 7). Chapters 8, 9, 10 and 11 look at more specialised topics.

199

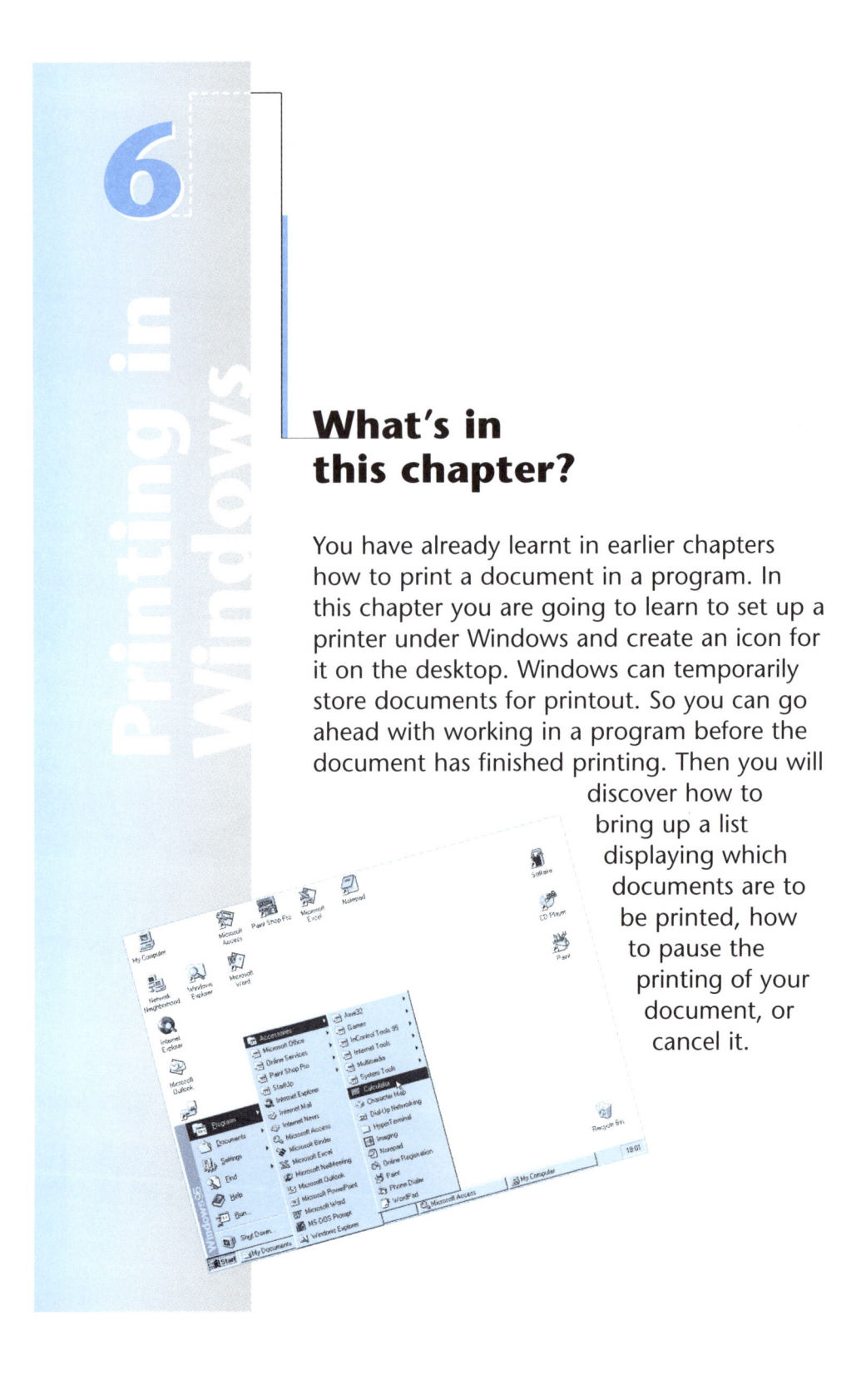

6

Printing in Windows

What's in this chapter?

You have already learnt in earlier chapters how to print a document in a program. In this chapter you are going to learn to set up a printer under Windows and create an icon for it on the desktop. Windows can temporarily store documents for printout. So you can go ahead with working in a program before the document has finished printing. Then you will discover how to bring up a list displaying which documents are to be printed, how to pause the printing of your document, or cancel it.

YOUR PROGRESS METER

Your already know how to:

Work with windows	23
Start a program	47
Switch between programs	51
Close a program	53
Print documents using Notepad	143
Print documents in Wordpad	156
Print a picture in Paint	173

Your are going to learn how to:

Set up a new printer	202
Put a printer icon on the desktop	209
Print	212
Change printer settings	215
Take control of the printer	218

201

Setting up a new printer

Windows supports a wide range of printers by various manufacturers. You can connect any of these to your computer. But they need to be installed before you can use them. To do this, a **printer driver** is installed in Windows. This is a program which 'traps' the documents you want to print and processes them for the printer. Windows uses what it calls a 'wizard' to install a printer. The wizard is a small program that leads you through the steps you need to take. You access the wizard via the *Printers* folder, which you can open either from the *Start* menu or the *My Computer* window. Carry out the following steps to install a printer. You may need files from the Windows 95 CD-ROM, so make sure you have this to hand.

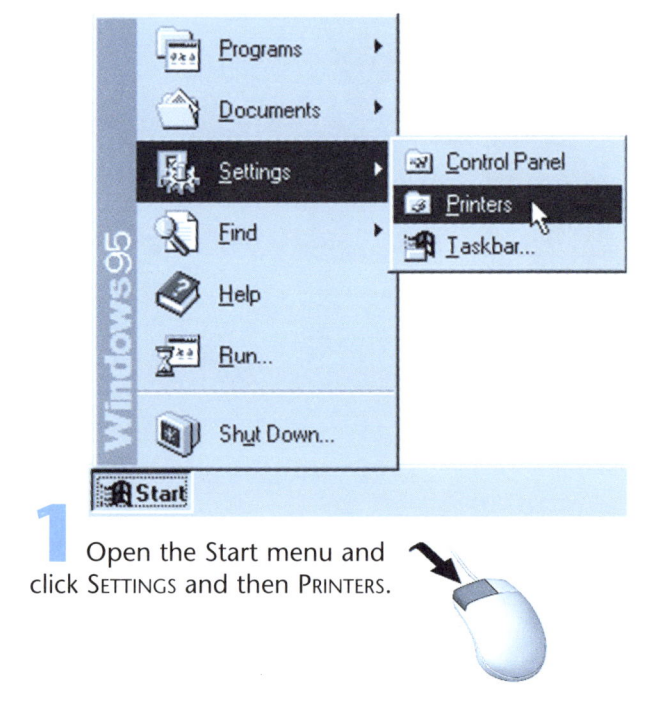

1 Open the Start menu and click SETTINGS and then PRINTERS.

The *Printers* window opens, showing the icons for the printers that have already been installed, plus an *Add Printer* icon.

SETTING UP A NEW PRINTER

2 Double-click on the icon *Add Printer*.

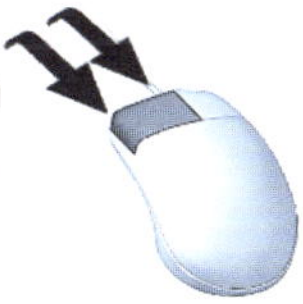

Windows starts up the wizard, which takes you step by step through the installation of the new printer. You will often encounter wizards in Windows. They are easy to use. You use the *Next* button to advance through the pages of the wizard. If you find you have forgotten to enter something, or want to go back and check, you can use the button labelled *Back*. The wizard will display the previous page. As you may have guessed, you can use the *Cancel* button to cancel the process of configuring a new printer, and shut down the wizard. You start carrying out the steps to install the printer when you see the opening page of the wizard.

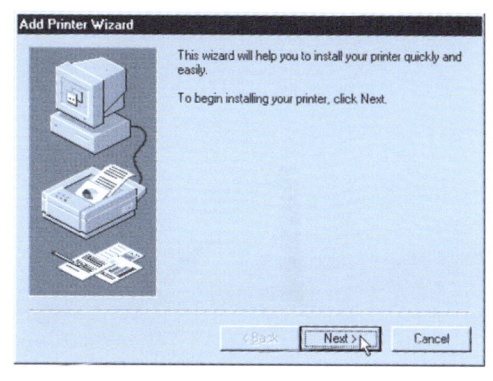

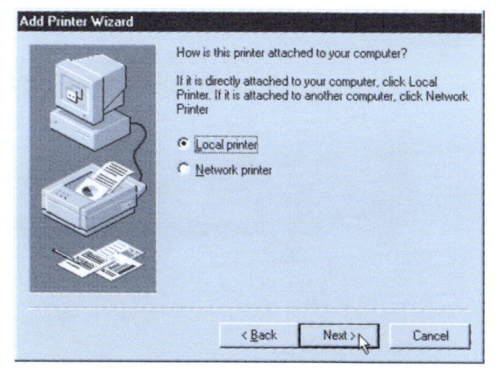

For a printer on a network you select the second option (see Chapter 9).

1 If the printer is just attached to your own computer, click the option 'Local printer' on this page.

203

2 Click *Next*.

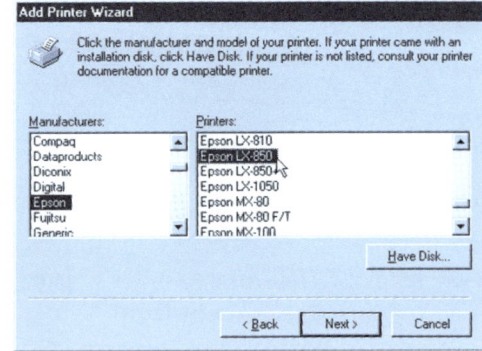

3 Select the manufacturer of your printer from the list on the left.

4 Then click on the model of your printer in the list on the right.

5 Click *Next*.

If your printer does not appear in the list, and you have a floppy disk or CD-ROM from the printer manufacturer, you can install the printer by clicking the *Have Disk* button. Windows opens a dialog box for you to select the floppy disk drive. This is rarely necessary so we won't bother with it here.

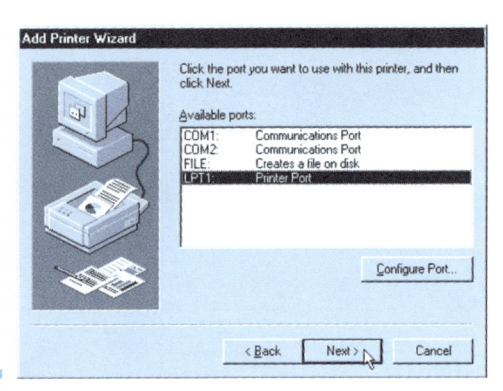

6 On this page, you select the port on your computer which your printer is connected to.

204

SETTING UP A NEW PRINTER

Most printers are connected to a parallel port, which is called LTP1:

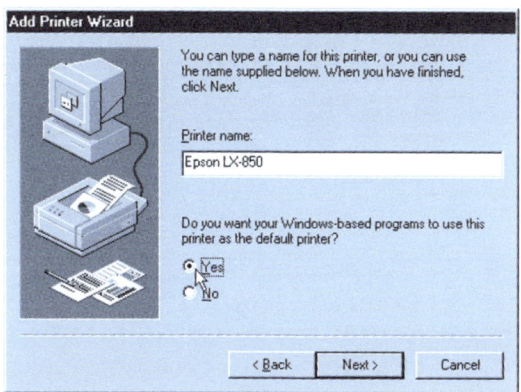

7 Click *Next*.

8 The printer name is specified, but you can alter the name if necessary.

9 Specify whether this printer will be used as the default printer for all Windows applications.

10 Click *Next*.

> Windows programs normally output data to the default printer, which can be specified in the above dialog. This is the printer which is preset after start-up of the program. Some systems have more than one printer attached to them. In that case, in each application you can select which printer to use via the *Print* dialog box. For example, the output could be sent to a colour printer for a graphics program, and the default printer for a word-processing program could be a laser printer.

205

This step completes the installation of the printer. But you have not yet checked whether all the settings are correct. Once a printer driver has been installed, Windows can print a test page. If this test page is correctly printed on the right printer, all is well (your printer is ready for use).

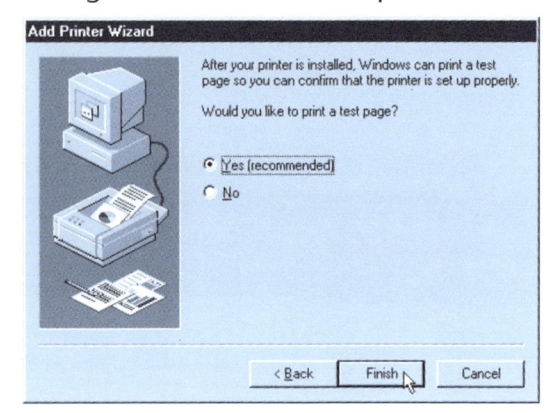

1 Set (or leave) the option 'Yes (recommended)' if at all possible, so that a test page to be printed.

2 Click *Next*.

Windows will now copy the printer driver files onto your hard disk.

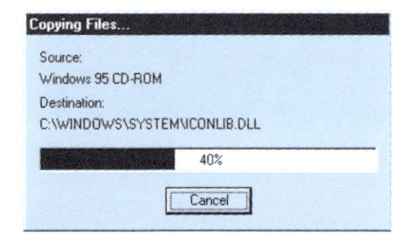

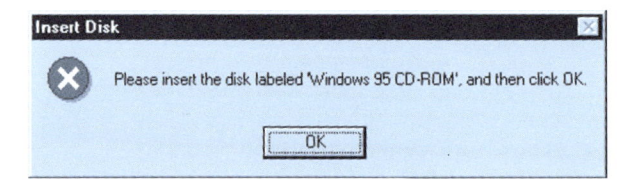

If this message appears, you need your Windows 95 installation CD-ROM.

SETTING UP A NEW PRINTER

1 First put the required CD-ROM into the drive.

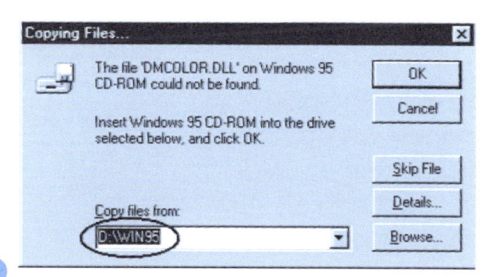

2 If this dialog appears, type in the name of the drive and path for the installation files into the *Source* box.

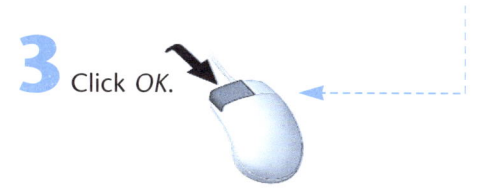

3 Click *OK*.

On the Windows CD-ROM, the printer drivers are in the \Win95 folder. In the above illustration, the CD-ROM was installed in the D: drive. If you do not know the name of the CD-ROM drive, you can use the *Browse* button to look for the available drives or folders on the drive.

If you see this message on the screen:

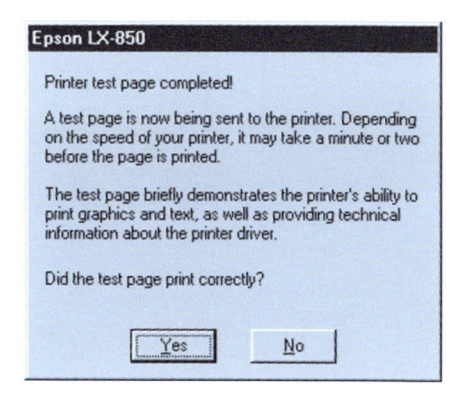

1 Check whether the test page has been printed correctly.

2 Click on the *Yes* button if everything is correct. If there are any problems, select *No*.

207

If the process has been successful, the icon for the new printer will appear in the *Printers* folder. You will now be able to use the printer.

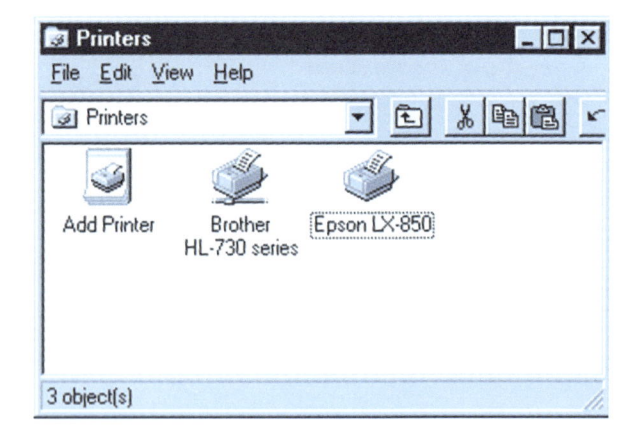

Did you select *No* in the message box just shown, because the page did not print out as it should? If so, Windows will automatically open the Help window shown alongside. You can obtain further information to help you track down and correct the fault by using the buttons in this Help window.

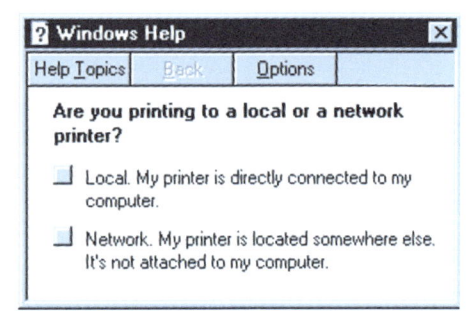

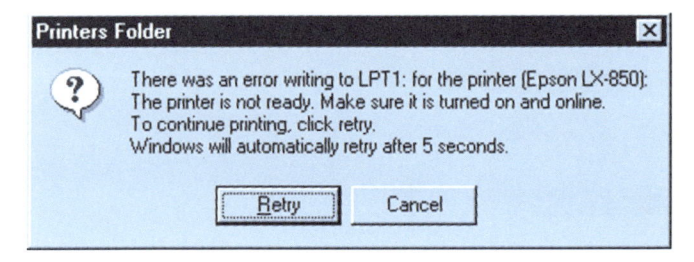

If, on the other hand, you see the *Printers* folder message box shown here, the fault is simply with the printer.

208

1 Check whether the printer is connected and switched on.

2 If necessary, set the printer to *Online*.

3 Check whether there is paper in the printer.

As soon as the fault has been corrected, Windows will resume output to the printer. This message box also appears if a printer fault occurs while printing a document. You should then check the printer.

> Sometimes something goes wrong during printing, and you have to cancel the print job in progress. You simply need to switch off the printer, and click the *Cancel* button. Windows will then delete all the data that have not yet been printed.

Putting a printer icon on the desktop

The next steps you are about to learn will show you how Windows manages the output to the printer, and how the printer settings can be changed. To do this, however, you need to open the Print Manager window for the machine in question. As a basic principle, this means opening the window of the *Printers* folder and double-clicking the icon of the desired printer to select it. So it is better to create the icon for the printer on the desktop.

1 Open the Start menu, and then from the SETTINGS menu, select PRINTERS.

2 Keeping the right mouse button depressed, drag the icon for the desired printer to a free spot on the desktop.

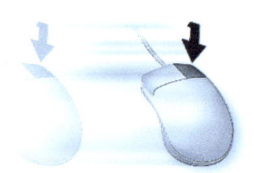

3 Release the right mouse button.

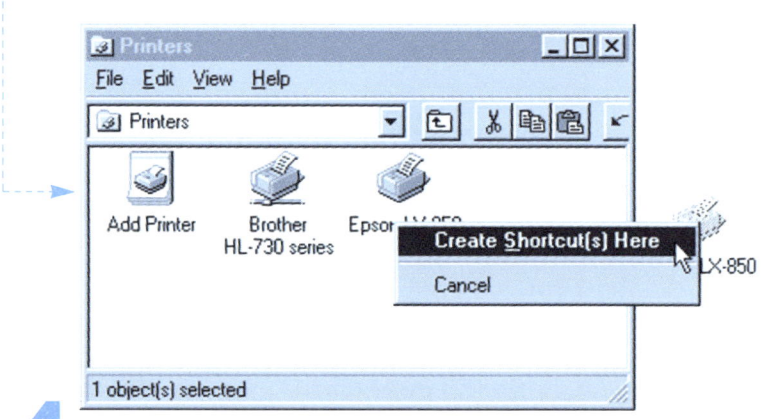

4 In the context menu, select the command CREATE SHORTCUT(S) HERE.

PUTTING A PRINTER ICON ON THE DESKTOP

5 Windows has created a shortcut to the printer. Rename the icon for this printer if you need to.

Now the icon for the printer concerned is created on the desktop. From now on you will be able to open the window, drag documents to the printer icon and print them.

You might like to have the icon in the Start menu as well as on the desktop.

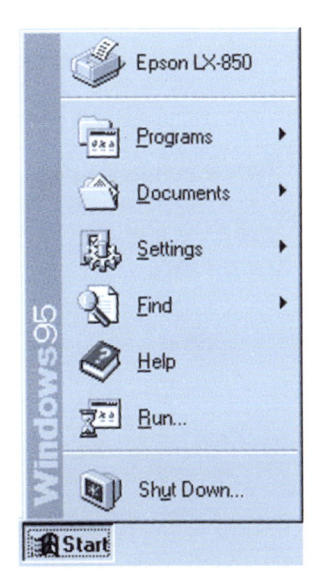

1 Drag the printer icon out of the Printers folder to the START BUTTON, keeping the left mouse button depressed.

2 Release the mouse button.

The icon is now created in the Start menu.

211

How to print?

There are several ways of printing offered by Windows. There are unfortunately slight differences between the various Windows applications in the way they behave when printing. You will usually print from a program.

1 If the program has a toolbar with a *Print* button, click on this.

In general, using the *Print* button will print the complete document as it stands, with no further questions. You met this option in Chapter 4, with the *WordPad* program. If there is no toolbar, take the following steps:

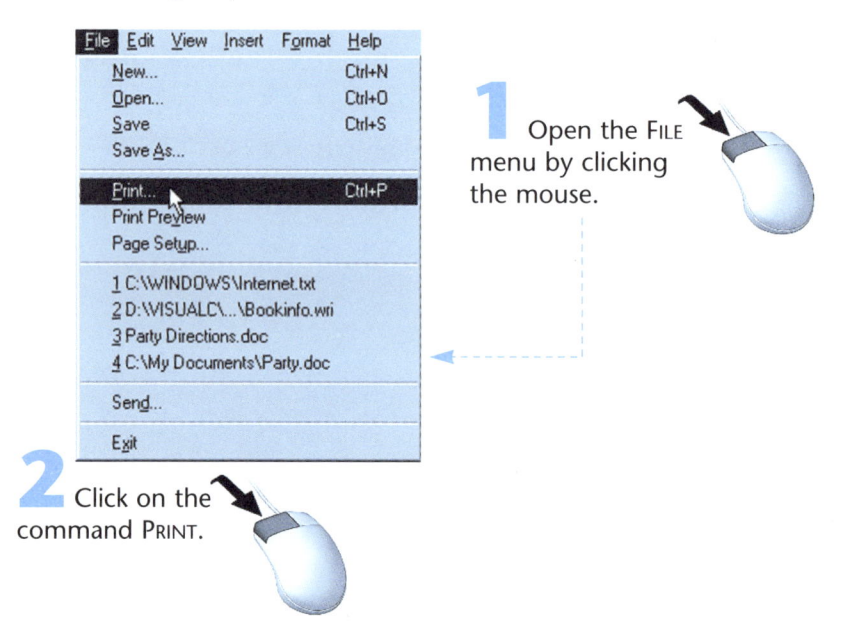

1 Open the FILE menu by clicking the mouse.

File	Edit	View	Insert	Format	Help
New...					Ctrl+N
Open...					Ctrl+O
Save					Ctrl+S
Save As...					
Print...					Ctrl+P
Print Preview					
Page Setup...					
1 C:\WINDOWS\Internet.txt					
2 D:\VISUALC\...\Bookinfo.wri					
3 Party Directions.doc					
4 C:\My Documents\Party.doc					
Send...					
Exit					

2 Click on the command PRINT.

If the menu lists the key combination Ctrl + P, you can also access the print function directly by using these keys.

How to print

```
Print                                    ? X
┌Printer─────────────────────────────────────┐
│ Name:   [Brother HL-730 series  ▼] [Properties]│
│ Status:  Default printer; Ready            │
│ Type:    Brother HL-730 series             │
│ Where:   LPT1:                             │
│ Comment:                    □ Print to file│
└────────────────────────────────────────────┘
┌Print range──────┐ ┌Copies──────────────────┐
│ ⊙ All           │ │ Number of copies: [1 ⬚]│
│ ○ Pages from:[1]│ │                        │
│        to: [ ]  │ │ [1][2][3] □ Collate    │
│ ○ Selection     │ │                        │
└─────────────────┘ └────────────────────────┘
                              [  OK  ] [Cancel]
```

3 Set the desired **print options**.

4 Click *OK* to start printing.

> All Windows programs should have the PRINT command listed in the FILE menu. There is a convention that, when you access the Print function via this menu command, you are saying that you want to set the **print options** (e.g. the pages to be printed, or the printer to be used) before the program sends the output to the printer. But in Chapter 4, you saw that Notepad, for example, does not keep to this convention. This program starts printing straight away, as soon as you click the PRINT command in the FILE menu. There are other programs which also operate on the 'all or nothing' principle and start printing immediately the PRINT command is selected.

Chapter 5 deals with handling documents. It says there that Windows recognises the file type from the filename extensions. So some documents can be loaded directly in the right program by double-clicking on the file. For anyone in a particular hurry, Windows offers a similar, very neat option for printing a document directly from a file.

1 Open the window of the folder containing the document file to be printed.

213

2 Select the document file with a click.

3 Click on the selected file using the right mouse button.

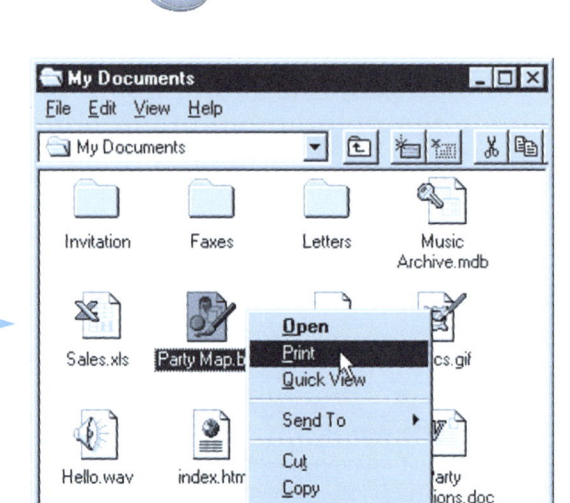

4 Click with the left mouse button on the PRINT command in the context menu.

Windows then automatically opens the document in the right program and starts the print operation. The program is closed as soon as the document starts to print.

> You can also drag a document file from the window of a folder to a printer icon using the mouse. When the icon for the document is over the printer icon, release the left mouse button. This procedure is called **drag and drop**. In most cases, Windows will print the document concerned using the application associated with it. Windows will only report an error if it cannot find an application that can work with this type of document. Drag and drop is an especially neat way of printing if you have created a shortcut to the printer icon on the desktop.

Changing printer settings

You might want to print a page in landscape format instead of portrait. You might want the printer to pick up the paper from the envelope tray. Perhaps you have several printers, and want to send the output to a different printer? Windows offers several options for changing the printer settings.

For this, you need to have the *Print* dialog box open (see previous section).

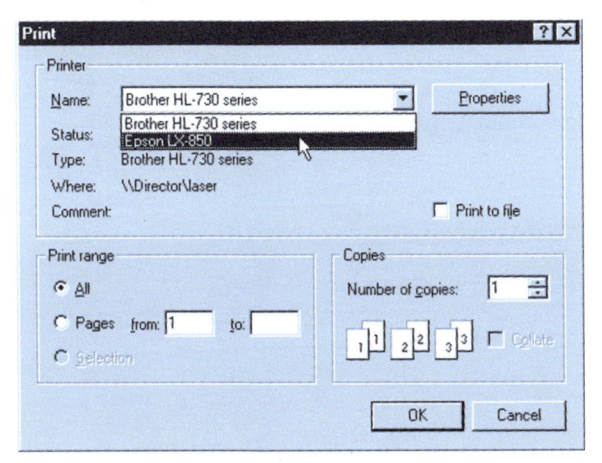

1 To change the printer, click the *Name* list box.

2 Select the name of the desired printer from the list.

215

You can then define the options for this printer or for the current document, and start printing by clicking on *OK*.

> **TIP**
>
> When installing a new printer (see above) you are asked if this is to be installed as the default printer. You will see in the *Print* dialog box that Windows lets you have several printers installed. But a program can only output to one printer at any one time. If you open the Print dialog box, the name of that printer is shown in the *Name* box. If you select another printer, this setting remains for that particular session using the program. If you close the program and start it up again later, the default printer will once more be used.

> **CAUTION**
>
> There are unfortunately some older Windows programs which can only use the default printer. If you select another printer in the *Print* dialog box for these programs, that other printer is automatically set to be the default printer. In that case, you will have to remember to set it back again after printing.

In the *Print* dialog box, you will see the *Properties* button. Clicking this will open the *Printer Properties* sheet, with various tabs (*Paper, Graphics* etc.).

1 Click on the *Properties* button in the *Print* dialog box.

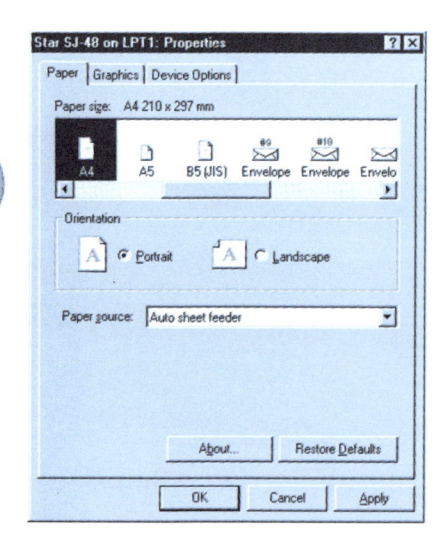

Alongside you can see the properties sheet of a printer.

216

CHANGING PRINTER SETTINGS

The number of tabs and the contents of each will depend on which printer you're using. But the most important options are similar for most printers.

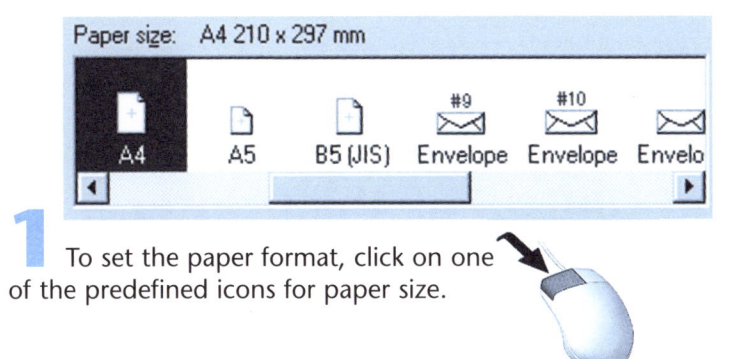

1 To set the paper format, click on one of the predefined icons for paper size.

Some printers even allow you to define and set your own paper formats.

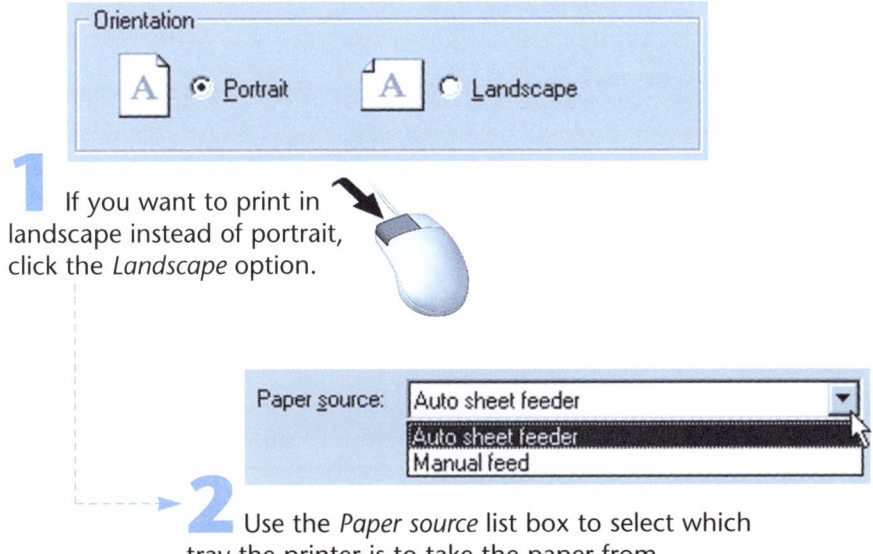

1 If you want to print in landscape instead of portrait, click the *Landscape* option.

2 Use the *Paper source* list box to select which tray the printer is to take the paper from.

TIP: The *Restore Defaults* button resets the printer properties to the ones set by the manufacturer. If something fails to print properly, you could try going back to these default settings.

217

> **TIP**
> It is worth repeating at this point that the options shown in the dialog boxes below the tabs depend on the printer chosen. This applies, for example, to the paper source (the names of paper trays may vary. The illustrations above relate to the Star SJ-48 printer.).

Taking control of the printer

If you are printing a document of several hundred pages, it will take some time before the last page rolls out of the printer. But the program you used to print the document usually only takes a few seconds to do its job. So from that point of view you do not need to sit around waiting for the printer to finish. Windows stores print data temporarily on the hard disk, and works away in the **background** passing them on to the printer as required. In other words, the data for output to the printer are held as **print jobs** in a **print queue**.

Whenever there are data waiting to be printed, a small printer icon appears next to the time display in the taskbar.

If there is a **problem** with the **printing**, this is usually indicated by a tiny question mark on the printer icon.

This means that you can always see how printing is coming along, and can carry on working in the program in the meantime. You can also open other documents, or even close the program you had been printing with. Some users use several programs at a time, or send several documents in succession to the printer. How do you find out which documents are in the queue? How do you pause a print job? Or cancel it altogether?

To do this, you have to open the Printer window (not the same as the *Printers* folder: do not confuse these).

1 Double-click on the printer icon

> You can use either the printer icon in the right-hand corner of the taskbar or the icon for the printer in the **Printers** folder for this. If you have created a shortcut which displays the printer icon on the desktop, select this by double-clicking.

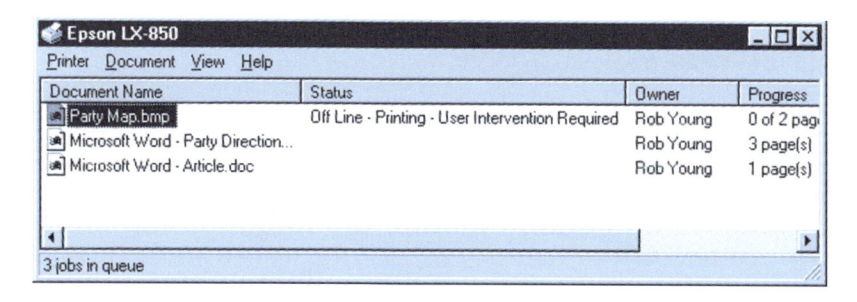

Document Name	Status	Owner	Progress
Party Map.bmp	Off Line - Printing - User Intervention Required	Rob Young	0 of 2 pag
Microsoft Word - Party Direction...		Rob Young	3 page(s)
Microsoft Word - Article.doc		Rob Young	1 page(s)

3 jobs in queue

The window shown here will open. It lists the print jobs in the print queue, in other words, all the documents which have not yet been completely printed. There is one line for each print job, with the one which is actually being printed at the top. Reading across the line, the window provides information under various categories:

- The first category title is **Document Name**. This name is given by the program through which the document is being printed. It is usually the same as the filename of the document.

- Under **Status** you find information about the status of the particular print job. Here, for example, on the top line about the document being printed, there is currently a problem, and a message shows this. You can see from the jobs in the queue whether the job has been paused.

➡ Under **Owner**, you can see which user in a network wants the job printed. This is helpful if there is a printing problem. Then the person concerned can be told.

➡ Under **Progress**, you can see how many pages of a multi-page document have been printed.

➡ The last category, **Started At**, gives the time when the program sent on the document to begin printing.

You can manage what happens to print jobs via the menu bar. For example, you can pause them:

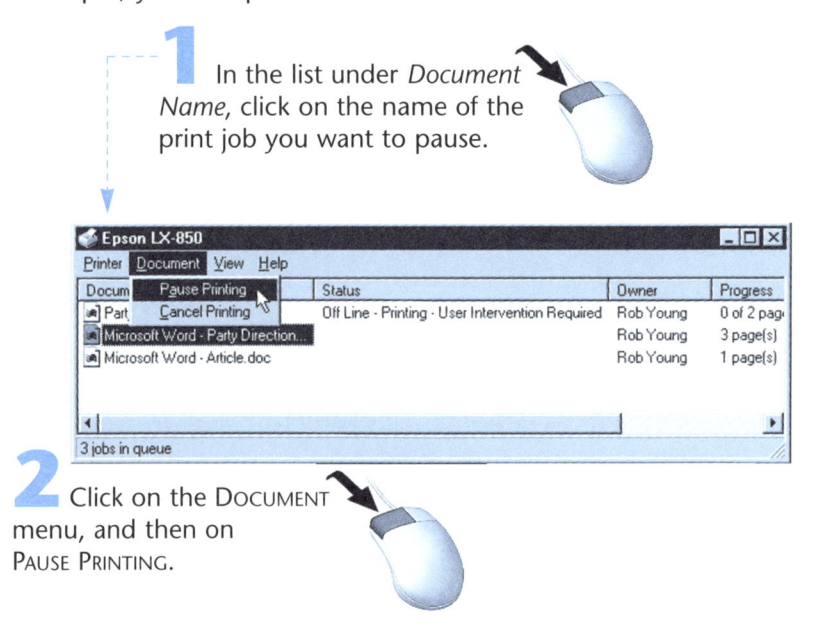

1 In the list under *Document Name*, click on the name of the print job you want to pause.

```
Epson LX-850                                                    _ □ X
Printer  Document  View  Help
Docum    Pause Printing      Status                              Owner      Progress
  Part    Cancel Printing    Off Line - Printing - User Intervention Required  Rob Young  0 of 2 page
  Microsoft Word - Party Direction...                             Rob Young  3 page(s)
  Microsoft Word - Article.doc                                    Rob Young  1 page(s)

3 jobs in queue
```

2 Click on the DOCUMENT menu, and then on PAUSE PRINTING.

Under *Status*, you will see the message 'paused'. The print job will not be sent to the printer until you resume printing it again.

TAKING CONTROL OF THE PRINTER

This facility means you can hold up the printing of a very long document in a queue to get a letter printed first, for example. To resume a paused job, follow these steps:

> **Tip:** You cannot do this with a document that is already being printed. A print job in progress cannot be paused to allow another one to be printed first.

1 Under *Document Name*, click on the name of the print job you want to resume.

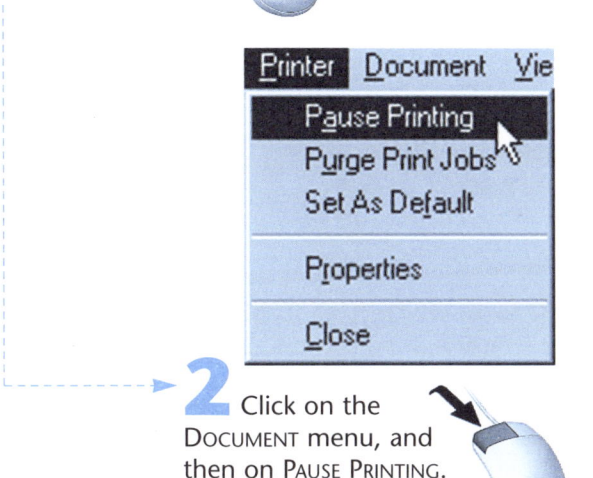

2 Click on the DOCUMENT menu, and then on PAUSE PRINTING.

You can see whether the print job was paused, because there will be a tick next to the command. By clicking again, you are releasing the print job to resume printing. Windows searches down the list of print jobs, selects in order the next one to have been released, and sends that to the printer.

You sometimes need to cancel a print job. This may be because you selected the print command by accident. Or there may have been a problem with the printer and you had to switch it off to correct it.

221

Cancelling a print job takes just a few steps:

1 Under *Document Name*, click on the name of the print job you want to cancel.

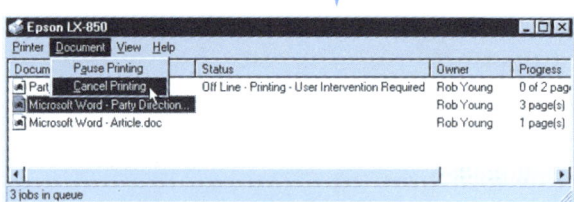

Docum	Pause Printing	Status	Owner	Progress
Part	Cancel Printing	Off Line - Printing - User Intervention Required	Rob Young	0 of 2 page
Microsoft Word - Party Direction...			Rob Young	3 page(s)
Microsoft Word - Article.doc			Rob Young	1 page(s)

3 jobs in queue

2 Click on the DOCUMENT menu, and then on CANCEL PRINTING.

It will take a few seconds for the job to be cancelled and the revised list of print jobs to appear on screen.

> **TIP**
> If you want to cancel all print jobs, it is quicker to select the command PURGE PRINT JOBS from the PRINTER menu.
> Alternatively, you can use the PAUSE PRINTING command in this menu. Then Windows will interrupt processing of the whole print queue. This can be very useful if the printer is out of use or disconnected for a while.

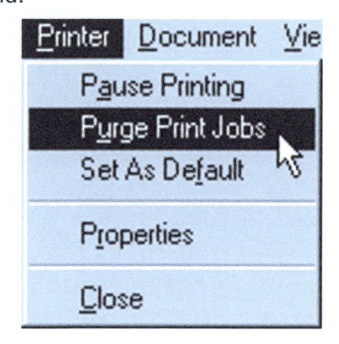

Printer menu:
- Pause Printing
- Purge Print Jobs
- Set As Default
- Properties
- Close

In the PRINTER menu you can also see whether this printer is set as the default. If it is, there will be a small tick next to SET AS DEFAULT. If it is not, click this command, and Windows will set it as the default printer.

The section 'Changing Printer Settings' showed how to open the Printer Properties sheet from the Print dialog box, by selecting the *Properties* button. You can also click on the PROPERTIES command in the PRINTER menu. You will find additional tabs in the Printer Properties sheet, giving the settings for the printer and connections.

7

Fun with Windows

What's in this chapter?

You can use Windows for entertainment and relaxation as well as work. Games are a big topic of course, and in Windows they are fun. With the Windows CD-ROM, you have all sorts of choices: not only playing cards and hunting for mines, but you'll also find the Hover! program, where you can race through a maze in a bumper car. Would you rather listen to music CDs while you work at your computer? No problem. No problem either if you want to use Windows for watching video 'films' and sequences. This chapter will tell you about all these.

Your already know how to:

Work with windows	23	Deal with files and folders	58
Get Help	34	Create a document using Notepad	126
Start a program	47		
Switch between programs	51	Edit the document in Notepad	128
Close a program	53	Create pictures in Paint	159

Your are going to learn how to:

Play music CDs on the computer	226
Work with sound files	234
Watch videos in Windows	239
Play Minesweeper!	245
Relax with Solitaire	248
Play Hover! through the maze	252

Playing music CDs on the computer

Does your computer have a CD-ROM drive? If it has, you can play music CDs while you work. You just need to plug a headset into the headset socket of the CD-ROM drive. Computers with an in-built sound card can play music CDs through the sound card's speakers. There is a small program in Windows that allows you to play music CDs. Below we explain how to use this.

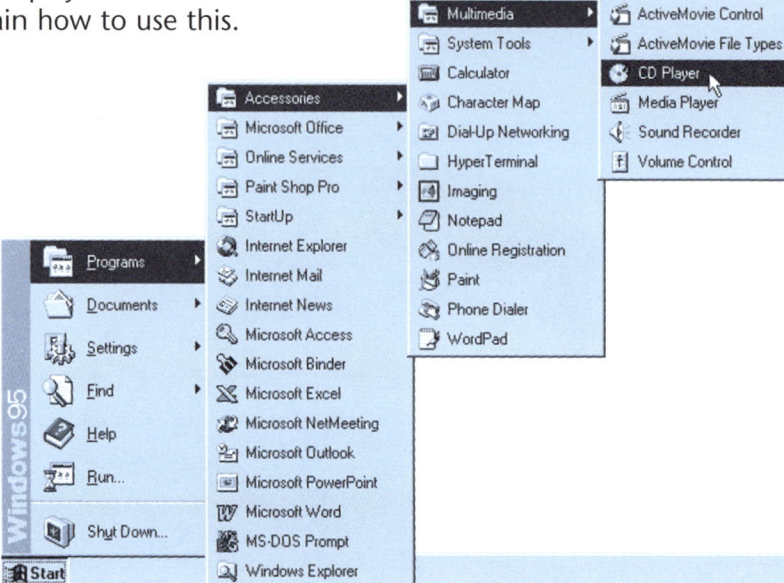

1 Open the Start menu, move the mouse up to PROGRAMS, and then to ACCESSORIES.

2 Select MULTIMEDIA, and click on CD PLAYER.

PLAYING MUSIC CDS ON THE COMPUTER

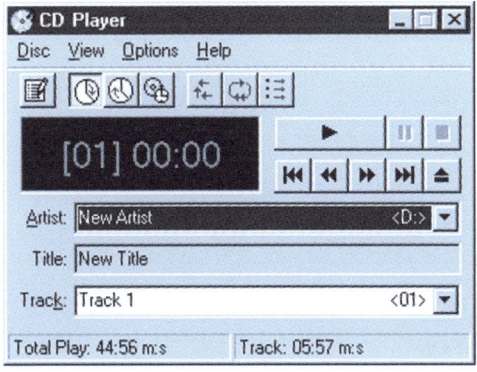

Windows starts up the CD Player program, and you will see this window.

3 Insert a music CD (audio CD) into the CD drive.

You will find a number of player controls in the *CD Player* window to use when playing a music CD.

Once a CD has been inserted, use this button to **start** to play your CD.

Pauses play.

Stops playing an audio CD.

Opens the **CD tray** of the CD-ROM drive.

Moves **forwards** and **backwards** within the track.

Moves to the **previous track** or the **next track**.

These controls may well be familiar from your hi-fi CD player. The big advantage of the *Windows CD Player* program is that you can put together your own list of tracks to be played.

227

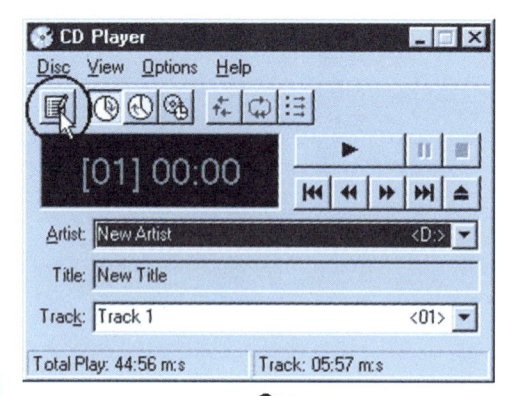

The first step opens a window where you can type in the **name** and **title** of the CD.

1 Click *Edit Play List* in the *CD Player* window.

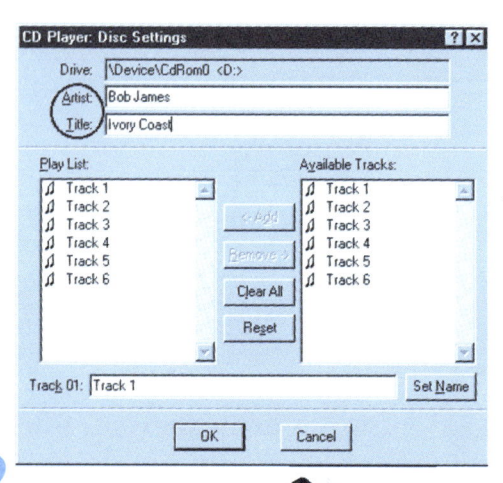

2 Click on the *Artist* text box, and type in the name.

3 Click on the *Title* text box, and type the title of the CD.

228

The names you type will appear in the *CD Player* window.

> If the toolbar is missing from your *CD Player* window, or if you cannot find *Artist* and *Title* shown, look in the VIEW menu. There you can find the commands to show or hide window items (e.g. toolbar).

When you first start the program, it shows all the tracks of the CD as Track 01, Track 02 and so on. The next step enables you to type in the names of the tracks on the list. This is how it is done:

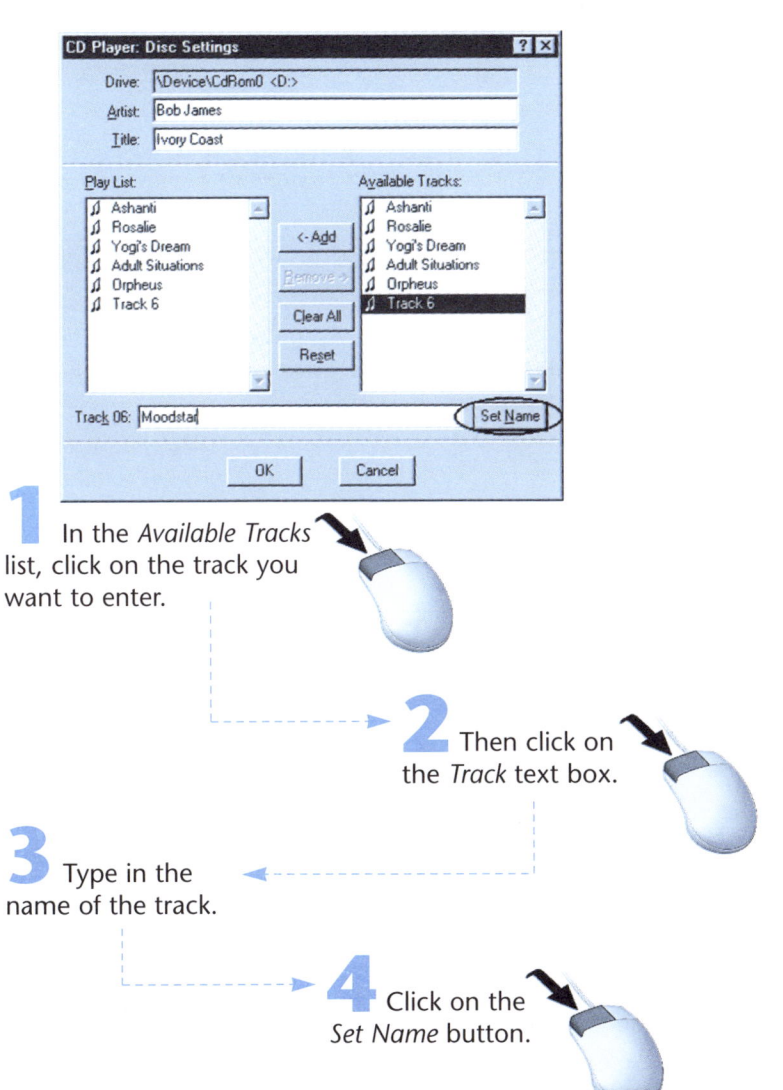

1 In the *Available Tracks* list, click on the track you want to enter.

2 Then click on the *Track* text box.

3 Type in the name of the track.

4 Click on the *Set Name* button.

229

The program enters the name you have typed and highlights the next track on the list. You can repeat these steps as required, to enter the names of all the tracks.

In the left-hand list, *Play List*, you can specify the order in which tracks of the audio CD are to be played.

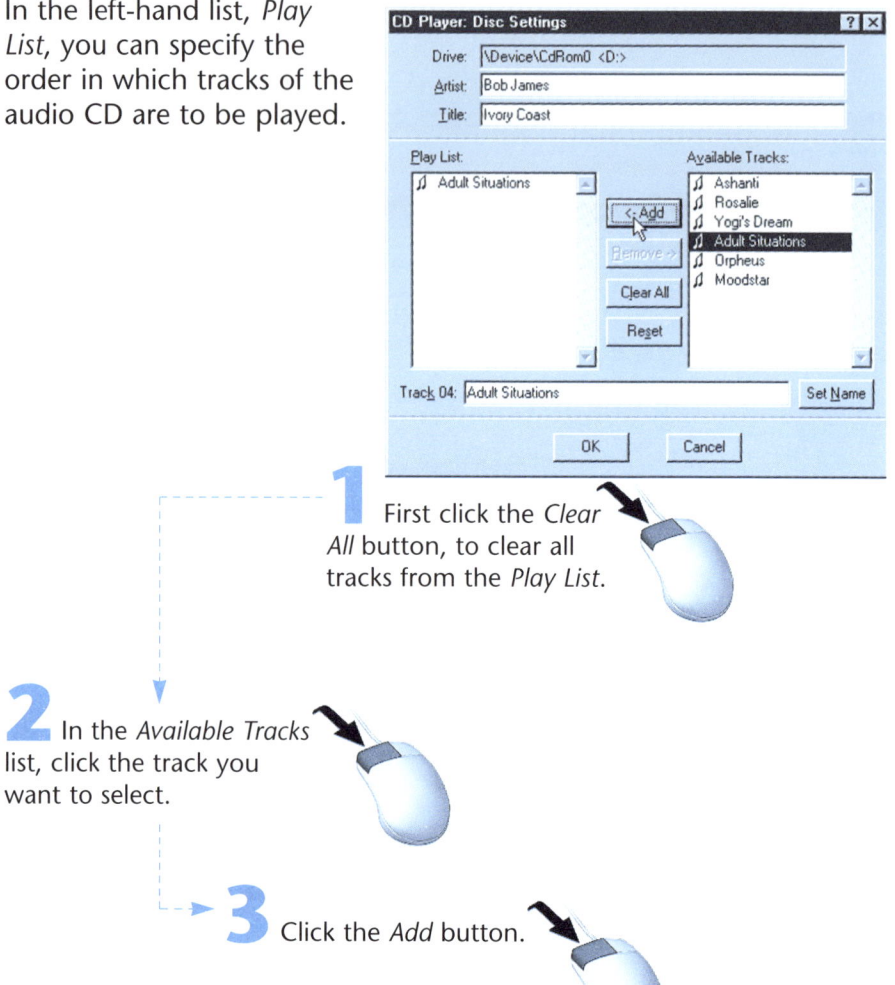

1 First click the *Clear All* button, to clear all tracks from the *Play List*.

2 In the *Available Tracks* list, click the track you want to select.

3 Click the *Add* button.

The program now adds that title to the Play List. Repeat these steps until all the tracks you want to put on the Play List have been added.

PLAYING MUSIC CDS ON THE COMPUTER

To remove a track from the Play List, follow these steps:

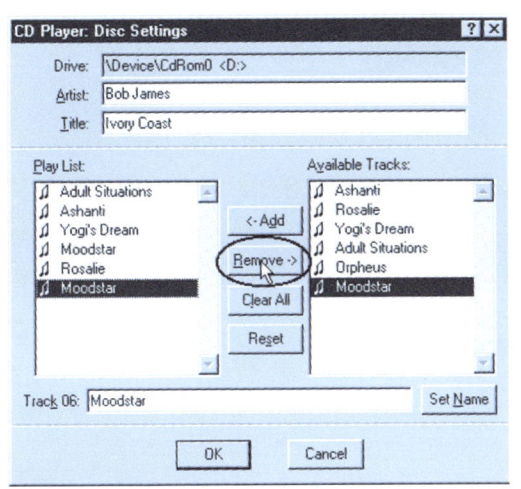

1 Click on *Edit Play List* in the *Disc menu*.

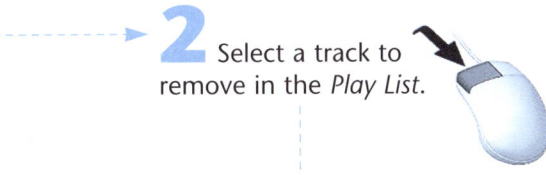

2 Select a track to remove in the *Play List*.

3 Now click the *Remove* button.

4 When you have removed all the tracks you wish, close the dialog box by clicking on *OK*.

When you start to play your CD the program will play the chosen tracks in the set order.

231

You also have the option of directly selecting a particular track in the **CD Player** dialog box.

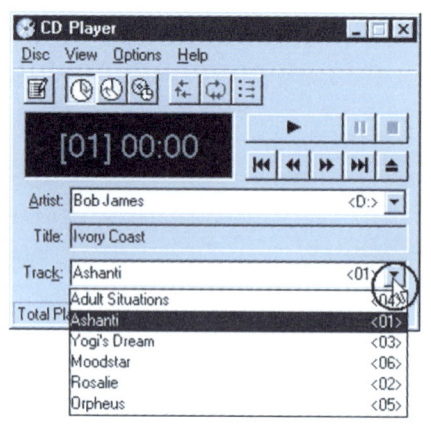

This shows the tracks selected in the above procedure.

1 Open the *Track* list box.

2 Click on the track you want to select.

In the toolbar above the CD player controls, there are icons which operate the digital display in the CD Player window.

The left-hand icon displays the track time elapsed for the track being played. The right-hand icon switches the display to the track time remaining for that track.

This icon displays the time remaining for the whole CD in the **Timer** field.

The next group of three icons controls audio CD play. You can select one of these icons, followed by the Play icon, and the program will then play the tracks in the mode you selected.

PLAYING MUSIC CDS ON THE COMPUTER

Selecting this icon will play the tracks on the Play List in random order.

If putting in a new CD is too much effort, select the **Auto Repeat** icon. This plays the tracks continuously in the order set in the Play List.

You might want to hear a sample of each track of a CD to help you choose an interesting one.

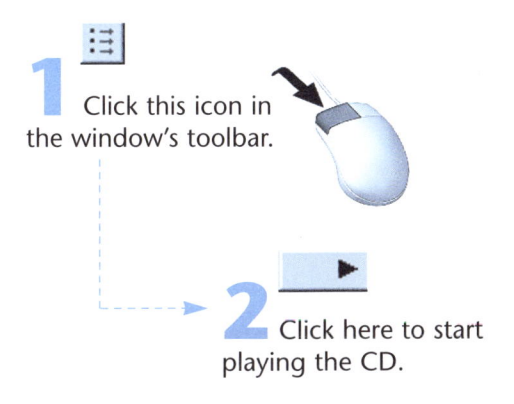

1 Click this icon in the window's toolbar.

2 Click here to start playing the CD.

The CD Player will play just the opening section of each track. This is **Intro Play** mode.

This is how to set the length of play time for the Intro sections in Intro Play:

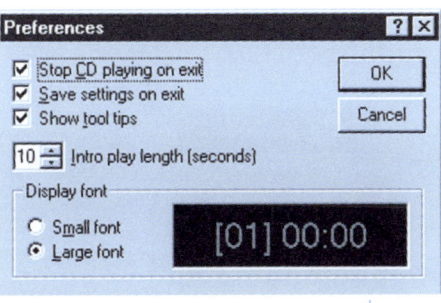

1 Select the SETTINGS command in the OPTIONS menu.

2 Specify the **Intro Play Length** in the *Settings* dialog box.

> **TIP**
> You can either type in the length of the play time or adjust it up or down by clicking the buttons. This display is called a **spin box**.

233

Working with sound files

Windows has a Sound Recorder program which can be used to record and play back sound documents. These documents are stored in sound files, which frequently have a *.wav* extension. All you need to play back sound documents is a computer which has a sound card. To record them, you also need to have a microphone.

> **TIP**
> If you do have a sound card to play back sound documents, Windows usually displays a tiny loudspeaker in the taskbar. Double-clicking on this opens the **Volume Control** window.

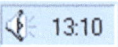

It takes just a few mouse clicks to open the Sound Recorder:

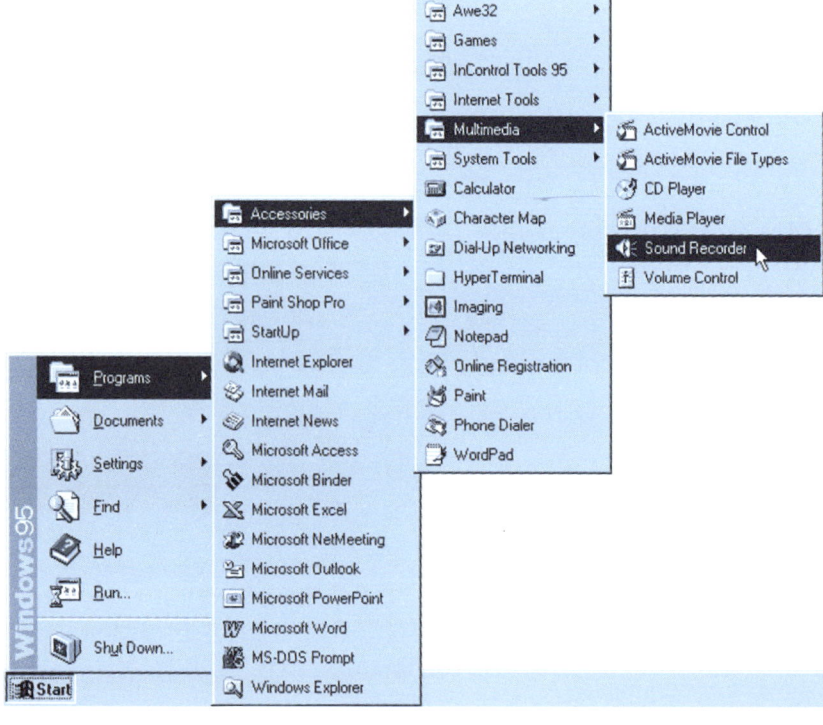

1 Open the Start menu, and go to PROGRAMS/ACCESSORIES.

WORKING WITH SOUND FILES

Windows starts up the program, and you will see this window.

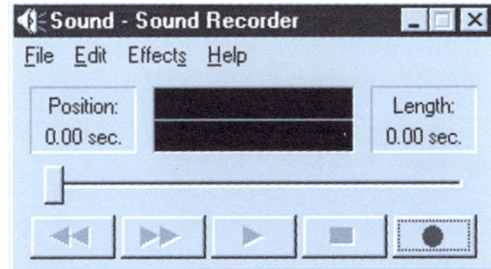

2 Move to MULTIMEDIA and click on SOUND RECORDER.

You can now record your own sound files. The following steps show you how:

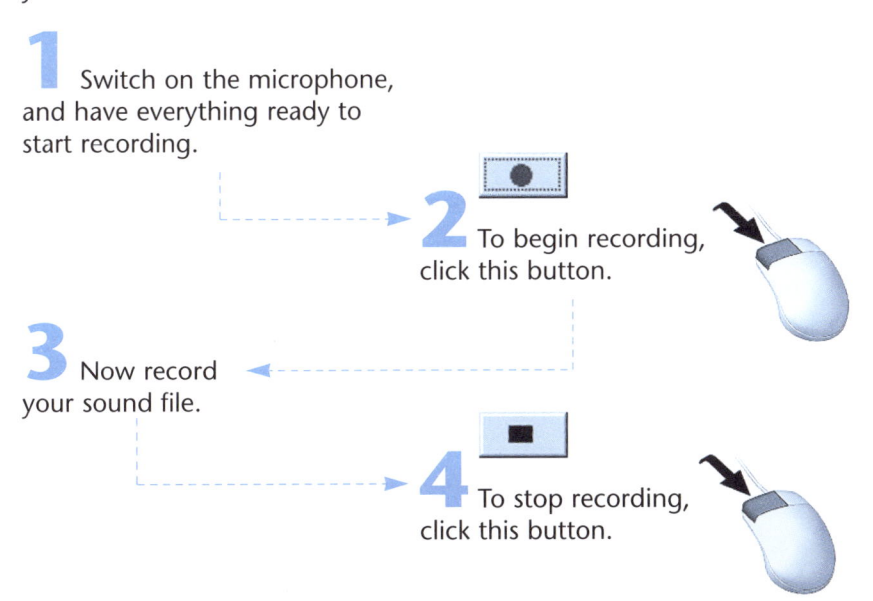

1 Switch on the microphone, and have everything ready to start recording.

2 To begin recording, click this button.

3 Now record your sound file.

4 To stop recording, click this button.

The illustration here shows the Sound Recorder window after recording has been stopped.

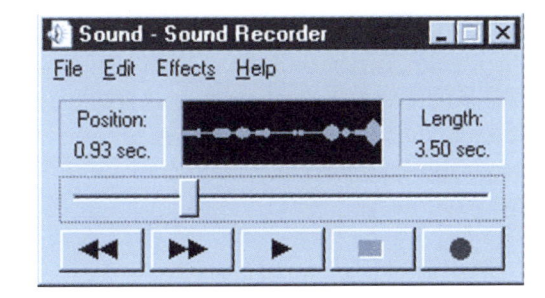

235

You can then play back, edit or save the recording. Sound files, as mentioned earlier, are saved with a *.wav* extension. To save them, follow these steps:

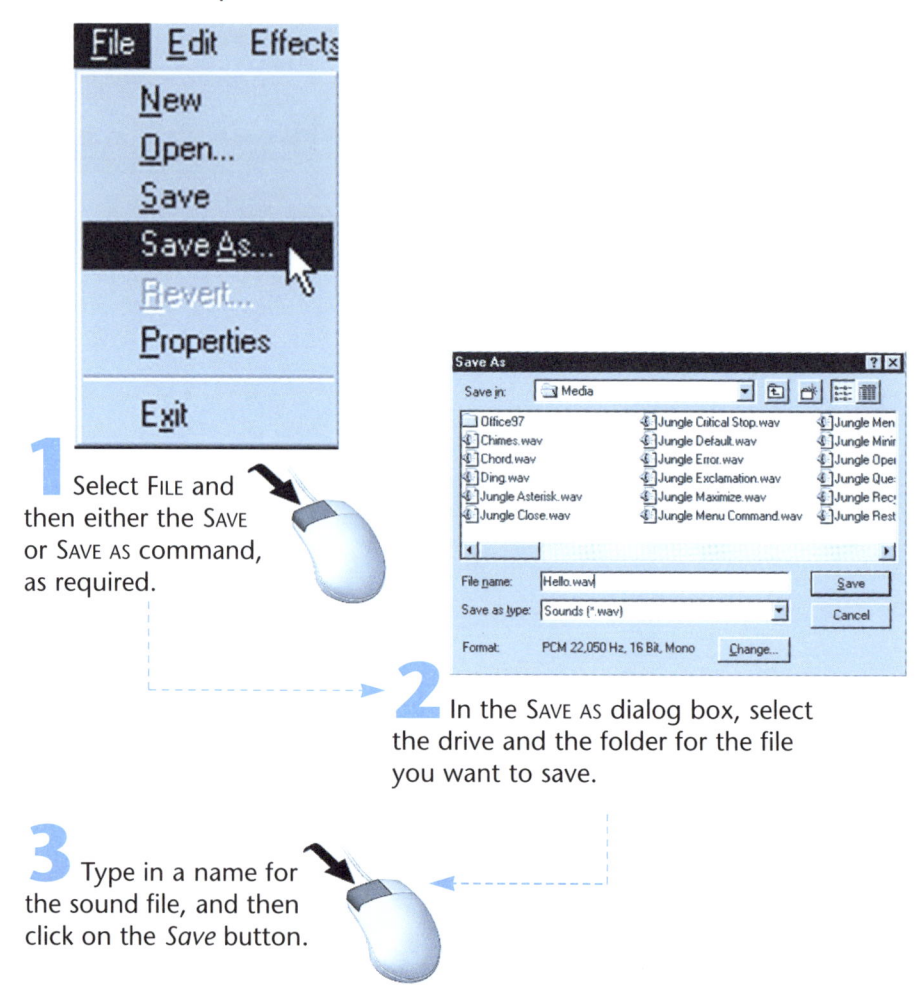

1 Select FILE and then either the SAVE or SAVE AS command, as required.

2 In the SAVE AS dialog box, select the drive and the folder for the file you want to save.

3 Type in a name for the sound file, and then click on the *Save* button.

Sound Recorder will then save the current recording in the file with the name you typed in. If you select the SAVE command again on a later occasion, the file will be saved straight away. SAVE does not offer any dialog. If you use the command SAVE AS, you can save it under a new filename.

236

Working with sound files

There are different types and qualities of recording (telephone, radio, CD) you can use to save a sound document. The better the sound quality, the bigger the file will be. You will find a *Change* button in the *Save As* dialog box. This opens the *Sound Selection* dialog box, in which you can specify the quality in the *Name* text box.

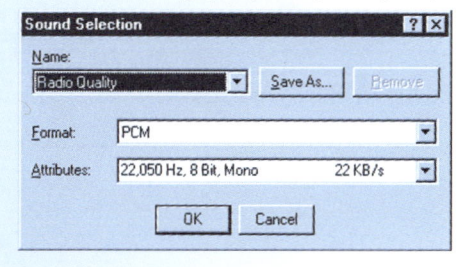

Once you have sound files, you can play them in the **Sound Recorder**. This means loading the file, and then playing it back.

1 Click FILE in the Sound Recorder menu, and then click on the OPEN command.

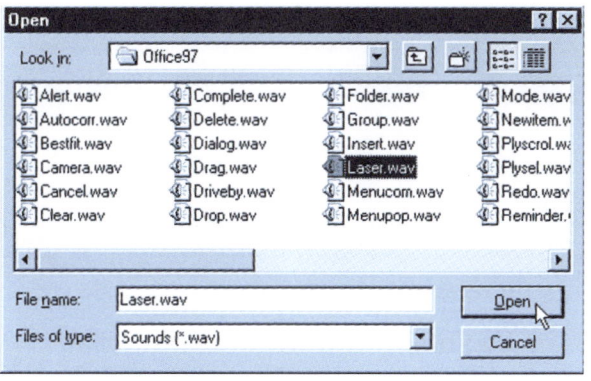

2 Select the drive and folder where the *.wav* files have been saved.

237

3 Click the file you want, and then click on *Open*.

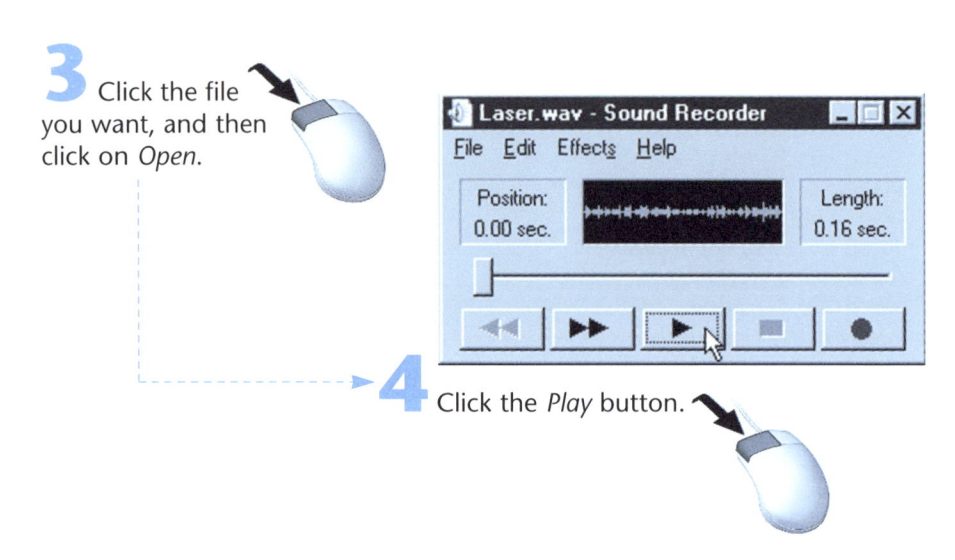

4 Click the *Play* button.

The sound document is played. The overall playing time of the sound document and the time elapsed are displayed in the Sound Recorder window.

1 Click this button to stop playback.

In the Sound Recorder window, there is a slide control which moves along during playback. You can also move it along with the mouse to any point in the sound document. You can use it to move to the beginning or end of the document. A better way of doing this, though, is with these buttons:

Returns to the **beginning** of the sound document.

Advances to the **end** of the sound document.

238

Sound Recorder offers two menus, EDIT and EFFECTS, which enable you to change sound documents once you have recorded them. You can 'cut' a sound document, change the playback speed, run it backwards or mix more than one sound document. You will find details in Sound Recorder Help.

Fun as it is to use sound documents, the real plus is being able to insert your own voice recording into a text document and send it to someone. The recipient can access the sound recording directly from the loaded text document. You can see an example of how this might look in WordPad at the end of Chapter 4.

Watching videos in Windows

Windows contains a *Media Player* program. You can use this to play audio CDs or (as in *Sound Recorder*) sound documents from *.wav* files. This section will mainly deal with a particularly interesting subject: the functions that enable you to play video files. You can turn your computer into a sort of home cinema. A fast enough computer (e.g. 133MHz Pentium PC) with sound card can play these videos at full-screen size, with sound. There is now a vast range of CDs with videos of this type.

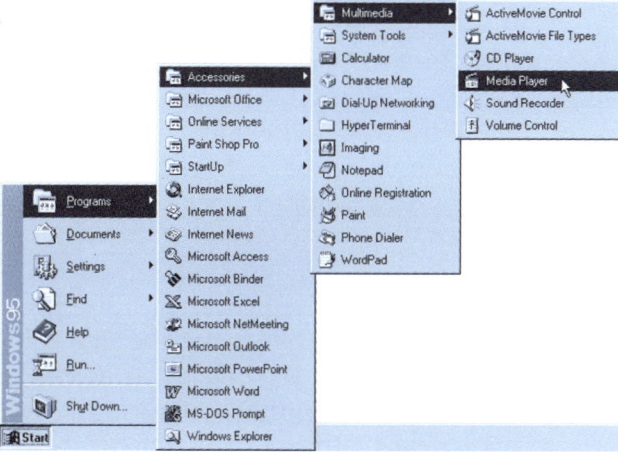

1 To start the program, first click PROGRAMS/ACCESSORIES in the Start menu.

239

1 In the ACCESSORIES sub-menu, select MULTIMEDIA and then MEDIA PLAYER.

Media Player has a quite simple opening window.

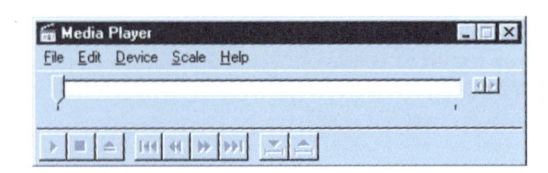

The play controls are similar to the ones shown for CD Player at the beginning of the chapter.

▶   Use this button to **start** to play an audio CD, sound document or video.

❙❙   **Pauses** play. This button replaces the Play control as soon as playback begins.

■   **Stops** playing an audio CD, sound document or video.

▲   **Ejects** the CD. You can close the CD tray of the CD-ROM drive by clicking a second time on this button.

◀◀ ▶▶   These two controls activate the **forward** and **backward** direction of playback. You can move the playback point step-by-step within a track of an audio CD, a sound file or a video.

◀◀❙ ❙▶▶   These move to the **previous** or the **next** set point. In a music CD, they shift to another track. In sound documents, they take you to the beginning or end of the document. In videos, they shift to set points in the video. This is the beginning or end of the video, or the beginning or end of a defined section.

WATCHING VIDEOS IN WINDOWS

Using *Media Player* is as easy as using CD Player. On the Windows CD-ROM, you will even find some *.avi* files in the *\Funstuff\Videos* folder, that you can use to try out video playback.

1 Click FILE in the Sound Recorder menu, and then click on the OPEN command.

2 If a tick is not displayed in front of the command VIDEO FOR WINDOWS, click this entry.

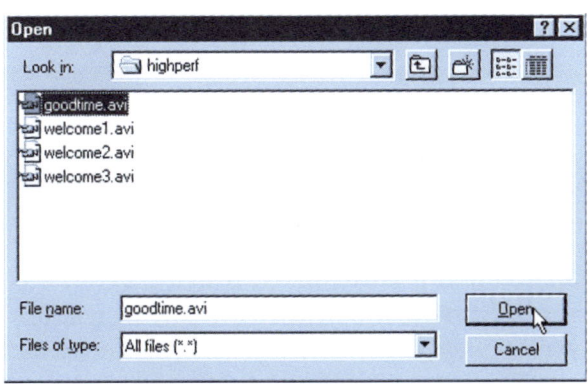

3 Select the command OPEN from the FILE menu.

4 Look for the *\Funstuff\Videos* folder on the Windows CD-ROM.

241

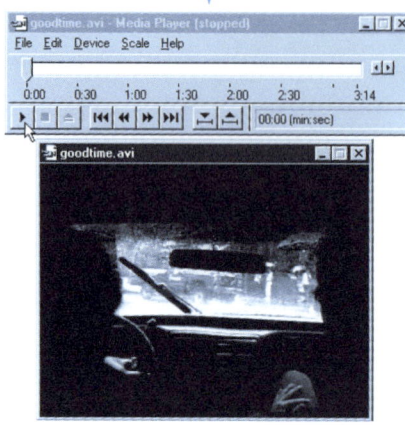

5 Click on one of the video files, and then on the *Open* button.

The video will be shown in a second window. You can use the controls described above to pause or run backwards or forwards in the video.

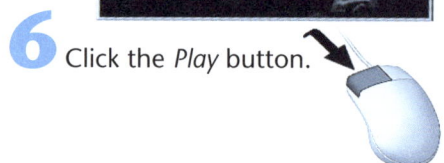

6 Click the *Play* button.

To view single frames in the video, first stop the video using the *Stop* button. Next to the slide control, you will see two buttons, which will run the video *backwards* or *forwards* frame by frame. You could, alternatively, shift the slide control to the desired point in the video file using the mouse.

Do you find it awkward to watch a video the size of a postage stamp or postcard? It is not possible to alter the size of the window in the normal way, unfortunately, but you can adjust it.

WATCHING VIDEOS IN WINDOWS

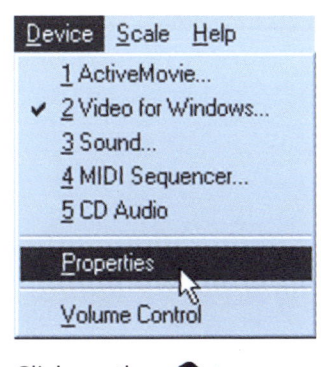

1 Click on the PROPERTIES command in the DEVICE menu.

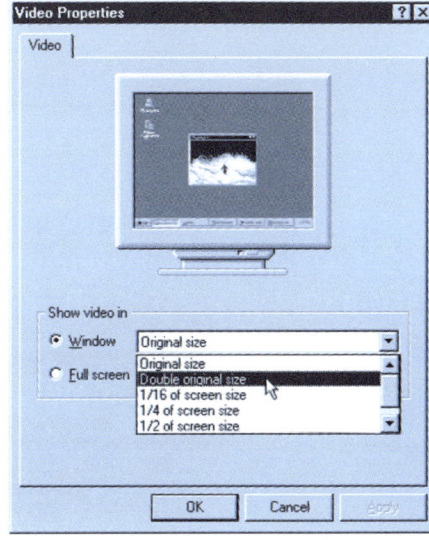

2 Click the option box beside Window.

3 Open the list box and select the window size you want.

4 Close the dialog box by clicking on *OK*.

TIP
The window sizes are available in stages from Original size to *Maximized*. Select the size which gives you the best playback quality and speed.

243

If you are interested in a particular section of the video, you can define that section.

1 Start playback of the video.

2 Click on this button at the beginning of the section.

3 Use this button to mark the end of the section.

The section you have defined will be marked by a blue bar in the slide control.

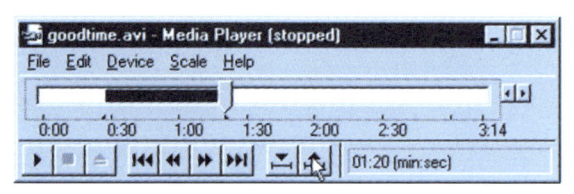

> **Tip**
>
> A single frame can be marked by using the CLIP command in the EDIT menu. The OPTIONS command in the EDIT menu opens a dialog box in which you can, for example, select automatic frame reverse or automatic repeat. You will find further details about the Media Player functions in its online Help.
>
> Videos can be inserted into a letter or text document, just like a picture or sound document. You can, for instance, create a letter in WordPad and insert a video. The video can be accessed and watched on the recipient's computer. Bear in mind, though, that video files are very large, and the file with the letter may not fit onto a floppy disk.

Minesweeper!

Windows comes with the Minesweeper program, a game in which you have to find out the safe areas in a minefield in the shortest possible time. The playing area is divided up into squares. You can find out by clicking the squares whether they are free of mines, and if there are mines nearby.

The **number 1** in a square means that **one** of the neighbouring squares has a mine in it. The number tells you how many mines there are in neighbouring squares.

To play Minesweeper, follow these steps:

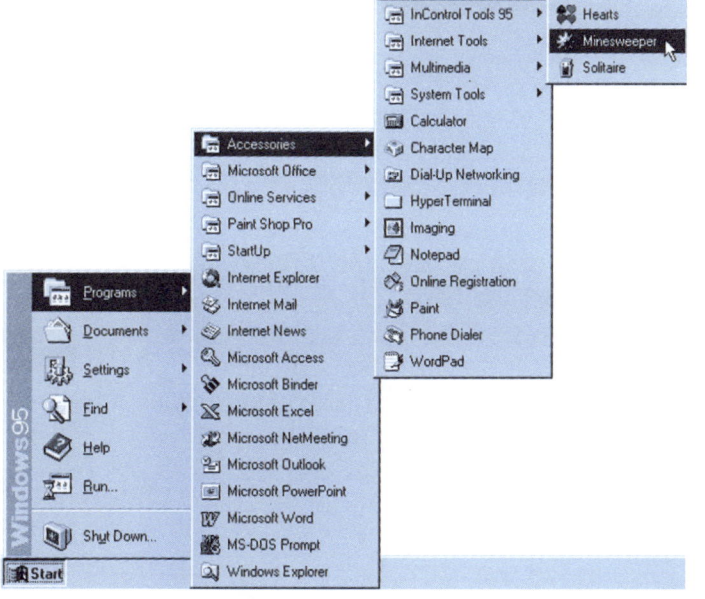

1 Click on PROGRAMS in the Start menu, and then on ACCESSORIES.

245

2 Select the entry GAMES, and then MINESWEEPER.

Minesweeper starts up, and you see this window. Now you can begin minesweeping.

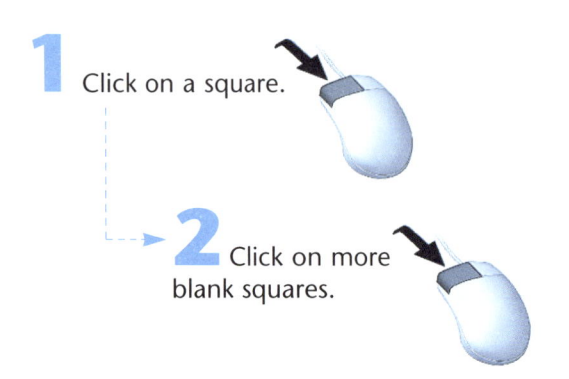

1 Click on a square.

2 Click on more blank squares.

Each square you select is 'uncovered'. The aim is to uncover as many squares as possible that are free of mines in the shortest possible time.

If you click on a square with a mine in it, you have lost the game (as here). Here you can also see how the numbers in the squares match up with the number of mines in neighbouring squares. The time elapsed since you began minesweeping is shown in the digital display top right.

MINESWEEPER!

> If you suspect that a square contains a mine, point to another which you think could be free of mines. Now hold down the left and right mouse buttons together, and Minesweeper will uncover all the neighbouring squares that do not contain mines. When you release the mouse buttons, these squares are covered up again, and you can 'sweep' the squares one at a time. If you think the particular square contains a mine, click it with the right mouse button, and Minesweeper will mark it with a flag.

Here you can see some of the squares that have been marked with **flags**.

1 Click on the face to begin again.

This face is a **Smiley**!

The world of computing often uses **Smiley** faces to express various emotions (as well as smiling faces, you can get sad and angry ones, etc.). Minesweeper uses three different 'luxury versions' for this Smiley button. In electronic mail (e-mail), you find ordinary versions being used (see Chapter 8).

> You will find a number of commands in the GAME menu for beginning a new game or setting the level. You can get further information in the game's Help, which you access via the **?** menu.

247

Relax with Solitaire

Solitaire is the card game Patience, which Windows has taken up and turned into a computer game on the same lines. The aim in Solitaire is to take the cards from the starting deck, and place them in four stacks, in which they are laid out in order from ace to king.

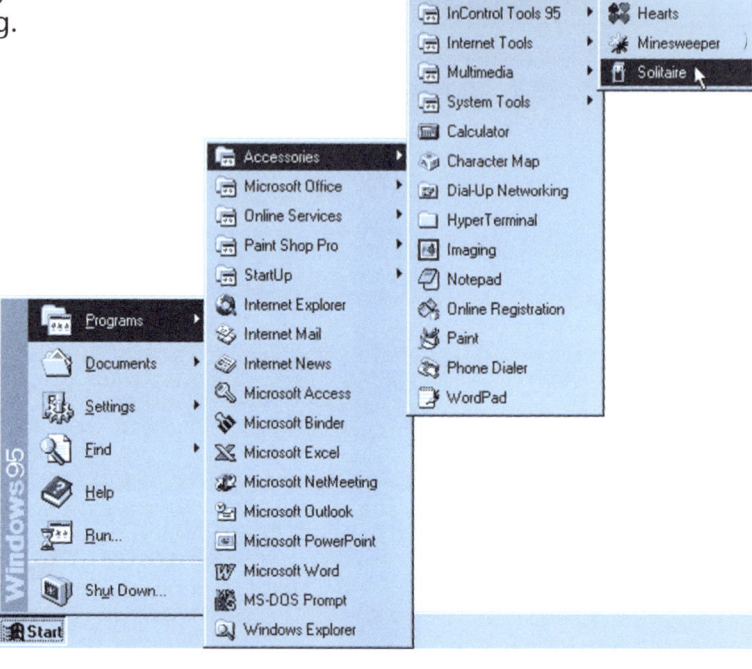

1 Click on PROGRAMS in the Start menu, followed by ACCESSORIES.

2 Select the GAMES group from the ACCESSORIES menu.

3 Click on SOLITAIRE.

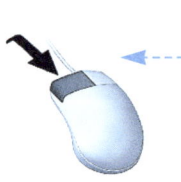

248

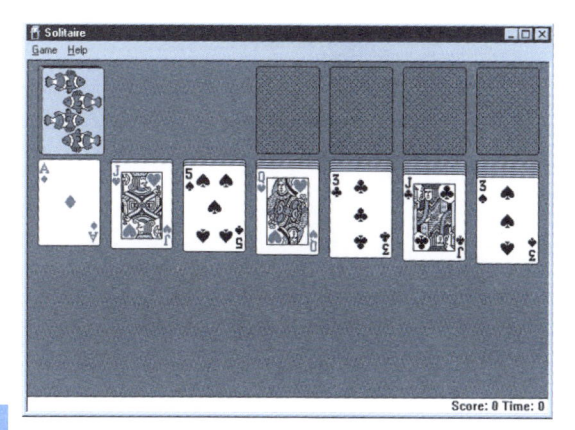

4 When you start the program the first time, it lays out the cards automatically. When you start a new game, you click on the GAME menu, and then on the command DEAL.

The program then deals out a new set of cards from the stack.

In the bottom row, you can see seven cards laid out face up. You can use the mouse to drag cards which are face up to a suitable stack.

The deck with the rest of the cards is face down in the top left-hand corner.

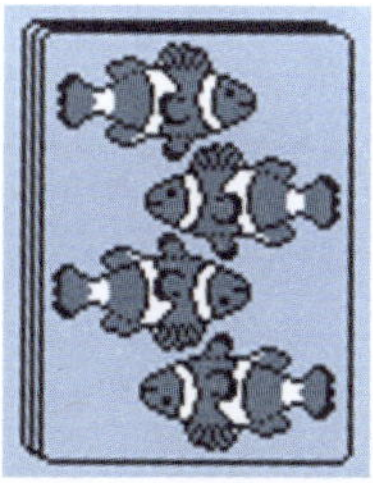

The positions for the four final 'suit stacks' are also marked out. This is where you are going to lay the cards, in the right order, beginning with the aces.

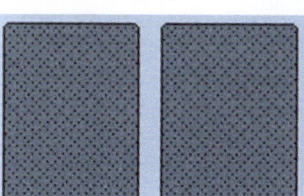

249

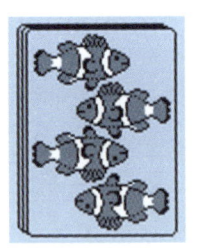

1 To pick up a card, click on the deck in the top left-hand corner.

2 Cards which are face up in an existing stack can be picked up and dragged to a suitable stack in the bottom row, using the mouse.

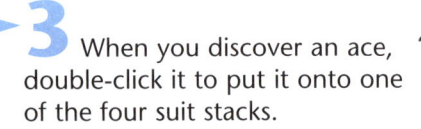

3 When you discover an ace, double-click it to put it onto one of the four suit stacks.

4 You can 'turn over' a face-down card at the top of a stack by double-clicking.

Continue in this way. You have to make valid moves as you sort the cards and place them on the stacks. The cards must be arranged as alternately black and red in any one stack.

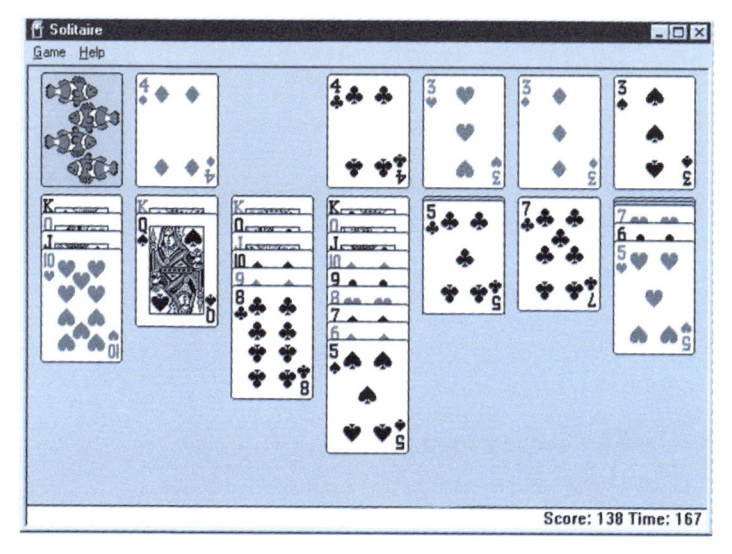

You also have to put the cards in the right order (King, Queen, Jack, ten, nine, eight, seven, six, five, four, three, two, ace). So, on top of a black five of spades, you can only put a red four (hearts or diamonds). The program rejects invalid moves. The game ends when you have either arranged all the cards in the right order in the four stacks, or when there are no more valid moves you can make.

> You will find further information about the game in Help for this program. You can access it via the **?** menu. The GAME menu gives you a number of commands for dealing the cards, undoing the last move, or setting options.
>
> SUGGESTION: The CARD BACK command on the GAME menu opens a window in which you can choose the design for the back of the cards. Try using the 'robot' card back some time, and see what happens!

251

Action, Hover! through the maze

You will have Hover! if you obtained your copy of Windows on CD-ROM. 'Hover' is strictly speaking a hovercraft, but here Hover is a sort of bumper car, which you steer through a maze. The aim of the game is to collect your opponent's flags scattered about the maze before they collect yours. Follow these steps to play Hover!

1 Put the Windows 95 CD-ROM into the drive.

2 Click on the *Hover!* button in the *Windows 95 CD* window.

> If the *Windows 95 CD* window does not appear when you insert the CD-ROM into the drive, select the CD drive in the *Explorer* window. In the *\Autorun* folder of the CD-ROM, you should start up the *Autorun.exe* program by double-clicking the mouse. The window you need should then appear.

ACTION, HOVER! THROUGH THE MAZE

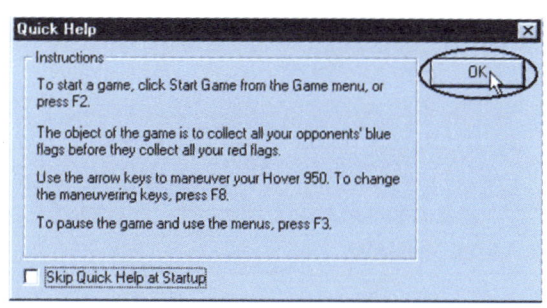

1 The *Quick Help* window can be closed by clicking on *OK*.

2 Press the function key F2 to start the game.

The game is loaded, and you can now steer the bumper car through the maze. You can opt to use a **joystick** or the keyboard for this.

> Many games use a **joystick** steering device. It is a small lever, like the control used in a traditional-style plane, which can be moved in various directions. It controls the direction of travel.

If you have to opt for the keyboard, use these keys:

The **function key** F3 interrupts play.

253

Use the **function key** [F2] to resume play.

[↑] moves the vehicle forwards. The longer the key is depressed, the faster you travel. So it also acts as the accelerator.

[↓] enables you to go backwards.

The [→] and [←] keys steer to left and right.

In the numeric keypad are four more keys you can use to control travel direction:

[Home] takes you backwards and left,

[Page ↑] takes you backwards and left,

[Page ↓] takes you forwards and left, and

[End] takes you forwards and right.

ACTION, HOVER! THROUGH THE MAZE

The first thing you see when you start the game is the vehicle's cockpit, with a view ahead into the maze. Various items in the cockpit are important for the game.

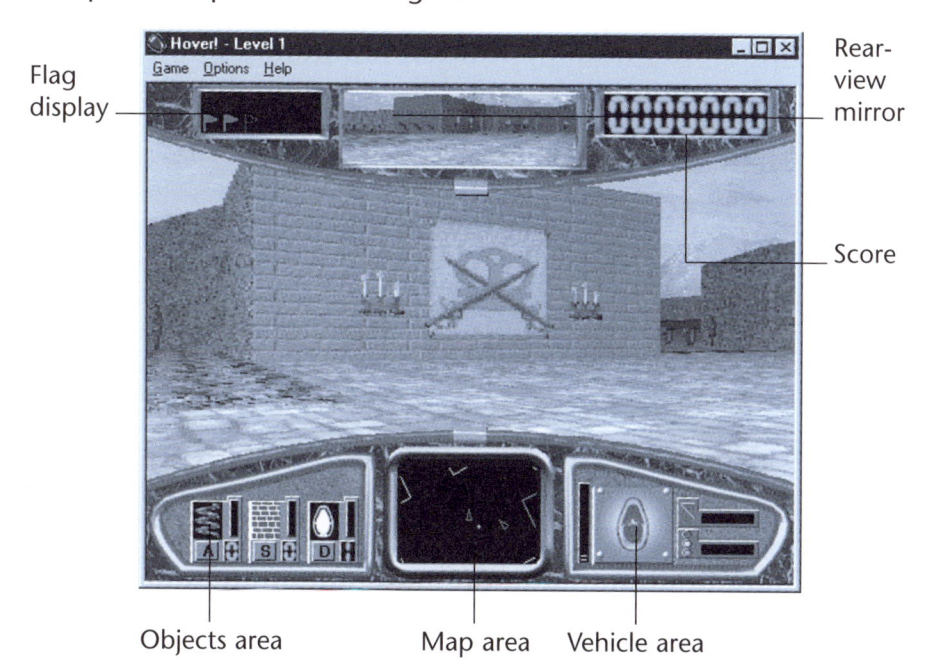

Flag display — [screenshot of Hover! - Level 1 showing cockpit view] — Rear-view mirror

Score

Objects area   Map area   Vehicle area

- At top left you see the box with the **flag display**. This shows the blue flags you have collected, and how many red flags your opponent has collected.

- At the lower levels, you receive 1000 points for every one of your opponent's flags you collect, and 2500 points for every one of your own flags still in your possession at the end of the level. Your **score** is displayed at top right, next to the rear-view mirror.

- In the **rear-view mirror** you see what is happening behind you. It helps to see if an enemy pilot is approaching.

255

- You can see an aerial view of your current surroundings in the **map area**. You can enlarge the map section using the plus key, and reduce it using the minus key. The red triangle is your vehicle. Green, yellow and blue triangles represent other pilots. Red and blue flashing spots are flags. In this game, you collect your opponent's blue flags by driving over them.

- Below, left, is the **objects area**. You can access the functions you need to jump, build walls, or make yourself invisible here. But for you to do this, they have to be available at this stage in the game. This is shown by the number in the relevant box. If the number is more than zero, the object is available. Press the key shown in the box for that object to perform the function (e.g. A to jump). The number 3 alongside means you can jump three times.

- Below, right, is the **vehicle area**. This shows direction of travel, speed, and the time periods remaining for 'invincibility' or higher/lower speed.

> If you forget what an area signifies, click it with the right mouse button, and then select the *Help* button. Hover! will present a small Help window with additional information.

You will see a number of objects on your way through the maze, and you may be attacked by enemy pilots.

This is one of the flags in the maze. Red flags are yours, blue ones have to be collected by driving over them.

Action, hover! through the maze

If you get a cloak like this from a pod, it makes you invisible to enemy pilots for a time. The vehicle area shows you how much invisibility time you have left.

Enables you to build a wall to stop an enemy pilot.

Enables you to jump and look over a low wall, or jump over an enemy.

Indicates a mystery pod. You can pick these up when you find them in the maze. They may contain 'good' or 'bad' objects.

There are 'skid pads' on the ground. They act like a patch of oil if you drive over one, and you skid in a random direction. If you collide with anything, you will be thrown back in the opposite direction.

This is a 'hold pad' on the ground. It will stop your vehicle for a while if you drive over it.

There are other objects you might find in the maze. The game's Help gives further details. You will also find tips for playing. Now you can *Hover!*

Take a break now, just 'for practice', and try out the Windows games for yourself. Have fun!

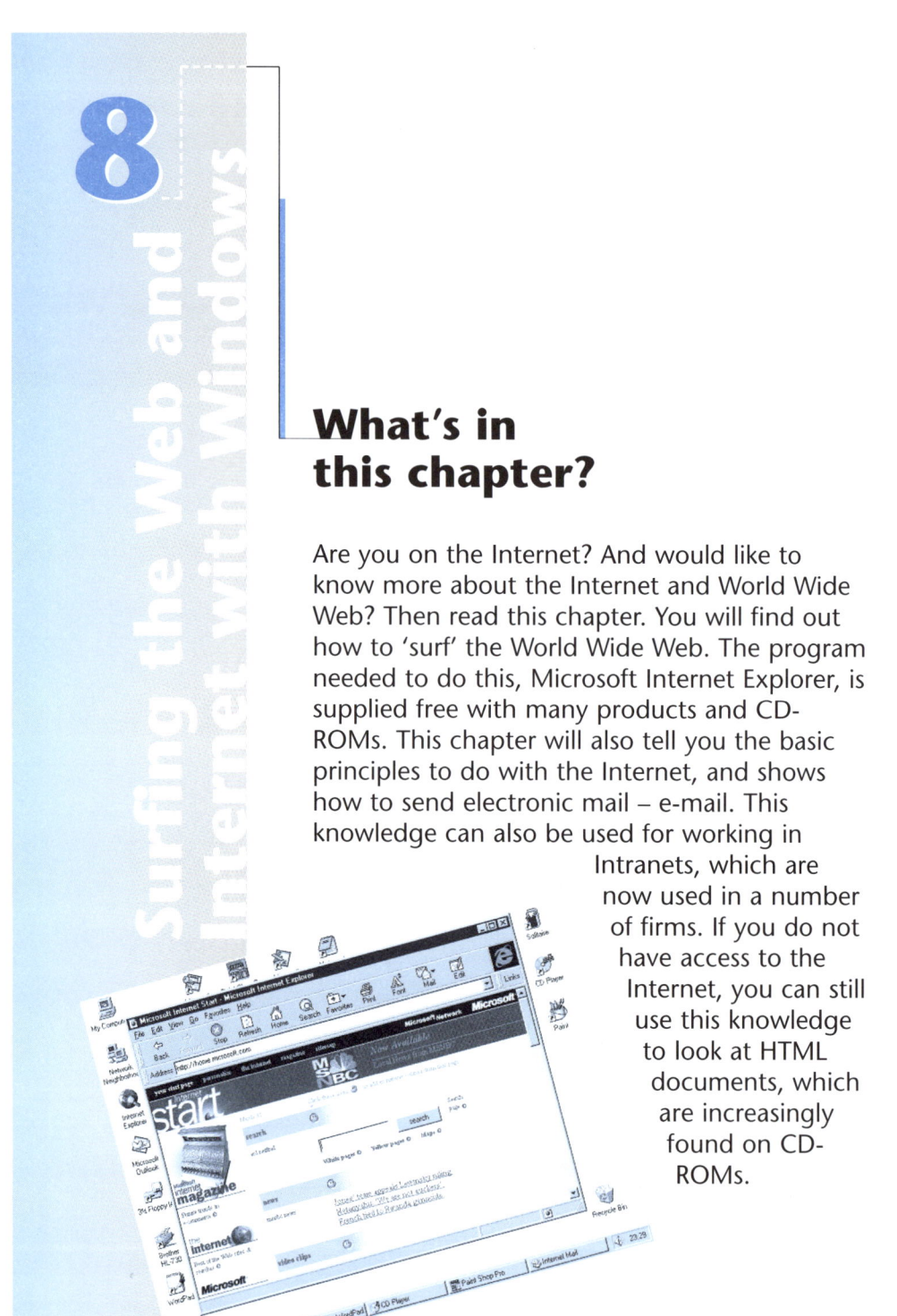

8

Surfing the Web and Internet with Windows

What's in this chapter?

Are you on the Internet? And would like to know more about the Internet and World Wide Web? Then read this chapter. You will find out how to 'surf' the World Wide Web. The program needed to do this, Microsoft Internet Explorer, is supplied free with many products and CD-ROMs. This chapter will also tell you the basic principles to do with the Internet, and shows how to send electronic mail – e-mail. This knowledge can also be used for working in Intranets, which are now used in a number of firms. If you do not have access to the Internet, you can still use this knowledge to look at HTML documents, which are increasingly found on CD-ROMs.

You already know:

Working with windows	23
Getting Help	34
What is the Start menu?	46
Opening a program	47
Switching between programs	51
Closing a program	53
Dealing with files and folders	58
Producing a text in Notepad	126
Producing pictures in Paint	159

Your are going to learn:

What are the Internet, Intranet, World Wide Web and browsers	260
Taking the first steps with the Internet Explorer	264
Marking Web sites	272
Saving, loading and printing document pages	275
Setting up the home page and other options	280
Searching on the Internet	282
What is e-mail	284

What are the Internet, Intranet, World Wide Web and Browsers?

Everyone these days is talking about the **Internet**, but do you know where the name comes from, and the idea behind it? The word is made up of two ideas, *Inter(national)* and *Net(work)*. A **network**, then, stretching beyond national boundaries across the globe. This

> A network is a system linking several computers with each other by lines or cables, for the transfer of data. It means that computers can exchange files or data. This is a facility which is often used by companies. The staff do not have to send files such as letters and other documents on a floppy disk, but can send them via the network. Chapter 9 shows how Windows supports such network functions.

idea was taken a logical stage further in the Internet. It is possible not only to link the computers within a company, but to link those in different towns or countries. A computer in San Francisco, for example, can exchange data with a computer in Rome or Rio. The link between the systems in this case is normally the public telephone network.

Originally, only a few computers in various universities were linked by Internet. Anyone with access to one of these computers would also be able to reach every other computer on the Internet (and through these computers, their users). All you need to send a file or message to another user, as for the ordinary mail, is an address. Since the exchange of data on the Internet is so simple, quick and inexpensive, more and more computers were linked with each other worldwide.

What are the Internet, Intranet, World Wide Web and Browsers?

What can you do on the Internet, and what are the benefits? Like the postal service before it (where you could telephone, send letters, packets and parcels, or carry out financial transactions), the Internet offers various services (like the exchange of messages, sending files, telephoning, etc.). A large proportion of Internet users really only use two functions: sending e-mails and 'surfing', as it is known, on the World Wide Web.

> E-mails are simply letters written and sent electronically. You write a text on your computer, put on it who is to receive it, and send the message as an e-mail to your nearest Internet computer. For this, you just need a telephone line and a modem – a device for transmitting messages down telephone lines. The Internet does the job of putting the message in a mailbox for the recipient to pick up. They can download it onto their own computer, read it, edit it and pass it on. You can attach other files to an e-mail, to be passed on with it. E-mails are cheap; what you pay is the Internet subscription and the cost of the call to the nearest Internet computer. So you do not have to pay international telephone charges to the USA, as you would for fax. E-mails are quick (compared with the post), so a letter to the USA takes a few minutes to arrive.
>
> The World Wide Web is a further service, which enables you to access so-called Web pages. These might contain the latest weather information, exchange rates, or a firm's publicity, for example. To display them you need a special program called a browser.
>
> As well as the Internet, the term Intranet is increasingly heard. Intranets are networks using similar programs to the Internet, and are often installed in large companies. Since only employees of the company can use this network, the Inter part of the name was changed to Intra. If you are familiar with Internet functions, you will be able to work with a company's Intranet straightaway.

That just leaves the question, How does the World Wide Web work? What is so special about the World Wide Web that makes it so popular? Here are a few ideas: there are many thousands of computers in the Internet, with countless files in them. Looking for a particular document produces a few problems. Think about looking for a particular file on your own computer.

Now think of millions of users. Once you have found that distant file, how will you read it if it has been produced using a different program? (Do you know which word processing format someone in, say, India, is using, and do you happen to have it on your computer?)

The World Wide Web, or WWW or Web for short, was created to simplify finding documents and displaying them on screen.
The documents themselves are spread as far and wide as ever, but each has an address, which states exactly where the file is (think of it as being like the address on a letter). All the documents are stored in a special format, with the file extension .htm or .html. Programs like the Microsoft Internet Explorer can read and display these files.
These programs as a whole are called browsers. Using the predefined 'address' and 'file format' makes easy access to the documents by browser possible.

> **WHAT'S THIS?**
> You will probably come across the term HTML in this connection. This stands for Hypertext Markup Language. Documents can be produced with this 'page description language' (similar to PostScript) in such a way that they can be displayed on different computers using a browser. HTML documents are stored in files with the extension .htm or .html.

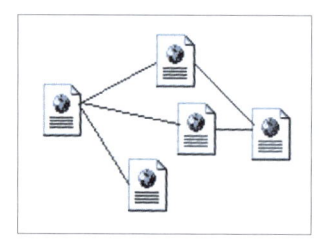

The HTML language makes it possible to leave in a document references to further documents. These references are called Hyperlinks.

WHAT ARE THE INTERNET, INTRANET, WORLD WIDE WEB AND BROWSERS?

> **TIP**
>
> You only need to be concerned with the niceties of HTML if you are producing documents for the World Wide Web yourself. But this language does enable anyone putting out Web pages to define a connection between different documents.

Once you know the address of a document, you can specify it in the browser. The browser downloads the document from the World Wide Web and displays it on your computer.
This illustration shows a 'Web page' in Microsoft Internet Explorer. If you point at an underlined item, a stylised hand will appear, directing you to the hyperlink. If you 'select' (click) the hyperlink, the follow-up page will appear.

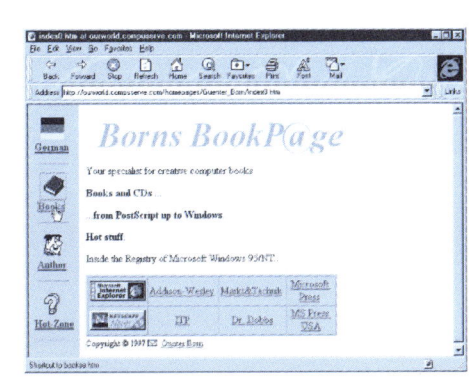

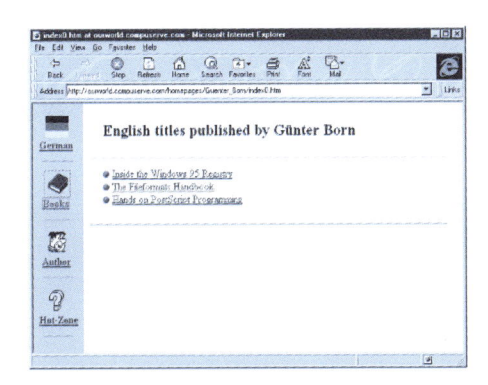

On the follow-up page shown here, you can see further hyperlinks, leading to yet more documents. So, using hyperlinks, a person or organisation putting out Web pages can link together a collection of documents for the 'readers'.

> **TIP**
>
> It may not matter to you, the reader, where these files are actually located. If you find an interesting page, you can access further pages via hyperlinks. When you select a hyperlink, the browser conducts its own search for the document it refers to, and downloads it into your computer, whether it comes from a computer in Rome, Tokyo or Sydney. This movement from page to page is called surfing the Internet. You will discover in the next section how this works in practice.

263

Taking the first steps with the Internet Explorer

The Microsoft Internet Explorer is not contained in all editions of Windows 95, but it is in Windows NT 4.0, and in Microsoft Plus!, the additional package available for Microsoft Windows. The program is also on many CD-ROMs, in Microsoft Office 97 – a package of programs for office work – and in (almost) every access package from online service providers such as CompuServe or America Online (AOL). The next few pages explain the basic steps for calling up Web pages using Microsoft Internet Explorer 3.0.

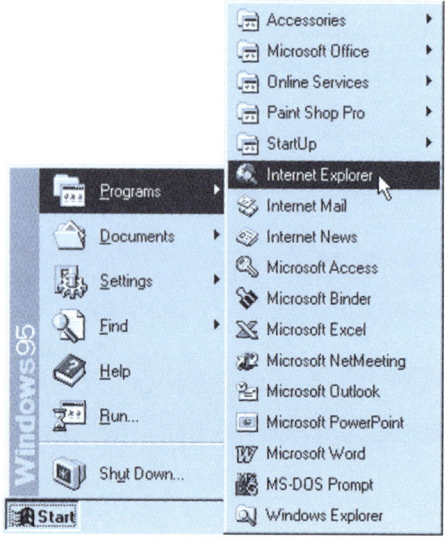

You may have a different version of Internet Explorer, or be using Netscape Navigator as your browser. They are similar to use. The only difference is in some of the commands or buttons. But it is still worth trying out the following steps.

1 The Internet Explorer is opened from the Start menu via the entries PROGRAMS/INTERNET EXPLORER.

If you have an icon for the Internet Explorer on the desktop, you can start it from there, by double-clicking the icon.

264

TAKING THE FIRST STEPS WITH THE INTERNET EXPLORER

The program opens up this window, with a start page; here the page is empty. The window has a title bar, menu and toolbar. There is also a status bar and a text box for the address.

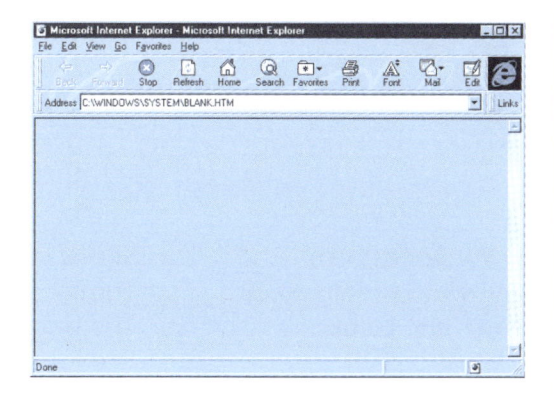

Here is the text box for the address.

> If the Internet Explorer tries to establish a connection with the Internet straight away when you start it up, and then delivers an error message that it cannot find the address, then the wrong start page is installed. You will find out further below how to alter it. Meanwhile, these steps assume that you do have a working connection to the Internet. If you install AOL or CompuServe, this connection is automatically installed. For AOL, you first need to start up the access software and log on. As soon as you are 'online', you can use the built-in browser. Alternatively, you can then start the Internet Explorer and work using this.

Accessing up and working with Web pages is the same for all documents in the Microsoft Internet Explorer. You need the site address of a Web document. These addresses are usually given in the form:

http://www.xxx.com

http:// shows that the document is on the Web (or in an Intranet). The letters which follow are the address proper.
The only possible problem is that you must know the exact address. You may, for example, discover Web site addresses from firms' advertisements.

265

> The abbreviation URL is sometimes found. It simply stands for an address on the Internet.

There are also magazines and other sources which publish such addresses. The following table gives some addresses (though these may change over time).

www.stones.com	Site of the Rolling Stones
www.virginradio.co.uk	The Virgin Radio site
www.bbc.co.uk	The huge BBC site
www.itv.co.uk	Site for the ITV network
www.channel4.com	The Channel 4 TV site
www.telegraph.co.uk	The Daily Telegraph online
www.designercity.com/cosmopolitan	Home of Cosmopolitan magazine
www.erack.com/select	The Select magazine site
lottery.merseyworld.com	The UK National Lottery site
www.number-10.gov.uk	Inside the home of the Prime Minister
www.sporting-life.com	The Sporting Life magazine site
www.eu.microsoft.com	Microsoft's UK web site
www.moneyworld.co.uk	For financial news and dealings
www.whatson.com	Current stage shows, films and entertainments
www.yell.co.uk	The Yellow Pages online
www.bonus.com	Vast activity site for kids
www.prenhall.com	The Prentice Hall web site

If you know the address of the document, type it into the browser's address box. The document is then downloaded, and you can reach any follow-up pages using the hyperlinks already mentioned. You are about to see how, as an example, to access a popular games site. The Web address is http://www.gameshows.com

Taking the First Steps with the Internet Explorer

1 Click the address box in the Internet Explorer window.

Address |http://www.uk-calling.co.uk/frame.html

2 Type in the address exactly as given.

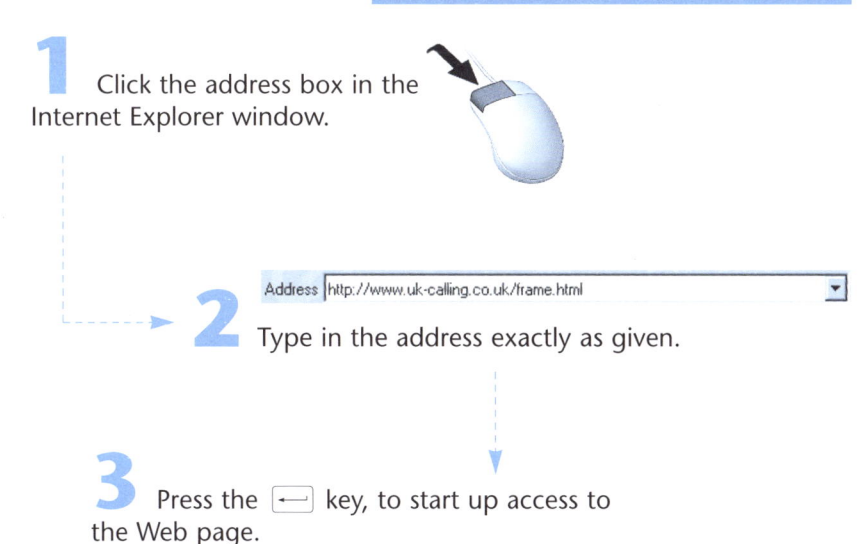

3 Press the ⬅ key, to start up access to the Web page.

It may take several seconds for the browser to find the page. Remember, it may be fetching it from the other side of the world. That need not worry you. Your job is just to type in the correct address.

> **CAUTION**
> On occasion, it can take a very long time to make the connection with the computer which has the required page. You can cancel the browser request by selecting this icon in the toolbar.
>
> ⊗ Stop

> **TIP**
> If a page is not completely downloaded, or to repeat a request, select this icon in the browser toolbar. It will request the page again on the WWW.
>
> Refresh

If a valid Web address has been given, the browser will find it and download the information onto your computer. The page is then built up step by step in the browser window. This could take a few minutes, depending on the size of the document and the number of graphics contained in it.

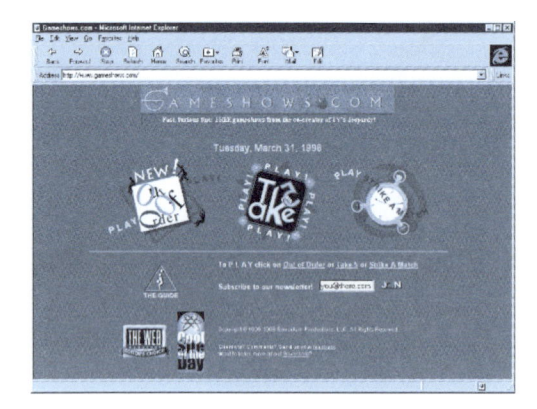

Here is the Web page with the address http://www.gameshows.com. There are pictures on the page featuring the names of the games. The names are also given below and underlined. The underlining shows that these are hyperlinks.

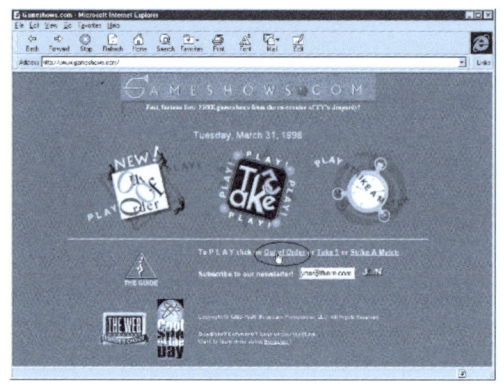

The mouse indicator becomes a tiny hand.

1 Point at an item which has a hyperlink.

2 Click on the hyperlink Out of Order.

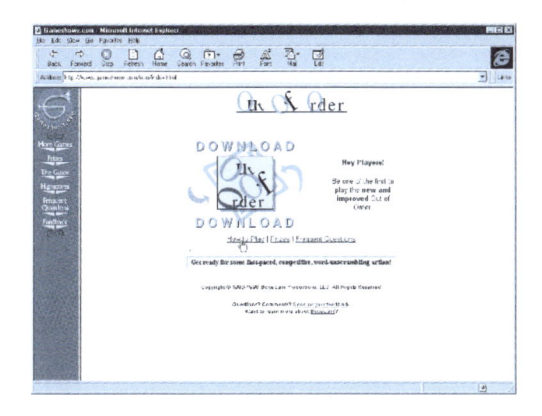

Taking the First Steps with the Internet Explorer

The browser will now request the document that the hyperlink referred you to. Here is the page displaying the information just requested. If this page too contains hyperlinks, you can reach the next one by clicking on it in just the same way. So 'surfing' WWW pages is child's play. The most difficult part is knowing the right address for the start page.

Sooner or later, though, there are two further questions you will encounter. Say you want to return to a Web page you have visited previously. Do you need to type in the whole original Web page address?

No, the browser 'remembers' the moves you have made. It automatically records the addresses of pages you have visited.

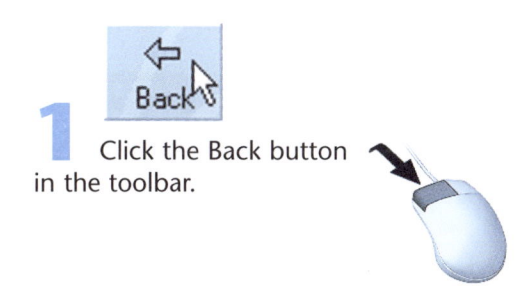

1 Click the Back button in the toolbar.

Now, the browser will display the previous Web page. Would you like to go on a page?

269

2 Click the Forward button.

In the example used here, the browser will show you the page you have just visited, the Web page with the Out of Order game.

TIP The Forward and Back buttons can only work when you have visited more than one page in the current session. When you start a new session, they will be greyed out (unavailable). Bear in mind, too, that you may need to click several times to get to the page you want, because the browser only moves one page at a time. Sometimes it helps to open the Address list box, and call up the address stored there.

Hyperlinks often appear as text underlined in blue on Web pages. But that need not necessarily be so, as the next example shows.

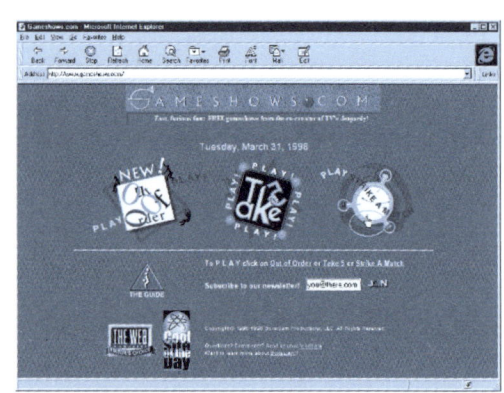

1 Point to the picture for the Strike a Match game.

270

Taking the First Steps with the Internet Explorer

The stylised hand appears, showing that a hyperlink exists. There is also a reference to the target page in the status bar.

2 Click on Strike a Match picture.

The browser calls up the page with the next document, loads and displays it. You can now use the various hyperlinks to access further documents.

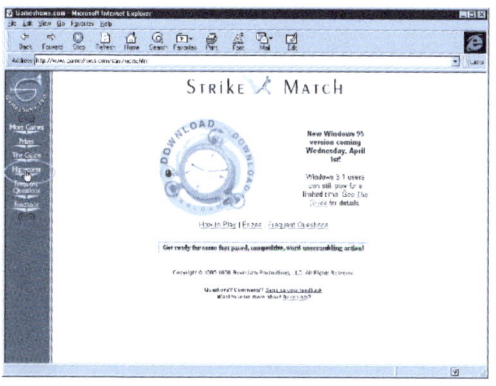

1 Click on Highscores.

The page relating to this has been divided up into several windowpanes. You can call up extra information via the hyperlinks, but this time they are displayed in one of the panes of the window.

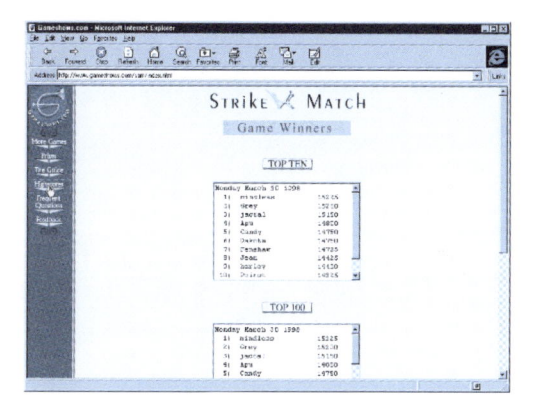

271

> **TIP**
> The design of a document, whether the window is divided up, and the position of hyperlinks, is all decided by the issuer of the page. There is often a graphics page which refers on to pages of text.

> **CAUTION**
> When you no longer want to go on surfing the Web, disconnect from the Internet. Otherwise, you will continue paying telephone charges for online access. Often (but not always!) it is enough to close the Internet Explorer window in order to terminate the connection. You may need to obtain details from the online access support service.

Marking Web sites

If there is a Web site that you particularly like or visit frequently, it can be a tedious job to type in the address every time. It is also all too easy to forget the addresses of interesting Websites (writing them down takes time). The Microsoft Internet Explorer has a function for storing the addresses of interesting Web sites. It is sometimes called Bookmarking, because you are, as it were, putting a bookmark in the WWW page to look it up later. This function in the Microsoft Internet Explorer is called Favorites.

1 Click on the FAVORITES menu or button.

2 To select a favourite you have defined already, click the entry in the FAVORITES menu.

272

Marking Web Sites

3 To define a new favourite, select the command ADD TO FAVORITES.

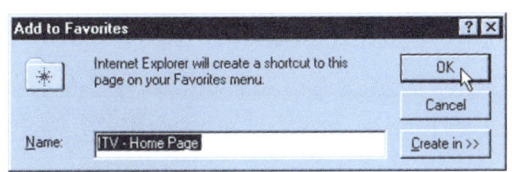

4 Change the name as needed, and then click on OK.

The new name is then added to the list of favourites. You can access this page from now on by selecting its entry.

> When you are defining a number of favourites, you can do this more efficiently by grouping them together in batches. Use the button Create in >> in the dialog box Add to Favorites. The dialog box is extended, and there is then a specific button for creating a folder to put the favourites in.

Maybe you forgot to add the favourites, or maybe you would like to read a page from a site you have just visited at your leisure later on? The Microsoft Internet Explorer can usually help you here, too. It is also possible to read the pages offline.

273

WHAT'S THIS

While there is still a connection between your computer and the Internet, you are said to be online. This is easy to spot, because you pay telephone and online charges for it. When you disconnect from the Internet, your computer is offline.

The browser registers the pages you visit, using its internal temporary memory. If you use Forward and Back to turn onward or back a page while you are online, the browser can load the pages from this temporary memory. The Web pages can then be displayed more quickly. If at a later stage, when you are offline, you want to see the Web pages you have visited, this is what to do:

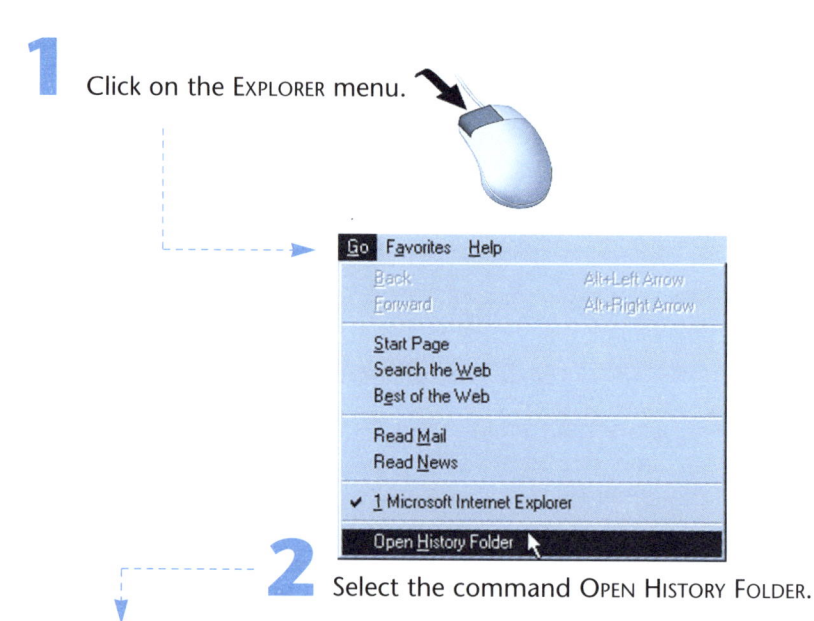

1 Click on the EXPLORER menu.

2 Select the command OPEN HISTORY FOLDER.

In the History folder, the names of the pages which are still in the temporary memory are listed.

3 Click on one of the entries.

274

The Internet Explorer now loads the page from its internal memory. You can then read it at your leisure.

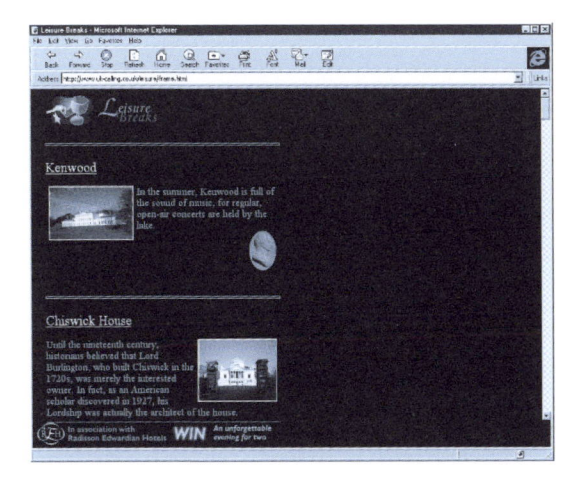

TIP: There are times when not all the information in the document is still there. Pictures may be missing, or you may click a hyperlink and find that it reconnects you to the Internet to load the page it refers to.

Saving, loading and printing document pages

Would you like to save the text of a page deliberately, in order to read it again later? This can be done in just a few steps with the Microsoft Internet Explorer:

1 Click on the command SAVE AS in the FILE menu.

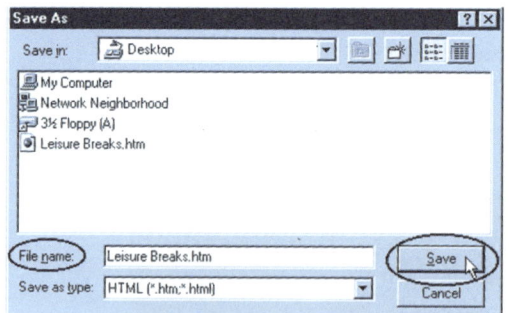

2 In the Save as dialog box, select the folder that the file is to go in.

3 Enter the filename in the Filename text box.

4 Click on the Save button.

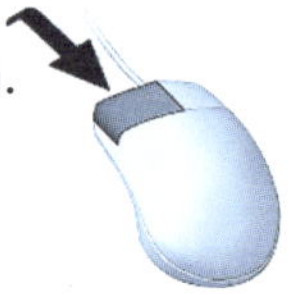

The Internet Explorer saves the text of that page under the name you have specified, and with the extension .htm or .html. Unfortunately, the pictures contained in the document are not saved along with the text. Would you like to save pictures?

1 Click the picture, using the right mouse button.

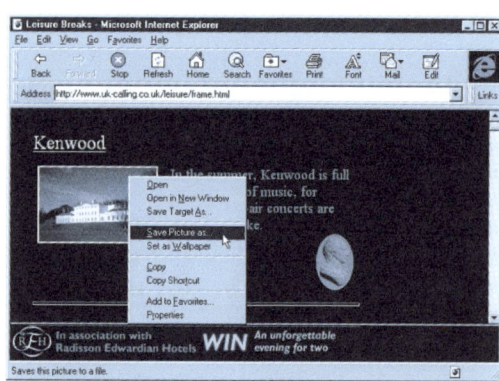

2 In the context menu, select the command SAVE PICTURE AS.

SAVING, LOADING AND PRINTING DOCUMENT PAGES

The pictures are automatically saved with their filenames. Of course, the browser can only display the pictures in the HTML document if the right name for the picture folder was used.

You may be asking, is it possible to reload a document page that was saved in HTML format? That, too, can be done with no problem. You will find these files more and more on CD-ROMs or program floppy disks, as the HTML document format is very popular. There are two ways of displaying an HTML file:

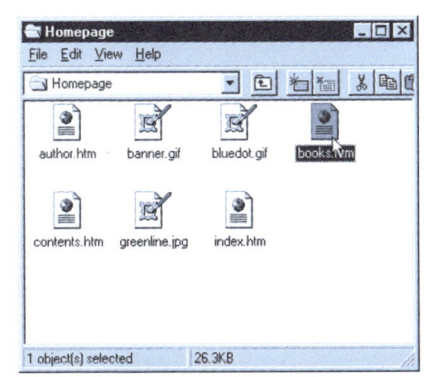

1 In the Explorer window, or the window of a folder, simply double-click on the icon for the file.

The file will automatically be displayed in the Internet Explorer (or in the default browser).
Or:

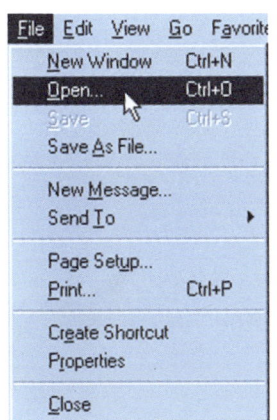

1 If the Internet Explorer window has been started up, select the OPEN command in the FILE menu.

A further alternative is to press the key combination Ctrl + O to access the function.

277

The browser displays the
Open dialog box, for you
to enter the address of
the document.

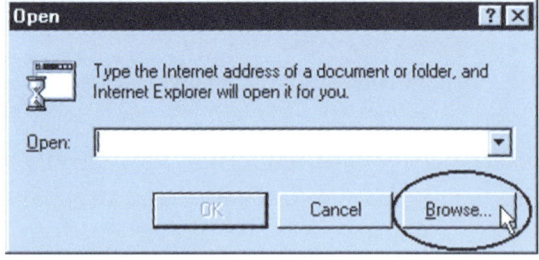

2 In the Open dialog box, select the Browse button.

3 In the Open dialog box, select the folder with the HTML files.

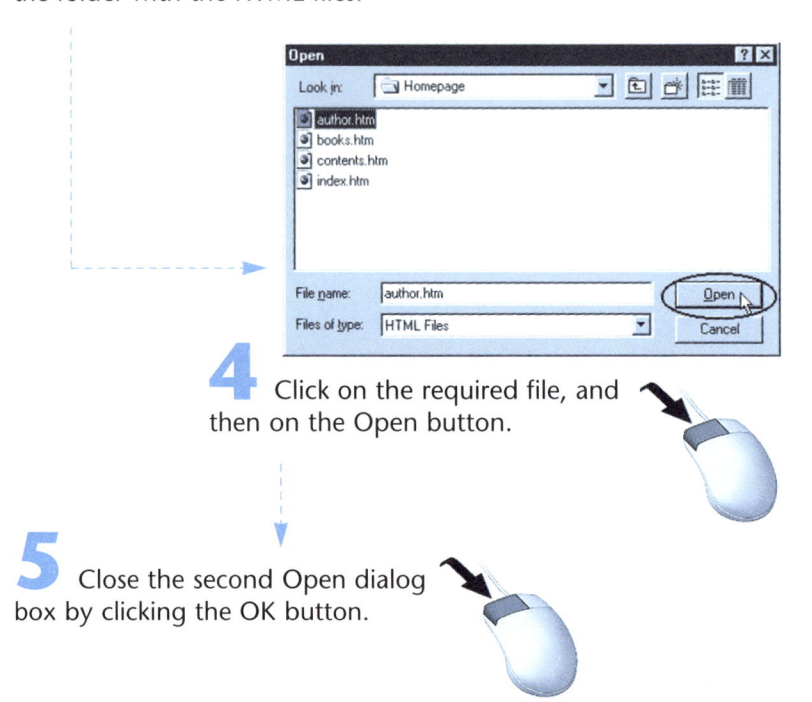

4 Click on the required file, and then on the Open button.

5 Close the second Open dialog box by clicking the OK button.

The Internet Explorer will now load the required HTML file and display it like a Web document.

278

Saving, Loading and Printing Document Pages

Printing HTML documents once they have been loaded is also very easy.

1 To print a page in the Internet Explorer, click the Print button.

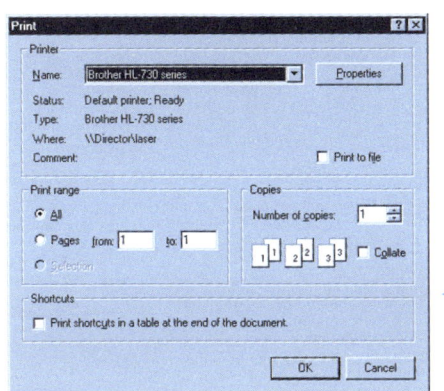

2 Set the required options in the Print dialog box.

3 Click on OK.

The browser will now print the contents of the document page which is currently displayed, together with the graphics. Should the display window be too small to display it all, the browser will print those parts of the document which are not visible.

> **TIP**
> Mark the check box 'Print links as a table at end of document'. Then the browser will print a list at the end of the document page, giving the addresses of all the hyperlinks contained in the document. You can discover some interesting Web sites this way.

279

Setting up the home page and other options

When the Internet Explorer is started up, it automatically loads its own start page. This is also often called the home page. Another way to reach the home page is by clicking its icon on the toolbar.

This gives you the opportunity to define a regularly used page. If you are lost in the Internet 'jungle', this icon will bring you back to familiar territory. But you have to specify the relevant home page for the Internet Explorer. On installation, the address of an Internet Web site is specified. To change the home page address (and adapt other options to suit your needs), follow these steps:

1 Select the desired Web page in the Explorer

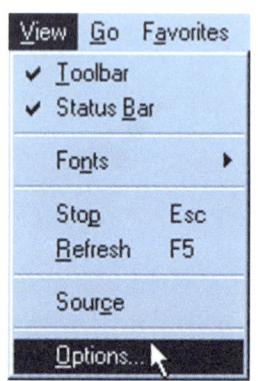

2 Click the command OPTIONS in the VIEW menu.

Setting up the Home Page and other Options

The Explorer displays the Options sheet.

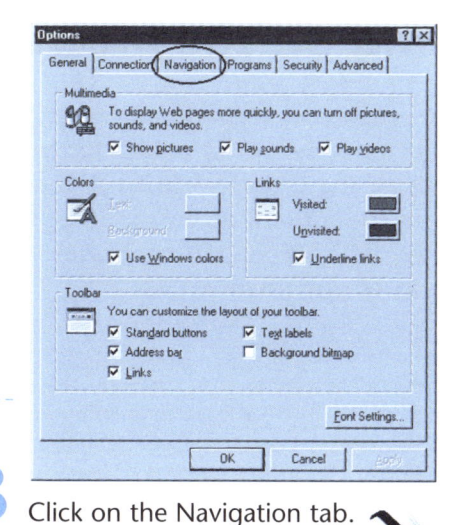

3 Click on the Navigation tab.

4 In the Page list box, select the specification home page

5 Click on the Current page button.

6 Close the window by clicking OK.

> You can enter either a valid Internet address or a file on your computer as your home page address. WWW addresses usually begin with the letters http://, whereas the address file://<drive:folder\file> specifies a computer file.
>
> You can also define the search page via the Page list box. Once you have selected this entry in the list box, you can type in the address of the search page. The Default page button sets the home page predefined by Microsoft, or the search page in the Address text box.
>
> The History group informs you how many days the Internet Explorer has been storing the pages in the History folder. You can delete the contents of this folder using the Empty History folder button.

281

Searching on the Internet

The problem when you are trying to access individual Web pages is that you need to know the addresses for them. With many millions of documents on the World Wide Web, that is a problem, if only because of the sheer number. Fortunately, there exist what are called search engines, which you can command to search for specific items in the contents of documents.

> Search engines are computers which browse Web sites, to detect HTML documents and save particular key words. When a search request is made, it collects the documents in which the words you have entered as search topics occur as key words. These are examples of search engine addresses: http://www.yahoo.com or http://www.lycos.com. You can enter the address of one of these search engines on the search page (see previous pages). This page is called up when you select the Search function.

The Microsoft Internet explorer supports your search by calling up a search page, which can be defined in advance. In what follows, it is assumed that a such a search page has been defined. Here, this is http://www.yahoo.com.

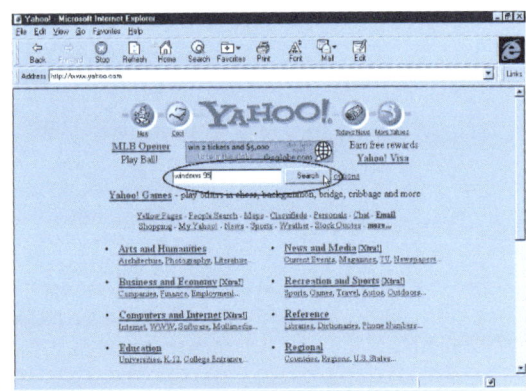

1 Click on the Search icon in the toolbar.

2 Type in the search topic in the text entry box.

SEARCHING ON THE INTERNET

3 Click on the Search button.

The search engine displays the documents found, listed on a page in abbreviated form.

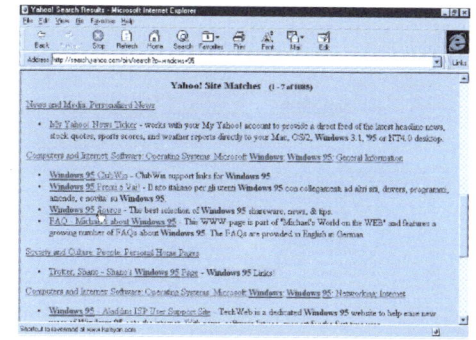

4 Click on the hyperlinks to access the documents you want to see.

> The search engines make it very convenient to search for key words on the Internet. How you enter the key word depends on the particular search engine. If you enter more than one key word, some search engines require you to put a plus sign between them. Others need the key word to be put in inverted commas. The search engine Yahoo has the advantage of access to the information of other search engines, such as Altavista. So you may sometimes receive back the results as a page from one of these other search engines.

283

What is e-mail?

'Give me your e-mail address'. This request is one we hear more and more; sending e-mails is an everyday matter for so many people now. But what is the reality behind the name, and how do you use this function of the Internet?

An e-mail is no different from an ordinary letter, except that you send the message in electronic form. As with an ordinary letter, you need to give the address it is to be sent to, and your own address as the sender. On the Internet, these are expected to be in a special form, as in name@transportservice.com. If you typed hugox@aol.com, for example, your message would be received by a fictitious user on America Online. The message you had written would be sent on its way on the Internet, and deposited in the mailbox of the recipient. They can then download it from the mailbox onto their own computer and read it.

> To send e-mails, you need an authorisation. This is normally supplied by the online service provider, together with your e-mail address. You can send such e-mails on internal company networks (e.g. Intranet), as well as the Internet. Unlike the sending of fax documents, the Internet automatically delivers the message to the mailbox of the particular person. This may in some circumstances save considerable telephone charges. E-mails also have the advantage that you can attach quite large files to the message, and transmit them together (which cannot be done with fax).

WHAT IS E-MAIL?

Is the Microsoft Internet Explorer on your computer set up to send e-mails? If so, you will be able to try out the following steps for creating and sending e-mails.

First, you need to access the function for creating the message in the Internet Explorer window.

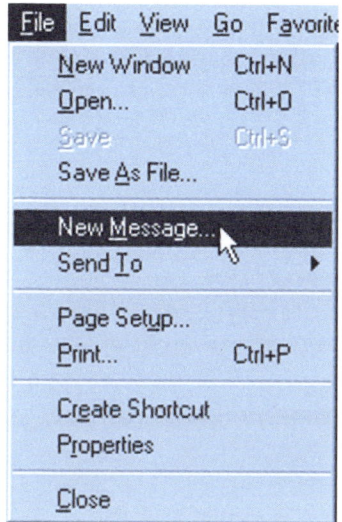

1 In the FILE menu, select the command NEW MESSAGE.

The Microsoft Internet Explorer will now start the program used to process messages (e-mails). Here, the *Outlook* program from Microsoft Office 97 will be used for this.

285

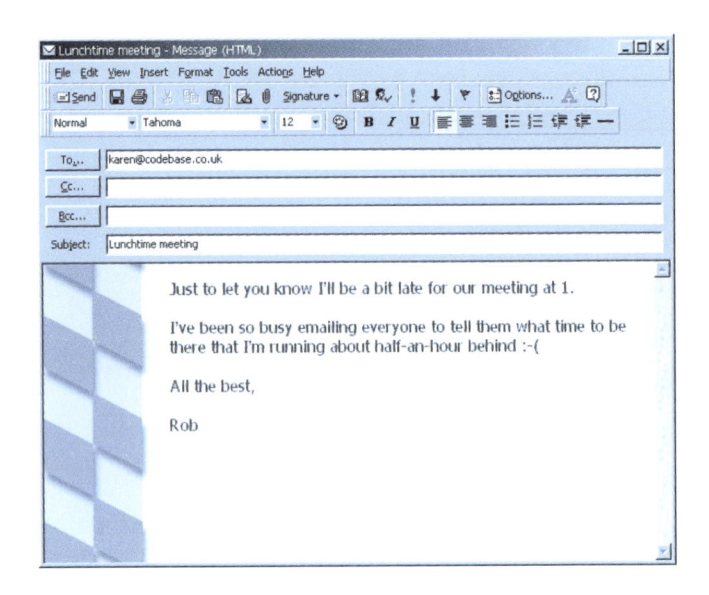

Now enter the address of the recipient in the To box (and if necessary, another in the CC box to send a copy to a second recipient). The message program will automatically supply your address as the sender.

Next, you can enter the subject of the message in the box provided, and then type the message.

> The window may look slightly different, depending on the e-mail program used. The arrangement of the boxes for the addresses and for the message should be similar, however. Most programs also have an address book function, which allows you to manage the e-mail addresses of individual users.
> In Outlook, this address book can be accessed using the *Address book* button on the toolbar.
> To attach a file to a message in Outlook, select this button . A dialog box enables you to specify the file to be sent.

WHAT IS E-MAIL?

> You often find symbols like this :-) in these messages. They are generally known as **Smileys**, and represent stylised faces, tipped over onto their side. They are handy for expressing emotions in the message. Here are some samples:
>
> :-) joy/humour   :-(sad
> ;-) wink   :-o surprise/shock

2 When you have composed the message, click the *Send* button in the Outlook window.

That message is then sent.

> If you use another program to create and edit messages, you may find that the buttons used to access the function are arranged slightly differently, or that it does things by using a menu. Reading the mail received is also carried out by the e-mail program. It is not dealt with in this book.

287

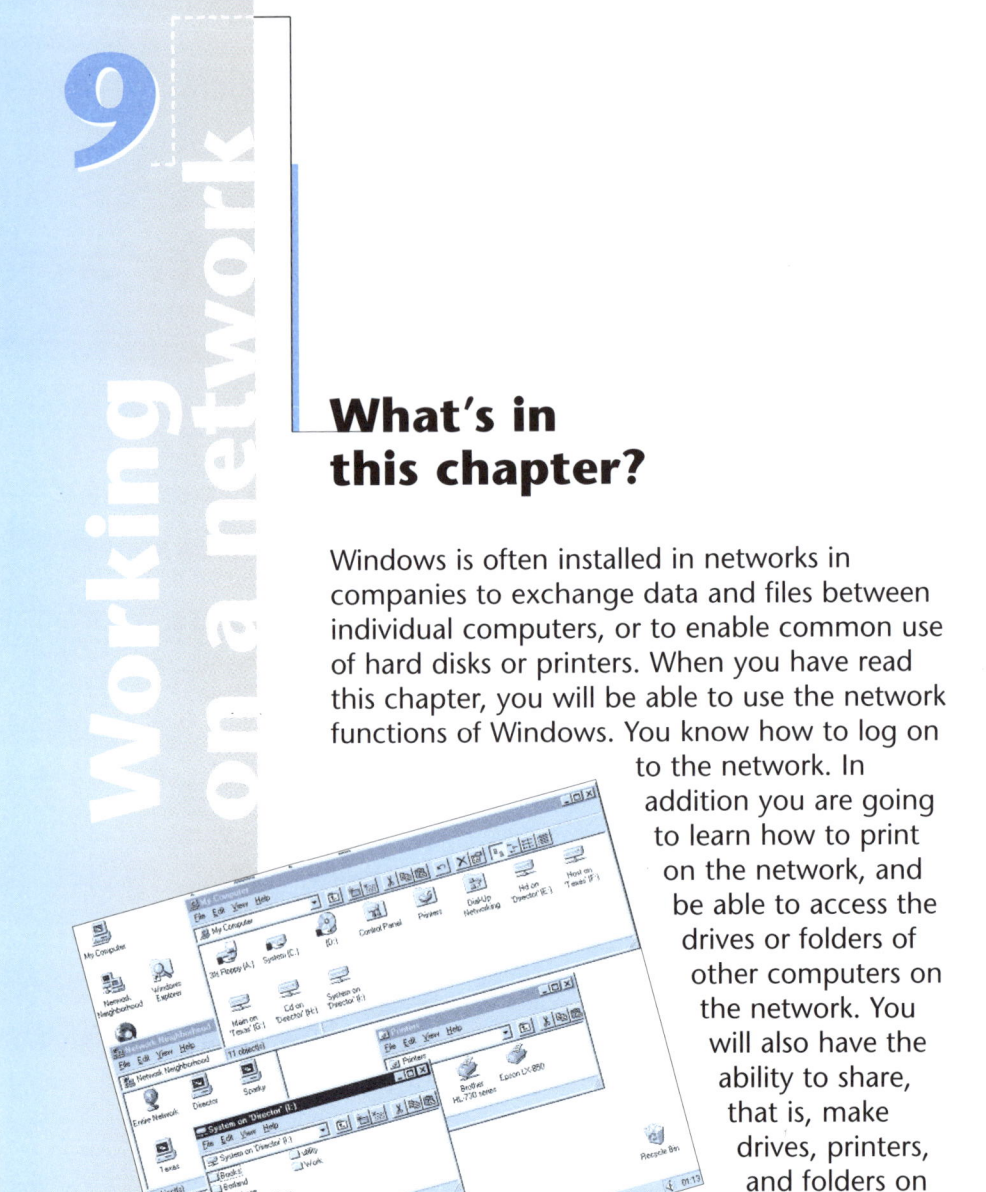

9

Working on a network

What's in this chapter?

Windows is often installed in networks in companies to exchange data and files between individual computers, or to enable common use of hard disks or printers. When you have read this chapter, you will be able to use the network functions of Windows. You know how to log on to the network. In addition you are going to learn how to print on the network, and be able to access the drives or folders of other computers on the network. You will also have the ability to share, that is, make drives, printers, and folders on your PC available for general use by other network users.

Your Progress Meter

You already know:

Dealing with files and folders	58
Displaying files and folders in the Explorer	76
Installing a new printer	202
How to print	212
Changing printer settings	215
Managing the printer	218

Your are going to learn:

A brief survey of networks	290
Working on a network	292
Mapping and disconnecting network drives	301
Printing on the network	303
How to install a network printer	305
How to share a printer	309
Sharing drives and folders	312

A brief survey of networks

You may have come across the concept of networks (in this book at least, the idea has been mentioned). Why do we need networks, and what are they really all about? Suppose that Jones & Co. run a small architect's office with a number of employees. There is Mr Jones, Mrs Brown, the secretary, and a second (part-time) employee, Mr Smith. They each have their own PC, located in two separate rooms. There are unfortunately a couple of problems: for reasons of cost, there are only two printers available. If Mr Smith wants to print something, he has to copy the files onto a floppy disk, and print it using one of the other computers. There are also problems when Mr Jones and Mr Smith want to exchange drawings, because the size of the file means that it cannot be copied onto floppy disk. (Methods like this would be simply intolerable in any larger firm, as you can imagine.) Mr Jones therefore decides to link the individual computers in the offices together by cables, to create a **network**.

One possibility would be to use one computer as the **main computer** (called the **server**) of the **network**. All the files needed for common use are stored here. The printer is also connected to this computer. Every user of the network can access this printer and the drives of the **server**.

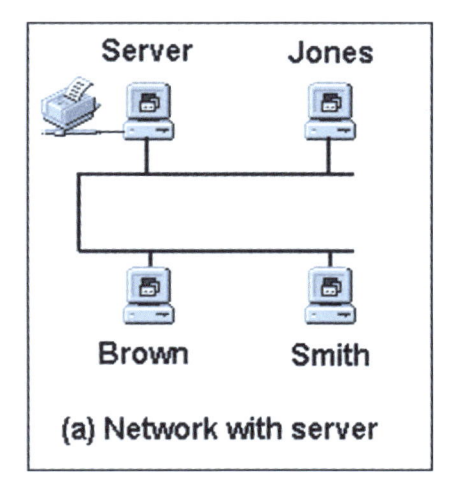

(a) Network with server

> A **server** is the main computer in a network. It offers its resources (printer, drives) to all the users in the network. The other computers in the network are then known as **clients**, since they use the resources of the server. (This is easy to remember: a waiter (server) serves the guests (clients) - though we usually use the word "client" in a business or professional context.)

A BRIEF SURVEY OF NETWORKS

> **TIP**
>
> **Servers** are frequently **used** when **a large number of users** work on a **network**. The server provides the computing function for the network users. Administration of the network is also done by the server, a considerable advantage in a network of more than ten to twenty users. **Windows NT Server** and **Novell Netware** are two products which are often used to run a PC client–server network.

Mr Jones, however, feels that it is too complicated and expensive to run a network with its own dedicated server and the necessary software for his office. Files only occasionally have to be exchanged, and he would like all the computers to be in use. He has just employed Mrs Harrison, and purchased a new computer. So he decides on what is called a workgroup network. Here, too, the computers are linked with each other. Devices such as printers can be connected to any of the PCs, however. Users can allow other network users to share their resources, such as printers. Drives or folders can also be made available for general use.

> **WHAT'S THIS?**
>
> **Resources** in this connection is a collective term for devices or other items which are available on a computer. Devices may for example be printers, floppy disk drives, hard drives or CD-ROM drives. Other items would be folders and the sub-folders within them. It simplifies matters to group them all together under the term **resources**.

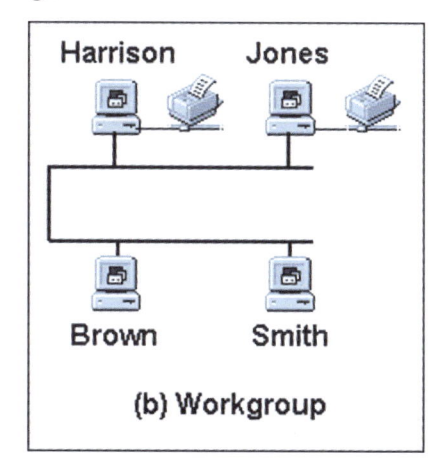

Harrison   Jones

Brown   Smith

(b) Workgroup

> **TIP**
>
> Since networks of this type do not require a dedicated server, they are often installed in smaller work groups such as small firms and departments. All that is needed in practice is a cable, and what is termed a network card for each PC, to connect it to the network. The network functions for workgroup networks are already contained in Windows. This makes it possible to install a network very cheaply. Each user in the network decides which of the resources on their own computer they will share, to make them available for general use on the network. There are problems, though, if too many users try to access one computer, and someone is working on it at the same time. Also, the sharing of resources by more than ten to twenty users can no longer be administered very efficiently.

TIP

To prevent unauthorised access to the server or the workstations, each user must log on using a password (this was mentioned in Chapter 1). User names and passwords offer a way of specifying, for example, who has access to certain drives or printers.

Working on a network

If your computer is connected to a network, it offers some additional functions for accessing the resources. You will notice the first change the moment you start up Windows. On Computers which are being run, say, on a NETWORK, Windows expects you to log on in the Welcome dialog box. This prevents unauthorised users from gaining access to the network. It is possible to bypass logging on by pressing the Esc key, but if you do that, not all Windows functions may be available to you. Here are the steps for logging on:

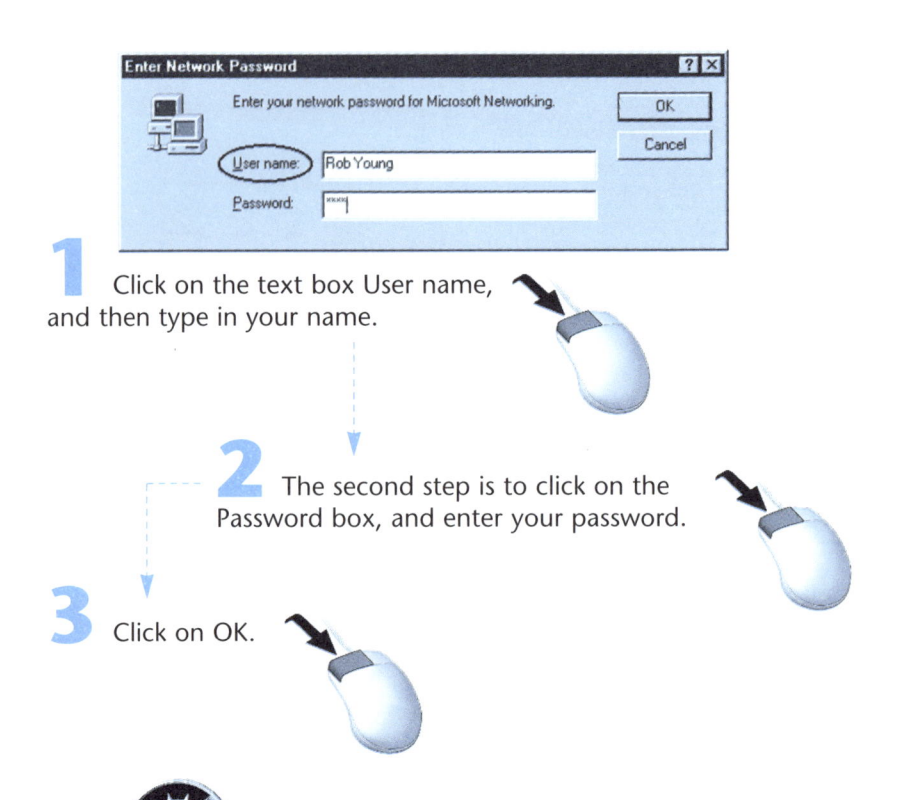

1 Click on the text box User name, and then type in your name.

2 The second step is to click on the Password box, and enter your password.

3 Click on OK.

Working on a Network

The letters of the password are not shown, but simply represented by asterisks (*). This prevents an outsider from being able to read the (secret) password. Once you have typed in your name and password correctly and closed the dialog box by clicking on OK, you are logged on to Windows and the network. (You should not be annoyed if the log-on dialog looks different from the one shown here. It is possible to set this under Windows.)

> **TIP**
>
> Your name and password are saved when you first log on. A second dialog box appears when you do this, where you have to type in the new password again by way of confirmation. Take note of your user name and password, as you will need both when you log on again. In networks, there is usually a particular person, often called a system administrator, who is responsible for the running of the computers. In this case, you need to be allocated a user name and password by the administrator.

The next sections give a concrete description of working with resources in a workgroup network. Using a server, procedures are largely similar. If you encounter difficulties with logging on or using the network functions, ask your system administrator (this is the person who is responsible for the running and administration of the network). This person is normally the one who tells you your user name and (secret) password.

When you have logged on to Windows, the Network Neighborhood icon will appear on the desktop.

This icon gives you access to the resources of other computers on the network, and enables you to use any printers, drives or folders available to you. Procedures for using these are very similar to those for the My Computer window.

Network Neighborhood

1 Double-click the Network Neighborhood icon.

293

Windows will now open the Network Neighborhood window. The structure of this window is like the My Computer window, which is already familiar. You will find a menu bar, a toolbar and a status bar. Working in this window corresponds to using the My Computer window (see Chapter 3).

The only difference will be that the icons in the network neighbourhood look different from the ones in the My Computer window. Whereas in that window you see the drives of your own computer, the Network Neighborhood window contains the resources (that is, the computers or workstations) of the network.

Entire Network   A network can contain a large number of computers. The Entire Network icon shows you the workgroups or servers in the whole of the network.

Texas   The computer icon shows you which server or workstations you can access within your own workgroup.

Each computer (server or workgroup computer) has a unique name, which is used to access it. In the window shown above, for example, you can see the three workstations Director, Sparky and Texas belonging to the current immediate workgroup in a workgroup network.

294

WORKING ON A NETWORK

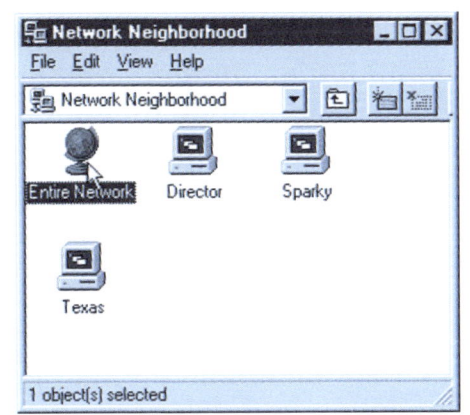

1 Double-click on the Entire Network icon.

The associated window is opened, to display the servers and workgroups of the entire network.

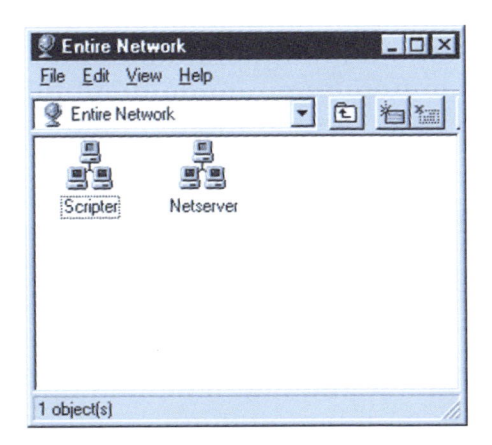

Here, the network contains just two workgroups, with the names Scripter and Netserver.

2 Double-click the icon of a workgroup (here, Scripter was selected).

295

The window now displays all
the computers in the
workgroup (here, this is the
Scripter workgroup,
containing the Director,
Sparky and Texas
workstations).

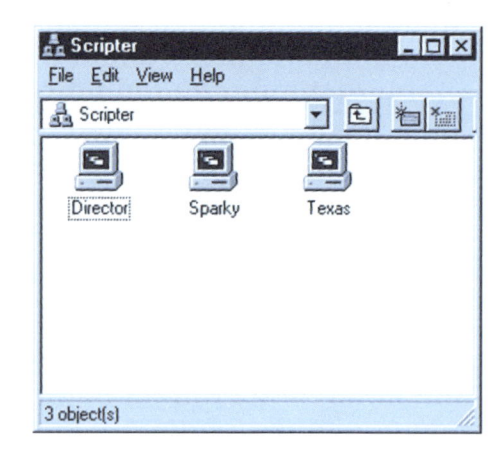

> You will perhaps have noticed that this window is displaying the same computer names as those shown in the Network Neighborhood window. In a workgroup network, different computers (e.g. Sales, Marketing and Development) can be connected to form a workgroup, and each given its own name. You are assigned your computer as a user in a workgroup. You can of course (with the relevant authorisation) access the computers of another workgroup, but you are more often likely to be working with printers or drives on the computers of your own workgroup. Having to select the Entire Network icon every time, followed by your workgroup, would be a tedious way of going about this, so Windows displays the individual computers of your own workgroup in the Network Neighborhood window, to give you quicker access to them.

The following steps show how to access the resources of a workstation in the workgroup. So you can go back to the Network Neighborhood window.

1 Click on the 🔼 button in the toolbar, or press the ⌫ key.

This takes you to the level above whichever one is displayed (to the folder above the file or, here, to the window above this one in the hierarchy, the one with the workgroups).

Working on a Network

2 Double-click the icon for a workstation.

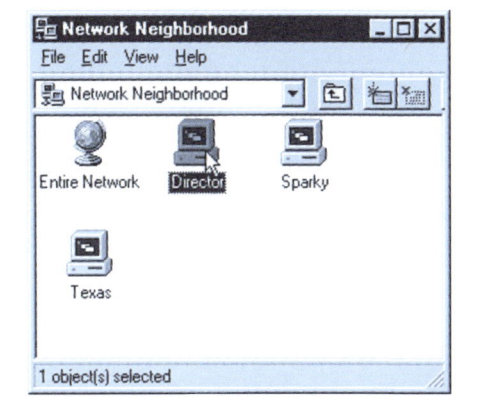

Here, the Director workstation has been selected. The ones in your network will obviously have different names.

The resources of that workstation are now displayed in a window. Only the shared resources, those which have been made available by the user of that workstation for general use on the network, are shown. A computer icon stands for a shared computer or a shared drive on this workstation.

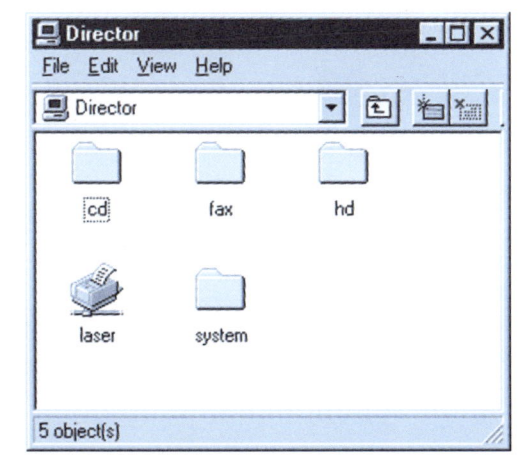

If the computer in question has a printer that is available for general use within the worksgroup, you will see the icon for this.

297

The icon for a drive or computer does not indicate which it actually is. Since you are only interested in the data held in a particular computer, it is not really relevant to know. In Comment column of the Details display, you can find further information about the item, if that information has been provided. This information is typed in when the resource is set up to be shared (see below). If only two folders are shown, it does not mean that these are all that is on the computer; simply that the user has not made the others generally available.

To use a shared resource (for example, a folder), follow these steps:

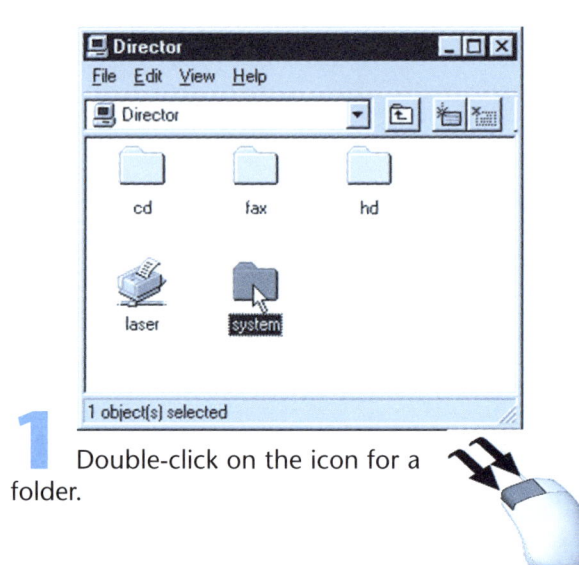

1 Double-click on the icon for a folder.

Here, the folder *system* has been selected.
The next steps depend on whether use of a password has been agreed to allow access to the resource.

298

WORKING ON A NETWORK

Here, a password is required.

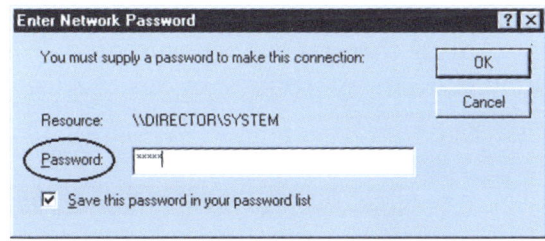

2 Click the Password text box, and type in the password.

3 Click on OK.

Windows now displays the contents of the resource selected (here, the contents of the folder). You can then work with the files and subfolders of the resource.

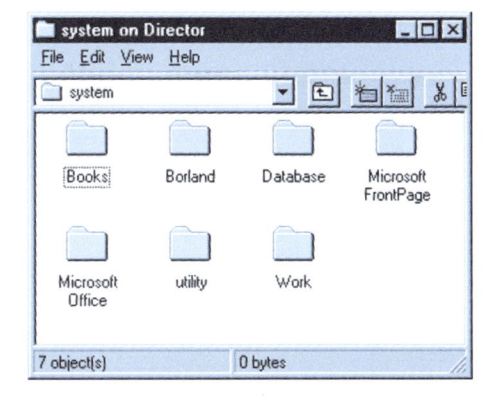

This works in the same way as was shown in Chapter 3, using the example of the My Computer window.(The only difference is that you will not see any drive icons). So you can read folders and files, delete, rename and copy them, or load documents into programs.

However, the owner of a particular resource may well have protected the folders and files from being changed by other users, at the time they were shared. It is possible to make the resource read-only, or to

299

require a special password for write access before any changes can be made. If changes are not permitted, Windows will refuse all attempts to move, rename or delete a file or folder, and will display an error message.

Save As

⚠ \\Director\system\Work\chapter9.txt
This file cannot be accessed.
Make sure that you have security privileges on the network drive.

[OK]

> **CAUTION**
>
> Look out for this when editing files using a program. If you load a letter, for example, from a read-only network resource, you cannot save any changes to this document back into the original file. Windows will block the saving of the document on the resource concerned.

> **TIP**
>
> Using the Network Neighborhood icon on the desktop is not the only way of reaching a resource on a network. Open the list box Change folder in the window displaying the folder or in the Explorer window. In this list box, you will also find the Network Neighbourhood icon, and the icons of any network resources currently in use.

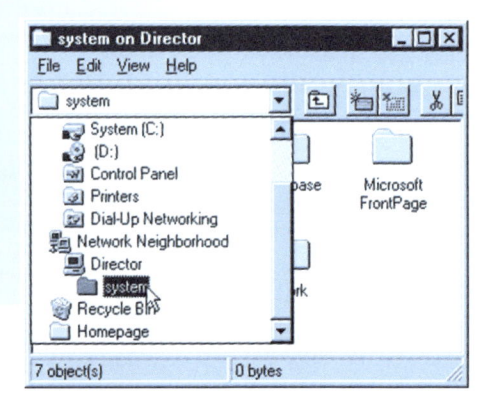

system on Director

File Edit View Help

system

- System (C:)
- (D:)
- Control Panel
- Printers
- Dial-Up Networking
- Network Neighborhood
- Director
  - system
- Recycle Bin
- Homepage

base Microsoft FrontPage

7 object(s)   0 bytes

Mapping and disconnecting network drives

Do you prefer to work with drive icons in the Explorer, or in the My Computer window? Do you still have older programs which do not support access to network resources, or only support it inadequately? 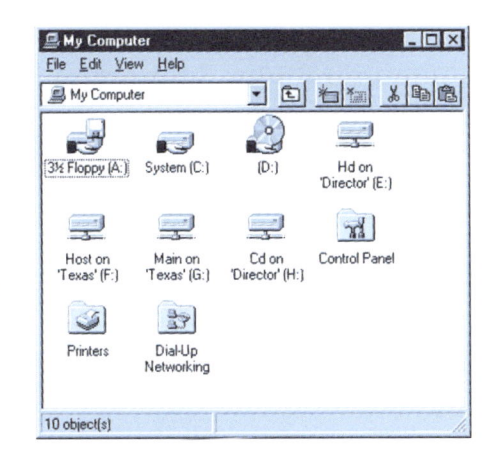
If so, you can allocate a drive name to a shared folder on the network. This drive is displayed in the My Computer folder. The stylised network cable shows you that it is a network resource. To connect ('map') one of these drives to a shared drive or shared folder from another workstation on the network takes just a few steps:

1 Open the window of a folder, or the Explorer window.

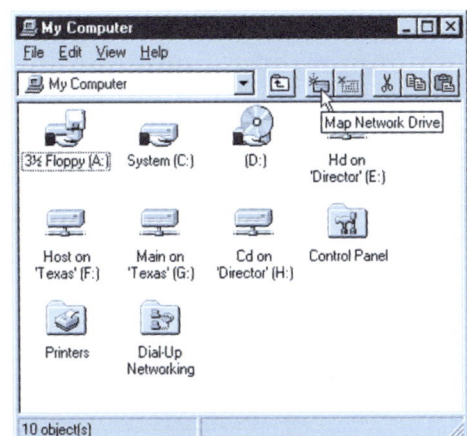

2 Click on the Map Network Drive button on the toolbar.

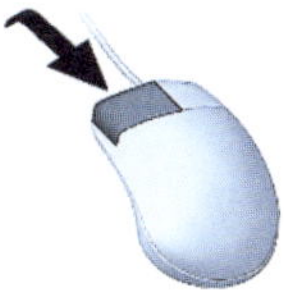

301

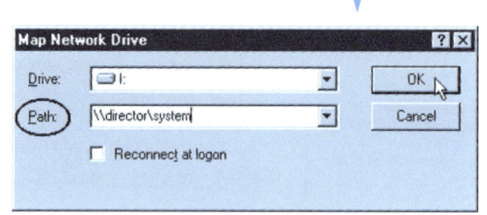

3 In the Drive list box, select a drive letter which is free.

4 In the Path box, enter the path for the network resource.

The path for a network resource is generally given in the form \\computername\folder. So the path for the system folder on the computer called Director, for example, would be \\Director\system.

> If the network resource has already been put on a drive, you can open the Path list box and select the path by clicking on it.
> If you mark the check box 'Reconnect at log-on', Windows will automatically set up the connection when you next restart. However, for this to happen, the network computer involved must be ready for use.

To disconnect an existing connection for a network drive takes just a couple of steps:

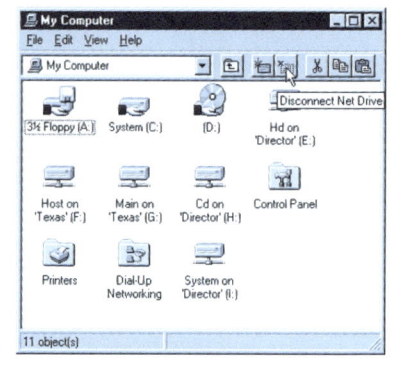

1 In the folder window, click on the button Disconnect Network Drive.

302

PRINTING ON THE NETWORK

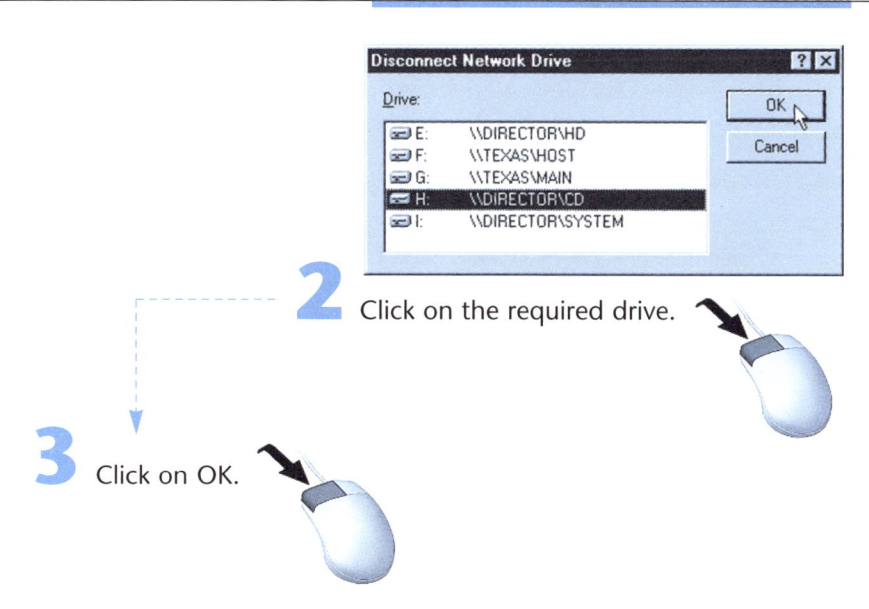

2 Click on the required drive.

3 Click on OK.

Windows breaks the connection to the network resource, and the drive icon disappears from the My Computer folder.

Printing on the network

Does your computer have no printer attached? Or perhaps you wish to use a special printer (e.g. colour printer) to print documents? If your printer is part of a network, you can use any shared printer on the network. Selecting one is as easy as using the local printer attached to your own computer.

1 Click on the PRINT command in the FILE menu of the application window. Alternatively, you can press the key combination Ctrl + P .

303

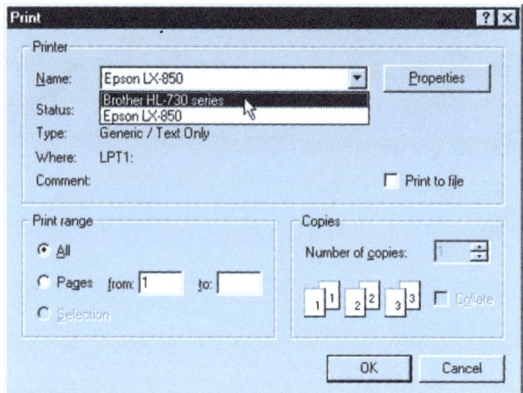

2 In the Print dialog box, click on the Name list box.

3 Select the desired network printer.

4 Click on OK to start printing.

> Before you can use a printer on the network, it must be installed on your computer. If you do not find a network printer in the Name list box, you will first need to install it.

How to install a network printer

In order to use the shared printer of another workstation on the network from your computer, you first have to install it. Here is how you do this:

1 Open the Printers folder (e.g. via the SETTINGS command in the start menu).

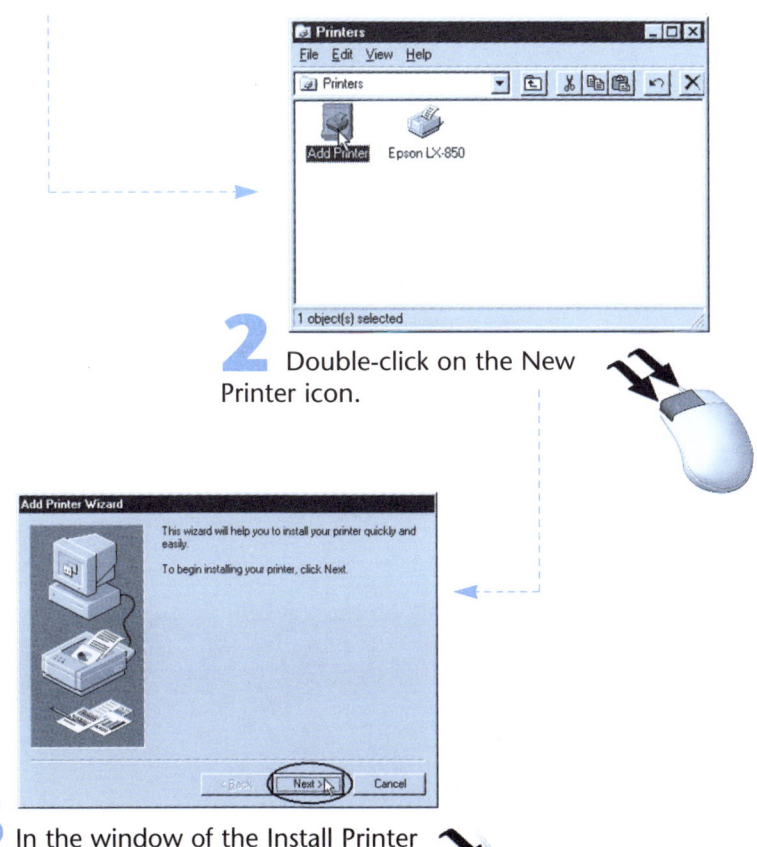

2 Double-click on the New Printer icon.

3 In the window of the Install Printer wizard, click on the Next button.

4 Click on the option Network Printer.

5 Click on the Next button.

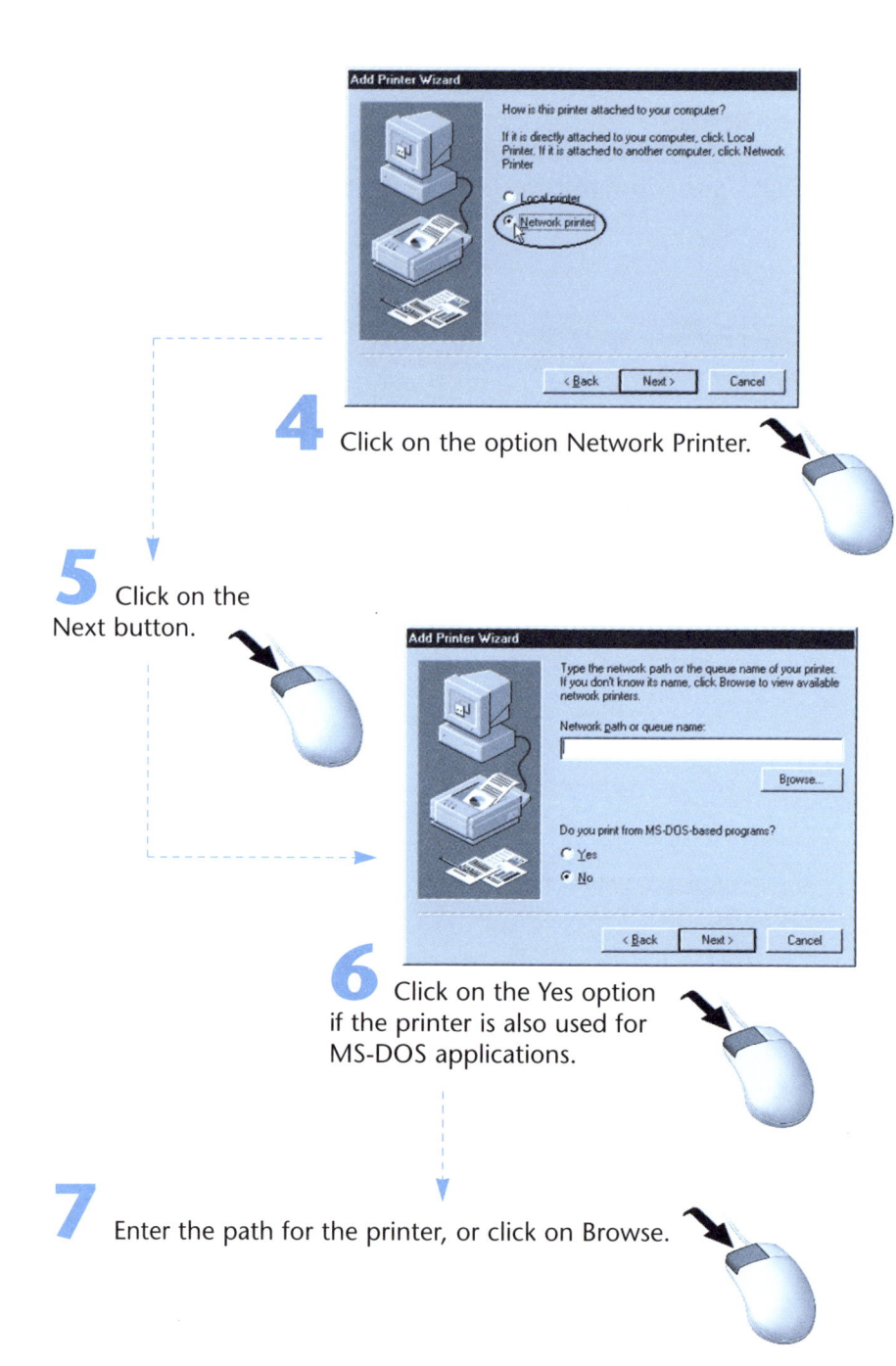

6 Click on the Yes option if the printer is also used for MS-DOS applications.

7 Enter the path for the printer, or click on Browse.

How to Install a Network Printer

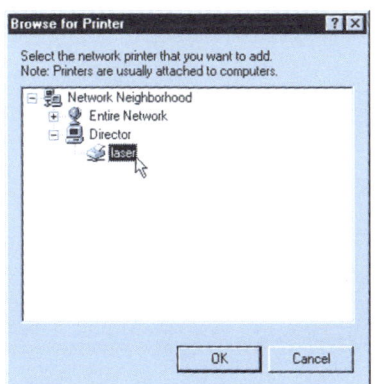

8 If you clicked Browse, look for the printer belonging to the workstation, and mark it with the mouse.

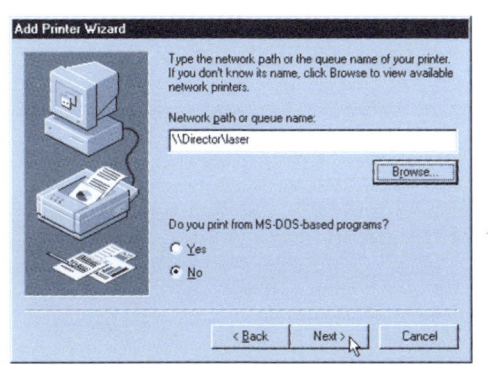

9 Click on OK.

10 When the path for the network printer has been specified, click on Next.

307

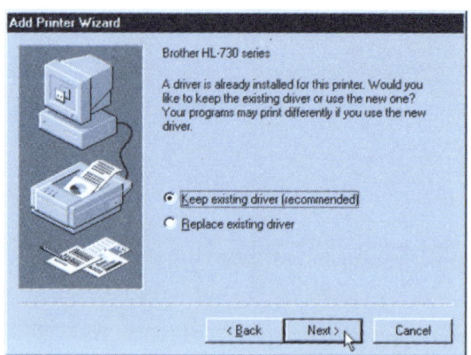

11 Select whether Windows is to use a new printer driver or the existing one.

12 Click on Next.

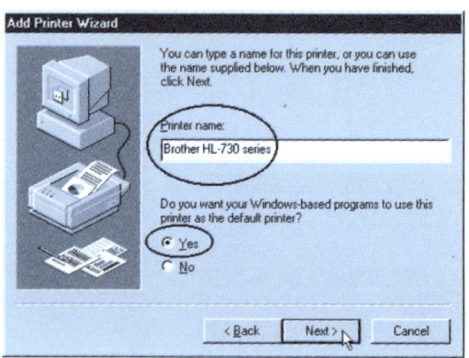

13 If you wish, change the name of the printer.

14 If you intend this printer to be the default printer for all Windows applications, specify this.

15 Click on Next.

308

How to Share a Printer

16 The last step is to select whether you want Windows to print a test page, and then to confirm when the test page has been correctly printed on the chosen network printer.

The last steps are very similar to the procedure described in Chapter 6 for printer installation.

The newly installed network printer is now displayed as an icon in the Printers folder. From now on, you can use this printer just like any other (local) printer.

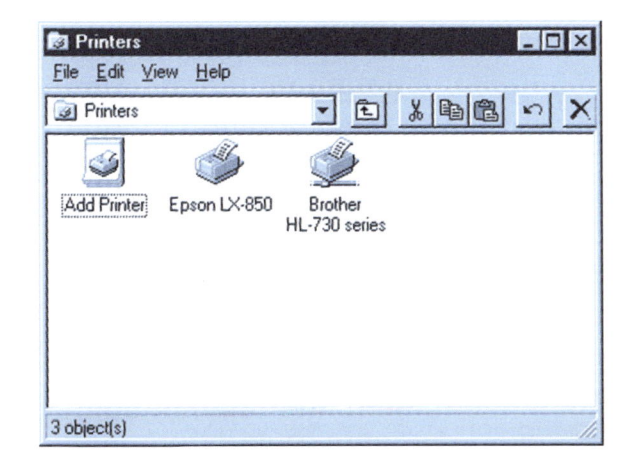

> **Tip**
> If you drag the icon to the desktop, using the right mouse button, and select the command CREATE SHORTCUT(S) HERE in the context menu, the icon will be installed on the desktop. This will enable you to open the window for this printer very quickly, and keep track of the queue of print jobs waiting for the network printer it relates to (see also Chapter 6).

How to share a printer

You can allow others on the network to use the printer attached to your PC. To do this, however, you need to share it.

1 Open the Printers folder.

309

2 Click using the right mouse button on the icon for the printer to be shared.

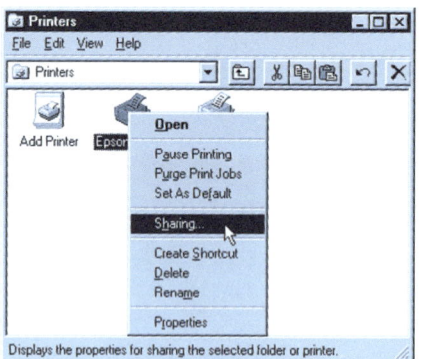

3 Select the command Sharing in the context menu.

The window displaying the properties of this printer is now opened. Only one is of interest in this case, the Sharing tab, which is displayed straight away in the foreground. You need to set the sharing options in the dialog box for this tab.

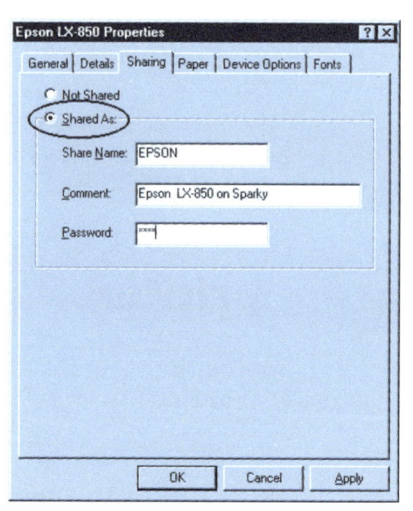

1 Click on the option Shared As.

How to Share a Printer

2 Type in the name for the printer to be shared (maximum 12 characters).

3 Enter a further comment, describing the printer.

4 Specify a password, if one is to be used, and then close the window by clicking on OK.

Windows makes the printer available as a 'share' on the network. A tiny hand appears on the icon for the printer in the Printers folder, to indicate sharing.

To cancel sharing, open the Sharing tab, and select the option Not Shared.

> **TIP**
> The other network users will see the name you have typed in, displayed in the Network Neighbourhood window when they select the computer. If the user selects the Details display, they will also see the comment you typed in. This comment can give further information about the type of printer. If you do not want every user on the network to use the printer, enter a password in the relevant box. When you close the Sharing window, Windows will ask you to reconfirm this password. Other users on the network will see a request for a password when they select that printer. If they do not know the password, they will not be given access to the printer.

> **CAUTION**
> If you have shared your printer on a network, you need to take care over what you do with it. You cannot simply switch it off, to interrupt a print job, for example. It may be another user's print job. Also, if you decide to clear all print jobs (see Chapter 6), you need to check for other users, and inform them if necessary.

Sharing drives and folders for multiple use

You can make an entire drive available for general use on a network, or just one folder (along with the subfolders it contains). This takes just a few steps:

1 In the My Computer window, or another window, click with the right mouse button on the icon for the drive or folder.

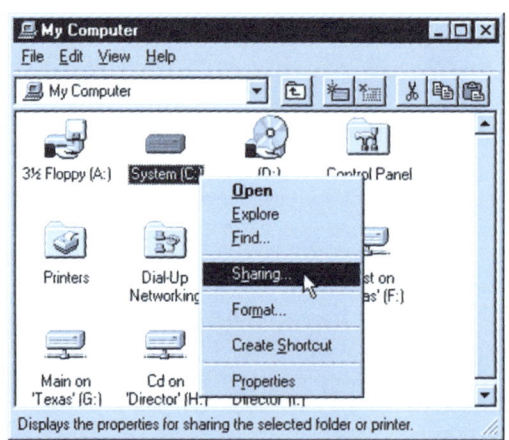

2 In the context menu, select the command Sharing.

Windows will open the Sharing tab. You now specify the options for sharing the drive or folder.

Sharing Drives and Folders for Multiple Use

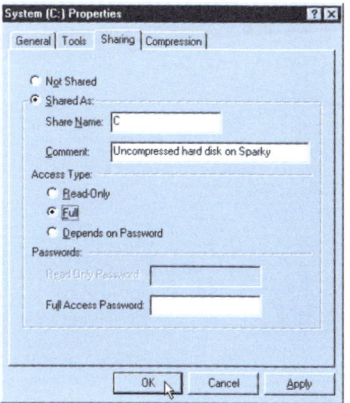

1 Click on the option Shared As.

2 Enter the 'share name' for the drive or folder to be shared.

3 Specify a comment describing the shared resource.

4 Select the type of access, and give the password, if necessary, for access to the resource.

5 Close the dialog box for this tab by clicking on OK.

Windows makes the resource available as a 'share' on the network, with the options you have specified. Shared drives can be recognised by the stylised hand displayed in the left-hand lower corner of the icon.

> **TIP**
> If you select the access type 'Read-only', other users can only ever read, but not change, the data on the shared resource (it is write-protected). If the users do need to change as well as read the data, select one of the other options, 'Full' access, or 'Depends on Password'. You then specify one or two passwords, depending on the option selected. This enables you to allow read-only access to one group of users, and full access under the other password. If you leave the boxes blank, every user on the network can access the resource, and open or change drives or folders. You will find further information about network functions in Windows Help.

313

10

Care of your hard disk and defragmentation

What's in this chapter?

While you are working with programs and files, the data on the hard disk is frequently being changed. Errors may arise, which can even sometimes lead to the loss of data. You will find out in this chapter how to use a program to scan drives for errors, so as to locate and correct, and avoid loss of data. You will also discover how to clean up the hard disk with a defragmenting program. This enables Windows to read and save files more quickly.

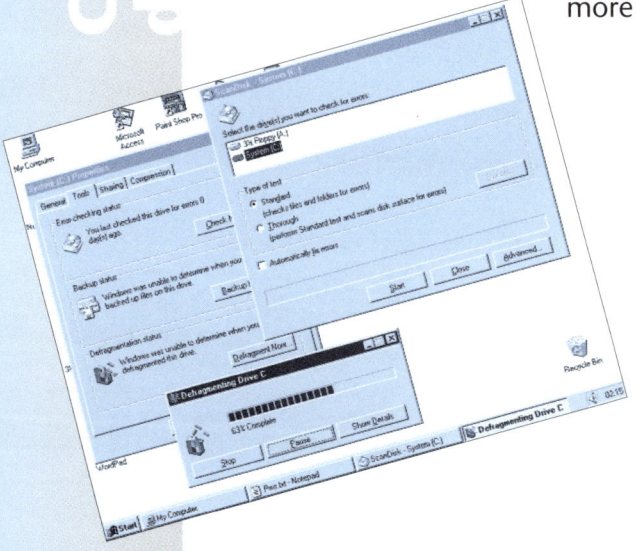

Your Progress Meter

You already know:

Starting a program	47
Closing a program	53
Displaying drives, files and folders	68
How much data is stored on a disk	106

Your are going to learn:

Scanning drives for errors	316
Defragmenting drives	321

Scanning drives for errors

Chapter 3 showed how to work with drives and floppy disks. If you look back at this chapter, you will see that, when you format a floppy disk, a summary of the disk data is displayed. This summary may also give a figure for the number of defective sectors. These are areas of the disk where data cannot be saved.
What applies to floppy disks can also apply to other drives, such as hard disks. A hard disk may display damaged areas, for example, a defective directory, etc. A whole variety of causes may be to blame:

- The hard disk is damaged in places, and cannot accept data in that location (this can happen, if, for instance, you 'quickly' try to move the computer while it is on, or give it an accidental hard blow with your knee).

- The computer may be switched off without exiting Windows first, or a power cut may have the same effect.

- Sometimes, a program may even fail to work (it is said to have 'crashed'), and you can only make the computer work at all by switching it off and on again.

These and other factors gradually develop into errors on the hard disk or file system.

> Windows uses a particular file system for saving folders and files on a hard disk or a floppy disk. The file system determines how the data are saved. Thus the file system groups together the file and folder names in a directory. The file system also determines that filenames may have up to 255 characters. Since filenames in older DOS versions consisted only of eight characters, plus a full stop and three characters for the filename extension, Windows additionally saves these short filenames (also called '8.3' filenames) on the hard disk. The actual data of the files are saved in blocks, also called sectors, on the medium. The data system notes which sectors are used, and which files they belong to. But the situation can arise where the hard disk has occupied sectors which do not belong to any file (known as cross-linked clusters), or where the long and short filenames do not match.

SCANNING DRIVES FOR ERRORS

These and other errors lead to problems as time goes on. So you need to detect such errors, and correct them if necessary, using the programs which exist for the purpose.

1 In the My Computer window, click on the icon for the drive you wish to scan.

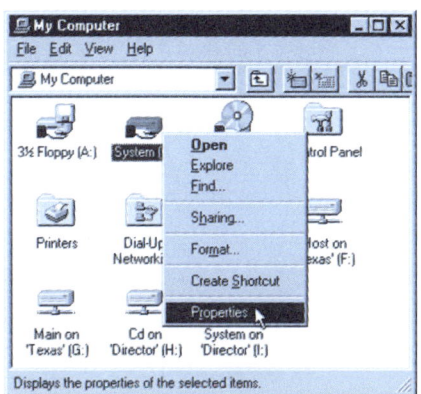

2 In the context menu, select the command PROPERTIES.

3 Select the Extras tab.

> **TIP**
> The dialog box for the Extras tab shows you the state of the drive, as regards the last error scan, the backup status and the last time defragmenting was carried out.

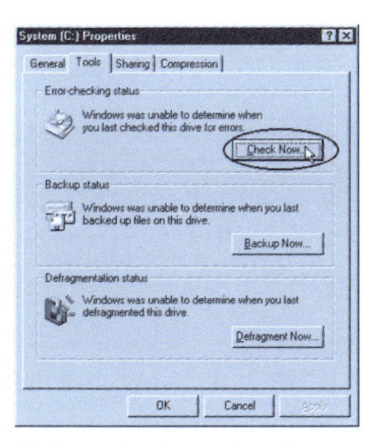

4 Click on the Scan Now button.

317

Windows starts up the ScanDisk program, which displays this window.

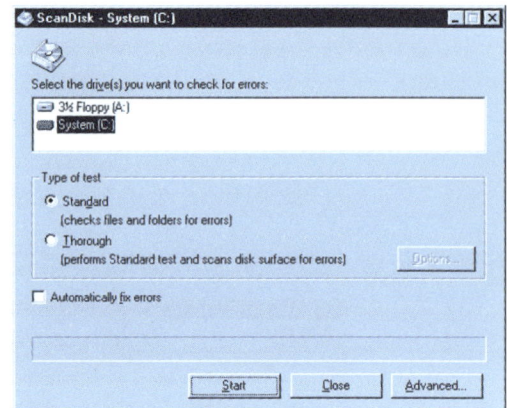

1 Change the selection of drive to be scanned, if necessary.

2 Click on the Standard Testing option.

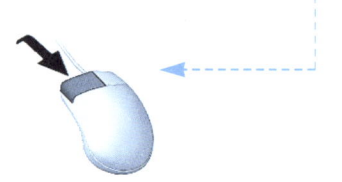

The ScanDisk window contains the Advanced Testing option, which allows you to access a window with additional options.

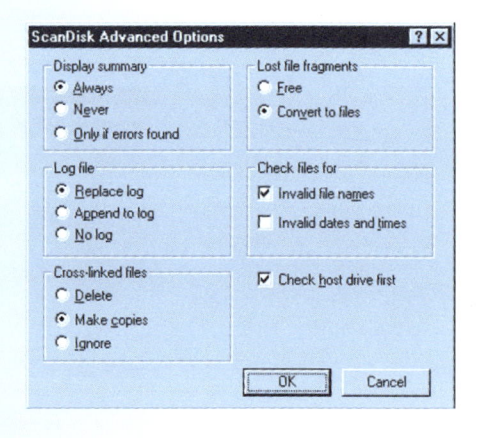

3 If necessary, specify the further options.

318

SCANNING DRIVES FOR ERRORS

4 Click the Start button to begin the scan.

The window's progress display shows you how the scan is progressing.

If ScanDisk finds errors on the drive, a window appears with message about this.

In the example shown here, errors have been found.

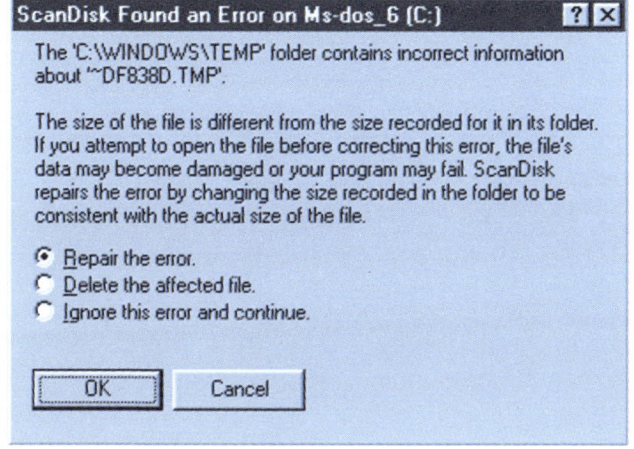

> **ScanDisk Found an Error on Ms-dos_6 (C:)**
>
> The 'C:\WINDOWS\TEMP' folder contains incorrect information about '~DF838D.TMP'.
>
> The size of the file is different from the size recorded for it in its folder. If you attempt to open the file before correcting this error, the file's data may become damaged or your program may fail. ScanDisk repairs the error by changing the size recorded in the folder to be consistent with the actual size of the file.
>
> ● Repair the error.
> ○ Delete the affected file.
> ○ Ignore this error and continue.
>
> [OK]   [Cancel]

1 Click on an option to select how the error is to be corrected.

2 Confirm your choice by clicking on OK.

> The safest option is to save sectors with errors in files. You will find these files afterwards in the main folder of the drive, with names like File001.chk, File002.chk etc. If you have any lost texts, you may be able to rescue them out of these files. Otherwise, you can delete the files.
> Sometimes, when the scan program is started, Windows displays a message that the medium is blocked. You should then close the window with the drive from which you opened the properties sheet.

319

At the end of the scan, a summary of the data medium is displayed.

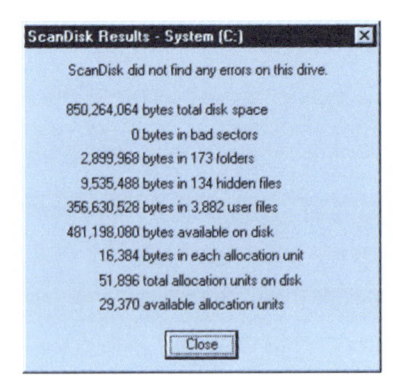

```
ScanDisk Results - System (C:)

ScanDisk did not find any errors on this drive.

850,264,064 bytes total disk space
         0 bytes in bad sectors
 2,899,968 bytes in 173 folders
 9,535,488 bytes in 134 hidden files
356,630,528 bytes in 3,882 user files
481,198,080 bytes available on disk
    16,384 bytes in each allocation unit
    51,896 total allocation units on disk
    29,370 available allocation units

            [ Close ]
```

Various options are available to specify whether the summary appears, and how the scan is carried out.

If you select the option Thorough in the ScanDisk window, a test of the surface of the storage medium will also be carried out.

This test detects not only errors in the file system, but also defective areas on the floppy/hard disk. If the Thorough testing option is selected, the following window can be opened using the Options button.

In this dialog box, you can choose the areas which ScanDisk will include when testing the surface.

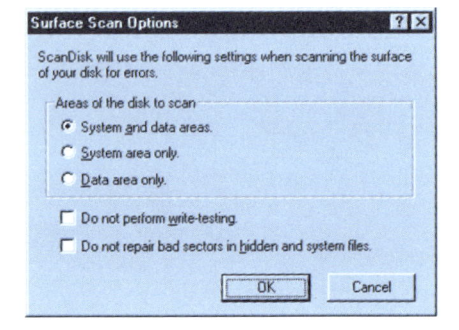

```
Surface Scan Options

ScanDisk will use the following settings when scanning the surface
of your disk for errors.

 Areas of the disk to scan
   (•) System and data areas.
   ( ) System area only.
   ( ) Data area only.

   [ ] Do not perform write-testing.
   [ ] Do not repair bad sectors in hidden and system files.

              [   OK   ]   [ Cancel ]
```

> **TIP:** You should scan the drives of your computer for this type of error on a regular schedule. This prevents loss of data, and means that problems with a hard disk or drive are identified at the start.

Defragmenting drives

A floppy disk or hard disk is subdivided into separate blocks. These blocks are used by the file system to save files. When it does so, the file system always uses free blocks for the file data. If you change or delete files, this leads to a situation where a file rarely occupies adjacent blocks. Instead, the data of that file are scattered 'randomly' over the blocks of the hard disk. The effect of this is that Windows becomes slower and slower in reading and saving files.
(All the separate blocks that go to make up the file first have to be looked for.) There is, however, a program which reorganises, or 'defragments', the files on a hard disk. The program arranges the data of the files so that they are located in neighbouring blocks.
To defragment a drive, these are the steps to take:

1 Open a window which displays the drive.

2 Click with the right mouse button on the icon for the drive.

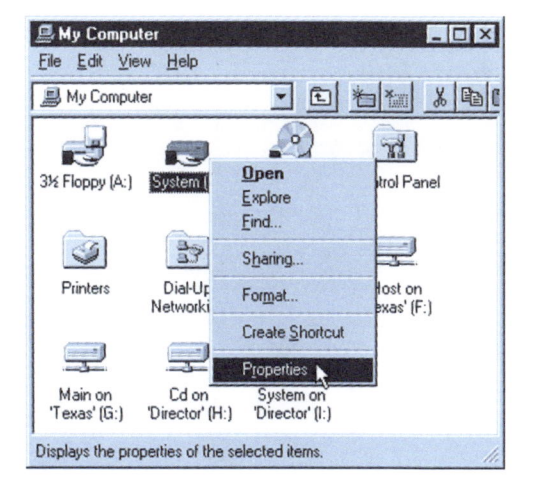

3 Select the command PROPERTIES.

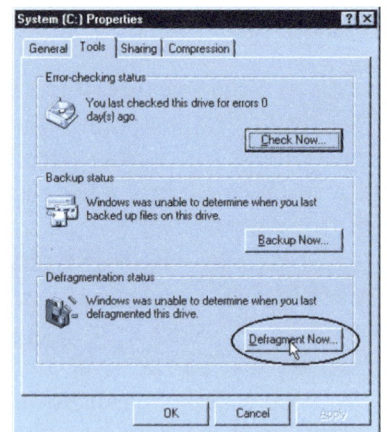

4 In the Extras dialog box, click on the Defragment Now button.

The defragmenting program now checks to what extent the files are distributed in blocks scattered across the hard disk. This scattering is called fragmentation.
If defragmentation will help, this is shown in the Defragmenting dialog box.

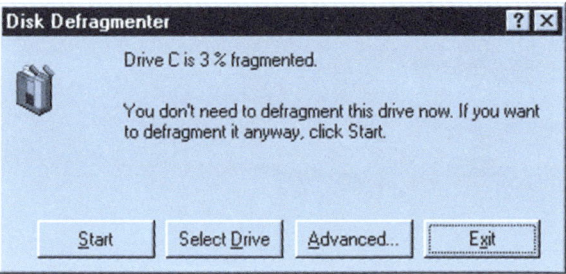

1 Click on the Start button to begin defragmenting.

DEFRAGMENTING DRIVES

TIP

The Advanced button enables you to choose the method of defragmentation. The default setting Complete Defragmenting takes longest, but produces the best results. But you can opt for it to group together only the free memory or only the files. This is quicker.

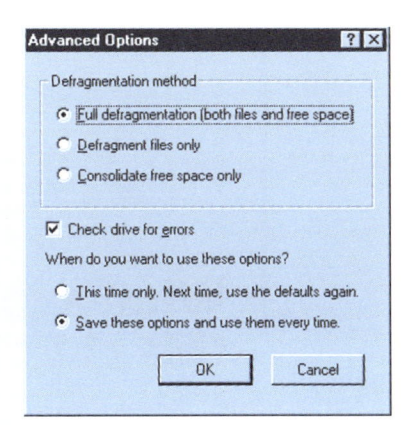

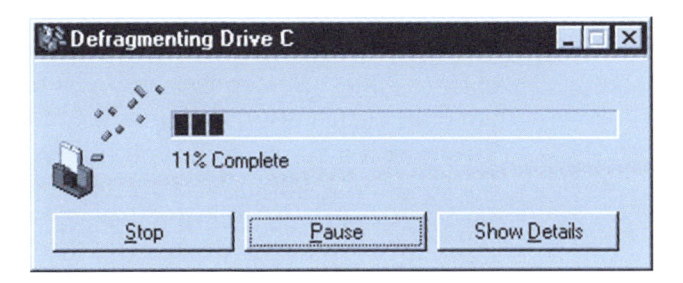

The status of the defragmenting process is displayed in the dialog box shown here. You can pause or end defragmentation as necessary, but only by using the buttons provided, not by switching off the computer!

CAUTION

A drive can only be defragmented if it is error-free. So you will, if necessary, need to scan for errors before defragmenting.

323

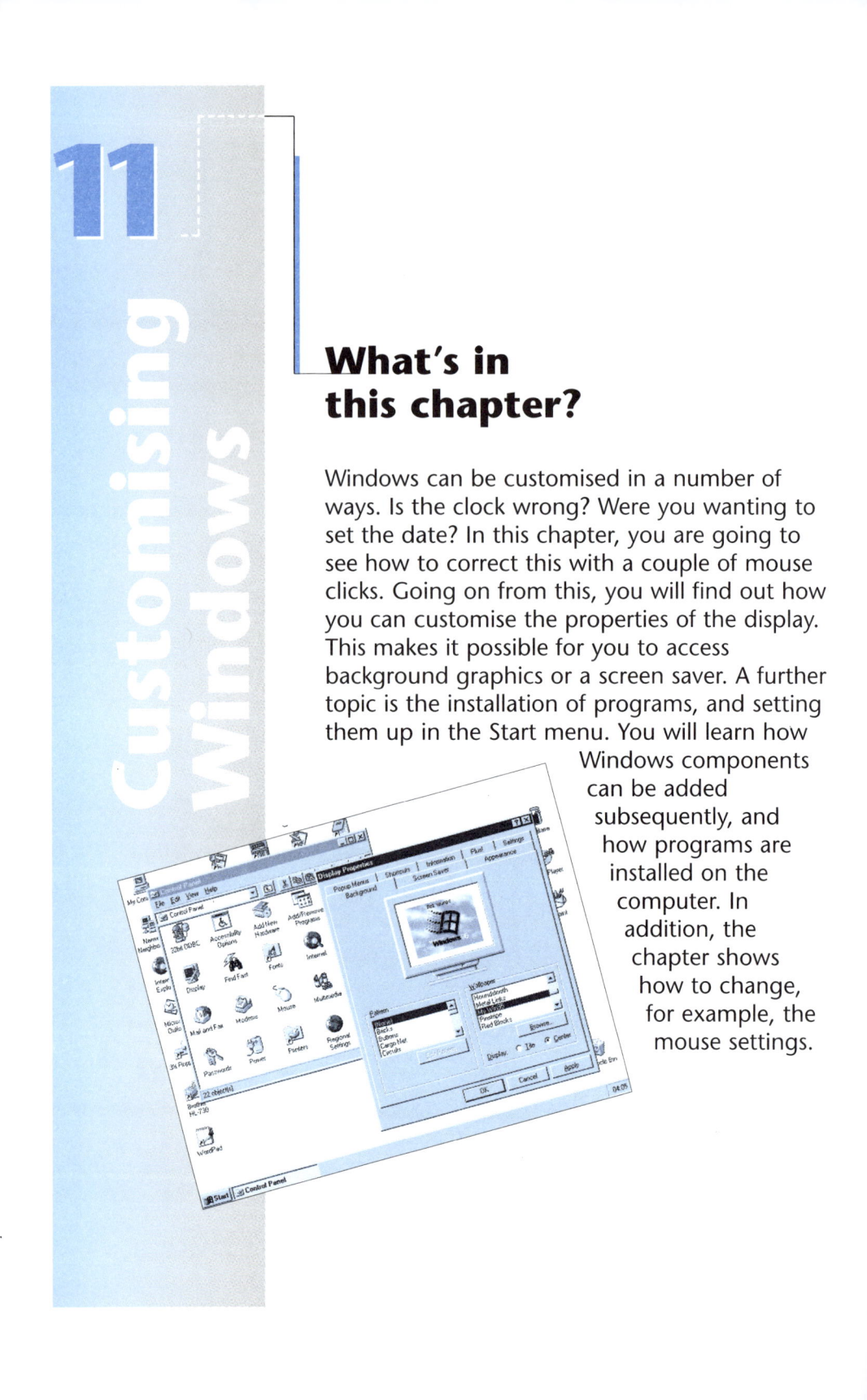

11

Customising Windows

What's in this chapter?

Windows can be customised in a number of ways. Is the clock wrong? Were you wanting to set the date? In this chapter, you are going to see how to correct this with a couple of mouse clicks. Going on from this, you will find out how you can customise the properties of the display. This makes it possible for you to access background graphics or a screen saver. A further topic is the installation of programs, and setting them up in the Start menu. You will learn how Windows components can be added subsequently, and how programs are installed on the computer. In addition, the chapter shows how to change, for example, the mouse settings.

Your Progress Meter

You already know:

Working with the mouse	17
Working with windows	23
Using the Start menu	46
Starting a program	47
Closing a program	53

Your are going to learn:

Setting the time and date	326
Changing the desktop background	330
Installing a screen saver	336
Changing the screen resolution	338
Installing Windows components	341
Installing programs	344
Changing the Start menu	346
Installing a program icon on the desktop	350
Installing DOS programs	352
Installing the mouse	356

325

Setting the time and date

Windows displays the time in the lower right-hand corner, and will also display the date on demand. You learnt this back in Chapter 1. But if the time or the date is wrong, what do you do? The problem is not a major one. All you need is couple of mouse clicks to put the clock right and set the date.

1 Double-click on the time displayed in the lower right-hand corner of the taskbar.

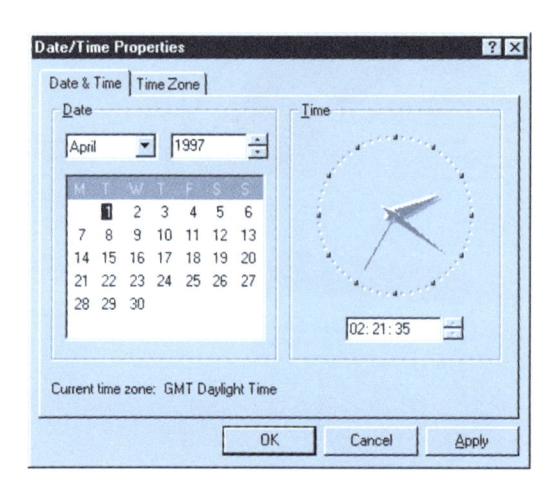

Windows opens the dialog box, displaying the current time, and the calendar, showing month and year.

To set the time, proceed as follows:

1 Click on the figures for the hours, minutes or seconds in the time display box.

SETTING THE TIME AND DATE

2 Enter the new figures. Alternatively, adjust the time by clicking on the two arrow buttons of the spin box.

3 Click on either the OK or the Apply button.

The clock face will display the time you have just set.

> **CAUTION**
> When you open the Date and Time tab, the time keeps running. You can tell this from the second hand ticking round. When you set the figures in the time display box, the clock stops until you click either OK or Apply.

To reset the date, you need to follow these steps:

1 Check the year display box, and adjust if necessary. You simply need to click on the arrow buttons of the spin box, by the year display.

2 If necessary, open the list box for the month.

327

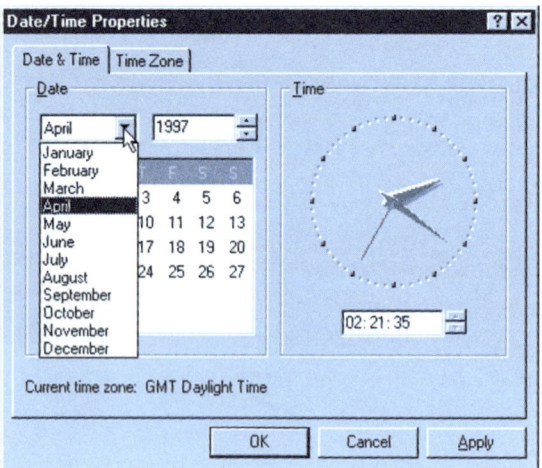

3 Click on the month which you want to enter.

The day is indicated by a coloured background for that date.

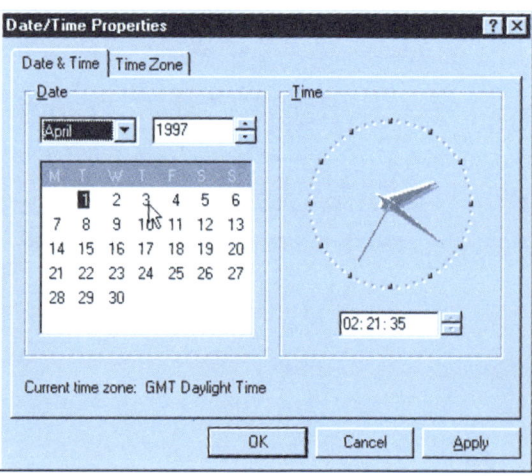

4 Now click on the required day of the week.

328

SETTING THE TIME AND DATE

5 Close the dialog box by clicking on OK.

> **TIP**
> You can use the Date and Time tab to find out which day of the week a particular date will fall on (between 1980 and 2099). You simply have to alter the year and the month. As soon as you alter the year, using the arrow buttons of the spin box, the right days of the week for that year will be displayed in the calendar. If you use the Cancel button to close the dialog box for this tab, the date set will be the actual current date.

The date/time dialog box has a second tab, which you can use to set the required time zone. This time zone also controls how the date and time are displayed. For Dublin, Edinburgh, London and Lisbon, Greenwich Mean Time is displayed. If you wish to alter the time zone, this is the procedure:

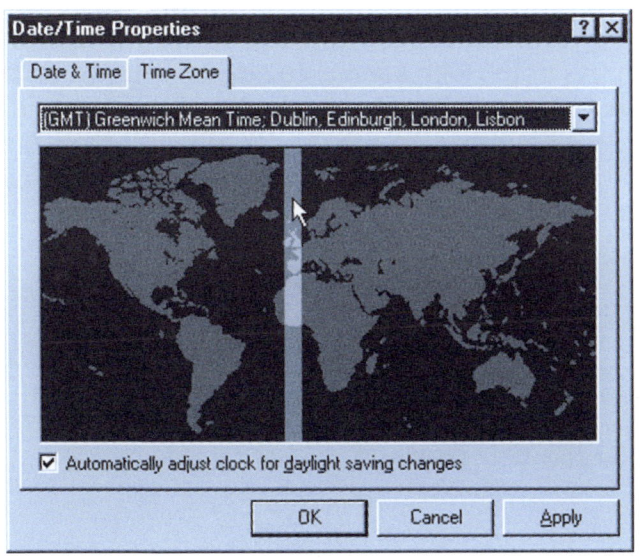

1 Point at the band with the light background.

329

2 Drag the band on the map in the required direction.

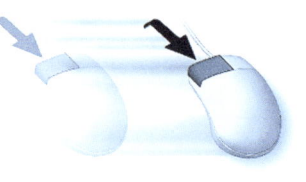

3 Click on the Apply button to set the time zone.

An alternative way of accessing the time zone is by using the list box in the tab for this feature. Opening the list box displays a series of predefined time zones, with the names of well-known cities in that time zone.

Changing the desktop background

The Windows desktop can be displayed with a white background (as in this book) with various colours or patterns or, if you like, with 'wallpaper'. This makes it possible to produce a desktop designed to suit your wishes. You could, for instance, scan in a holiday photograph and display it on the screen.

> Menu is a term you will often encounter in Windows. It is a small window, listing various topics. You can choose from it as you would from a restaurant menu. In Windows, you click an entry to choose it. You can use the Start menu to start programs or other Windows functions (see Chapter 2)

CHANGING THE DESKTOP BACKGROUND

Following installation, Windows will probably display a dark green desktop background. In this book, though, a white background was used because the icons stand out more clearly on it. If you would like to change the colour of your desktop background, this is how to go about it:

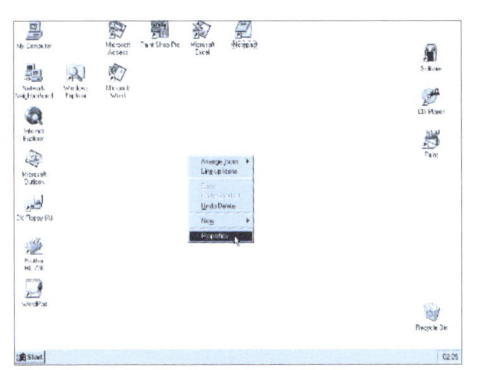

1 Click on an empty area of the desktop, using the right mouse button.

2 In the context menu, select the command PROPERTIES.

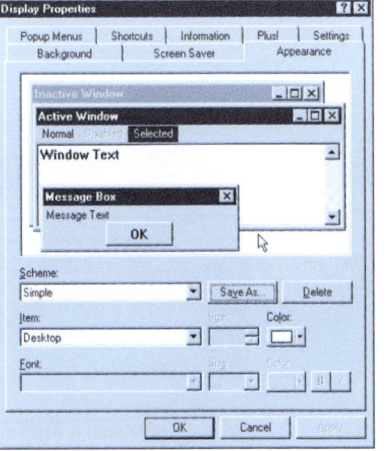

3 Click the Appearance tab.

4 A window displays a preview of the various window contents. Click on the area of this window which has the current background colour.

331

The word Desktop should appear in the Item box. If it does not, select it in the list box under Item.

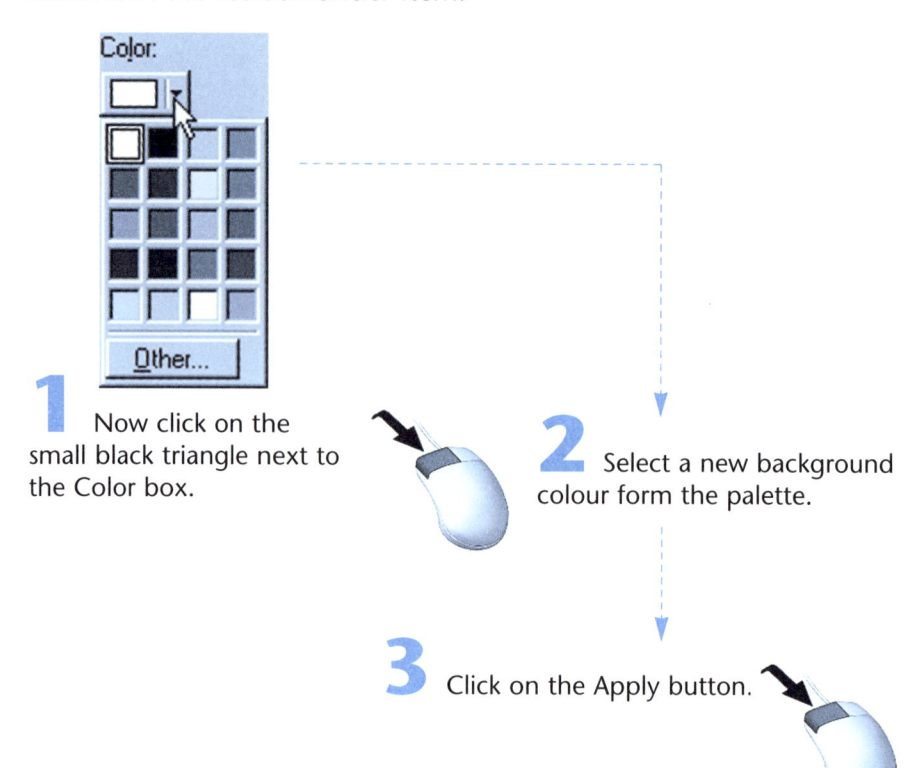

1 Now click on the small black triangle next to the Color box.

2 Select a new background colour form the palette.

3 Click on the Apply button.

Windows will then change the desktop colour to the one you have chosen.

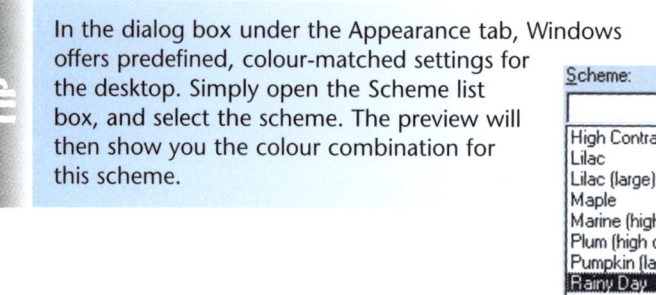

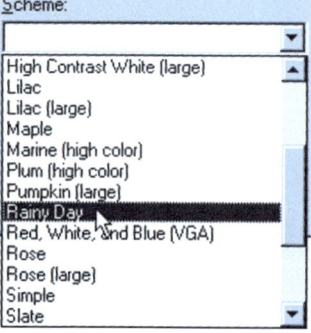

> **TIP**
> In the dialog box under the Appearance tab, Windows offers predefined, colour-matched settings for the desktop. Simply open the Scheme list box, and select the scheme. The preview will then show you the colour combination for this scheme.

Changing the Desktop Background

Your options include not only a single-colour background, but also patterns, and pictures ('wallpaper'). Choosing a pattern or wallpaper is easy. It simply involves saving the wallpaper in the Windows folder as the file type .bmp. Follow these steps to create a desktop background with a pattern or wallpaper:

1 Click on an empty area of the desktop, using the right mouse button.

2 In the context menu, select the command PROPERTIES.

3 Click the Background tab.

These steps are essentially the same as the procedure for changing the background colour, except that a different tab is used. The dialog box under the Background tab shows you a stylised image of a screen with a preview of the pattern or wallpaper you have chosen. You will also see two list boxes, for you to select patterns or wallpaper. The following steps enable you to choose one:

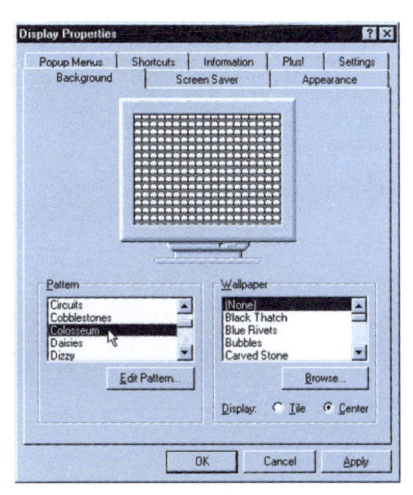

1 Look for a pattern you want in the Pattern list box.

333

2 Click on the relevant entry.

3 If you like the pattern, click on the Apply button, or on OK.

Here you see a desktop with background brick pattern. The icon titles appear in the colour you have selected for the background (see above).

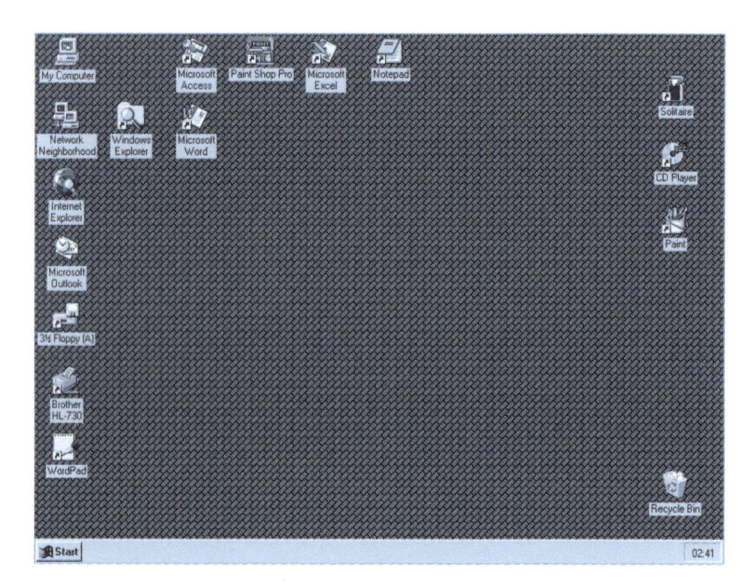

> As you can see from this example, a screen with a background pattern is less legible and less easy to manage. If you work at the computer for long periods, you might decide to do without background patterns. The white background used in this book is the easiest to work with.

CHANGING THE DESKTOP BACKGROUND

As an alternative, you could display a picture as wallpaper on the desktop background. Windows has some .bmp files which can be used as background wallpaper. But you can choose others. They can even be created or edited in the Windows program Paint. The following steps enable you to use a wallpaper:

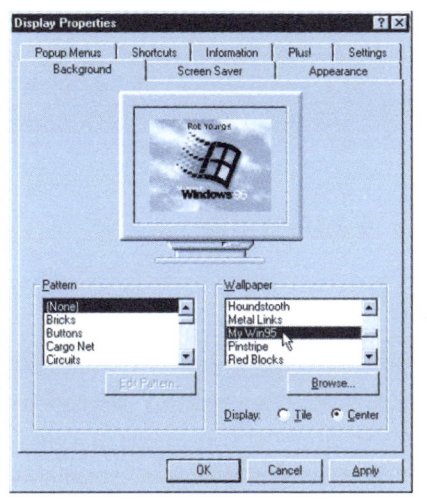

1 Click the Background tab.

2 Select the picture you want from the Wallpaper list box, and click on the relevant name.

3 If you like the wallpaper, click on the Apply button, or on OK.

Windows will now display the picture you chose as the background wallpaper for your desktop. Here, the Windows logo which was modified in Chapter 4 is used as the background.

335

To remove patterns or wallpaper, repeat the steps just shown, and set the option for the pattern or wallpaper in the Background dialog box to None.

> If the picture you have selected is a type of pattern, select the option Tile in the Background dialog box. Windows will then use it in a tiled arrangement across the whole desktop. If, on the other hand, it is an image (such as a holiday photograph), mark the Center option. If the image is smaller than the desktop, Windows will then place it in the centre. You can look for picture files in other folders, by using the Browse button.

Installing a screen saver

Windows offers a SCREEN SAVER function. This is a program which recognises when the computer has not been used for a length of time (that is, when nothing has been entered using the keyboard or mouse). The program then changes from the desktop display to a moving design of your choice. Depending on the monitor being used, this can be switched to energy-saving mode after a certain period.

> Older screens sometimes have burned-in 'patterns', which can be seen when the screen is off. The screen saver is designed to prevent the pattern of images which are often displayed (e.g. the desktop) being 'burned in' in this way.

To use one of the Windows screen savers, you first need to configure it. You do this in a similar way to changing the wallpaper:

1 Click on an empty area of the desktop, and in the context menu, select the command PROPERTIES.

INSTALLING A SCREEN SAVER

2 Select the Screen Saver tab.

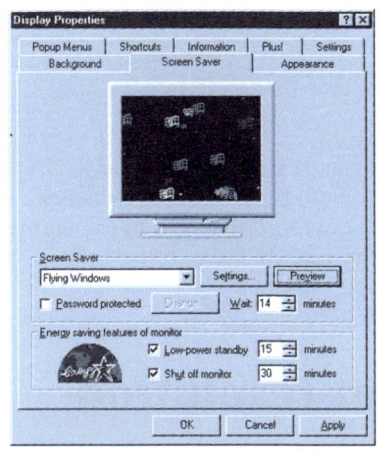

This dialog box lists the options from which to choose your screen saver.

1 Open the Screen Saver list box, and click on your chosen entry.

2 Enter how long you want the screen saver to wait (in minutes) in the Wait box.

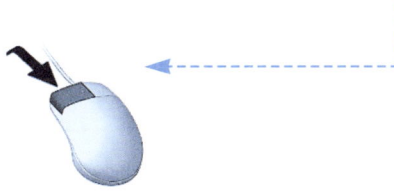

3 Click on OK.

Windows will now apply your settings for the screen saver. It will be activated when the screen has been idle for the waiting time you set. When you press a key or move the mouse, the previous desktop display reappears, and you can continue working on your computer.

337

> The images used for the screen saver are displayed for preview when they are selected in the Screen Saver dialog box. If you click on the Preview button in this dialog box, the selected screen saver will be displayed full-screen. Simply moving the mouse will return you to the dialog box. You can set various options via the Settings button, depending on the screen saver chosen.
> If your monitor supports energy-saving functions, the options in the 'Screen Energy-saving functions' group become available. You can choose and set the time period before these functions come into effect.

> The Password Protected check box allows you to activate the use of a password for the screen saver. The password can be set using the Change button. If this option is on, you will need a password to return to the normal desktop from the screen saver. It is therefore wiser to leave the option switched off, or to be suitably cautious about setting it.

Changing the screen resolution

Windows allows you to select the screen resolution. The higher the resolution, the more items there will be room for on the desktop. On the other hand, as screen resolution increases, the desktop items and windows will become smaller. The standard resolution setting following installation of Windows is 640 x 480 pixels. However, depending on the size of monitor being used, and the built-in video adaptor, you can set higher resolutions.

> The screen contents are displayed using a pattern of coloured dots, arranged in rows. The number of coloured dots per row, and the number of rows, is called the (screen) resolution.

To do this, carry out the following steps:

1 Click with the right mouse button on an empty area of the desktop, and select the command Properties in the context menu.

CHANGING THE SCREEN RESOLUTION

2 In the Display Properties sheet, select the Settings tab.

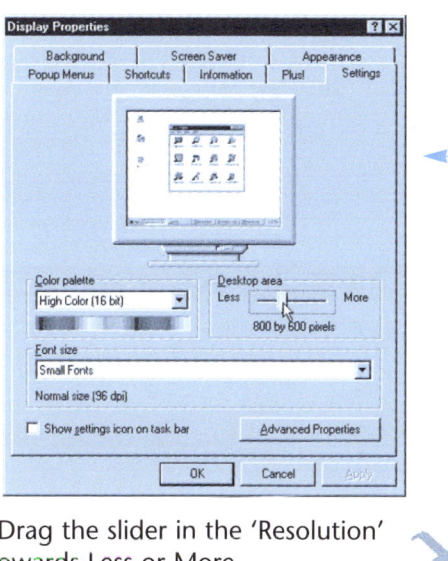

3 Drag the slider in the 'Resolution' area towards Less or More.

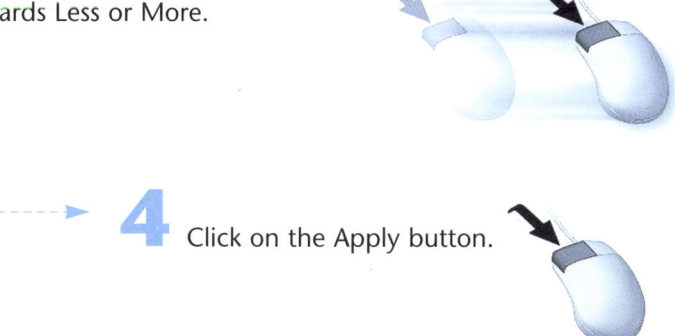

4 Click on the Apply button.

In step 3, you can only select resolutions which are actually supported by the video adaptor built into the computer. Windows has to switch over the display to alter the resolution.
For this reason, a number of dialog boxes are shown before and while the switching over occurs. Select the buttons in the dialog boxes in each case.

339

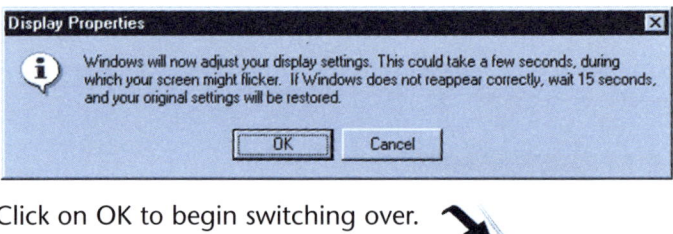

1 Click on OK to begin switching over.

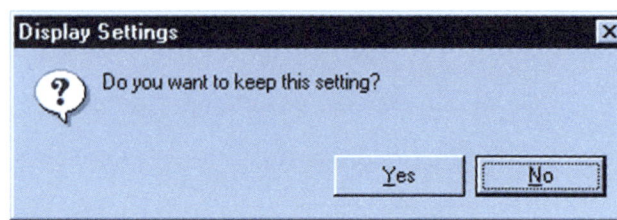

2 When the resolution has been switched over, this dialog box appears. Select Yes to preserve the new resolution.

3 If the desktop is not properly displayed using the new resolution, select the No button.

If the screen remains dark after switching over, or if you can make nothing out, you need wait only 15 seconds. Then Windows automatically switches back to the old resolution.

> **TIP**
> Where the switch of resolution has been successfully carried out, you should try out whether the new resolution is easy to work with. Especially at high resolutions, the icons and texts become very difficult to read. A lower resolution of 640 x 480 or possibly 800 x 600 pixels is then preferable.

Installing Windows components

Windows is installed with certain programs and functions as standard (this is mostly carried out when the computer is still at the manufacturer's). Possibly, on your system, certain functions (e.g. games, desktop backgrounds, screen savers, etc.) are missing. If you have the Windows CD-ROM, you can still very easily install these later.

1 Insert the Windows CD-ROM into the drive.

2 If Windows opens the CD-ROM 'Welcome window', this can be closed straight away.

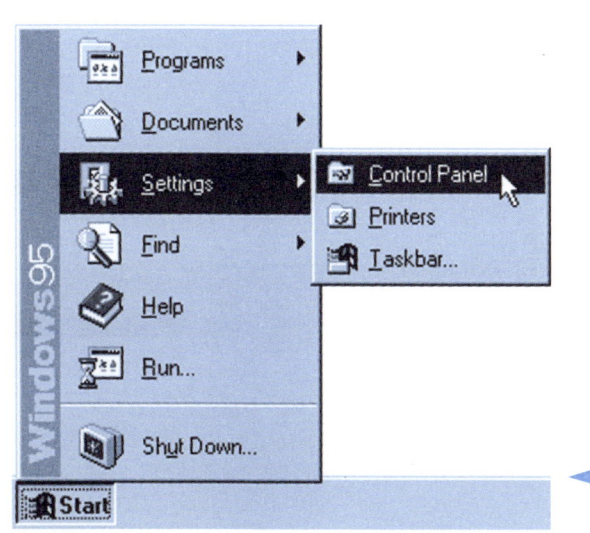

3 In the Start menu, click on the command SETTINGS/CONTROL PANEL.

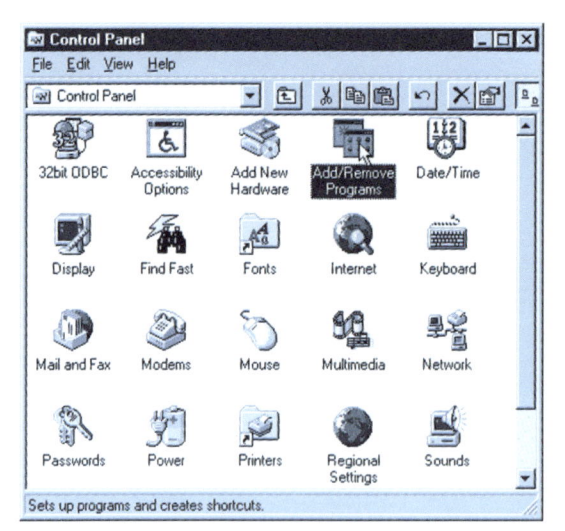

4 In the Control Panel window, double-click on the Software icon.

5 Select the Windows Setup tab.

Under this tab, you will see the individual groups of components which it is possible to install or delete subsequently in Windows. If there is a tick in the check box in front of a particular entry in this list, then at least one component from that group has been installed.

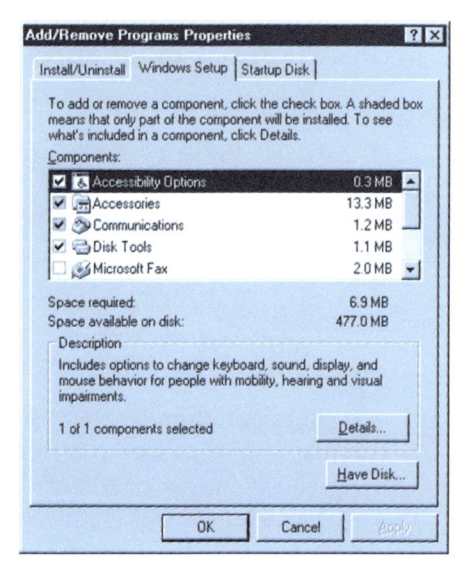

INSTALLING WINDOWS COMPONENTS

To select the components of a group, carry out the following steps:

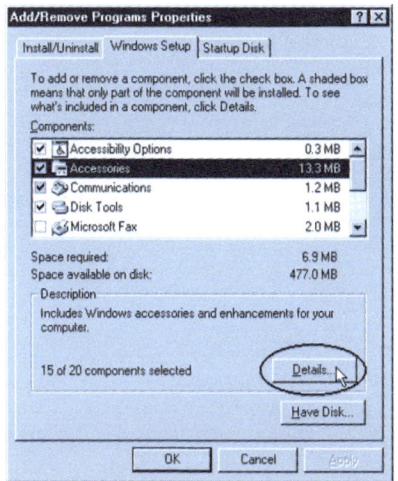

1 Mark the check box of the component you want in the dialog box for the Windows Setup tab.

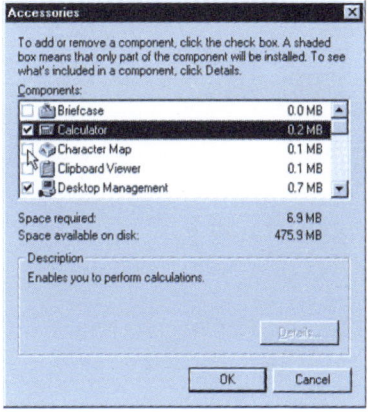

2 Click on the Details button.

If the entry consists of several separate components, you can use the Details button to open a further dialog box and mark the components.

3 Mark the check boxes of the components which are to be installed, in the list which is displayed.

343

4 Now close the open dialog boxes, by clicking on OK in each.

5 In the dialog box under the Windows Setup tab, click on the Apply button.

Windows will carry out the necessary changes to the configuration.

> Windows checks through all the changes you have made in your choice of components. Where an option had been marked, but is now deleted, the component it relates to will be deleted. Where you have newly marked a component, Windows will install the missing files from the CD-ROM. If the mark against a component is deleted, Windows will delete the functions concerned. In the case of some components, you will need to start up again before the changes can take effect. If so, there will be a dialog box to tell you about the need to restart. You can use the Yes button to start up again immediately, or select No, and carry out the restart later.

Installing programs

If you wish to use a new program under Windows, you will normally need to install it from a CD-ROM or floppy disk. It takes a only few steps:

1 Place the CD-ROM or floppy disk in the appropriate drive.

2 Open the My Computer window, and double-click on the icon for the drive.

INSTALLING PROGRAMS

3 Look for the installation program in the drive window.

4 Start the program by double-clicking the icon.

5 Follow the instructions given by the installation program.

> **TIP**
> The installation programs usually have names like Setup.exe of Install.exe. If you see a file like this in the main directory of the CD-ROM or floppy disk, that should be the program you are looking for. You will often find information on the name of the installation program in the documentation files of the program concerned. Files of this sort often have names like Readme.txt. Chapter 4 describes how to display a text file like this in Windows Notepad.
> The installation steps vary from one program to another, so no further account will be given here. Instead, you should look for this in the program documentation.

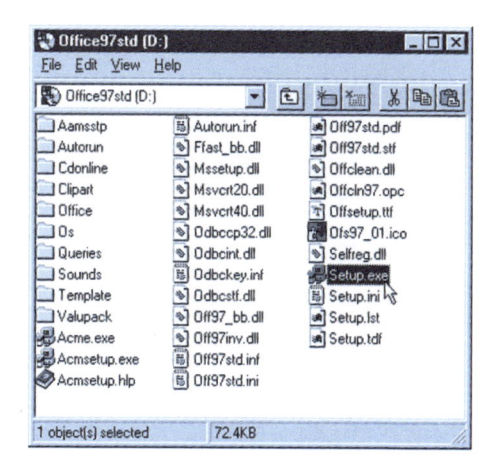

The window shown here gives the contents of the Microsoft Office CD-ROM, with its installation program. With many CD-ROMs, a window is opened automatically when the CD is inserted. The installation programs can often be selected via a button in this window.

345

Changing the Start menu

When programs are installed, an icon is often entered in the Start menu. But the situation often arises where entries in the Start menu need to be changed. This may be to remove entries which are no longer needed. In other cases, a program is being put into a previously existing group, or into a newly created group in the Start menu. To remove a folder (or a group) or a program entry from the Start menu, the following steps are necessary:

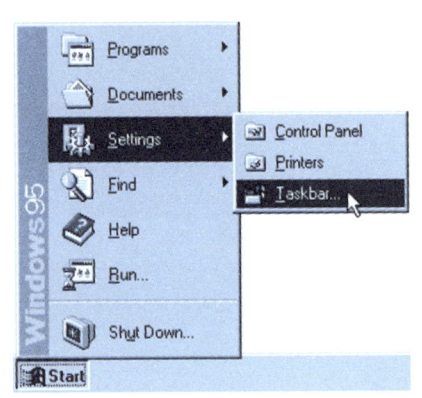

1 Click on the commands SETTINGS/TASKBAR in the Start menu.

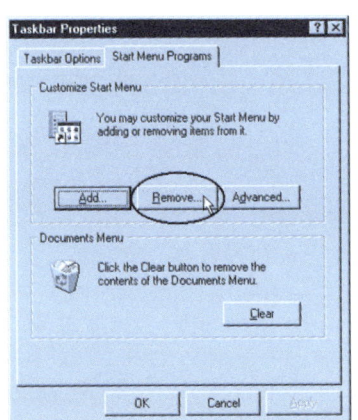

2 In the dialog box for the Start Menu Programs tab, click on the Remove button.

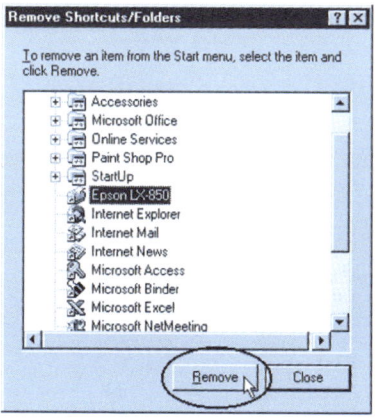

CHANGING THE START MENU

3 In the Remove Shortcuts/Folders dialog box, highlight the entry to be deleted.

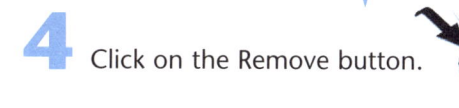

4 Click on the Remove button.

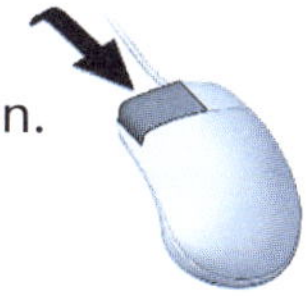

Since the Start menu is ultimately a folder (of a special sort), you can look in the display, as in the left-hand pane of the Explorer window. The folders for a group of programs can be opened by double-clicking on the relevant icon.
To add a program to the Start menu, carry out the following steps:

1 Select the commands SETTINGS/TASKBAR in the Start menu.

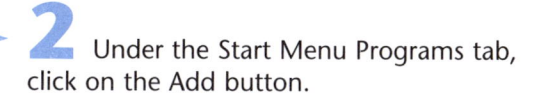

2 Under the Start Menu Programs tab, click on the Add button.

347

Windows starts a wizard, which leads you through the remaining steps of installing the program in the Start menu. The following example puts an entry for the Windows Notepad directly in the PROGRAMS menu.

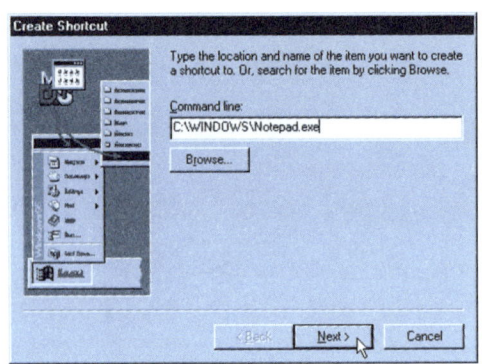

1 In this dialog box, enter the command to access the program. The Browse button can be used if necessary to look for the file containing the program.

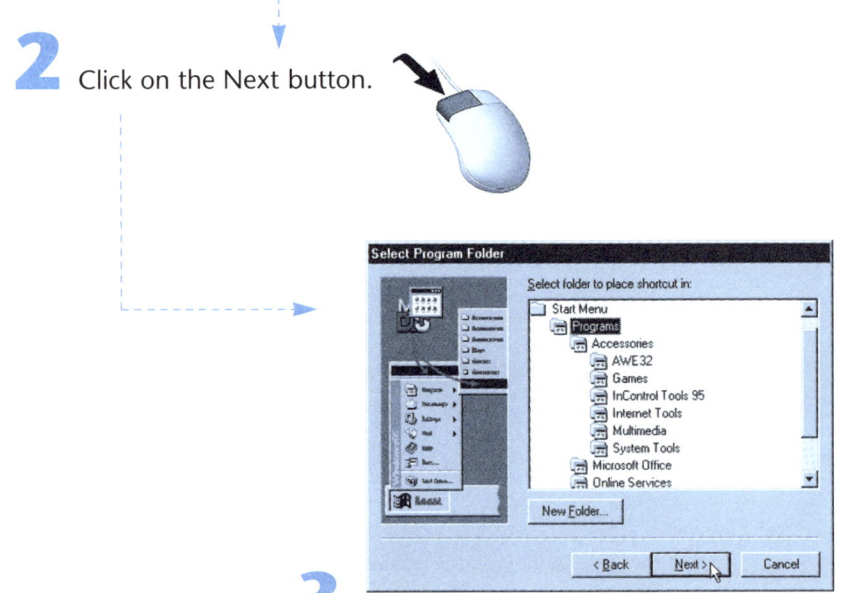

2 Click on the Next button.

3 Select the folder where you want to enter the file. You can create a new folder by using the New Folder button.

348

CHANGING THE START MENU

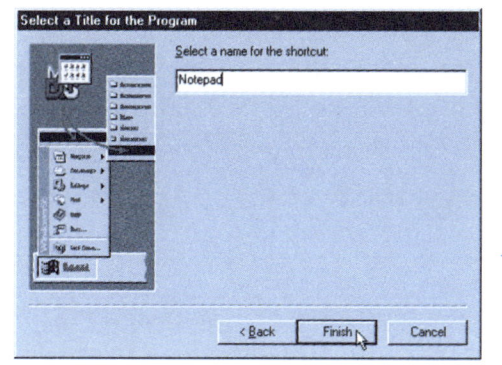

4 Click on Next.

5 Enter the name which you want to appear as the command in the Start menu.

6 Click on the Finish button.

7 Close the open window.

Now, when you open the Start menu, you will see the (new) entry NOTEPAD in the PROGRAMS menu. You can use this method to create a new entry for any program in the Start menu.

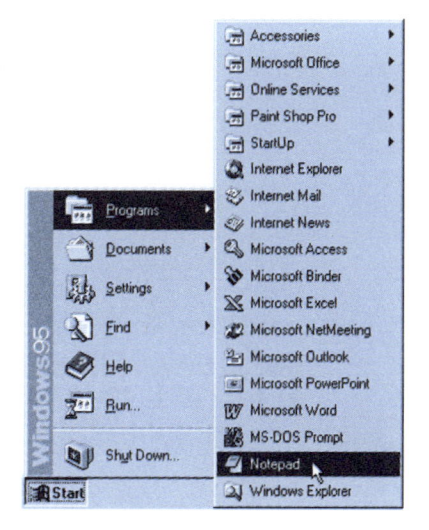

349

TIP

If the method shown above seems too longwinded, here is an alternative. In the dialog box for the Start Menu Programs tab, click on the Advanced button. The window displaying the Start Menu folder will then open. You can work in this window in exactly the same way as you can in the windows of other folders, and can add or delete programs or folders. If you open a second window, displaying the folder with the program you are interested in, you can drag the icon for it to the Start Menu folder, keeping the right mouse button depressed. You can then use the CREATE SHORTCUT(S) HERE command in the context menu to install the new entry.

Installing a program icon on the desktop

You can create shortcuts to frequently used programs on the desktop. That enables you to start the program by double-clicking the icon.

WHAT'S THIS?

Shortcuts are a technique especially used by Windows. They link an icon and a name to a program or document file. You can put a shortcut on the desktop, for instance. Then all you need is to double-click the icon to load the document or program it relates to.

1 Double-click on the My Computer icon.

2 In the My Computer window, double-click the icon for drive C:.

350

INSTALLING A PROGRAM ICON ON THE DESKTOP

3 In the drive C: window, select the Windows folder by double-clicking.

4 Find the icon for the Notepad.exe program in the window for Windows.

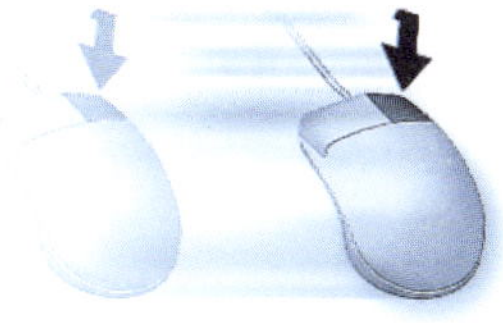

5 Drag the icon for the Notepad.exe program out of the window onto the desktop, keeping the right mouse button depressed.

6 Once the icon is clear of the window and on the desktop, release the right mouse button.

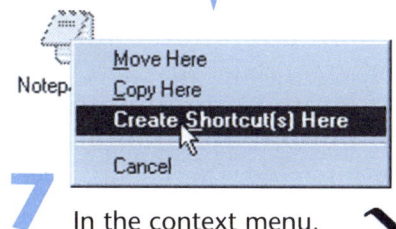

7 In the context menu, click on the command CREATE SHORTCUT(S) HERE.

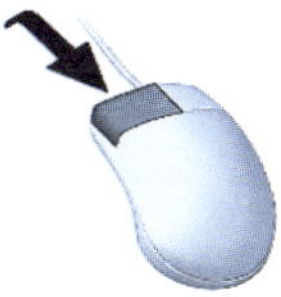

WHAT'S THIS? Context menus are opened by using the right mouse button. Windows puts together the commands available for the particular situation in this menu.

351

Windows now installs the icon as a shortcut on the desktop. All you need to do in order to start the Notepad program is to double-click the icon for it.

Shortcut to
Notepad.exe

> **TIP**
> You can create desktop shortcuts anywhere you like using the method described above. In Chapter 3, this is shown being done with files and folders. You will also see there how to rename (shortcuts).You can remove a shortcut by dragging the icon to the recycle bin.

Installing DOS programs

Do you still have DOS programs which you would like to install under Windows 95? This is often the case with games. DOS programs can be started by double-clicking the icon for the .exe-, .com- or .bat- file, in the same way as Windows programs. You can install the icons as shortcuts on the desktop, or as entries in the Start menu.

However, as opposed to Windows programs, all DOS programs are carried out in a DOS window. The way in which Windows is to handle the DOS window can be set. The most important settings are dealt with below, using the example of the DOS program Edit.com. This program is found in the Windows sub-folder Command. To change the settings for the DOS window of a program, carry out the following steps:

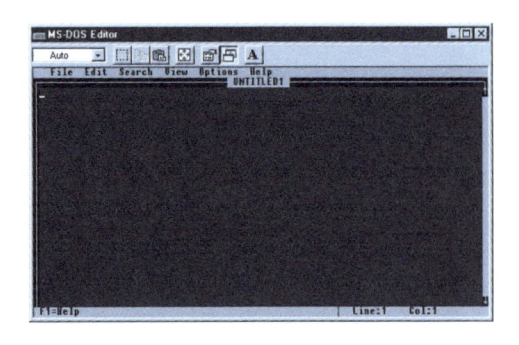

352

INSTALLING DOS PROGRAMS

1 Open the window of the folder in which the DOS program is stored. (here, it is the Windows subfolder Command).

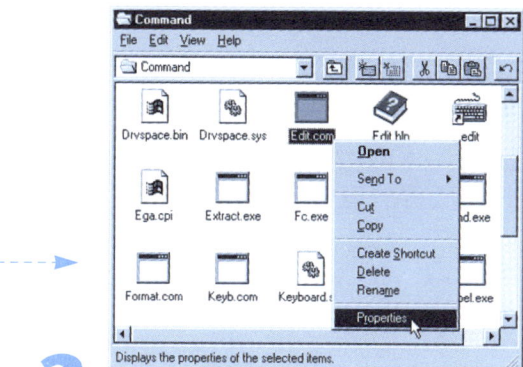

2 Click using the right mouse button on the icon for the DOS program, and in the context menu, select the command PROPERTIES.

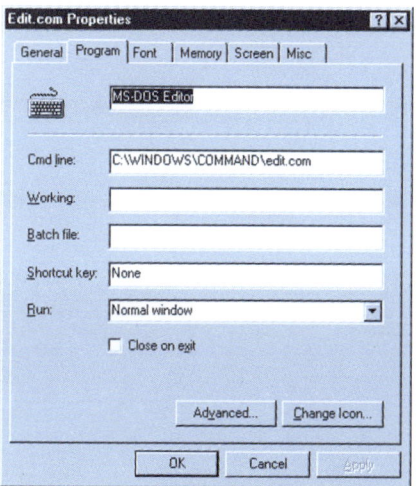

3 Enter the options for the DOS program in the dialog boxes for the individual tabs.

4 Close the window by clicking on OK.

353

When the program is next started, Windows will adopt the definitions you have laid down for the DOS program. You can choose in the dialogs, for example, whether the DOS program is to be run in a window, or to use the whole screen.

> Under the Program tab, for example, in the Command Line box, you can modify the command for starting the DOS program. You can specify here whether a program is to load a document file automatically. In the Run list box, choose whether the program is to appear in a window or as an icon after the start. Mark the check box 'Close on exit', so that Windows will close the DOS window automatically when the program is terminated. The check box should not be marked if you wish to continue seeing the program messages after the program has been terminated. In that case, you will have to close the window yourself after exiting the DOS program. All DOS programs are displayed using the same icon in the windows of folders. You can assign each DOS program an icon of its own from an icon library, using the Other Icon button.

However, some DOS programs do not run under Windows. In Windows 95, you can make sure that the program's own DOS version is automatically loaded when the program is started.

1 In the dialog box for the Program tab (see above), click on the Advanced button.

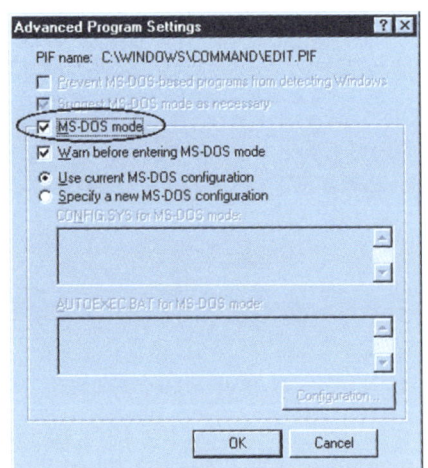

2 In the Advanced Program Settings dialog box, which then appears, mark the 'MS-DOS Mode' check box.

354

INSTALLING DOS PROGRAMS

3 Close the open dialog boxes by clicking the OK buttons.

Then, when you start the DOS program, Windows will be exited, and DOS loaded. When the DOS program is closed, the computer reloads Windows into its memory.

Many DOS programs use additional special memory areas, with names like EMS memory, XMS memory, etc. These memory options can be set in the dialog box for the Memory tab, after the entries on the manufacturer. The setting Automatic enables the program to request the required memory itself.

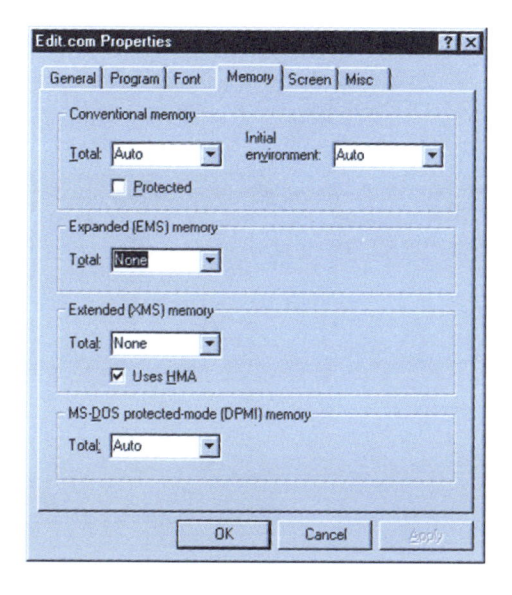

> **TIP**
>
> The setting None switches off the area of memory concerned. There is not room here to go into detail about the requirements of DOS programs with regard to memory settings. The manufacturer's program documentation usually contains information as to which settings should be selected for Windows.
>
> Information on the remaining options on the tabs can be found in Online Help. Click on the item, using the right mouse button, and then click with the left mouse button on the Help button. A window with further information is then opened.

355

Setting up the mouse

If you are left-handed, or if you have difficulty double-clicking the mouse, it makes sense to customise it to suit your needs.

1 In the Start menu, select the command SETTINGS/CONTROL PANEL

2 Mouse
In the Control Panel window, double-click on the mouse icon.

The properties sheet then opens, with the tabs relating to the properties of the mouse.

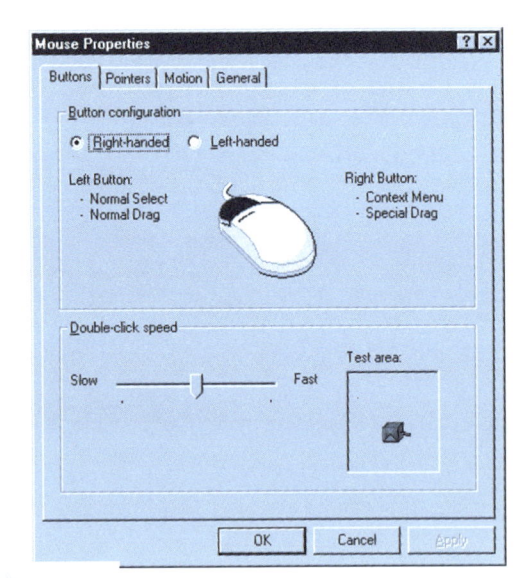

1 If you are left-handed, click on the Left-handed option.

2 To change the speed of the double-click, drag the slider in the 'Double-click Speed' area either to right or left.

3 To test, double-click on the test area with the picture of a box. If the head of the 'Jack-in-a-box' pops up, your double-click was successful.

When you close the properties sheet by clicking on OK, Windows adopts the new settings.

> **TIP**
> You can set further Windows options by using the other icons in the Control Panel. You will find further details in Windows Help.

Start-up problems

Nothing happens when I switch on
Please check the following:

- Are all the plugs in their sockets?
- Is the screen switched on?
- Are you sure the power is on?

The computer displays a message: Keyboard Error, Press <F1> key
Please check the following:

- Is the keyboard connected to the computer?
- Is anything (this book, perhaps) resting on the keyboard?
- Is one of the keys on the keyboard jammed?

  Then press the function key F1.

The computer displays a message: Non-system disk or disk error...
Drive A: probably still has a floppy disk in it. Take it out and restart the computer.

Problems with the keyboard and mouse

When I start up, the keys in the numeric keypad do not work properly

The right-hand side of the keyboard contains a keypad called the numeric keypad, which can be used to type in numbers. If no numbers can be typed in on it, press the [Num] key. This is also called the num lock [Num lock]. It is located in the top left-hand corner of the numeric keypad. Pressing the [Num] key a second time switches the keypad back over. Now, the cursor keys on this keypad can be used.

When I press a key, suddenly more than one character appears

The keyboard has a repeat function. If you press a key for a slightly longer time, the computer repeats the character you typed. You may be pressing the key too long. You can alter the time taken before Windows activates the repeat function.

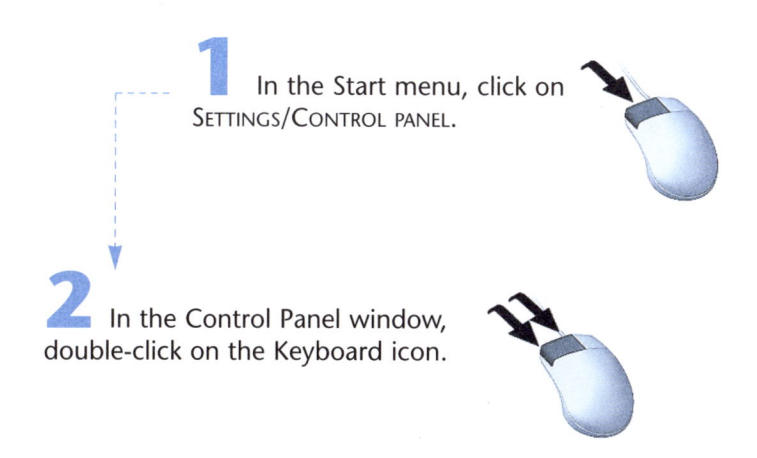

1 In the Start menu, click on SETTINGS/CONTROL PANEL.

2 In the Control Panel window, double-click on the Keyboard icon.

3 Click the Speed tab.

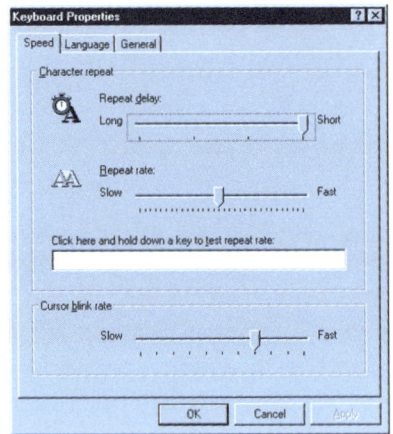

4 Alter the settings for Repeat Delay and Repeat Rate.

You can try out your settings in the test box, and then close the window by clicking on OK. If this does not solve the problem, check whether a key is jamming, or the keyboard is damaged (the key registers several times, and types several repeats of the character when pressed).

The UK English national keyboard driver is not installed.

1 In the Start menu, click on SETTINGS/CONTROL PANEL.

2 In the Control Panel window, double-click on the Keyboard icon.

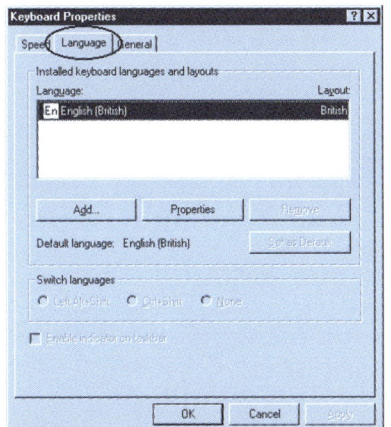

3 Select the Language tab.

Here, the keyboard layout must be set to UK English. If a number of languages are listed, select UK English and close the window. If the entry is missing, you will have to add it, using the Add button. Windows will lead you through the appropriate steps.

The mouse pointer does not move, or does not move properly
Please check the following:

- Is the mouse properly connected to the computer?
- Is the mouse on a mat?
- Is there dirt on the ball of the mouse?

After long use, the part of the mouse that detects movement becomes dirty. Remove the ball located on the underside of the mouse. You will see a number of small wheels. If these are dirty, clean them (e.g. with a Q-tip). The mouse should not be placed on a shiny surface, as it does not roll well there.

361

The mouse buttons function in reverse, or double-clicking does not work

Problem: if you click using the left mouse button, a context menu appears; the right mouse button has the effect of selecting things. In other words, the functions of the left and right mouse buttons are reversed. Reason: you have stumbled on a left-handed mouse. Solution: learn to use it left-handed, or:

1 In the Start menu, click on SETTINGS/CONTROL PANEL.

2 In the Control Panel window, click on the Mouse icon.

3 Select the Buttons tab, and set the Button Configuration to Right-handed.

When you close the window, the mouse buttons should work correctly. If you have problems with double-clicking, you can also change the double-click speed on this tab, to make working with the mouse easier.

> Do you work with a laptop? If so, select the Motion tab, and mark the check box 'Show Pointer Trails'. On this property sheet, you can also set the speed at which the mouse pointer moves.

Problems with the Windows desktop

The words 'Safe Mode' appear on the desktop

Windows detected a problem on start-up, and started the computer in Safe Mode. This occurs when the proper exit procedure for Windows was not carried out. Exit Windows, and try to restart the computer. Usually, all is then well.

The icons refuse to move across the desktop

If, when you move the icons with the mouse, they automatically spring back to their original position, take the following steps:

1 Click using the right mouse button on an empty area of the desktop.

2 In the context menu, select the command ARRANGE ICONS.

3 Remove the highlight on the command AUTO ARRANGE in the submenu, by clicking it with the mouse.

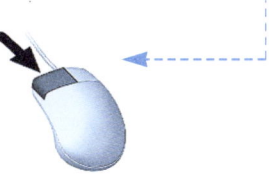

Now you will be able to move the icons.

A shortcut has been deleted by accident

If you have just accidentally deleted a shortcut, you can cure this if you immediately open the context menu using the right mouse button, and select UNDO DELETE. Otherwise, you will need to create the shortcut again (see Chapter 11).

The program is not in the Start menu

You need to enter the program in the Start menu yourself. You will find how to do this in Chapter 11.

When I open a program, Windows cannot find it

Problem: you are opening a program using a shortcut or the start menu, and this window appears. Windows cannot find the program. Either you have deleted the program file, or you have put it in a different folder. If the program is still on the hard disk, use the Browse button to set the path to the program.

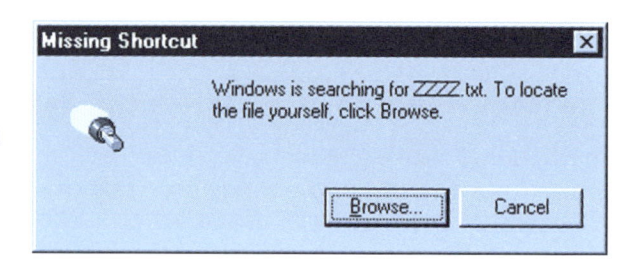

The taskbar is missing, or is in another place, or is too big

The taskbar can be moved to different locations on the desktop. You can drag it with the mouse to one of the four sides of the screen. You can also push it to the edge, so that all you see is a grey line. Use the mouse to drag the taskbar to the position you want. Sometimes the taskbar disappears when you set a window to full-screen size. You can adjust these settings of the taskbar, using the PROPERTIES/TASKBAR command in the Start menu. In the dialog box for the Taskbar Options tab, mark the check box 'Always on top'.

The time is not displayed

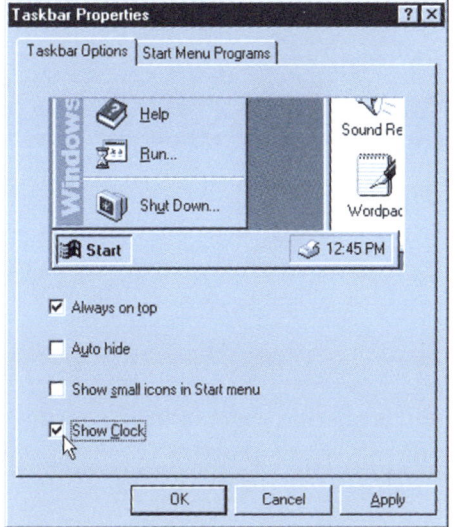

1 Click on SETTINGS/TASKBAR in the Start menu.

2 In the dialog box for the Taskbar Options tab, mark the check box 'Show Clock'.

3 Close the window.

Pattern or wallpaper appears/is missing

If you wish to change any settings for the desktop background, you can do this using the Display Properties sheet. Chapter 11 explains how.

The screen saver is not working

The screen saver is only activated when the computer has not been used for a period of time. If an application window is open, too, the screen saver is not always activated. If necessary, check the settings in the Screen Saver dialog box (see Chapter 11).

365

I have forgotten the screen saver password

You have set a password for the screen saver, but now cannot remember it, and the screen saver is activated. Crazy!
For the future, keep to the advice in Chapter 11, and decide not to set up an access password. To solve the present problem, take the following steps:

1 Switch off the computer (if you had been working in a file, and had not saved it, you have lost all the changes, but take it as fair punishment).

2 Restart the computer and log on.

3 Open the display properties sheet, and switch off the password protection (or set a new password).

Chapter 11 describes how to install a screen saver.

I have forgotten the Windows password

Do you need a password to log on under Windows? And what if you have forgotten it? You can bypass logging on by using the `Esc` key. Start the Windows Explorer, and find the files with the .pwl file extension (using the formula *.pwl to search). The Explorer will display a file with your name and the file extension .pwl. Delete this file, exit Windows and restart the computer. Now enter your name in the log-on box. Windows will ask you for a password. Enter a new password.

> **TIP**
> If you work on a network, you should first ask your network administrator for a new password. The trick shown here does not work with Windows NT. You need to ask your administrator for a new password.

PROBLEMS WITH THE WINDOWS DESKTOP

Not all the folders and files can be seen in the window

Sometimes the window is too small. You can use the scroll bars to move the page on in the window and display the files and folders you could not see before.

The toolbar is missing in the folder window/Explorer window

In a number of programs, you can display or hide the toolbar, using the VIEW menu.

A program refuses to work

It does sometimes happen that a program becomes unusable. It will not react to keyboard entries or mouse clicks.

1 Press the key combination Alt + Ctrl + Delete simultaneously.

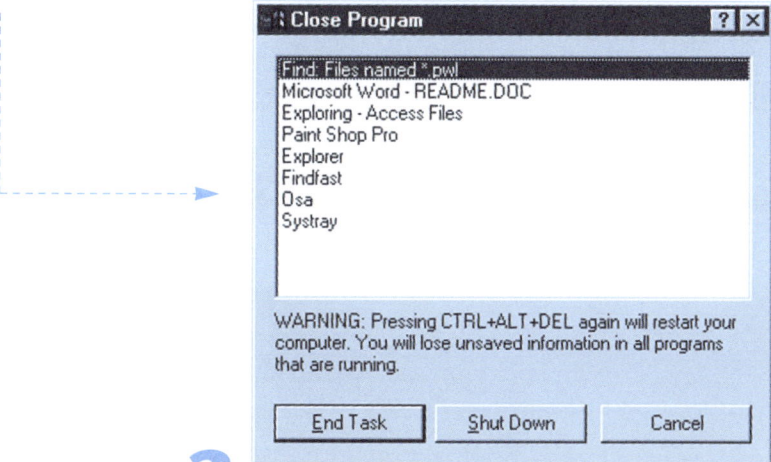

2 In the Close Program window, click on the name of the program which no longer works.

3 Click on the End Task button.

367

Windows now tries to close the program compulsorily. If this is not possible, a further window with a message appears, telling you that the program is not reacting. You must then select the button to close that program.

Folders and files

Filename extensions are not shown

Are the extensions for some filenames missing in folder windows, or in the Explorer?

1 In the VIEW menu, select the command OPTIONS.

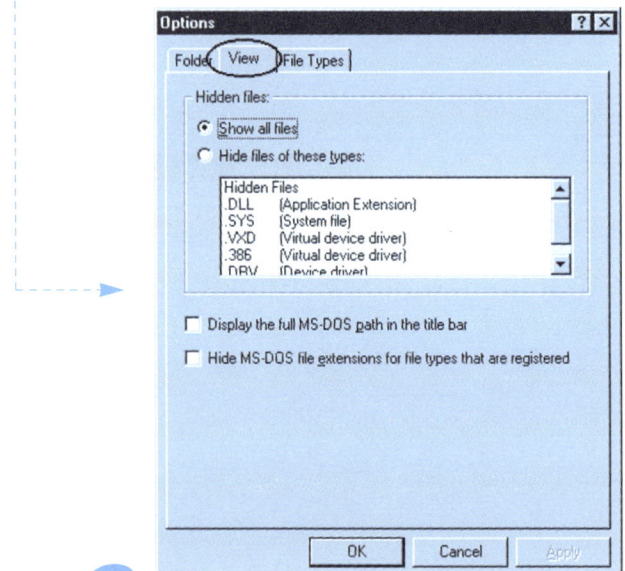

2 In the dialog box for the View tab, delete the mark in the 'Hide MS-DOS file extensions for file types that are registered' check box.

3 Close the window.

Some files are not shown

If you are certain that a particular file is in a folder, but it does not appear in the folder window or in the Explorer, open the View tab (VIEWmenu/OPTIONS). In the group 'Hidden files', the option 'Show All Files' should be marked. If necessary, you must press the function key F5 to update the display of the window.

Each folder is shown in its own window

A further window is opened for each folder icon you select by double-clicking. To change this, reset the option for 'View' in the dialog box for the Folders tab (which you can reach via VIEWmenu/OPTIONS) so that all folders are displayed in one window.

A floppy disk or CD-ROM cannot be read

When you double-click on the drive icon, a message appears, telling you that the drive is not ready. You should then check the following:

- Is there a floppy disk or CD-ROM in the drive?

- For a CD-ROM, open and close the drive, and wait a few seconds. Windows will then usually recognise the change of CD-ROM.

- Is the floppy disk inserted into the drive the right way round? If necessary, look back to Chapter 3, to check which way round to insert a floppy disk.

- If you used a new floppy disk, possibly it has not yet been formatted. In this case, you need to format the disk (see Chapter 3) before using it.

Once you have discovered what is wrong, correct the fault.

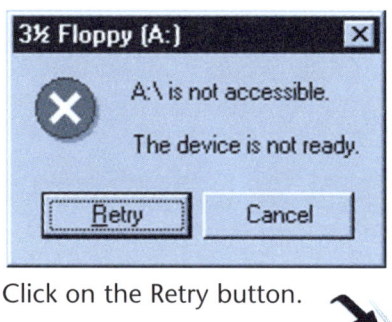

1 Click on the Retry button.

Sometimes, it is necessary to click on Retry several times. Alternatively, you could select Cancel and repeat the entire attempt.

It is impossible to write to the floppy disk

When you try to save a file onto a floppy disk, this error message appears. Take the disk out of the drive, and remove the write protection (see Chapter 3).

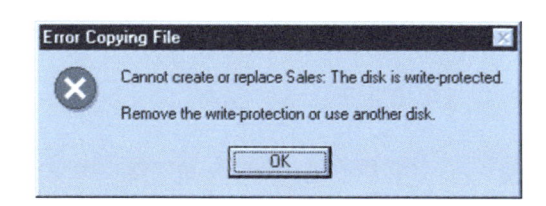

I am trying to change a file, and cannot

You have loaded a document file in a program, changed the contents and selected the Save function. The program opens the Save Under dialog box instead, and suggests a new filename. If you type in the old filename, the program tells you that the file is read-only. This will obviously happen with CD-ROMs, because you cannot change the contents of a CD-ROM.

FOLDERS AND FILES

If files are copied from a CD-ROM, the files are given write-protection. You can remove the write-protection on such floppy disks.

1 Click on the icon for the file, using the right mouse button.

2 In the context menu, click on the command PROPERTIES.

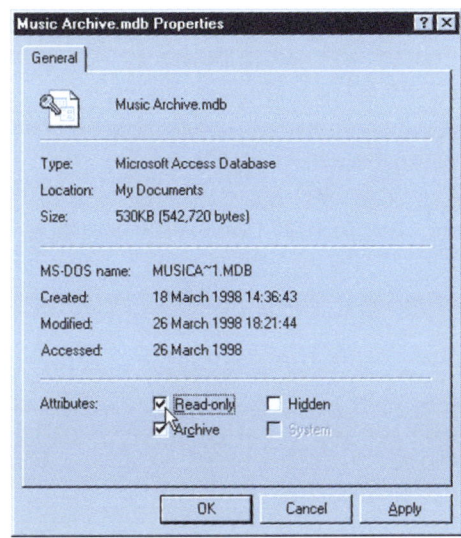

3 Remove the mark in the 'Read-only' check box.

4 Close the dialog box.

371

Printing problems

The printer will not work

The following message may appear when printing. There is a problem with the output to the printer. Remove the cause, and select the Retry button.

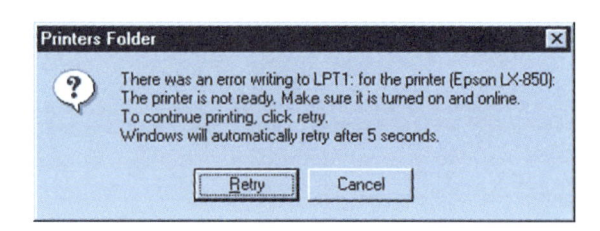

> **Printers Folder**
> There was an error writing to LPT1: for the printer (Epson LX-850):
> The printer is not ready. Make sure it is turned on and online.
> To continue printing, click retry.
> Windows will automatically retry after 5 seconds.
>
> [Retry] [Cancel]

You can also cancel printing, using the Cancel button. To remove the cause of the printer problem, you need to check the following:

- Is the printer switched on, and is it getting power?

- Is the printer cable between the computer and the printer connected?

- Is the printer set to Online?

- Does the printer have enough paper? Toner? Ink?

- Is there a problem at the printer (e.g. paper jammed)?

- Might you have selected the wrong printer (on a network)?

- Is the printer driver correctly installed (e.g. choice of printer port)?

Removing landscape specification

The pages are being printed with the lines running across the length of the page. In this case, you need to alter the print options from Landscape to Portrait. Chapter 6 contains an explanation of how to do this.

The printer is taking paper from the wrong tray (Letter, A4)

Change the printer options for the paper feed. Chapter 6 contains an explanation of how to do this.

Graphics are printed too coarsely

Graphics sometimes have a very coarse printed appearance.

1 In the Printers folder, click on the printer icon, using the right mouse button.

2 In the context menu, select the command Properties.

In the Printer properties sheet, it is possible to set the print options for many printers. You could, for instance, set the halftones on the Graphics tab to 'fine'.

Adjust the contents of the Resolution list box to suit. Under the Device options tab, you can also set the 'print quality'.

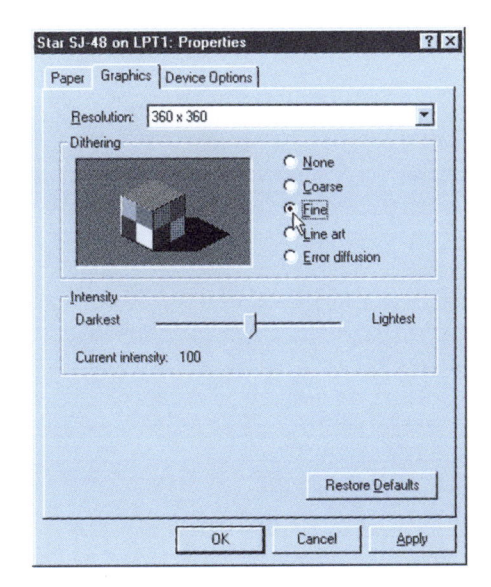

Every time I print, I get an empty page

Windows can add pages known as separator pages when printing. If you do not need these, switch off the issuing of these pages in the printer properties sheet.

1 Set the Separator Page option in the dialog box under the General tab to None.

This option should stop the empty pages appearing at the end of printing.

The Mouse

'Click...'
means: quickly depress a mouse button once.

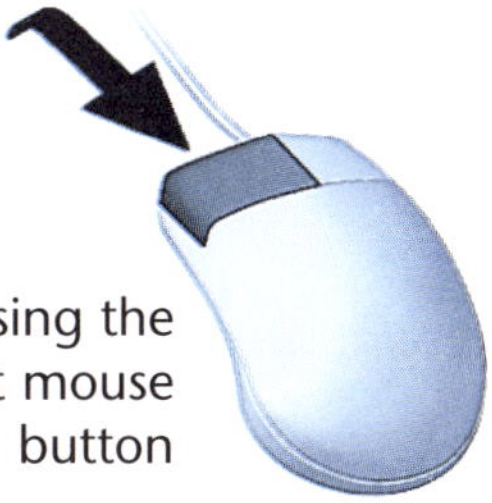

Click using the left mouse button

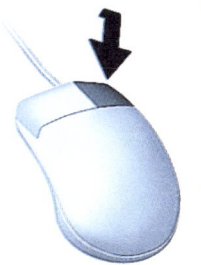

Click using the right mouse button

'Double-click...'
means: depress the left mouse button twice in quick succession.

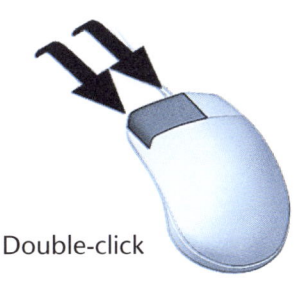

Double-click

'Drag...'
means: click on particular items on the screen, using the left mouse button. Keeping the mouse button depressed, move the mouse, and so move the item to another position.

Drag

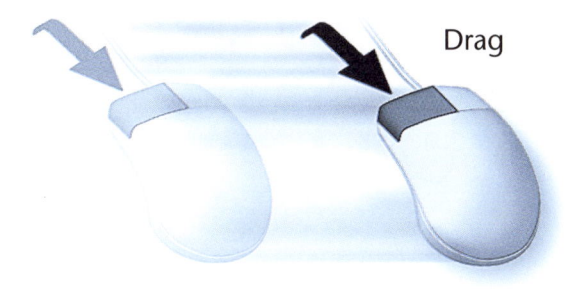

The Keyboard

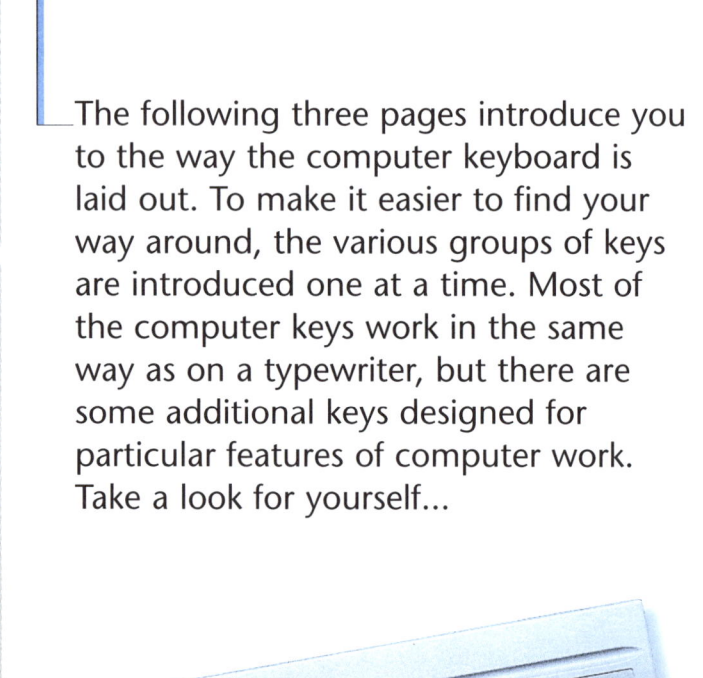

The following three pages introduce you to the way the computer keyboard is laid out. To make it easier to find your way around, the various groups of keys are introduced one at a time. Most of the computer keys work in the same way as on a typewriter, but there are some additional keys designed for particular features of computer work. Take a look for yourself...

THE KEYBOARD

Typewriter keyboard

These keys are used in exactly the same way as on a typewriter. The Return key also has the function of sending commands to the computer

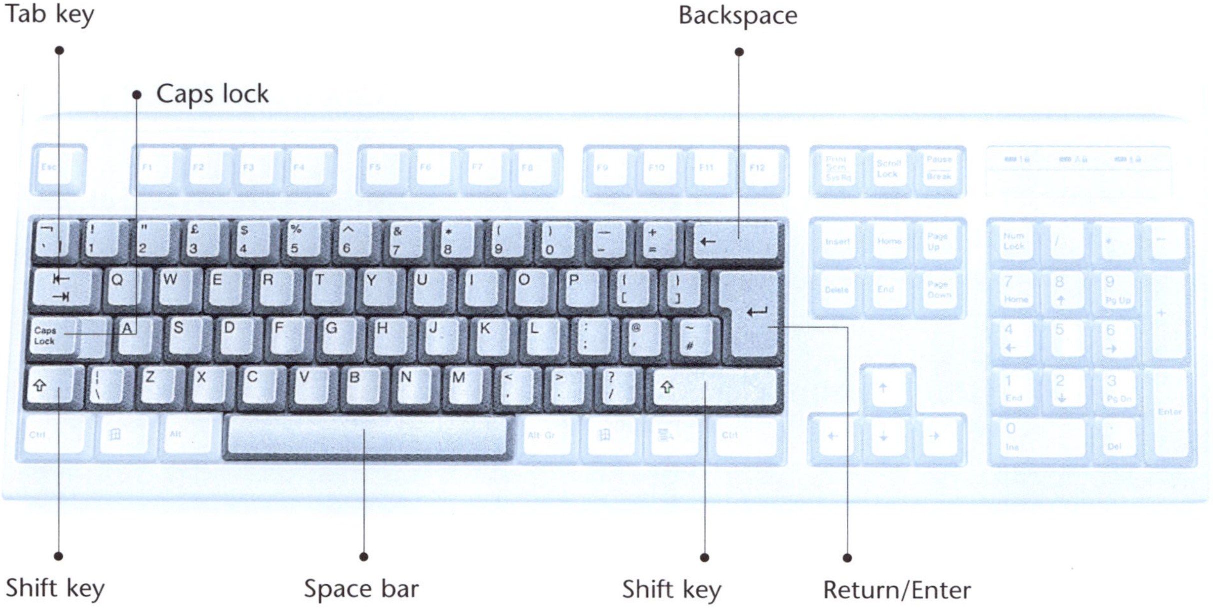

- Tab key
- Caps lock
- Backspace
- Return/Enter
- Shift key
- Space bar
- Shift key

377

Navigation keys

These keys are used to move around the screen

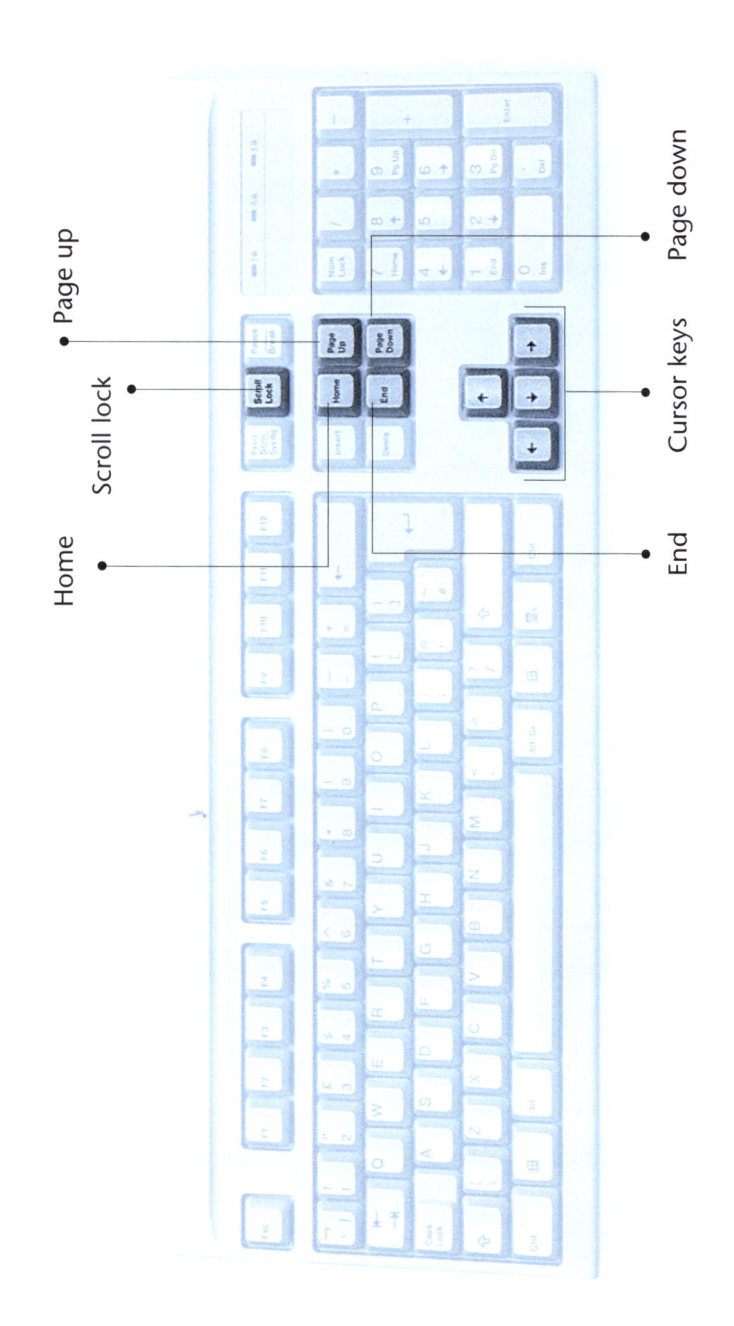

- Page up
- Scroll lock
- Home
- Page down
- Cursor keys
- End

Special keys, function keys, indicator lights, numeric keypad

Special keys and function keys are used to perform particular tasks on the computer. $Ctrl$, Alt and $Alt Gr$ keys are usually used in combination with other keys. The Esc key can be used to cancel commands, and the Insert and Delete keys insert or delete text, amongst other things.

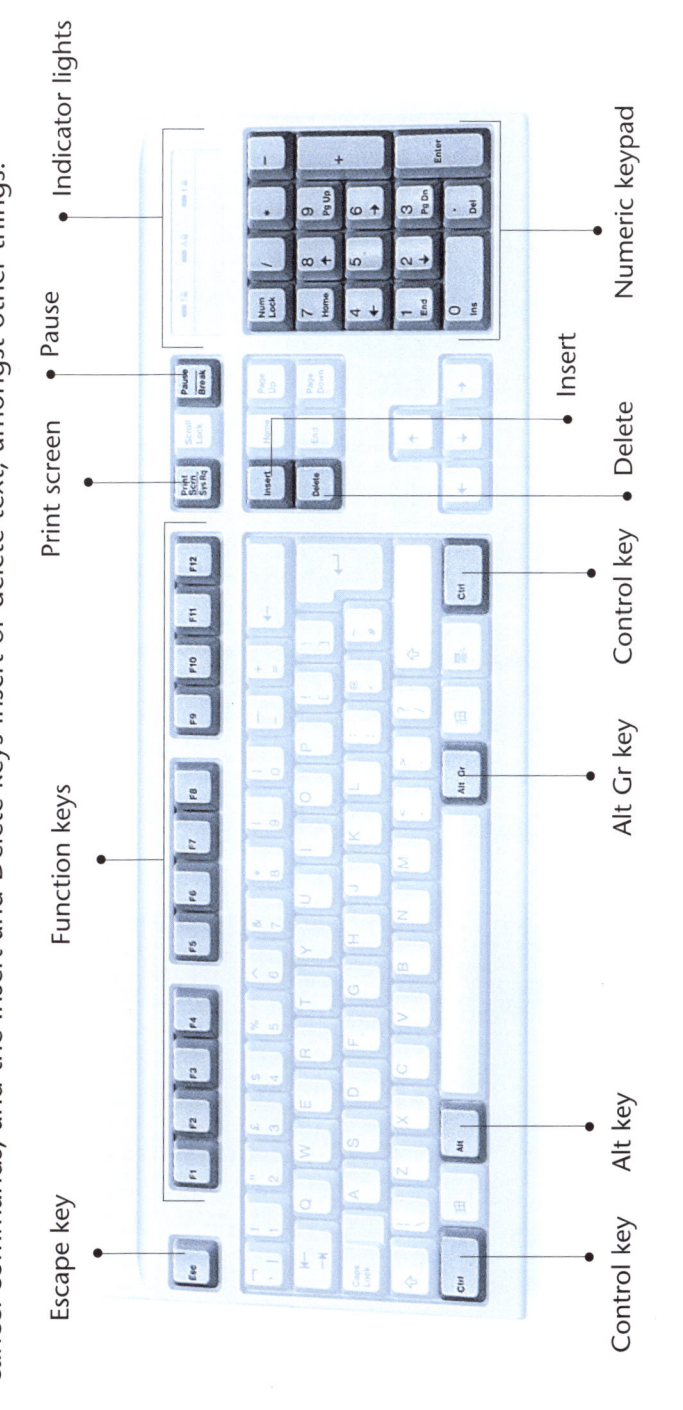

- Escape key
- Function keys
- Print screen
- Pause
- Indicator lights
- Numeric keypad
- Insert
- Delete
- Control key
- Alt Gr key
- Alt key
- Control key

THE KEYBOARD

379

Glossary

A

Access Microsoft Access 97 is the name of a Windows database.

Account authorisation to log on to a computer by data line, and e.g. surf the Web

Address Memory location in the address space (main memory) of the computer, or description of the location of a Website or recipient of an e-mail.

ANSI characters ANSI is the abbreviation for American National Standards Institute. ANSI characters define the characters used under Windows.

AOL Abbreviation for the company America Online, which offers access to online information services.

Application program Programs which can be used for working on a computer (e.g. Word, Excel, Access, Corel Draw, etc.).

Arithmetic/logic unit Special computing component for mathematical computing operations.

GLOSSARY

ASCII characters Abbreviation for American Standard Code for Information Interchange. The ASCII character set lays down 127 characters (letters, numerals and some special characters).

AUTOEXEC.BAT A special file used by Windows to adopt settings when the computer is started up.

B

Backslash The character \ used to separate the elements of a pathname (Drive:\folder\filename).

Backup Term for saving of data (files are saved onto floppy disk, tape or - recently - onto CD-ROMs).

BASIC Abbreviation for Beginners' All-Purpose Symbolic Instruction Code. BASIC is a simple programming language, which is easy to learn. A modern version has been incorporated into Microsoft Visual Basic.

Baud Definition of the speed of data transfer over serial lines.

Bit The smallest unit of information in a computer (it can have the value 0 or 1). 8 bits make 1 byte.

Bitmap Format for storing pictures or graphics. The picture is divided up (as on a screen) into individual dots, which are stored line by line.

Boot Start up the computer.

Browser The program which makes it possible to display pages on the World Wide Web.

Bug Software error in a program.

Byte Unit of information consisting of 8 bits. A byte is able to represent numbers from 0 to 255.

C

C Name of a programming language.

381

Character set The character codes which are available on the computer (ASCII, ANSI).

Chip General term for an electronic component.

CIS Abbreviation for the company CompuServe, which offers access to online information services.

COM Name of the serial ports of the PC (e.g. COM:1)

Command An instruction to the computer.

CONFIG.SYS Special file used in starting Windows.

CPU Abbreviation for Central Processing Unit, the computing unit of the computer.

Cursor The position indicator on the screen. It can take the form of a hand, an arrow, a vertical line, an hourglass, etc.

D

Database Programs for storing, managing and providing data.

Data com Abbreviation for data communication.

Density The recording density of floppy disks. There are two types: DD (Double Density = 720 Kb on 3½" disks) and HD (High Density = 1.44 Mb on 3½" disks).

Desk top publishing (DTP) The preparation of documents (leaflets, books, etc.) on the computer.

Download To load data into a computer by modem, e.g. from the Internet.

E

Editor A program for producing and editing simple text files.

Electronic mail (e-mail) Messages sent by electronic means (see Chapter 8).

EMS Abbreviation for Expanded Memory; describes a special technological method relating to memory.

Error Program fault.

Ethernet Technological method for transferring data on a network.

Excel Name of a spreadsheet program by Microsoft.

F

FAT Abbreviation for File Allocation Unit. It specifies how Windows saves files on the floppy disk or hard disk.

File A file is used to store data on floppy disks or hard disks (see Chapter 3).

Floppy disk Another name for a diskette.

Font The typeface used for the letters of a text (e.g. Times, Courier, etc.).

Font size Size of the letters in a text.

Freeware Software which can be used free and passed on at cost price only.

FTP Abbreviations for File Transfer Protocol. This is a function on the Internet, enabling files to be transferred between computers.

G

Gigabyte Also written Gb or Gbyte. Unit of 1024 Mb, or more than a thousand million bytes.

Gopher Name of a search engine on the Internet.

H

Hardware All the parts of a computer which can be handled. (As opposed to software).

High Memory Area (HMA) Part of the memory which lies immediately above the 1 Megabyte boundary.

Home page Start page of a person or company on the World Wide Web. Hyperlinks lead from the start page to further Web pages.

HTML Abbreviation for Hypertext Markup Language, the document format in the World Wide Web.

Hyperlink Reference in a Web document to another Web page.

I

Internal memory The memory (RAM) in the computer. The size is given in megabytes.

Internet Worldwide linkage of computers in a network (see Chapter 8)

J

Joystick A steering lever used for computer games programs.

K

Kilobyte Also written Kb or Kbyte. Unit of 1024 bytes.

L

LAN Abbreviation for Local Area Network. It refers to a network within a company (the opposite is Wide Area Network).

LCD Special type of display (Liquid Crystal Display) used for laptop computers.

Lotus 1-2-3 Spreadsheet program by the company Lotus.

M

Mailbox Electronic letterbox.

Megabyte Also written Mb or Mbyte. Unit of 1024 Kb, or 1,048,576 bytes.

Modem Auxiliary device used to enable a PC to send data down a telephone line. Needed to access the Internet.

MS-DOS An older operating system distributed by Microsoft.

Multimedia Technological means with which texts, pictures, video and sound can be combined and displayed on the computer.

N

Network Linkage between computers so that data can be exchanged between them.

O

Online Information Service Service which enables access to the Internet (e.g. T-Online, AOL or CompuServe).

Operating system This is the program (e.g. Windows) which appears immediately on starting up the computer.

Output unit Device which can receive output from the computer (e.g. screen, printer).

P

Parallel port Interface providing a connection between a computer and a device (usually a printer).

Pascal Programming language, which was often frequently used for the development of PC applications, but has now decreased in significance.

Path The route from a hard disk to a file in a particular folder (e.g. C:\text\letters).

Processor Another name for the CPU.

Public Domain Software which is publicly accessible, and can be freely copied or passed on with the author's permission (see also freeware).

Q

QWERTY keyboard Standard English-language keyboard (the name comes from the first six keys of the second row).

R

RAM (Random Access Memory) The name for the components which make up the main memory of the computer.

Resolution The measurement which gives the number of dots that make up a graphic (arranged as rows of dots). The resolution determines the number of dots per row, and the number of rows per picture (the same applies to the screen resolution).

S

Scanner Auxiliary device which enables pictures or written material to be read into a computer.

Screen saver Program designed to prevent the screen contents 'burning into' the monitor while the computer is not being used. No longer necessary with modern screens, but still attractive. Can to some extent be used as security to prevent unauthorised use of the computer.

Serial port Interface for connection of a device (e.g. modem, mouse).

Server Main computer in a network.

Shareware Software which can be handed on and tried out free. If the software is used regularly, it must be registered with the author of the program for a fee, usually quite small. This gives the user the chance to try out software thoroughly before making a commitment. The author is spared high distribution costs, and so can usually offer the software cheaply.

Software Another name for the programs and applications.

Spreadsheet Programs with which complex calculations can be carried out simply in table form.

U

UNIX Aa multi-tasking operating system, which is mostly installed in large networks.

URL Abbreviation for Uniform Resource Locator (Website address).

User interface The means by which the computer leads the user through the functions of a program, and makes it possible to use the computer.

V

VGA Graphics standard (16 colours and 640 x 480 pixels). Today, Super VGA is used, with considerably more colours and pixels.

Video adaptor Circuit board in a PC for managing the screen.

Viruses Programs (usually destructive) which replicate and copy themselves into other programs. Viruses usually 'strike' when a particular event occurs (e.g. on a particular date).

W

Word processing Programs for producing letters, reports, books and so on (e.g. WordPad or Microsoft Word).

WWW World Wide Web, part of the Internet, providing easy access to texts and pictures, using a browser.

X

XMS Term for the expanded memory of a PC beyond 1 megabyte.

Index

Symbols

.AVI 241
.BMP 61, 176
.DOC 61, 157
.EXE 61
.HTML 277
.PCX 176
.RTF 158
.TXT 61, 139, 158
.WAV 234

A

Access 380
Account 380
Address 380
ANSI characters 380
AOL 380
Application 380
Arithmetic/logic unit 380
ASCII characters 381
Audio CD 240

B

Background colour 163
Backslash 117, 381
Backup 381
BASIC 381
Baud 381
Bit 381
Bitmap 381
BMP file 174
Boot 381
Box 36

Browser 261, 381
Browser, Internet Explorer 264
Browser, Netscape Navigator 264
Bug 381
Bullet 152
Button 17
Button, Browse 116
Button, Cancel 55
Button, Change window size 25
Button, Close 53
Button, Close window 25
Button, Start 16
Byte 381

C
C 381
Calendar 329
Capacity 106
Capital letters, typing 128
CD, Intro Play 233
CD, Play list 230
CD Player 227ff.
CD-ROM drive 66
Character set 382
Characters, deleting 90, 130
Check box 41, 43
Chip 382
CIS 382
Clicking 19f., 375
Clipboard 100, 133
Clipboard, data exchange 136
Colour, infill 167
Colour printer 205
COM 382
Command 382
Command, undo 162
Computer, shutting down 43
Computer, starting up 14
Context menu 83, 351
Control Panel 356f.
Copying 100, 135, 171

CPU 382
Cursor 382
Cursor keys 130
Cut 100, 133, 135, 171

D
Data, exchange 51, 136
Data, exchange between windows 136
Data, exchange using clipboard 136
data com 382
Data loss 68
Data medium 60
Database 382
Date, changing 327
Date, displaying 19
Day of the week 328
Day of the week, displaying 19
Default printer 205, 216, 223
Density 382
Desktop 15
Desktop, arranging icons 75
Desktop, changing background 330
Desktop, creating shortcut 350
Desktop, graphics 333, 335
Desktop, installing program icon 350
Desktop, pattern 333
Desktop, problems 363
Desktop, removing wallpaper 336
Desktop, with printer icon 209
Desktop publishing 382
Destination disk 104
Destination folder 95
Dialog box 38
Directory 65
Display, drive contents 69
Display, Explorer 76f.
Display, expand 73

389

Display, list 73
Display mode 75
Display, sort 74
Display, sort criteria 74
Display options 73f.
DOC file 62
Document, desktop 192
Document, list 198
Document, loading 194
Document, marking text 132
Document, opening 190
Document, printing 157, 213, 215
Document, quick view of contents 197
Document, shortcut on desktop 192
Document file, display 188
Document list, deleting 199
DOS programs, installing 352
Double-click, changing speed 357
Double-clicking 22, 375
Double-clicking, to open window 22
Double-clicking, to start program 22
Download 382
Drag & drop 215
Dragging with the mouse 21, 375
Drawing, labelling 168
Drawing, moving 172
Drawing tool 160, 163f.
Drive, capacity 106
Drive, changing 79f.
Drive, defragmenting 321
Drive, display 68
Drive, displaying contents 68f.
Drive, naming 66
Drive, properties 107
Drive, types 65f.
Drive, scanning 316
Drive, scanning for errors 316
Drive, sharing 298
Drive, sharing on network 66
Drive contents, displaying 68ff.
Drive icons 65f.
DTP 382

E

E-mail 261, 284ff., 382
E-mail, sending 284
EMS memory 355, 382
Error 383
Error, Computer does not start 358
Error, Keyboard 359
Error, printer does not work 372
Ethernet 383
Excel 62, 383
Explorer 48, 76f.
Explorer, displaying files 76
Explorer, displaying folders 76
Explorer, setting icon size 77
Explorer window 76f.
Explorer window, folder hierarchy 77
Extension 61, 139

F

FAT 383
File contents, quick view 197
File display in Explorer 76f.
File icon 189
File size 108
File system 316
File type 74, 188
File type, not registered 190
File type, unknown 190
File type, .wav 234
Filename extension 61, 87
Filename extension, automatic 139
Filename extension, .bat 63

INDEX

Filename extension, .bmp 61
Filename extension, .doc 62
Filename extension, .exe 62
Filename extension, .hlp 62
Filename extension, icon 189
Filename extension, .txt 62, 139
Filename extension, .xls 62
Filenames, capitals/lower case 61
Filenames, icons 61
Filenames, rules 61
Files 60f., 368, 383
Files, copying 90, 95, 99
Files, copying in folder 99
Files, copying multiple 95
Files, creating 86f.
Files, display options 72
Files, displaying 68
Files, displaying in Explorer 76
Files, deleting 109
Files, establishing size 107f.
Files, file names 61, 87
Files, finding 114
Files, introduction 60
Files, moving 101
Files, opening 190
Files, organising 64
Files, quick view of contents 197
Files, renaming 88
Files, replacing 102
Files, restoring 111f.
Files, retrieving from Recycle Bin 111
Files, saving 86f.
Files, selecting 96f.
Files, sort criteria 74
Filling in colour 167
Find, accessing direct 117
Find, Browse button 116
Find, including subfolders 116
Find, limiting search 115
Find, using wildcards 115

Find files 114
Find folders 114
Floppy disk 60, 65, 67f., 370
Floppy disk, copying 90, 103ff.
Floppy disk, formatting 94ff., 117
Floppy disk, handling disks 67
Floppy disk, inserting 68
Floppy disk, labelling 67
Floppy disk, magnetic layer 67
Floppy disk, removing 68
Floppy disk, removing write-protection 94
Floppy disk, write-protecting 67
Folder, changing 79ff.
Floppy disk drive, icon 65
Folder, Explorer 76f.
Folder display in Explorer 76f.
Folder display, sorting 74
Folder display, sorting: reverse order 75
Folder icon 64
Folder name 64
Folder window, Details display 73
Folder window, displaying 70
Folder window, icon size 72
Folder window, List display 74
Folder window, scrolling 69
Folders 63f., 368
Folders, copying 90f.
Folders, deleting 109
Folders, discovering memory used 107
Folders, display in window 73
Folders, display options 74
Folders, displaying 68
Folders, displaying multiple windows 71
Folders, finding 114
Folders, introduction 60
Folders, minus sign 78
Folders, moving 101

391

Folders, names 64, 85
Folders, opening 69f.
Folders, plus sign 78
Folders, renaming 88
Folders, restoring 111
Folders, rules 65
Folders, saving documents 64
Folders, selecting 98
Folders, sharing 298
Folders, sort display 74
Folders, starting/creating 83ff., 138
Folders, subfolders 64
Font 151, 383
Font, bold 149
Font, italic 152
Font size 151, 383
Fonts 169
Formatting 94, 148f.
Fragmentation 322
Freehand line 160
Freeware 383
FTP 383
Function keys 379

G

Game, Hover! 252
Game, Minesweeper 245
Game, Solitaire 248
Gopher 383
Graphics file 61
Graphics sections, copy 170
Graphics sections, cut 170

H

Hard disk 60
Hard disk, correcting errors 319
Hard disk, defective sectors 320
Hard disk, defragmenting 321
Hard disk, fragmentation 322
Hard disk, scanning surface 320

Hard disk drives 66
Hardware 383
Help 34
Help, accessing 34
Help, accessing directly 39
Help, accessing Windows functions 35
Help, additional window 35
Help, displaying 34
Help, finding particular topics 36
Help, Help topics 35
Help, index 36
Help, search topic 36
Help, searching 37f.
Help, tabs 34
Help, text 36
Help command 34
Help function 34, 62
Help function, displaying 34
Help text, displaying 36
Help window 34
HMA 383
Home page 280, 383
Hover! 252ff.
HTML 262, 384
HTML document, printing 279
HTML file, loading 277
HTML pages, printing 279
Hyperlink 262, 268ff. 384
Hypertext Markup Language 262

I

Icon 25, 61ff.
Icon, for files 63
Icon, My Computer 16
Icon, Network Neighborhood 16, 293
Icon, Recycle Bin 16
Icons, arranging 74
Icons, dragging 21f.
Icons, specifying size 72

Icon size, specifying 72f.
Indent 128, 155
Indent, first line 155
Inserting objects 100
Inserting text 134
Installation CD-ROM 206
Installation programs 345
Installation of Windows components 341
Installing programs 344, 352
Internal memory 384
Internet 260, 384
Internet, mailbox 261
Internet, modem 261
Internet, searching 282f.
Internet, surfing 263
Internet, World Wide Web
Internet browser 261
Internet Explorer 264
Internet Explorer, home page 265, 280
Internet Explorer, loading document pages 277
Internet Explorer, options 280
Internet Explorer, printing document pages 279
Internet Explorer, saving document pages 275
Internet Explorer, searching 282f.
Internet Explorer, start page 265, 280
Intranet 261
Italic 152

J
Joystick 253, 384
Justification 149

K
Key combination 52
Keyboard 376
Keyboard, problems 359
Keyboard, setting repeat rate 359

L
LAN 384
Landscape orientation 215
Laser printer 205
LCD 384
Level, Up One Level icon 70
Levels, Hierarchy of 77
Line, adjust length automatically 148
Line, changing 128
Line, single indent 128
Line breadth, reducing 155
Line indent 153
Line length 154
Line length, adjusting 129
Line length, automatic return 147
Line length, carriage return 146
Line spacing 128
List box 82
Log-on: bypassing 14
Log-on box 14
Lotus 1-2-3 384

M
Mailbox 261, 384
Marking 20, 96f., 132f.
Marking, folders 98
Marking, multiple files 96f.
Marking, part of drawing 170
Marking, removing 20, 22, 89, 133
Maximising, window 26
Media player 239
Menu 21
Menu, Start 46
Menu bar 24, 77
Menus, accessing functions 24
Menus, working with 47f.

393

Message box 94
Microsoft Internet Explorer 264
Microsoft Word 157
Minesweeper 245ff.
Minus sign 78
Modem 261, 384
Monitor, energy-saving function 338
Mouse 17, 359, 375
Mouse, buttons 17
Mouse button, middle 17
Mouse, buttons reversed 362
Mouse, clicking 17, 19f.
Mouse, cursor 18
Mouse, double arrow 28
Mouse, double-clicking 22
Mouse, double-click speed 357
Mouse, dragging 21
Mouse, installing 356
Mouse, motion speed 363
Mouse, pointer 18
Mouse, pointer does not move 361
Mouse, pointer hard to see 363
Mouse, pointing 18
Mouse, problems with double-click 362
Mouse, selecting 20
Mouse pad 17
Mouse trail, displaying 363
Multimedia 385
Music CDs, entering tracks 229
Music CDs, playing 226
Music CDs, Play List 230
Music CDs, specifying order of tracks 230
My Computer 16

N
Navigation keys 378
Netscape Navigator 264

Network 260, 290, 385
Network, Client 290
Network, disconnecting 302
Network, folder icon 297
Network, installing printer 305ff.
Network, logging on 292f.
Network, log-on, avoiding 14
Network, log-on box 14
Network, mapping 301
Network, path 302
Network, printing 303
Network, resources 291
Network, server 290
Network, sharing drive 312
Network, sharing folder 312
Network, sharing printer 309ff.
Network, Workgroup 291
Network, working on 292
Network, write-protection 300
Network card 291
Network Neighbourhood 16, 294, 296
Network resource, path 302
Network resources as drives 301
Notepad 62, 126
Notepad, creating text 126
Notepad, editing text 128ff.
Notepad, loading file 139
Notepad, printing text 143
Notepad, saving text 136
Notepad, window interior 127
Num lock key 359

O
Object 25, 63, 84
Offline 274
Online 274
Online information service 385
Open with 195
Operating system 385
Option box 42

Output unit 385

P

Paint 61, 159
Paint, colour infill 167
Paint, colour palette 160
Paint, copying sections 170
Paint, cutting out sections 170
Paint, drawing area 160
Paint, drawing tool 160, 163f.
Paint, filling in colour 167
Paint, freehand line 160
Paint, formatting text 169
Paint, list of tools 160
Paint, loading graphic 174
Paint, new drawing 160
Paint, printing 176
Paint, saving 173
Paint, selecting brush width 161
Paint, specifying background colour 163
Paint, undo command 162
Paint, wallpaper 177
Paintbrush 161
Paragraph 147
Password, forgotten 366
Path 117, 385
Pathname 117
Picture in text document 181
Pictures, creating 160
Pictures, editing 159
Pictures, file types 176
Pictures, printing 176f.
Plus sign 78
Point 151
Pointing with the mouse 18
Port, serial 386
Port, parallel 205, 385
Portrait orientation 215
Print options 213
Print, cancel 158

Print job 218
Print job, cancelling 222
Print job, owner 220
Print job, pausing 220f.
Print job, releasing 220
Print job, status 219
Print Manager 209, 218
Printer, as desktop icon 209f.
Printer, cancel sharing 311
Printer, changing settings 215
Printer, default settings 217
Printer, install printer wizard 202
Printer, installing 202
Printer installation, test page 206f.
Printer, manufacturer 204
Printer, model 204
Printer, output to 212, 218
Printer, output to different 215
Printer, paper tray 217
Printer, port 204f.
Printer, print queue 218f.
Printer, properties sheet 216
Printer, setting paper orientation 217
Printer, sharing 309
Printer, status display 219
Printer, tabs
Printer driver 202, 207
Printer icon 209
Printer icon, in Start menu 211
Printer icon, installing 209ff.
Printer icon, on desktop 209ff.
Printer icon, problem 218
Printer icon, title 211
Printer output, cancelling 222
Printer output, directing 220
Printer port 204f.
Printer settings, changing 209, 215f.
Printer output, managing 209f.
Printing 143, 212

Printing, cancel (Notepad) 144
Printing, cancelling 222
Printing, changing printer 215, 303
Printing, key combination 212
Printing, network 303
Printing, start 213
Printing, store temporarily 218
Problems 358
Problems, files 368
Problems, folders 368
Problems, keyboard 359
Problems, mouse 359
Problems, printing 372
Problems, starting up computer 358
Problems, Windows desktop 363
Processor 385
Program window 52
Program file 62
Program group, Accessories 50
Program group, subgroups 50
Program icon 50, 57
Program icon, installing 350
Program window, button 52
Program window, changing 52
Program window, in foreground 52
Program group 50
Programs, crash 367
Programs, exchanging data 51
Programs, exiting 27, 53ff.
Programs, opening 22, 47, 55ff.
Programs, installing 344, 352
Programs, loading simultaneously 51
Programs, opening from desktop 56
Programs, Start menu 48, 347
Programs, switching 51
Public domain 385

Q
Quick help 19
Quick help window 19
Quick view 197
Quickformat 119
QWERTY keyboard 385

R
RAM 386
Recycle Bin 16, 109
Recycle Bin, emptying 113
Recycle Bin, icon 114
Resolution 386
Resource 16, 291
Restore 112
Rubber 162
Ruler 153

S
Save as 157
Saving 60, 65, 157
Saving, in new folder 138
ScanDisk 318
Scanner 330, 386
Screen background, changing 330
Screen resolution 338
Screen resolution, changing
Screen saver 336, 365, 386
Screen saver, installing 336
Screen saver, not working 365
Screen saver, password 338
Scroll bar 32f., 69
Scroll bar, horizontal 33
Scroll bar, scrolling page by page 33
Scroll bar, scrolling text 33
Scroll bar, vertical 33
Scroll button 32
Scroll button, dragging 32
Scrolling arrow 33
Scrolling a window 32

Scrolling, page by page 33
Scrolling, scroll bar 32
Search topic, help 36
Search (see Find)
Searching, on Internet 282f.
Searching, in text 141
Sectors, defective 316ff.
Selecting (see marking)
Server 386
Shareware 386
Shortcut 350, 352, 364
Smileys 247, 285
Solitaire 248ff.
Sound card 226, 234
Sound documents, editing 236
Sound documents, pausing playback 238
Sound documents, playback 237
Sound documents, quality 237
Sound documents, recording 235
Sound documents, saving 236
Sound file 237
Sound files 234
Sound quality 237
Sound Recorder 234f.
Source folder 95
Source disk 104
Spin box 233
Spreadsheet 386
Start menu 20, 46, 346
Start menu, adding program 347
Start menu, changing 346
Start menu, using 21
Status bar 25, 77
Subfolder, opening 70
Switching between programs 51f.
Switching between programs, key combination 52
Switching between programs, taskbar 52
System administrator 293

T
Tab 153
Tab, automatic 153
Tab, delete 154
Tab, ruler 153
Tab, manual 153
Tab, marking 154
Tab, moving 154
Tab stops 155
Tabs 34
Taskbar 16, 364
Taskbar, icons 52
Taskbar, programs 52
Taskbar, Start button 16
Taskbar, time 16
Text, combining with graphics 180
Text, copying 135
Text, correcting errors 128
Text, creating 126
Text, cut 133
Text, editing 128
Text, formatting 148
Text, highlighting 151
Text, indent 128
Text, inserting 128, 134
Text, italic 152
Text, justification 149
Text, loading 136, 157
Text, marking 132f.
Text, paragraph 147f.
Text, positioning in 136, 156
Text, printing 143
Text, removing marking 133
Text, saving 136, 156
Text, setting tab 155
Text, underlining 152
Text, undoing changes 133
Text, word search 141
Text box 36, 116
Text cursor 89, 90, 127
Text cursor, positioning 130

397

Text document, formatting 148
Text document, inserting video 244
Text document, printing 157
Text editing, key combinations 130
Text file, loading 139
Text document, loading 157
Text passage, highlighting 151
Time 16
Time, changing 326
Time, display missing 365
Time, time zone 329
Time, setting 326
Time zone, setting 329
Title bar 24
Toolbar 24, 77
Toolbar, displaying 71, 145
Toolbar, hiding 71, 145

U

Undo 111, 162
Undo button 112
UNIX 387
Up one level 70
URL 266, 387
User interface 15, 387

V

VGA 387
Video, display window 242
Video, set points 240
Video, setting window size 242
Video, watching 239ff.
Video adaptor 387
View page 159
Viruses 387
Volume control 234

W

Wallpaper 177, 330
Web pages 261, 272
Web pages, saving 275
Website addresses 266ff.
Websites, bookmarking 272
Websites, favourites 273
Wildcard 115
Window, arranging windows 30
Window, changing
Window, closing 27
Window, foreground 27, 30
Window, full-screen 26
Window, icon 26
Window, minimising to icon 26
Window, moving 30f.
Window, opening 22f.
Window, opening icon 23
Window, resizing 28f.
Window, scrolling 32
Window, status bar 25
Window, structure 24
Window, title 24
Window, title bar 24, 31
Window, toolbar 24
Window height, changing 28
Window size, changing 26, 28f.
Window size, maximising 26
Window size, restoring 26
Window width, changing 28
Windows 95: the window 23
Windows, accessing calculator 49ff.
Windows, drive 65
Windows, exiting 41f.
Windows, installing components 341
Windows, introduction 40
Windows, password forgotten 366
Windows, Start menu 20
Windows, starting 14

Windows, wallpaper 177
Windows calculator 49
Windows components, installing 341
Windows Help 34
Windows Help, accessing direct 39
Windows Help, displaying window 34
Windows Help, search topics 37f.
Windows Notepad 126
Windows tour 40
Word 157
Word processing 387
WordPad 62, 144
WordPad, indent first line 155
WordPad, loading documents 157
WordPad, printing documents 158
WordPad, saving documents 156
WordPad, setting tabs 155
Workgroup Network 291
World Wide Web 261f., 387
Write-protection, removing 94
WWW 262, 387

X

XMS memory 355, 387